SAP R/3 on the Internet

SAP R/3 on the Internet

Mario Pérez
Alexander Hildenbrand
Bernd Matzke
Peter Zencke

 Addison-Wesley

Harlow, England · Reading, Massachusetts · Menlo Park, California · New York ·
Don Mills, Ontario · Amsterdam · Bonn · Sydney · Singapore · Tokyo · Madrid ·
San Juan · Milan · Mexico City · Soeul · Taipei

First published by Addison Wesley Longman Verlag GmbH 1998
as *Geschäftsprozesse im Internet mit SAP R/3*

Pearson Education Limited
Edinburgh Gate
Harlow
Essex CM20 2JE
England
and Associated Companies throughout the World.

The programs in this book have been included for their instructional value. They have been tested
with care but are not guaranteed for any particular purpose. The publisher does not offer any war-
ranties or representations nor does it accept any liabilities with respect to the programs.

Many of the designations used by manufacturers and sellers to distinguish their products are
claimed as trademarks. Pearson Education Limited has made every attempt to supply trademark
information about manufacturers and their products mentioned in this book. A list of the trademark
designations and their owners appears on this page.

Translated by Jason M. Miskuly
Cover designed by The Senate, London
Typeset in 9.5/12pt Palatino by 30
Printed and bound in the United States of America

First published 1999

ISBN 0-201-34303-7

British Library Cataloguing-in-Publication Data
A catalogue record for this book is available from the British Library

Library of Congress Cataloging-in-Publication Data
Geschäftsprozesse im Internet mit SAP R–3. English
    SAP R/3 on the internet / Mario Perez ... [et al.] ;
    [translated by Jason M. Miskuly].
        p.   cm.
    Includes bibliographical references.
    ISBN 0–201–34303–7
    1. SAP R/3. 093. 2. Business--Computer programs. 3. Electronic
data interchange.   I. Perez, Mario, 1964–   .   II. Title.
HF5548.4.R2G47 1999
650' .0285'53769--dc21   99–10117
                                                             CIP

Trademark notice
iXOS and iXtrain are registered trademarks of iXOS Software AG, Bretonischer Ring 12,
85630 Grasbrunn, Germany.
SAP, R/3, ABAP/4, SAP Archivelink and SAP Business Workflow are registered trademarks
of SAP Aktiengesellschaft Systems, Applications and Products in Data Processing,
Neurottstraße 16, D-69190 Walldorf, Germany. The publisher gratefully acknowledges
SAP's kind permission to use its trademark in this publication. SAP AG is not the publisher of
this book and is not responsible for it under any aspect of press law.

Preface

As a new medium of communication, the Internet has conquered the world with breathtaking speed. Its strengths lie in its ability to integrate both numerous existing technologies and those created specifically for it. Even today, basic knowledge of the Internet flourishes and business applications that benefit from the Internet add to the profusion. With its R/3 System, SAP AG has already begun to build a road in the right direction. Internet business applications have an almost unlimited potential to change the way that enterprises communicate with each other.

The structure of this book reflects the many-sided nature of that basic knowledge in many ways. It also recognizes that the sheer multiplicity of topics will force some of them to the margin. The book offers a complete guide. It seeks:

- to understand the Internet as a business platform for the R/3 System;

- to introduce the Internet functions of the R/3 System;

- to provide a solid foundation for business decisions.

The book provides a good understanding of the Internet, although it avoids technical details for the most part. The presentation ensures that readers can reproduce integration of the R/3 System into the Internet in addition to the business and technical possibilities that integration offers. Highlights of the book include a thorough introduction of the SAP Internet applications already usable today. This book addresses users and enterprise management concerned with the optimization of business processes.

In addition, the book serves the IT manager as a handbook for the implementation of specific Internet solutions. Programmers will find the presentation of complete applications of interest, especially because the applications contain technical information. The programming guidelines offer a detailed view of developing Internet application components for the R/3 System. We treat in detail the technical background of the R/3 System's ability to work on the Internet. The background enables readers to estimate the essential options, the possible risks and the required effort. The programming guidelines end with an introduction of the multimedia and interactive possibilities available today with the use of enhanced HTML tools.

This book is a compendium that reliably answers all the relevant questions on the selection, creation and use of R/3 business applications on the Internet.

Mario Pérez

Foreword

Globalization of markets and the resulting competition are forcing enterprises to optimize business processes even further. Demands for optimization and greater efficiency become particularly urgent when the flow of business information extends beyond the borders of the enterprise.

The Internet offers international enterprises not only new sales and distribution channels, but also innovative business processes. The worldwide penetration and high level of standardization of the Internet also contribute to increasing globalization.

The business processes of the SAP R/3 System are optimally suited to operating worldwide processing chains without breaks in media. Synchronized communications between individual enterprises become an important factor in these chains. Optimization applies not only to the flow of information within one enterprise, but also to the entire flow of business.

In understandable language, the authors introduce the essential aspects of the Internet and indicate the possibilities of SAP business solutions on the Internet with practical examples. To give application developers the ability to implement R/3 Internet components, they also concretely present technical implementation in detail.

The active collaboration of many SAP and iXOS developers, especially from the ALE/WEB team, made this book possible. Without the very open information policies of SAP AG and cooperative collaboration with Addison Wesley Longman, timely publication would have been impossible.

We thank all our colleagues who have contributed to the successful implementation of business applications on the Internet.

Bernhard Hochlehnert
Walldorf
Hans W. Strack-Zimmermann
Grasbrunn

Acknowledgements

Its timely subject and the extremely rapid cycle of technological development have made this new book necessary. Peter Lipps provided the basic idea for the book, an idea successfully transformed into reality by a previous work.

Since the first version of the Internet Transaction Server, the ALE/Web Team, a cooperative venture of SAP AG and iXOS Software AG, has provided significant further development. Here we particularly thank Michael Heckner and the entire development team for their indispensable contributions to the current architecture of the Internet Transaction Server. We offer special thanks to Thomas Hantusch, who agreed to the use of important portions of *SAP R/3 im Internet* and contributed to the success of this work.

However, only the active and open support for this book provided by SAP AG made the publication of extensive revisions possible. Among many others, Bernhard Hochlehnert, Claus Neugebauer and Peter Lorenz offered valuable support and decidedly unruffled collaboration. Their work again expressed the positive and constructive partnership between SAP AG and iXOS Software AG.

The hand of Andres Pérez produced the professional graphics. His work ensured success in the overall quality of the book and in the depictions of various user scenarios.

The rapid publication of this book owes much to the uncomplicated collaboration we enjoyed with the publisher, Addison Wesley Longman.

Mario.Perez@munich.ixos.de
Peter.Zencke@sap-ag.de
Alexander.Hildenbrand@munich.ixos.de
Bernd.Matzke@ixos-leipzig.de

Contents

1 Information technology and networked business

In the closing decade of this century, information technology has become the most important innovative factor in, and driving force of, business development.

The advances in information technology have unfolded at an unheard-of dynamic. Constant developments render each other obsolete at an ever-increasing rate and accompany us on the path to the clearly recognizable information society of the twenty-first century.

The Internet or, more precisely, the World Wide Web, belongs to these innovative factors. What we know today as the WWW began with basic research in a strategic project of the American government in the sixties, ARPANET. It then underwent a long maturation period in scientific laboratories (such as the CERN physics lab in Geneva) and an initially slow beginning among public users. The commercial use of the WWW, however, has made almost explosive headway in the past few years.

In the past thirty years, information technology has always functioned as the forerunner for new business approaches. Technology runs ahead of business. The use of new technologies for business solutions presented a constant challenge. Among the new achievements of information technology, the Web may well possess the greatest potential for change among business processes. Enterprises increasingly use the Web as the backbone of business operations with their customers and partners.

How rapidly such usage becomes normative essentially depends upon the presence of an efficient infrastructure for communication transmission: the data highway. The United States has doubtlessly pioneered the building of an infrastructure for the information society at a national level. Such a highway displays an increasingly rapid and close-meshed exchange of information between consumers and companies, citizens and institutions, and companies among themselves.

The Internet and progressive globalization obviously exist within the same context. The internationalization and globalization of enterprise-oriented business activity has also developed without the Internet, in an ever-larger area of economic opportunity. The Internet, however, supports globalization by enabling completion of business activities over great distances within seconds and by creating market transparency between widely separated suppliers and consumers.

Ever more global companies and networked companies design their cross-border business operations to include a general supply chain. This type of supply chain creates a unified process, beginning with the procurement of resources, continuing with specialized intermediate producers and distribution systems, and ending with the consumer. Such integration accelerates globalization and forces into commerce those who do not want to miss its benefits. Information technology for cross-company business processes and the efficiency of the supply chain represent a competitive factor of growing importance.

The performance characteristics of successful standard business software include the ability to incorporate new technology rapidly, to transform the technology into solutions and to make the solutions available to customers as early as possible. The success story of the SAP R/3 System rests on this ability. In 1993, SAP pioneered the first client/server concept for enterprise business use with its R/3 System. Since then, the approach of open, configurable and adaptable standard business systems to support the operation of permanently changing business processes has become the norm. From the beginning, the design of the R/3 System supported cross-border and cross-company business processes. The system's three-level client/server architecture has always supported networked end users, providing them with a connection to business data processing even when they work remotely.

In 1996, SAP took a large but evolutionary step in opening the R/3 System to the Web and to data processing on a cross-company network. The new Internet technology quickly brought with it new business scenarios that used multimedia to address previously unreached users of business data: the anonymous end customer and the sporadic IT user within the company.

The use of the Internet for processing business activities between independent companies, bound only by information technology and a common business model, places users in a new dimension. A business must step away from itself; it must change the focus from its traditional center within the enterprise to cross-company processes.

This book provides details on the new possibilities for business provided by the use of the SAP R/3 System and the Internet.

1.1   Revolutions in the information age

Despite the rapid changes in information technology, three levels provide a basis for an outline of its range. In general, the following questions describe information processing:

- What medium stores the coded information?

- What technology transforms and distributes data?

- What user interface provides information to users?

Finally, the range of coverage and speed of information transmission, as well as the size of the human community using the information define the development stage of the information society.

A backward glance at the development of the information age from Gutenberg to the present shows the technological leaps that justify speaking of an Internet Revolution. The Internet characterizes itself by the digital coding of every sort of information, by a technology of networked computers for the transformation and transmission of data, and by a multimedia user interface.

Today the Internet moves along a dynamic process of expansion and improvement. The essential characteristics of this movement include increasing bandwidth, and growing tendencies to join coded information and compress it into multimedia data. In the business area, bandwidth along the backbone will soon cross the 100-gigabit limit. Users can also recognize a paradigm shift: a transformation from specialized and limited data processing systems to systems that convey knowledge and distribute information more widely. It becomes increasingly important to make information accessible and useful for all concerned.

For the new information society, the Internet means as much as did the printing for the Reformation book for the Enlightenment and long-distance communications the telephone for the Industrial Revolution.

Those interested might like to read Stefan Zweig's miniature, 'The First Word on the Ocean,' from *Humankind's Greatest Moments* in light of the above comparison. Zweig closes with the words: 'Thanks to its victory over space and time, humankind would now stand gloriously united for all time. It would no longer find itself incessantly confused by the disastrous delusion of trying to destroy this grandiose unity and exterminate itself with the very means that power over the elements has given it.'

To understand the dynamic development of the Internet, bear in mind that the consumer market, more than any other factor, drives forward its spread. General political, legal, and structural conditions influence only the speed of its adoption. The disadvantages of location threaten those slow to adopt the Internet. The Internet revolution and the PC revolution share links to the consumer market. New electronic equipment with impressive performance characteristics enters the market steadily. The new equipment includes new usage possibilities for both the private and commercial area.

Note the convergence of different systems. The previously divided areas of television and computing grow ever more clearly together. A challenge faces the systems technology level: to integrate new equipment, each with its own technology, into a common communications platform.

In addition to technological integration, a constant challenge exists to configure standard software more specifically and flexibly to the requirements of end users: *user-centric computing*. Employee workplaces must become as adaptable as possible to individual needs. The essential requirement: progressive standardization of business processes must also provide the end user with uncoupling and flexibility. Both the technology (equipment) and the ultimate design (form and layout) must remain adaptable to customer wishes.

The R/3 System has turned in this direction and will continue to do so. The *configure-to-order* paradigm at SAP includes the ability to configure the system in three dimensions: implementation of the system, upgrades and the needs of end users. As its goal, personalization seeks to increase employee productivity, especially as more and more responsibility for data and processes shifts from the back office to the employee directly concerned. In the end, the person responsible might function purely as a virtual worker:

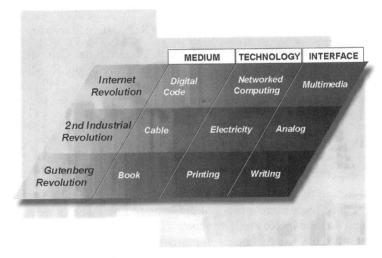

Figure 1.1   IT revolution in the information age

Figure 1.2   Consumer electronics: new equipment for network access

an independent contractor, or as an employee of a vendor or customer. For such an eventuality to become a reality, however, systems must become much more intuitively understandable and not require involved training programs. As it moves toward personalization, the R/3 System differentiates between the following areas:

1. The Internet applications, which comprise the special attention of this book. These applications include a new feature: their appearance as delivered serves only as an example. Customers themselves perform any adjustments required by their own needs, such as corporate design. The functions of the basic business application remain unchanged.

2. The standard GUI features configuration by the individual user. For example, as of release 4.0 of the R/3 System, users can move, pre-fill or hide fields to adjust the desktop to meet the workflow and the needs of the employee. The same ability exists for both the Microsoft PC platform and the new Java GUI of the R/3 System in web browsers.

3. Electronic forms created outside the R/3 System. Users can use Outlook, Visual Basic or even HTML to design entry templates independently of the R/3 System, which allows for decentralized, uncoupled processing. Users then transfer the results directly to the business processes of the R/3 System with Business Workflow, for example.

1.2   New enterprise structures

In recent years, large enterprises have seen a strong dissolution of traditional, hierarchical structures and turned to more strategically oriented organizational units and business branches. These units focus more on special products and market channels; they perform with greater agility. They increasingly function as independent business units and deal with each other much like external business partners. Each new business unit experiences external market pressure. The group therefore becomes more market-driven with flexible units and increased proximity to customers. At the same time, the synergy within an enterprise must maintain, improve or even intensify itself.

Integrated information systems for business control occupy an important place among strategic synergy factors. In the past, fragmented, uncoordinated information systems often resulted directly from overzealous attempts at decentralization, which lost sight of process transparency and integration. When building smaller, but more flexible business units today, a homogenous information system for the company must also build a parallel process of coordination and cooperation.

An examination of the development of networks in enterprises reveals that the first step creates an Intranet. The Intranet connects the employees of a group, independent of their location or business unit, with a common business information system based on client/server technology. Today's global enterprise has already built a worldwide network that connects the various locations and functions of the group. The demands made by the number of users, the size of company-wide data and the corresponding through-put of transactions make it clear that a central or mainframe system can no longer cover the requirements of a global enterprise. Besides the technical limitations involved, the complexity of such a system would render it unworkable.

The old contradiction between central and decentralized data processing belongs to the past. The evolution of client/server systems has created a communications technology similar to the one that IBM wanted to develop at the end of the 1980s with SA architecture and later implemented with open systems. SAP made allowances for such a system in 1993, when it developed the first scenarios for loosely coupled R/3 Systems. This strategy, using application link enabling (ALE), does not involve a new connection technique. Rather, it displays an application design that allows for the creation of cross-system business processes in the R/3 System. The design also addresses crucial questions. Which business functions should continue to require central processing at the group level? Which would benefit from decentralized processing? In either case, the benefits of integration must remain. The greater the demands placed on the operative processing level in the plant locations for sales, production, warehousing and distribution, the more appropriate decentralization becomes. Nonetheless, components for planning, controlling and

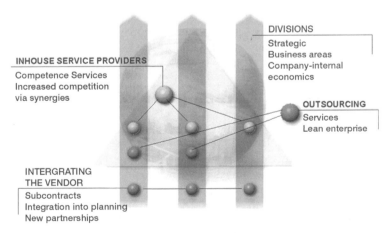

Figure 1.3   Dissolution of traditional enterprise structures

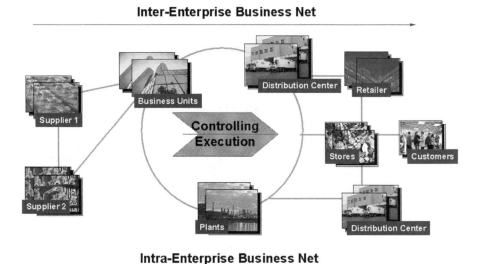

Figure 1.4   Business components in an intranet

strategic decision support must operate with uniform data throughout the enterprise. These components therefore require central control. Some accounting components, for example consolidation, remain functions of headquarters by definition.

Ultimately, an enterprise must decide for itself how much decentralization and centralization, and autonomy and regimentation it requires for its own operations. When making such decisions, the structure of the information system employed by the group plays a decisive role. Until now, the level of the technology has impeded rather than promoted progress. Responsibility for decision making becomes much easier to decentralize when doing so does not lose transparency and the ability to create a uniform layout. Even far-reaching decentralization should ensure that everyone retains knowledge of organizational structures and responsibilities, results remain transparent, and risk becomes evident early. The enterprise must retain the ability to judge efficiency across all lines. Finally, if the employees of the group are to remain teachable, they must participate actively in the dynamic changes of the enterprise. Only informed employees can work creatively. Such an understanding creates a completely new task for business information systems.

1.3   The Internet and the SAP R/3 System

The possibilities offered by the Internet for new business processes and applications have become evident only recently. During the first broadly based discussions on the topic in 1995–96, participants took very contrary positions. The Internet and client/server stood in opposition to each other. Many saw a renaissance of mainframe systems with new NC terminals. Others saw a future with free, self-distributed objects that would render integrated applications such as the R/3 System obsolete. The discussions proved premature. Three-level client/server systems have proved themselves capable of evolutionary expansion into Internet systems when they open their business functions internally with Application Programming

Interfaces (API). This became the hour of the SAP Business Application Programming Interface (BAPI), which had developed into architecture for the business framework.

Today, numerous reasons exist for joining client/server and Internet technology into a new, distributed transaction technology:

- The Internet and client/server computing both use the identical transfer protocol.

- The browser technology of the Internet greatly corresponds to the light client in three-level client/server architecture.

- The current browser language allows you to the imbedding of traditional input masks into richer multimedia presentations. In the next step, browser dialogs will enable intelligent direction by current PC applications.

However, the new Internet transactions will differentiate themselves from earlier mainframe transactions just as they do from current PC applications. They will no longer operate exclusively from a well-determined data source, either the enterprise data of the mainframe or the personal data of a PC. The new Internet transactions will operate on data from various sources: distributed systems of the enterprise units or from personal data, stored in laptops or in partner systems.

For this reason, two parallel approaches come into play. SAP included both in its Internet development. The inside-out approach makes the transaction of the R/3 System accessible to the Internet. The outside-in approach enables embedding external data and R/3 System data in traditional transactions. In the future, both approaches will grow together into a unified architecture.

1.4   Supply chain management

The change from a seller's to buyer's market in the last few years has effected changes most strongly in the supply chain. Markets have become much more competitive. This development makes customer demand for a product increasingly unstable and decreasingly open to accurate forecasting. Since the accuracy of meeting customer demand primarily affects sales quantities, enterprises respond with a sharper focus on the market and the individual customer. This focus renders obsolete large companies' product programs that could broadly influence stable markets. The push principle replaces the pull principle when market demand controls provisioning via the supply chain. Production and distribution must adjust themselves to changed demand flexibly, and not exclude the risk of higher inventories of products that may no longer sell. Discussion of the pull principle is not new. The Toyota concept of lean production, KANBAN control, and just-in-time management have influenced the discussion significantly. Bear in mind, however, that the discussion limited treatment of the Toyota concept to production with tight integration of component suppliers, and even there, expected relatively stable demand.

The supply chain describes the entire flow of goods, from the first supplier to the final consumer. Completely different kinds of business partners participate in the process: partners from the enterprise's own group and partners from external enterprises, with whom external market relationships exist. The essential challenge of supply chain management consists of integrated coordination of information and goods flow along the entire supply chain. This challenge particularly affects groups that operate globally. In recent years, such groups have transformed their affiliated production systems into an internal supply chain. New, cross-group information systems constitute a strategic portion of supply chain management.

Traditionally, business information systems within the confines of an enterprise have limited themselves to the supply chain processes that each link in the chain managed for itself. In the future, we will not deal with the isolated systems of closed organizational units. Rather, the future will bring cross-unit systems that use tight information exchange to regulate the transfer of goods and services as well as the corresponding payments. This approach involves an integrated optimization of the supply chain. Its ultimate goal seeks to achieve maximum customer satisfaction with marketable products at a profitable cost.

An abstract view would describe the supply chain as a communicative system of transformation. Participants in the supply chain act as independent units. By performing their part within the whole process of creating value, they contribute to the transformation of goods and services into products. They no longer act in isolation. A constantly controlled and directed flow of information joins them to their partners in the supply chain. The flow of information serves to coordinate the behavior of the networked entities among themselves as rapidly as possible. The coordination of the transformations provided by each participant should occur independently and correct itself in the process, so that, as a whole, the supply chain behaves as a self-regulating system. To illustrate the process, writers have introduced the term 'business ecosystem', an analogy to systems that exist in nature. Natural systems display the self-regulation of complex systems. Within a community of individuals of diverse sizes and species, a stable and functioning whole exists to provide benefit to all participants.

Until now, information systems have supported only the concerns of individual participants. The systems had not yet developed adequate coordination between the individual links. Accordingly, each participant sought to strengthen within the market and to shift risks to partners closer to the start of the process chain. This typical practice ignored the improvement potential of synergies. The true challenge consists of the integration of all the partners and the motivation of all to improve processes. The individual links should not pay for partial improvements by creating disadvantages for the others.

The essential problem of supply chain management involves use of information to coordinate the desired behavior of partners. For the information itself, the question of technical information exchange plays only a secondary role. Each transmission of infor-

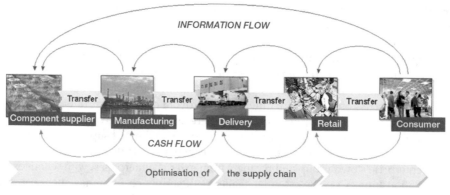

Figure 1.5   The cross-group supply chain

mation between business partners means an exchange of data. Obviously, the participants cannot understand each other without the presence of common semantics. Within the confines of a company or group with unified information systems, the enterprise-wide database established itself as the norm that provided a common level of linguistic definition for the objects of the enterprise. Without a similar, predominant level of semantic definition, coordination within the supply chain could not occur. Given its nature, the problem of semantic integration in a cross-enterprise becomes more difficult to solve. All current information systems build upon their own data structures. If the partners in a supply chain use different information systems, the links in the chain can understand each other only after translation or transformation of their data. In the past, the use of Electronic Data Interchange (EDI) served as one approach to solving the problem. EDI defines standard messages for data exchange. Each transaction system then translates the data into its own structures. The lack of EDI support by partner applications, however, caused little acceptance of EDI in the past. Every strategy for standardized norms suffers from a handicap: norms become the standard only after several generations of products.

An alternative solution to the problem of semantic integration of the supply chain exists in the use of a *master data broker* that prepares common reference data on partners, customers and products over the network. Common semantic references become important for the exchange of transaction data such as product orders. They become even more important when needs require common access to plan data, historical data and current data such as inventories. SAP will expand its Business Information Warehouse with these needs in mind. Consistent information will span the entire supply chain, from statements on the current availability of items in inventory to prognoses of market developments.

1.5   The extended supply chain on the Internet

The opportunities it offers for expansion of the supply chain on the Internet marks one of the most important contributions the R/3 System makes to new customer benefits.

Electronic commerce, a new consumer channel, signifies the first expansion of the supply chain. Electronic commerce enables companies to use the WWW to reach customers and consumers directly with product and reference information. Consumers, on their own, can trigger the sales and distribution process on the Internet.

Shopping on the Internet probably does not strike most people as particularly exciting. Even with multimedia enhancements, it cannot compete with the physical experience of shopping. It would, however, certainly strike most people as practical to have the seller come to a customer's home, rather than to have the shopper go to the supermarket. This option becomes available when the offerings on the Internet expand to include logistic and general services. Digital payments from bank accounts provide additional thrust to the concept of Internet shopping. Some estimate that the volume of electronic commerce in the Unites States will reach billions of dollars at the turn of the millennium.

Estimates on the volume of Internet-based business-to-business electronic commerce increase that figure by a factor of ten. Commercial and private use of the same technology will strengthen growth mutually in both application areas.

The R/3 System's ability to use the Internet will provide end consumers with direct access to the system's functions for sales and distribution. Companies can place price and catalog information on the Web automatically. Internet customers will have access to the information and companies can provide it without additional data maintenance. Product information will feature a new, multimedia presentation. An order placed on the Internet automatically initiates completion of a sales order that does not at all differ from an order produced manually in the sales department. Internet shoppers receive all the up-to-date information contained in the R/3 System's Supply Chain Management automatically. Customers have immediate access to information on the availability of a product, for example. The design of this new consumer channel for order processing in the R/3 System features high throughput. Today many firms optimize the throughput of their logical systems for rapid and precise delivery reliability. Automatic processing of order and delivery information, along with a high-performance warehouse and transportation system, provides the end consumer with a new dimension of service.

Customer service will become all the more attractive when the Internet offers not only standard goods from the catalogue, but also configurable products. Internet shoppers can examine a broad spectrum of options and configure a product designed for their particular wishes. The Supply Chain Management system routes the sales order triggered on the Internet directly into the assembly process, where individual assembly of the configuration ordered by the customer takes place. Before the order system on the Internet promises delivery to the customer, it must check to see if the plant can manufacture the special product and on the availability of its main components. The PC industry has already developed this configure-to-order process. In Germany, the Vobis company, a principal European distributor of personal computers and IT equipment, leads the way with its Internet shopping service and online configuration. Vobis bases its services on the R/3 System.

The first step toward improvement of individual customer services consists in storing information on an Internet customer taken from a previous business contact. Companies can then use the information to create an individual offer for a customer. The clothing industry, for example, will soon have the capacity to use information on the age, tastes and size of customers to respond to their individual wishes and provide custom-made articles.

The second expansion of the supply chain consists in the use of the Internet shopping for company purchasing. The Internet makes market offerings much more transparent for a company's purchasing department. Earlier systems would have manually created broad categories of data relating to sales offerings in an internal purchasing system. Now the purchasing department can access suppliers' offerings electronically on the Internet. Both the central purchasing department and the user departments have direct access to such information. On the Internet, strategic purchasing links general search functions, pre-qualification and condition negotiations into one networked purchasing and information system.

The Internet expansions of the R/3 System enable a direct connection between the processing systems of a company's purchasing department and the supplier's catalog. When creating an order, users access the external vendor's catalog directly. Orders that users create within the company's own purchasing system therefore use the most up-to-date product and price information available from the supplier. If, at the very beginning of the process, all data comes from the supplier, many steps in the purchasing process become superfluous. The purchasing department no longer needs to request proposals, and other processing steps, such as invoice verification, can, to a great extent, take place automatically. The processing of business-to-business purchasing can also go further. Complete integration of Internet sales and distribution with Internet purchasing consists of new Internet transactions. With the new transactions, an Internet order synchronizes updates in two systems. It places an order in the customer's system and a purchase order in the supplier's system.

Because they differ from today's asynchronous EDI integration of customer and supplier systems, the new Internet transactions signify a revolution similar to what occurred in the shift from batch operations to online systems twenty years ago. At that time, SAP earned a great reputation in the business world with its introduction of real-time processing. The capital 'R' in the name of the R/3 System testifies to this heritage. It seems only appropriate that the unbroken innovative power of SAP today makes it a pioneer in the development of distributed business-to-business Internet transactions.

The situation as it existed twenty years ago, however, has undergone a significant change: development of the new business-to-business transactions can no longer limit itself solely to business-oriented systems. If business partners wish to network themselves freely on the WWW, developers must assume a heterogeneous application landscape, in which various application systems nonetheless understand each other.

The developments made by SAP today within the R/3 System product family for business-to-business transactions represent only the first step toward use of the Internet in the supply chain. True establishment of a networked supply chain requires business communications standards for distributed transaction processing. The leading application systems must support such standard, much as they do current EDI standards.

SAP, the leading supplier of standard business systems, remains aware of its special obligation to provide open systems. The Internet functions as an open system that requires open standards for its success. The new commerce between networked system will differ from today's business. We stand at the very beginning of dynamic developments. As does current business practice, new networked commerce will require open, standard software.

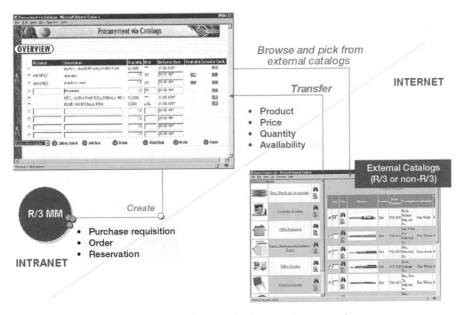

Figure 1.6   Business-to-business order processing

2 Internet basics

2.1 Motivation: the information society

The victorious march of the Internet in recent years has made the unstoppable shift in our society to an information society self-evident. (Remarks made here about the Internet also refer to the World Wide Web. Readers may consider the terms equivalent, as does general usage.) The success of the Internet has contributed to this shift more than any other factor. Information has become the fourth largest economic factor, as important as raw materials, labor and capital (Bundesministerium für Wirtschaft, 1995). Formerly, only a few could use or access the heterogeneous sources of and information presented on the Internet. Today, however, the Internet has become open to the public. What began with the military and soon spread to scientists has resulted in a tendency toward complete penetration of all areas of life (private, public, and professional) by the various information and communications technologies offered by the Internet. The interests of the subscribing groups do not lie in the global telecommunications network itself, but in the products of knowledge and the information that the groups can derive from the network. Accordingly, the evolution of an Internet market makes it more important to focus on an informed society, rather than on computerizing the society.

In the past, employers required competence in data processing. Today, in addition to the skills demanded earlier, employers also require information competence in the production, formatting, distribution, and use of knowledge and information. The job market makes such skills necessary and indispensable. Almost without exception, the criticism of the Internet, found repeatedly in the press, refers to its data processing problems, not to a societal or political problem with the commercialization of knowledge on a global, decentralized network. Press reports frequently note the poor response time of the World Wide Web (see Section 2.3.3), caused by excessive burdens on the network, as a criterion for its unsuitability. The media also attempt to justify a negative evaluation with the security problems that exist. Many consider the possibility of a break-in into an internal network sufficient reason to reject the Internet completely and thus ignore its benefits and potential. Information specialists recognize the additional problem of overwhelming *information overload* that makes it difficult to localize and provide a context for the desired information. Standard practices of *information retrieval* find no use on a distributed network such as the Internet. The situation demands new practices.

Although today's technical restrictions certainly lead to problematical situations during working hours, the difficulties by no means lessen the actual benefits that the Internet can provide. In any case, the problems restrict themselves to limited times. We will see that whatever weaknesses of the Internet we call to mind, they do not justify complete rejection of the Internet. The Internet does not enjoy central organization. Rather, it consists of the contributions of all its subscribers. Every enterprise that contributes to the Internet in the form of a new application helps to improve its overall structure. In a special way, the integration of SAP R/3 System applications on the Internet provides such a contribution.

Recent strong interest in the Internet and its value-added services shows that its problems no longer revolve around restrictive communication between experts, as in the case of traditional *online retrieval* from online databases. (*Online retrieval* means calling information from various databases via telecommunications connections by end-users. The process uses special Boolean operators.) The problems have come to affect all subscribers in the business and everyday worlds. In the past, the vast majority of enterprises already recognized the great need for internal communications and created solutions in many areas that provided the efficient production and use of enterprise-wide information. The SAP R/3 System exemplifies such a solution that comprehensively allowed enterprises to rationalize their information by better administration. Despite the possibilities already present, the Internet opens new, previously unimagined possibilities with its boundlessness and absolute transparency of available resources. Providers can decentralize the creation and administration of information, without even knowing anything about those who access it from anywhere. Especially for users of the SAP R/3 System, the Internet means access to information and information services for previously excluded groups. Geographical location or the complexity of the standard interface to the R/3 System (SAPGUI) prevented such groups from using the SAPGUI.

Many enterprises today seem to base their needs for the Internet as a provider of information and services on a 'nice-to-have' or 'me-too' syndrome. A delight in technical innovation and marketing considerations trigger such desires. These wishes, while less than admirable, should not blind anyone. A presence on the Internet should derive from the strategic measures of an enterprise and follow specific business goals. The people of today's information society constitute the most important parameter of this strategy. They base their informational autonomy on the desire to obtain information on an area of interest at any time and on the use of particular services. These wishes increasingly shift the relationship between providers and consumers. The demand for interactive information offerings on the Internet has risen and lightened the load for organizations. Companies or other information providers can now leave responsibility for the creation of information to consumers.

This trend becomes increasing notable in the banking industry. Competition has forced banks to limit the services they provide in the form of direct banking. At the same time, however, they have released the use of information services to the general public, services previously reserved to the banks' own employees. As an example, consider the possibility of setting up and maintaining your own automatic debits from a checking account. Various scenarios in the R/3 System also use the concept of self-service transactions. The primary significance of such an option does not come from the self-service itself, but from individual customer service, since the system meets customers' needs exactly. Travelers along the Internet do not look for generic information, but for specific information and service offerings tailored to their needs. The concept of value-added information (see Section 2.3.1) considers this need and generally seeks to measure the added value of a particular piece of information with varied parameters. The ability to access an R/3 System at home via the Internet at no additional cost has a distinct value-added component: completely current information at any time of the day.

Perhaps the remarks above already provide some idea of the inexhaustible new possibilities and hidden potential of the Internet. In this book, we can introduce only a few ideas that can function only for very specific types of enterprises. The standard software of the SAP R/3 System offers a broad spectrum of transactions, depending on individual use of the application modules. In theory, all these transactions can become serviceable on the Internet.

The task here consists of identifying the application areas within the R/3 System that would offer the most benefits if used on the Internet. The first chapter provides the reader with the knowledge required to understand the Internet enough to clarify its use for users of the R/3 System.

2.2   The Internet: a brief introduction

To many, the Internet seems an invention of the 1990s. In fact, however, development of the Internet began in 1969 with the creation of a military network that would not fail in case of sabotage or other damage. Before long, however, the Internet pushed its way into our living rooms. The Internet – who had ever heard or read of such a thing – became a topic of everyday conversation.

This chapter explains the most important terms relating to the Internet as they apply to specific applications. It provides a clear understanding for those without any previous knowledge. This indispensable material permits readers to comprehend the strategic and technical possibilities of an Internet connection from an R/3 System. Above all, the discussion of the Internet capabilities of the R/3 System (see Chapter 3) occurs within a rather technical context and requires knowledge of the Internet. A general and application-oriented understanding of the Internet also helps an enterprise decide on any strategic use of the Internet. Readers, however, may elect to skip over this chapter, along with Section 2.3, and use this material for later reference.

2.2.1   Foundations

The Internet functions as a chain of networks. Network nodes (routers), link the networks and permit subscribers to access all the resources of the entire network. Each subnetwork displays interest only in its own connection or crossover point to the other subnetworks. Any information requested over the Internet travels along numerous subnetworks before it appears on users' computers. In any case, users need not know the location – among the almost infinite number of subnetworks throughout the world – of the information or service they seek. Nor do they need to know the route the information takes as it fights its way to users through the thicket of several networks.

The Internet therefore recognizes no political or geographical borders. This feature makes it a thorn in the side of totalitarian systems, which often strictly control access to

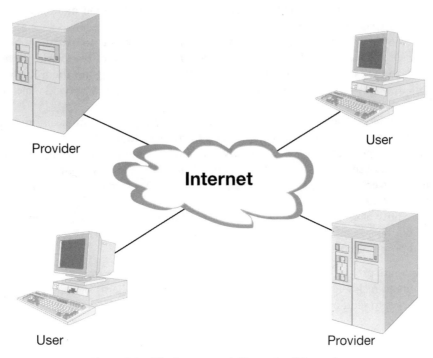

Figure 2.1   The Internet – A Network of Networks

the Internet. Information providers on the Internet, however, seek to offer exactly this worldwide coverage.

The network speaks a common language, or at least uses a uniform protocol family: Transmission Control Protocol/Internet Protocol (TCP/IP). The protocol serves two purposes. First, in preparation for transmission, it breaks the information into small, practical packets and provides it with the required address information (IP). This protocol transmits the information and ensures the ability to reassemble it at the other end. Second, it controls connection-oriented transmission and corrects faulty transmissions (TCP). Individual packets can then take various routes to their destinations. This process guarantees that the overall network, as a whole, does not suffer interruptions or outages.

Enterprises or private users who wish to subscribe to the Internet must have access to one of these sub-networks. As a rule, a service provider offers such access (see Section 2.2.2). Until a few years ago, only higher education institutions offered access to the Internet. No one intended commercial use of the network. Obviously, this situation has changed. Today, commercial offerings have far outstripped academic Internet offerings in both quantity and quality. Nothing will stop the commercialization of the Internet.

Generally, the Internet functions according to the client/server concept (see Figure 2.2). The principles on which the Internet works do not differ in any significant way from those used in the SAP R/3 System. In an R/3 System environment, the application server functions as a server and the SAPGUI on the users' computers functions as a client. To make correct decisions on questions involving the Internet, enterprise management must understand the client/server concept.

'Clients' enable the use of Internet offerings. The web browser (for example, Netscape Navigator or Microsoft Internet Explorer) functions as a client of the World Wide Web, which can receive multimedia documents from the Internet, transmit them further and, above all, display them. To receive anything at all, the client needs a 'server,' which makes the data available.

The client that subscribes to the Internet addresses the server with a unique Internet address. The server then returns the requested documents to the client. A web server (for example, from the Netscape Server Family) functions as the opposite of a web browser. All other Internet services (see Section 2.3) operate according to this client/server concept. Note that 'server' can refer to both the server software programs and the hardware that runs the software.

The quantity of services (see Scheller, 1994) built on the client/server concept increases steadily on the pulsating Internet. A brief summary of important servers follows. Note that an appropriate client must address each server.

- Mail servers provide central reception of all incoming mail messages and make them available to recipients when requested. Authorized mail clients of course, can use the mail server to send messages throughout the world.

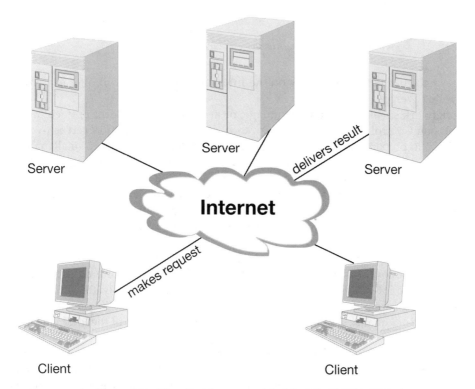

Figure 2.2   The client/server model of the World Wide Web

- Mailing list servers send mail messages to group of persons defined in a list. Special interest groups can use such servers to hold a discussion on a particular topic or to send information periodically to customers.

- News servers enable discussion on particular subjects (newsgroups). Both closed and open groups (at last count over 100,000) exist with some 10 million users (Aboba, 1993). All readers can read and answer all contributions (see Section 2.3.2).

- Gopher servers preceded development of the World Wide Web. They feature a hierarchical information system similar to FTP. Users can obtain any text or binary files via the menus of a gopher servers.

- FTP servers offer all types of files (programs, texts, images and so on) for download.

- Directory servers provide central administration of e-mail addresses and offer search functions.

- Certificate servers administer and generate certification of Internet subscribers. Certificates authenticate participants.

- Payment servers regulate payment for services and goods obtained on the Internet. Such servers connect to a banking network.

- Web servers constitute the most important link on the Internet today. Upon the request of a client, they transmit the desired HTML pages. Interfaces enable the generation of dynamic documents (*on the fly*) that the server returns to the client as the result of external program runs.

In the context of the R/3 System, the World Wide Web occupies a position of central interest. The World Wide Web offers a special value-added service that can integrate other basic services, such as FTP (see Section 2.3.3).

A Uniform Resource Locator (URL) represents a worldwide, unique address for an information or service provider on the Internet. With this address, users can obtain all the resources available at that site. By now, resource formats include all types of media: text, images, sound and film. The web browser of the World Wide Web therefore serves as an important integrator and delivery system for many of these document types. Appropriately, users can characterize the browser as a 'universal viewer.' Consider the homepage address of iXOS Software AG (*http://www.ixos.de*).

A Domain Name Server (DNS) converts this address into a unique IP number (149.235.30.50). These URLs also contain the Internet protocol intended for use. In the example, the entry addresses the HTTP protocol of the World Wide Web. An address might also point uniquely to other Internet services (see Section 2.3).

The Internet features a special characteristic: it operates completely independently of hardware and software. If a web server must provide services throughout the world, it has no interest in the client platform or software it addresses. Use of a common protocol (for example TCP/IP and HTTP for the World Wide Web) remains the only important consideration. The enormous number of web browsers on the market clearly shows that users can work with the most varied platforms. Hardware specifications deal only with questions of the performance required for handling specific tasks.

For an enterprise, this means that it can operate internally with extremely heterogeneous hardware. In most cases, companies do not need to purchase any additional hardware. The same holds true for external service providers and all other subscribers to the Internet. An enterprise that wishes to offer its services on the Internet receives an important gift. It must pay no attention to the network itself or to the equipment used by clients. A worldwide standard already exists. There is one exception: mainframe systems, such as those used in many large enterprises, for example insurance companies. Terminals attached to these systems cannot accept the client software required for the Internet.

2.2.2   Online services and Internet service providers

Two relatively clearly divided classes of providers can create an online presence for an enterprise: online services and Internet service providers. Each option possesses its own completely different characteristics. Users must first become aware of the different services that each offers. A decision depends directly upon the goals set by the enterprise for its presence on the Internet. Here we assume that an enterprise offers services, that it wishes to provide information to its global client base, and that users may appear anonymously or as familiar clients. The appropriate level of connection to the Internet differs from that of a private user, who only occasionally reads e-mail or examines the latest issue of an online magazine. The online presence of an enterprise must supply a satisfactory response time, even in periods of high load. If a company wishes to sell and distribute products and services, it must also investigate a method for processing payments.

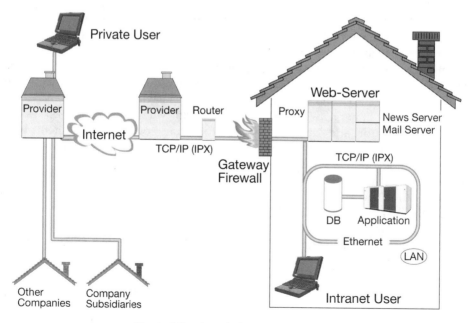

Figure 2.3   A typical Internet landscape

Online services

Online services feature a primarily closed group of users and a closed information area. Only direct members of the service can access its functions. The majority of formats and services remain proprietary today, although an increasing trend toward open standard also exists. For a long time, only subscribers of special online services had access to e-mail. Gateways have meanwhile made the mail servers of other online services and of the Internet accessible. Since all online services provide well-established payment methods, they can rather easily support the creation of *electronic marketplaces*. They can also calculate and bill the cost of goods and services sold online. As long as potential customers must wait for similar payment methods on the Internet in general, the Internet will not possess comparable commercial offerings.

For many years, a user-friendly interface provided online services with a decided advantage over pure Internet providers. Internet services almost exclusively possessed alphanumeric command lines until the end of 1994. Online services have long offered graphical interfaces. Although the situation has improved for the Internet providers, the online services still have a limited advantage.

The explicit collection and adaptation of information defines the second major advantage of online services. They actively endeavor to collect providers of information and entertainment (infotainment). They also use their systems and design to create an appropriate environment. The group that comes together in the process forms a type of virtual community.

As a rule, online services depend on centralized network structures. Central computers store information and make it available to users over a proprietary network. This network consists of direct connections. Compared to the Internet, these networks offer greater security. As seen above, the Internet transmits IP packets over an open network.

In the United States, the most important online service providers include *America Online* (AOL), *CompuServe, Prodigy* and *Delphi. Microsoft Network* (MSN) appears to reconsider its role as an online service. In Germany, Deutsche Telekom offers *T-Online* (formerly Btx), which differs from its pure Internet connection, *T-Internet*. Online services exist in almost all countries.

Online services handle their information offers more restrictively than the Internet itself. As compensation, however, they provide users with better commercial services. Fees for online services generally run higher than on the Internet. For example, many services charge for each outgoing and incoming e-mail message. Enterprise presence on an online service can become very expensive. These services do not provide the free publication of information and information services found on the Internet.

Online services have recently opened themselves to the Internet, so that their customers can use some Internet services, primarily the World Wide Web. Marketing strategy produced this development. The services sought to keep current customers and gain new ones who wished to enjoy the benefits of two worlds. Until recently, the poor connections provided by the online services overshadowed the already problematic transmission time on the Internet. Subscribers do not enjoy the free choice of a browser, but must content themselves with older or proprietary browsers. Users often have the ability to offer information themselves, in the form of a homepage.

The most significant disadvantage of online services remains the inability of external networks to access the information that the services provide. Homepages on the World Wide Web constitute the only exception. The owners of limited-access online services can hardly rejoice in the growth of an Internet community that will soon form part of their clientele.

Enterprises planning a presence with an R/3 System on the Internet need not even examine the question of connecting to it via an online service. The architecture of such systems makes a connection both impossible and meaningless. To connect an R/3 System to the Internet, an enterprise requires a web server that offers itself to the Internet community either wholly or in part and that permits access to the company's own R/3 System. The next section describes how such a server can connect to the network.

Internet service providers (ISP)

To connect its own web server to the Internet, an enterprise requires a suitable Internet service provider (ISP). An ISP offers access to the Internet primarily as a means of data transport. It does so more globally and more neutrally than online services. To guarantee availability of the complete range of offerings on the Internet, these providers must also run additional mail and news servers for their customers. Anonymous FTP servers merely imitate the habits of earlier, academically oriented services.

Internet providers first received financing from research grants and government funds. Universities, educational institutions and research facilities ran the services themselves. Today, commercial enterprises own and operate these systems. The providers tend to prefer industries and large enterprises as their clients, in addition to the traditional educational organizations. Most large ISPs ignore the private customers and small firms so heartily courted by the online services. Most often, small, local providers serve these customers. Smaller providers then purchase capacity and network access from the large providers. At least in Europe, such providers lack the support structure needed to serve a large number of customers who have no special knowledge of the Internet. Some small providers have begun to develop the necessary support, but often progress slowly, if at all.

Today, every country displays a wide range of Internet Service Providers. In addition to the major providers who serve business customers, many smaller providers address the private customer. The Internet itself offers the best way to search for providers and the services they offer. A search on the World Wide Web (for example, with AltaVista and the search terms 'Internet service provider' and the country name) reveals rich information about ISPs. Web sites offer a valuable overview of the available ISPs. For example, see *http://www.ispa.org.uk/frame.htm* for the most important ISPs in the United Kingdom or *http://www.crac.com.au/crac/isplist.htm* for Australia. Well-known global providers in the US include *BBN Planet, MCI* or *UUNET*. In addition, every state or region features local providers. The following web site offers a search of all ISPs in the US and Canada by area code: *http://boardwatch.internet.com/isp/*. An interesting global service today uses satellites to connect virtually every location in the world directly to US backbones. The service focuses on markets outside North America, where Internet bandwidth offers poor quality, unreliable service or limited availability. For example, InterSatCom (*http://www.intersatcom.net/*) offers a reliable, cost-effective solution for these services to reach the Internet with high-speed connections from anywhere.

Among European countries, Germany, for example, already has an appreciable number of providers including *EUnet, Xlink, MAZ, ECRC GmbH*. German providers function much like their American counterparts. Many providers possess particularly good connections to the backbone of the Internet, its main arteries. The connection enables enterprises or private users to use the services made available by the providers. More commonly, however, providers lease networks from large network operators.

A provider's regional proximity or point of presence (POP) forms the most important criterion for potential users to consider when they choose a provider. Providers establish POPs in various areas so users can access the Internet for the cost of a local telephone call. The advantage of a local POP becomes most obvious in the United States, where many telephone companies offer local calls at no charge.

The costs of the Internet include the following areas:

- fees charged by the provider;

- cost of telephone service;

- cost of individual infrastructure.

Interestingly, the costs associated with the Internet do not depend on the distance from a desired document or the distant country in which an e-mail correspondent lives. The only costs incurred reflect the connection between enterprises and the Internet service provider. Depending on the individual provider, costs arise based on the amount of data, the length of connection or, in many cases, at a flat rate. An enterprise will have to negotiate for the best deal from any given provider; no standard answers exist. If you expect a high volume of data, a flat rate, calculated independently of the amount of data, can provide the most cost-effective service. If you expect less demand, or if the quantity of data varies considerably, volume-oriented charges can prove less costly.

Finding a good provider can present difficulties. Ignorance of the Internet within an enterprise often leads officers to negotiate unfavorable contracts. To compare the services of several providers, you must have a rather exact idea of your needs. Enterprises should pay particular attention to service interruptions. A good provider will have few, if any, periods of downtime. This consideration has important implications for an Internet connection to an R/3 System. Otherwise, online purchases of articles maintained in the R/3 Sales & Distribution module could come to a standstill and anger a (potential) customer. Accordingly, a first-class support hotline becomes indispensable. You should also consider the following points before initiating a conversation with a service provider:

- What level of performance do you require? Consider the size and frequency of transmission of your documents.

- What services (see Section 2.3) do you require?

- What special technologies do you require (for example, for payment transactions)?

- What do you consider the minimum acceptable level of transmission performance?

Many potential users estimate the level of transmission performance without including a calculation of the current load. The larger the number of users sharing a common connection, the lower the throughput. The guaranteed throughput, rather than an impressive maximum network capacity, becomes the important factor. A 2 Mbit connection has a rated output of 2 Mbit. However, each additional user occupying the line decreases the throughput. An enterprise should take precautions to ensure that it does not become the weakest link in the long transmission chain on the Internet. Turning such a link off can prove difficult.

An enterprise must consider the following elements when it attempts an optimization:

- the capacity of the web server in use;

- the transmission capacity between the enterprise and the provider;

- the promised capacity of the Internet connection offered by the provider.

Most providers offer several options for online presence. An enterprise can then install the web server in various ways:

- On-site at the enterprise; the server can then have a dial-up or leased line connection to the provider.

- On-site at the provider; no connection costs incur.

- As a virtual web server with its own identity on the provider's web server.

- As a static Internet presence with rented/leased disk space on the provider's web server.

An enterprise operating an R/3 System would generally consider the first case. An R/3 System with an integrated web server requires special installation as well as maintenance by trained professionals.

If the web server operates on-site at the provider, two options exist. First, the provider's staff must learn the technology required to maintain the server and its applications. Second, the employees of the enterprise operating the R/3 system must have the ability to control and maintain the web server remotely. As the programming portion of this book makes clear, development of Internet scenarios can prove a complicated endeavor. It demands a great deal of delicate coordination between application development in the R/3 System and its transfer to the World Wide Web, or web server.

This approach offers two essential advantages. First, it saves connection costs between the enterprise and the provider. Second, it offers the possibility of leaving technical operation of the system to the provider.

However, the first advantage soon reveals itself a phantom: a connection between the provider and the enterprise's R/3 System must always exist. To guarantee good throughput, we recommend use of a leased line or a very good ISDN dial-up connection. You should also consider encryption along the line. Such a system already exists, as designed for the traditional connection of the SAPGUI to the application server (see the remarks on security issues for R/3 Systems in Chapter 3). The second advantage becomes usable only when the provider indicates a willingness to learn and deal with the Internet technology of an R/3 System.

For a traditional Internet presence, this solution remains completely practicable. If the web server is operating on-site at the provider, the staff there deals with the associated technical problems. Interaction with the R/3 System itself (and its internal database, for example), however, becomes impossible.

A virtual server receives its own identity in the form of an Internet address (for example, *http://www.ixos.de*). Unnoticed by users, however, it shares a computer with others. Such an approach makes sense if you expect a rather light load and do not require interaction with the internal R/3 System.

The rental of disk space on the provider's web server marks the last, and least expensive, option. This solution, however, has a disadvantage in the URL that the enterprise will receive. The URL would consist of the name of the provider and a suffix indicating the enterprise. For example:

http://www.xyprovider.de/provider/ixos

The name would not the meet the goal of individual presence on the Internet. After all, the Internet offers an opportunity for firms, regardless of their size, to establish their own identity. No one can estimate the size of a company from its URL.

The assignment of a domain name also has significance. Network Information Centers (NIC) assign domain names centrally; hierarchically distributed organizations assign domain names within a specific branch of the hierarchy. For example, you can reach the German NIC via *http://www.nic.de*. Every country has a corresponding local network information center that assigns all domain names within its top level domain. For example, one control center handles all domains within the top level domain 'uk' (*http://www.nic.uk/*). You can reach the world's leading global network information center over the Internet at *http://www.internic.net/*. Assignment of an individual domain naturally incurs additional, but relatively low, costs. You can then use the name in a URL on the World Wide Web instead of the IP address. *Domain Name Servers* convert the domain name into the proper IP address. The choice of a name clearly has strategic implications. The possibility of reserving and name, without having to use it, no longer exists. For example, a travel agency that applied for the name *www.travel.com* would have a tremendous advantage, even if it did business under another name. When searching for an online travel agent, many users would land at this site. The right to a specific domain remains problematic, especially when others lay claim to the same name. Only one Internet subscriber can demand and use the name 'travel' under the top level domain (TLD) 'de.' The real world of business permits the same name in various branches of industry without hesitation. Users have seen the addition of some top-level domains in the recent past (.firm, .store, .web, .arts, .rec, .info and .nom) and can expect more in the future. If a company spends enough money, it can even reserve a top-level domain for itself. The Coca-Cola Company, for example, might consider it wise to reserve 'coke' for its exclusive use.

2.2.3 The connection

Once you have found a suitable Internet service provider, you must address the question of the desired connection type. Since the type of connection greatly influences the fees charged by the provider, you should make a decision before contract negotiations with the service provider. You will find choosing the correct type of connection no less complicated. The choice depends directly upon the services expected.

The following overview shows the most important connection types (Emery, 1996):

- *Analog modem connection.* An analog modem connection offers the weakest features of all connection types. This connection uses a modem to convert binary data and transmit it over an analog telephone network. The recipient's modem then reconverts the signal into binary data. Only private Internet users will find this type of connection advisable. Such a connection would make professional offerings on the Internet next to impossible. With a normal v.34 modem and an ordinary telephone line, you can reach a bandwidth of 28–33 kBit/s, a speed suitable for light use by a few workstations. With a K56 Flex modem and an ordinary telephone line, you can reach a bandwidth between 33 and 52 kBit/s, suitable for heavier use by a few workstations.

- *ISDN dialup connection.* An ISDN dialup connection satisfies the minimum requirements for a commercial connection. You can choose between various configurations: a basic connection (two channels, each with 64 kBit/s) or a primary multiplex connection (30 channels, each with 64 kBit/s; over 2 MBit/s total operating performance). Normal telephone costs apply in addition to fixed, basic charges. It takes relatively little time to establish an ISDN connection.

- *Dedicated connection.* Instead of a dialup connection, you can also choose a dedicated connection. The options here include different levels of performance: 64 kBit, 128 kBit, 1.54 MBit/s (T1) or 45 MBit/s (T3). The distance between the provider and the enterprise constitutes the most important cost factor. The type of connection also directly affects the fees charged by the provider. In some circumstances, the provider might have to install special communications equipment. How can you determine if a dialup or hard connection offers a more favorable rate? The answer depends primarily upon the use of the connection. As a rule, ISDN hard connections become advantageous with high usage levels that otherwise would lead to high variable costs for a dialup connection.

- *Frame relay.* A shared connection over a high-speed line (T1 or faster). Each company sharing the line enjoys a guaranteed minimum speed of 56 kBit/s. Distances play no role in determining the costs for frame relay connections.

- *T1 connection.* Large enterprises that require high bandwidth often use this type of connection. T1 refers to the predefined capacity of the connection at 1.54 MBit/s, approximately 27 times the capacity of a 56 K line. A T1 connection uses a four-conductor wire consisting of a pair of standard telephone lines wrapped around each other in a plastic sheath.

- *T3 connection.* The use of modern, fiber-optic networks enables this connection to operate with a high transmission speed. To use the capacity of such a connection to its fullest advantage, the Internet provider should possess an even better connection to the Internet itself. The T3 connection typically has a capacity of 45 MBit/s. It is a costly, high-capacity trunk line, usually used only by large Internet Service Providers.

- *ATM.* 155 MBit/s. Asynchronous transfer mode (ATM) represents the most recent accomplishment in the world of the Internet. It addresses future needs for more rapid transmission rates. The ever-increasing transmission of video, graphics and audio will soon overwhelm the capacity of current networks. Large networks currently use ATM connections.

The correct choice of connection also involves calculating the future growth of the enterprise and allowing the capacity of the connection sufficient leeway.

2.2.4   The potential of the Internet

Two particular areas have by no means yet exhausted the potential of the Internet:

- number of connections for companies, government agencies, private users and households;

- number of value-added services available and usable.

User potential in enterprises

The numbers of users in small and large enterprises will very likely increase markedly, once more extensive solutions appear for current security and settlement questions. Many companies have already begun a broadly based program to equip their employees with workstation computers. Some computers replace existing mainframe terminals, others arrive as the employee's first system. Such equipment actually networks all workstations with a LAN and provides ideal ground for further growth of the Internet.

Besides finding cost-effective access to the Internet, enterprises must also address the problems of security and settlement. Security concerns include the following (see also Section 2.6):

- Security against unauthorized penetrations of the network. A firewall system usually covers such break-ins, but installation of a firewall consumes a great deal of resources and requires special knowledge.

- Security for data transported over the Internet.

- Security against accidental or malicious transfer of confidential or secret data to external parties by a company's own employees. The increasing availability of sensitive data and information in electronic form expands the risk of theft even as the information itself becomes more valuable and critical for a company. The means currently available make it difficult to control or stop illegal withdrawal of data sufficiently. For settlement, firms often require a system similar to that used with telephones, where the equipment records the cost of calls made by each telephone. Such a practice remains difficult in network situations and has little meaning in large firms, where private telephone networks generally have static costs. A similar situation exists for hard connection to the Internet. The demand for cost settlement will grow along with a more intensive use of services that add value and generate costs.

In addition to the concerns noted above, the Internet must offer a much higher level of operational security (reliability) in the future than it does today to ensure broader commercial use.

Private user potential

The computer industry projects that the year 2000 will see worldwide sales of PCs exceed those of televisions. Experts expect sales of some 130 million PCs per year. In 1997, 272 million PCs already operated, compared with 7,000 in 1970 (source: DPA News). Such figures allow the large potential of the consumer area alone to emerge. Up until now, only 7% of the households in the USA and about 4% of those in Germany have network connections (online services or the Internet). Approximately 80% of PCs and workstations sold in the future will have online capabilities without adding any additional equipment.

Experts expect that some 15–20% of households will possess network access by 2000. According to Dataquest, 82 million PCs had Internet access at the end of 1997. In Europe, high telephone and connection costs continue to hinder Internet usage, as high basic charges by Internet service providers for private household use did until recently.

A strategy for the implementation of new application areas must also include the intended clientele. Section 2.4.4 ('Electronic Commerce with the R/3 System') will address various application areas and the associated users in more detail.

2.3   Services on the Internet

Internet services include basic, value-added and meta-information services. Basic services enable the availability of value-added services. Basic services use a type of integration or agglomeration to add value to other services. Meta-information services provide information on the use and presence of existing services and thereby add significant value. The progressive computerization of business transactions will require new forms of communication and presentation to make the transaction transparent and communicable. Basic services can provide such forms of communication. Value-added services contribute to the integration of basic services and provide essential support for the visualization of business processes. Online forms enable users to order goods or services and even purchase them with the same medium, and simplify the ability to 'close the deal.'

A measurement of the usage potential of existing and future value-added services on the Internet requires concrete consideration of the term 'value added' (Kuhlen, 1995). The particular value added by any given characteristic often remains unclear. The search for new value-added services, which may place users of the R/3 System on the road to the Internet, makes an understanding of the term essential.

2.3.1   Value added

The Internet possesses considerable potential to expand current services and to create a host of new value-added services (VAS). A theoretical consideration of the terms information and value-added provides a foundation for concrete ideas and a better evaluation of expected benefits.

Information differs from knowledge and possesses a pragmatic character. It is business-relevant and necessary for the solution of current problems. Information is knowledge in action. Although the Internet reaches a broad range of users, it has not yet become a medium of mass communications. To handle the information needs of the most varied users, it requires a user model. To achieve a specific added value (AV), information must orient itself to its implied targets. Various contingency factors come into play here: time, money, areas of interest, habits, traditional concepts of value, social environment, individual processing capacity and organizational goals.

Information depends upon its context, its goals and its users. It must gear itself to the speed, selectivity, currency, complexity and precision of its users. The added value of information occurs in the transformation of knowledge into information, the value-added processes, within the context of the assumptions noted above.

Value-added services on the Internet must display the added value of the information they provide. The added value depends most significantly on the user's viewpoint, rather than that of the system. The system must merely implement the technology required to supply the information. The user interprets the added value that can vary considerably among several users. Clearly, a new value-added service must target a specific clientele. As a rule, no absolute added value exists.

All new Internet applications (VAS) seek to provide more value than previous solutions and competitors. The Internet uses a processing chain (refinement services) to create informational added value upon the foundation of its basic services. The following distinctions between the four forms of added value can help categorize new value-added services.

Comparative value added

The first type of value added is that added by the electronic version over that of the corresponding conventional process.

Internet: This form of added value reflects each new VAS (such as online shopping) that seeks to provide additional value independently of other, already present value-added services. E-mail provides a good example of such value. The speed and currency of data transfer provides an advantage and therefore, an added value.

The added value of e-mail arose from asynchronous communication, no change of media, distribution, speed, costs, attachments and so on. Security questions regarding e-mail remain open, for example, concerns about the confidentiality of data and the safety of the data transport itself (too much data still becomes lost). The expected VAS and their business potential here remain varied depending on the application: online shopping, tourism and insurance applications to name a few. The greater the benefit to the user, the greater the promise of success offered by the VAS. Concrete listing of the values added helps the evaluation process.

Inherent value added

A higher value for information brought about by improvements to the individual components of an electronic product, is a particular service or to the entire service.

Internet: This form of added value reflects further development of or additions to existing Internet applications. Consider these examples: Veronica for Gopher, Archie for FTP, new search variables in WAIS and Yahoo, and other Web browsers or navigation programs for WWW pages. (WAIS stands for Wide Area Information Servers: an information system on the Internet that permits access to heterogeneous databases with a uniform retrieval language (Scheller *et al.*, 1994; Kuhlen, 1995).)

The examples show how often specific supplemental programs create the actual added value. Individual searches provide users with a personalized view of available offerings.

Numerous value-added services have already appeared in the area of navigation programs or search engines, all of which can still undergo further improvement. Searching (no indexing or classification procedure) still contains serious weaknesses (see online retrieval).

Agglomerate value added

A greater value of information is brought about by the agglomeration of originally isolated services or products.

Internet: These services refer to the general connection possibilities between the most varied applications and platforms. TCP/IP creates a context for added value, enabling different types of computers to communicate with each other with appropriate application programs. Telnet also offers access to different systems that previously remained available only to isolated, local users. Various meta-information systems permit central access to systems that actually operate independently of each other. Unlike VAS with integrated added values, these systems do not link individual services.

Connecting an R/3 System to the Internet provides a significant agglomerate added value, since it opens previously isolated services of the system to at least a portion of the Internet community. The added value exists in the views of both the supplier and the consumer. Suppliers enjoy simplified distribution of important information (such as product information and prices) that they can store and publicize without redundancy. Consumers enjoy the added value of reliable, up-to-date information prepared especially for them at any time (such as an individual price offer created with R/3 Pricing Model).

The value-added services in this area have only limited economic size. This type of added value improves the services provided by the original product by better access and improved choice among various individual services.

Integrated value added

A greater value of information is brought about by combining various types of information products or services.

Internet: This category includes almost all services and offers the highest potential for new lucrative value-added services.

Examples of extant VAS with integrated added value include:

- The WWW as a uniform user interface with access to every type of external data (multimedia).

- Internet services such as:
  - FTP, Mail and Gopher (Gopher integrates other Internet services including WAIS, HYTELNET and Telnet);
  - Special servers such as Archie, Veronica and WAIS.

In the arena of personal computers, such services include the various office packages on the market. These packages integrate diverse applications (word processing, spreadsheet and database) and allow them to work with each other.

The greatest potential of new value-added services becomes most apparent here. The manifold areas of integration, however, first require identification and development. To understand today's situation, consider the insufficient identification of possible areas of integration at the start of the PC boom. Connecting an R/3 System to the Internet aims specifically at such an integrated value-added. When various application modules of the R/3 System combine with the graphics and hypertext-specific properties of the World Wide Web, many users can enjoy simplified use of a previously complicated application. In fact, integration with the Web enables many users to put R/3 applications to use for the first time. The following chapter provides a particularly appropriate example with its 'who's who' scenario. A receptionist or security guard can search for a given employee in the data of an R/3 System without ever having to know the least thing about the system itself.

Summary

Comparative and integrated added values promise the greatest commercial advantage. However, the other forms of added value provide the comparative and integrated forms with important support. In any case, a personalized, individual information service (see user model) remains an important factor for any future business ideas on the Internet. These ideas must strive for the most universally accepted design for processing all types of business events. The design must also allow for integration of the Internet into a company's own data processing efforts. The Internet must offer users a clear advantage for the purchase of goods or services. The stimulus of a new technology will convince only a few to use it but will also cause others to shy away from it. For some, e-mail signifies inferior value.

2.3.2   Basic services

The triumphal march of the World Wide Web has left basic services in the shadows. Nonetheless, basic services also provide added value over and against traditional processes – if past practices provided them at all in this form. The following presents the services and the potential that each can develop in a modern electronic business world. Their use has meaning for the implementation of Internet transactions with an R/3 System. This presentation places the technical functions of basic services in the back seat, and discusses them from an application-oriented and strategic viewpoint. The following seeks to evaluate the decisive added value that any given service in any given form can provide by integration into an Internet application.

E-Mail

E-mail remains the most used service on the Internet, as it does on any network. Such an observation should not come as a surprise. E-mail possesses properties not present in traditional mail or in communication over the telephone. A comparison with traditional mail and telephone shows that e-mail offers decided advantages of speed, further processing (without a break in the medium) and distribution (replication). An enterprise that still exchanges important information with traditional mailboxes (or in and out trays) requires more time and suffers from a general disadvantage.

E-mail provides a form of asynchronous communication that does not require the actual presence of both partners. Therefore, e-mail operates independently of time zones. Recipients can process and answer a message during normal working hours, without consideration of when the other party sent it. Transatlantic partners can communicate quickly and without complication. Both parties enjoy considerable mobility of time and space. Normally, e-mail does not remain bound to the workplace. Travelers can also access their e-mail accounts while under way.

The ease of distribution offered by e-mail creates a special added value. The recipients included in a mailing list receive a message prepared only once and sent to all members of the group. A list server distributes the messages to individual subscribers.

The World Wide Web integrates e-mail particularly well. Numerous browser manufacturers already offer integrated mail clients (see Figure 2.4). The ability of the mail client to display HTML (see Section 2.3.3) shows its close fit with the World Wide Web. This function calls the recipient's attention directly to an HTML page on the Internet. One interesting possibility offered by the feature: HTML forms that recipients can fill out and return to the sender.

E-mail consists of a header and a message area. The message area contains the actual message, but the header contains important information on the sender and recipient. Support of only the US ASCII character set remains the primary limitation of e-mail. This limitation prohibits the use of German umlauts and other accented characters. However, enhancing the header area with the MIME protocol (*Multipurpose Internet Mail Extensions*) enables not only the use of special characters within, but also attachments of any desired type to the message. An attachment might include images, programs, video, audio and so on. Modern e-mail clients already integrate the MIME protocol transparently–users need not bother with it at all. E-mail itself uses SMTP (Simple Mail Transfer Protocol).

The most important header fields for an e-mail user include:

- *To*
  One or more e-mail addresses (separated by a comma). Consider the following as an example of an e-mail address: *office@munich.ixos.de.*

- *Subject*
  The topic of the message.

- *Cc Carbon Copy*
  The address entered here receives a copy of the message.

- *Bcc Blind Carbon Copy*
  As Cc, except that recipients entered in the 'To' or 'Cc' field do not know and cannot see the addresses of those entered in this field.

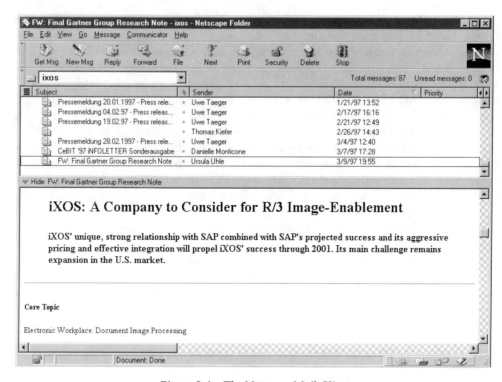

Figure 2.4   The Netscape Mail Client

- *Reply-To*
  The recipient can send a direct reply to the author of the previous message.

Within the World Wide Web, e-mail offers customers the opportunity to establish contact with an enterprise. Consider the following uses in the economic environment:

- customer requests to the enterprise;

- feedback for the enterprise;

- mailing lists for specific groups of clients;

- delivery of the requested information.

Newsgroups

News servers permit access to various newsgroups. Worldwide, an association of more than 40,000 news servers exchange messages among each other using the Network News Transfer Protocol (NNTP) protocol. Newsgroups operate within a topically ordered, hierarchical classification system.

Users can find a newsgroup on almost any topic today. Called bulletin boards in the United States, newsgroups also function like a blackboard. Users can read information already written or can add new contributions to a specific discussion. Within a newsgroup, threads identify the flow of a discussion and allow new readers to reconstruct it. In addition to countless public newsgroups, offered to customers by most Internet service providers, an almost infinite number of private discussions groups have arisen. In many cases, users require special authorization to participate in private discussions. Newsgroups can function with or without moderators.

An individual news server for an enterprise can markedly foster an exchange of information between its employees and its customers. In the latter case, a company can check the reaction to newly introduced software and test it for bugs. Users often discuss software-related problems and look to newsgroups for solutions. Companies can even spare themselves product support, since newsgroups provide a form of self-help for participants. Other economic sectors can also imagine appropriate uses for newsgroups. Newsgroups provide an added value similar to that of mailing lists. Newsgroups, however, demand active participation. Mailing lists often supply irrelevant messages to their subscribers.

Users create news messages as they do e-mail. They simply enter the name of the newsgroup, instead of a personal address, in the "To" field.

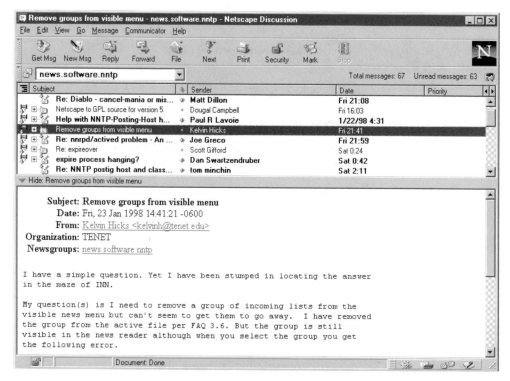

Figure 2.5   Newsgroups with Netscape Navigator

File transfer (FTP)

Before the appearance of the World Wide Web, File Transfer Protocol (FTP) served as the most important and most used service on the Internet. As its name implies, FTP permits the transfer of any kind of files between any computers on the Internet. The popularity of FTP arose from the reliable and free services offered by anonymous FTP servers. These anonymous computers offer access without a password. Users can then navigate within the file system of the remote computer as they do in their local systems. FTP allows the selection and transfer of both individual files and complete directories. An FTP session also operates according to client/server principles. The World Wide Web now serves as another client, in addition to traditional clients that use different operating systems.

Through browsers, the World Wide Web offers a function similar to FTP. Users can save documents referenced by hyperlinks to local disk drives. An FTP connection, however, provides the advantages of a control design, the ability to set parameters to personal preferences and a guarantee of secure transfer.

Many software firms currently offer software downloads with FTP. The transparency and elegance of the integration provided here often leaves users completely unaware of having had an FTP connection.

FTP remains indispensable for all enterprises that wish to transfer files of whatever sort (images, programs, audio, video and so on).

2.3.3   Value-added services

Value-added services offer navigation tools that provide users with an easy way to search for desired information among the various data available on the Internet. The World Wide Web has established itself as the leader among navigation services. The Web's integrated value-added character offers users a uniform interface not only to access other services on the Internet, but also to connect to different IT systems within a company. Our primary interest here lies in the connection to an R/3 System.

This marriage joins two quite different worlds to each other. The following section examines the basics of the World Wide Web and provides the preparatory work needed to understand Chapter 3 (The SAP R/3 System and the Internet). Unfortunately, this section cannot treat other value-added services, such as WAIS databases or Gopher servers.

World Wide Web (WWW)

The popularity of the WWW rests primarily upon its ease of use. The WWW also benefits from the excellent multimedia properties that lend luster to many application areas. These characteristics make the jump from a technical to an application-oriented world successful.

As the previous sections indicate, the WWW can not only integrate different media formats, but also additional protocols (e-mail, newsgroups, FTP, Gopher and so on). The WWW uses the HTTP protocol, but generally addresses documents in Hypertext Markup Language (HTML) format. For example, the URL *http://www.ixos.de/index.html* requests an HTML document named *index.html* from the server at iXOS Software AG. HTML rests upon the hypertext paradigm (see Kuhlen, 1991) if with somewhat limited functions. The use of this paradigm displays the primary added value of the WWW. The hypertext links used by the WWW enable the preparation of worldwide address information associated with a given user. This ability permits transparent access to the most diverse resources of the Internet. A hyperlink contained in the current document leads users to other documents that, unknown to them, wait for them on the same or a completely different web server.

The worldwide standardization of WWW pages with HTML ensures uniform handling of texts indented for transfer, including integrated hyperlinks. The WWW also uses GIF, a similar standard for graphics. HTML is a special Document Type Declaration (DTD) of the Standard General Markup Language (SGML). It describes the structure of a document rather than its format (see Riehm *et al.*, 1992). Each web browser (the client, for example Netscape Navigator or Microsoft Internet Explorer) interprets and presents the requested document according to available information on its structure. Accordingly, different browsers may well present the same structure information completely differently.

An HTML document uses *markup tags*, or simply *tags*, to store the structure language. The tags frame portions of the HTML document and thus describe its structure. A very simple HTML page would appear as follows:

```
<HTML>
<TITLE> The title of the WWW document </TITLE>
<BODY>
<H1> Heading 1 </H1>
     This is normal text.
</BODY>
</HTML>
```

The design of HTML originally foresaw the use of texts and hidden hyperlinks. The integration of interactive components has increasingly required supplementary tags, so that browsers require additional abilities to interpret the tags. Examples of such tags include JavaScript from Netscape or VBScript from Microsoft. To interpret these script languages, browsers require special preparation, which has led to considerable criticism. Proprietary solutions now endanger the original standardization desired by HTML. If a browser does not understand the tags in an HTML document, it usually ignores them.

Web servers often do not store HTML documents that users might request. Instead, the server must generate them on the fly. Various standard procedures exist to generate such documents. The Common Gateway Interface (CGI) permits users to call programs on the web server with hypertext links. Execution of the programs produces a prepared HTML document that the server then returns to the user. The integration of applications functions similarly with the Application Programming Interface (API) of the web server.

Our goal would produce a similar procedure for the integration of an R/3 System into the World Wide Web. The various possibilities for interaction with an R/3 System (see Chapter 3) result in various designs for implementing integration into the World Wide Web. In any event, all solutions must operate with the interfaces noted above. A web server must eventually possess a document in HTML format that it can return to the user's client for display.

use this technology to provide account applications on the Internet. With ActiveX, Microsoft offers an entire palette of interactive possibilities for integrating existing Microsoft applications on the Internet.

2.3.4 Meta-information services

Meta-information services have become indispensable for better use of the Internet services. They attempt to simplify and improve existing provision of information and services. The much-used Archie Server helps to find a given file on FTP servers. The World Wide Web uses an entire range of competing search engines. They differ from each other in how they organize information. Some pre-classify information. Others supply a large quantity of searchable sources, but here the user must often deal with a low relevance quota.

To make its presence on the Internet known, an enterprise must take some initial steps. Meta-information services can provide significant help in this process. An enterprise should make its own services known (in as classified a form as possible) to the most important search engines in addition to traditional marketing efforts such as advertising and direct mail. Some services use robots to find services offered by an enterprise, although the enterprise itself remains unaware of the robot's activities. The robots periodically search the Internet for new sources of information. In such cases, an enterprise should design its HTML pages to make their contents as clear as possible to the robot and, therefore, the search engine. The header area of an HTML page can include entries for content or keywords in meta-fields. The following servers enjoyed great popularity in 1997:

- AltaVista (*http://www.altavista.digital.com*);

- Lycos (*http://www.lycos.com*);

- Yahoo (*http://www.yahoo.com*);

- Infoseek (*http://www.infoseek.com*);

- Excite (*http://www.excite.com*).

For a good overview, consult the Netscape server (*http://home.netscape.com/home/internet-search.html*)

The large number of meta-information services has given rise to meta-meta-information services. They use a transparent user interface to search for information with the various search engines. In most cases users never know what search engine or system returned a particular hit.

A mall provides another option for integration of an enterprise's Internet offerings. Malls summarize various suppliers in different categories. The value of this approach depends on the popularity of the particular mall. A search within Yahoo for online shopping malls returns a large number of available shopping malls. American examples for such a mall include Empire Mall (*http://www.empiremall.com/*) and Emerald Mall (*http://www.emeraldmall.com/*). The EMB (Electronic Mall Bodensee) provides a good example of a regional mall that provides services across national borders to the Lake Constance area.

Many firms that create Web pages attempt to make their services more attractive by integrating them with meta-information.

2.4   The Internet in enterprises

The Internet is the basis of a new form of communication. The Internet will drastically change the way of doing business.

Enterprises continue to use the Internet primarily as a marketing instrument to supply customers and interested parties with information (data sheets, product descriptions, current company news and so on). However, additional application areas also present themselves: sales, distribution, support, service and logistics. Unlike use of the Internet for marketing, these applications require significantly more interaction and much greater integration of existing systems.

Viewed in isolation, the Internet remains an infrastructure for the distribution of information. Section 2.3 has already made that clear. Although the Internet provides a cost-effective means of distributing data, it cannot trigger any action to that data. Today you can order diverse products on the Internet, but you generally cannot check the status of the order or inquire about the remaining delivery time. Enterprises as a rule do not integrate their business systems into Internet applications. Today's 'standard' reflects isolated application systems especially dedicated to use on the Web. Such systems, however, also display all the problems inherent in a lack of integration, consistency and availability of data.

The R/3 System provides a particularly good basis for the integration of a business system into the Internet. As of release 3.1, the SAP R/3 System includes a design well prepared for connections to the Internet and well suited to the demands of Internet applications.

The Internet will not replace existing standard business software. Quite the contrary: it will increase the need for such systems. The success of Internet applications rests upon tight integration with these systems.

In addition, the R/3 System provides a basis for communication with business partners and other employees in the enterprise via electronic mail and newsgroups.

In the near future, access to these business systems over the Internet will drastically increase the number of system users. The Internet already boasts high numbers of users. According to IDC, a marketing research institute, the Internet currently has 53.3 million users. Some 44.2 million Internet users also use the World Wide Web. The remaining users limit themselves to e-mail. In general, the Internet grows at a rate of 100% each year. The astronomical numbers frequently encountered in reference to the Internet require some balance. Not all Internet users also use the World Wide Web. Rather, they actually do limit themselves to e-mail and other basic services. Users, however, belong to one of following classes:

- university-based WWW users;

- private users with individual Internet connections;

- users with a company connection to the Internet.

Some users belong to more than one user class simultaneously, thus further skewing the statistics. The groups also differ in the quality of the connections available to them and in the number of potential users (see Section 2.2.4, The Potential of the Internet).

An enterprise must therefore remain focused on its target group and develop its strategy accordingly. Section 2.4.4 (Electronic Commerce with the R/3 System) deals with these issues by distinguishing between business-to-business, consumer-to-business and Intranet applications.

The Internet saw sales of goods amounting to $60 million in 1994, $200 million in 1995, and, according to Forrester Research, $500 million in 1997. Forecasts place revenues in 2000 at between $70 and $200 billion.

By 2004, the Internet will handle revenues of between $600 and $800 billion, and account for 5–10% of retail sales (source: *http://www.magnamedia.de/*). According to its own figures, Dell currently reckons with $3 million in daily revenues from its Web site, about 10% of its total revenues. Seventy percent of revenues come from standard PCs, the remainder from notebooks and servers. An observation of expected market volume divided according to the business-to-business and consumer areas, provides the information in Figure 2.8. In the long term, much higher potential volume exists in business-to-business commerce.

The electronic marketplace of the Internet will continue to increase its market share and no one can continue to overlook it. In the future, the Internet will define the landscape of communications and replace current business practices, such as faxing (Gartner Group). A future enterprise without an Internet connection will soon become as unimaginable as one without a fax machine today.

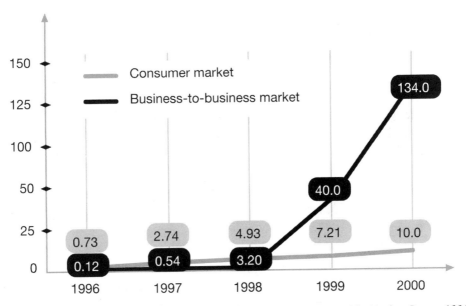

Figure 2.8   Expected market volume according to market segment (the Yankee Group, 1996)

The security of business transactions and a practical payment method (see Sections 2.5 and 2.6) constitute the essential factors for the complete and broad-based establishment of the Internet as a business platform.

2.4.1   Benefits of business on the Internet

Processing business transaction over the Internet or with the use of Internet technology offers several wide-ranging advantages. Different advantages apply to different enterprises, depending on the type and structure of the company (Lipps, 1995). More than anything else, the Internet offers a medium of communication. No enterprise can regard itself as self-sufficient in its supply of information. In various forms, both internal and external communication will always take place. The forms of communication provide different application area, each with specific characteristics and advantages.

Every enterprise should consider the suitability of using the Internet to process its own business transactions before it actually decides to do so. It must do so within the context of its strategic orientation (see Section 2.4.2). Regardless of the special potential offered by various application areas, some Internet-specific advantages exist for both customers and suppliers.

Consumers enjoy the following advantages:

- The Internet has no closing time. The customer has access to offerings at any time of the day or night.

- The Internet turns the world into a global village. A click of the mouse places every supplier in the world at the customer's disposal.

- Consumers have direct access to supplier systems in real time, assuming sufficient network throughput. They can make (purchasing) decisions immediately.

- The Internet displays current information, new offerings and additional suppliers as soon as they appear.

- Every computer and operating system platform uses the same WWW user interface, the browser, which serves as a 'universal client.' The browser features childishly simple ease of use and attractiveness. It clearly presents multimedia materials, such as business graphics, 3D animation, music, speech and video.

- The browser offers simple navigation within the information: a click of the mouse suffices. Search engines finds every occurrence of the search argument throughout the world.

- Internet technology offers an extremely good value. Browsers cost little, if anything, and often appear as part of the operating system. Transfer costs on the Internet remain much lower than the costs of WANs or proprietary online systems.

The advantages listed here for individual consumers also apply to business partners that sometimes act as customers. In addition, enterprises have the following advantages:

- The design and preparation of an Internet presence, a Web page, costs relatively little.

- Business processes extend beyond the limits of the enterprise. Customers can request warehouse stocks directly and place their own orders.

- Customers enter data without having to occupy an employee's time. Business processes take less time and therefore cost less.

- Use of these business processes does not require special client software or special training for users. Business partners simply use a browser, the same one they use to access every other Internet offering.

- Suppliers who appear on the Internet immediately gain a worldwide market of potential customers.

- The use of an Intranet, a Internet technology applied within and throughout an enterprise, offers employees the same advantages for internal information that customers have for external information:
  - Ease of use, even for occasional users;
  - Worldwide, immediate access at any time;
  - Multimedia contents.

From an economic viewpoint, these advantages must convert into financial advantages. Although many first think of increased profits for the enterprise because of increased revenue ('over 40 million Web users' as potential customers), reduced costs appear as the first effect. Cost reductions become most apparent in the human resources area, since the Internet automates many services and does not require a real person at the other end of the telephone. Consider the savings inherent in support services for software systems when new versions or corrections become available over the Internet.

Increased efficiency in communications within an enterprise leads to a smoother flow of business processes, the ability to make decisions more quickly and a rapid supply of important information. Section 2.3.2 made these benefits particularly clear for internal and external e-mail.

2.4.2   Strategic orientation of the enterprise

The use of new Internet technologies must result from the strategic orientation of the enterprise and may not serve the technology as an end in itself. Any attempt to use the Internet without integrating it into the general business policy of the enterprise and with no strategic design places the Internet on the level of technical fancy. The potential of the Internet remains unutilized or underutilized. The new multimedia and showy opportunities on the Internet lead to a considered application of the newest technological bells and whistles. Used properly, these applications make sense. However, inappropriate or incorrect use may well create a negative image in the rather critical Internet community. This factor becomes more important with the increasing commercialization of the Internet. Virtual enterprises can differentiate themselves based only on their appearance on the Internet. The actual size of the enterprise remains invisible.

Within the enterprise as a whole, the Internet takes on one or more roles as a communications medium. The task of any enterprise involves casting these roles with the technology currently available and developing concrete business ideas for the Internet. Technology provides a means to an end: innovation remains the order of the day.

The data processing department often suffers from poor communication with other divisions in an enterprise. This deficit leads to a one-sided argument for an Internet presence and affects the type of Internet applications chosen. The Internet, however, demands something completely different. As occurs occasionally with traditional data processing applications, all departments must converse with senior management around one table. All participants must contribute their own talents, ideas and viewpoints to the conversation and agree to the final decision. In such as case, the Internet presence of an automobile manufacturing enterprise might adroitly include a leasing or credit offer from the leasing subsidiary. The enterprise could tailor the offer of a particular vehicle to the needs and circumstances of the customer. Both divisions win here: the sales division sells a car and the finance division makes its own contribution to the profits of the enterprise.

Business areas that require a high level of communication generally profit the most from the Internet. An automobile manufacturer, for example, must communicate with potential customers interested in the technical specifications and availability of new models. The Internet gives customers information rapidly, without requiring them to travel to a dealership. It also provides them with an easy way to compare the offers of several manufacturers. Potential customers enjoy the additional service of an immediate, personalized purchase and financing offer.

An enterprise must, therefore, identify such areas and develop concrete business ideas for the Internet. Maximization of profits or minimization of costs provides a trustworthy basis for good ideas, even if such efforts do not yet display concrete numbers. It may prove difficult to design a marketing plan for the Internet that shows immediate, measurable increases in revenue directly attributable to the plan. Such measurements may require additional market research. Demographic measurement of Internet hits on particular Web pages can supply additional clarity.

An enterprise that uses the R/3 System extensively can use the system's new Internet functions to make the entire range of the system's modules available on the Internet. These modules (particularly SD, FI, HR and so on) correspond to the application areas noted above. Because some applications areas of an R/3 System must retain their particular focus, the integration of as many areas of the enterprise as possible into the Internet does not reflect a sensible goal. The greatest advantage of an R/3 System over isolated system lies in the direct linkage between the enterprise's internal systems and the application areas available on the Internet. The availability of as many transactions as possible on the Internet offers no particular advantage.

The example of an automobile manufacturer clarifies the advantages of an R/3 System further. To present any transactions on the Internet, an enterprise working with a traditional system would have to store and maintain its data, access logic and transactions twice. An enterprise working with an R/3 System, however, can permit direct access to the transactions themselves and, if necessary, trigger additional workflow. If the data or the transactions change in the R/3 System, they change simultaneously in the enterprise's Internet presence.

Users of an R/3 System must also identify and combine the deployment areas that new technology makes particularly appropriate for the Internet. *Internet Application Components* (IACs) already implement some of these areas. The standard R/3 System has contained these components since version 3.1. An entire chapter of this book discusses IACs in detail.

The following sections present Internet designs for the most promising areas of an enterprise. To enjoy a successful presence on the Internet, however, enterprises must also remain aware of the prevailing legal conditions within which they operate.

2.4.3   Prevailing conditions on the Internet

Almost overnight, the Internet changed. It opened a closed, unregulated system for universities to the commercial world. However, the scientific and research practices of university users no longer satisfy the requirements of business professionals. Heated discussions have recently arisen in some circles concerning the legal and social implications of the Internet. These discussions have brought several points to light: inadequate legal foundations and the absurdity of national laws in an area of global and international activity. The most important points include the following:

- legal force of business deals on the Internet;

- copyright on the Internet;

- censorship of content.

Business cannot operate in cyberspace without a legal foundation. Both parties to a deal must acknowledge the presence of a legally binding deal. Until recently, the Internet has operated without such a legal foundation. The primary problem involved the legal invalidity of an electronic signature, such as the one implemented with the public key method of encryption (see Section 2.5.1). The public key method has particular importance for electronic payment and for secure communications. Germany, for example, enacted a multimedia law in mid-1997 that regulates business dealings on the Internet, including the validity of a digital signature and includes encryption guidelines.

In traditional business dealings, the country or place in which the parties sign a contract provides the legal instance. The same clarity does not exist on the Internet. For various reasons, a server might exist in a completely different country than the actual supplier (either as a natural or as a legal person), the goods or services in yet another country. These considerations do not even begin to address the residence of the customer. Can the profits gained on a Web server in the Cayman Islands, for example, remain untaxed in Germany although the supplier is German, operates in Germany and has a German clientele? The effects of the German multimedia law on international business commerce on the Internet remain unclear.

In some respects, the Internet treats copyright as a stepmother. Users assume that they operate in an area without legal limitations. In reality, however, the national and international laws and guidelines for copyright that treat print media also apply to the Internet. The reuse of materials without proper authorization on the Internet reflects an area free of legal consequences rather than one of no laws. The law generally permits downloading of copyrighted texts for personal use. A problem of responsibility appears later, when other Internet users distribute the material further or make other use of it. The law remains unclear about the liability of the supplier who made the material accessible. However, clarity does exist for copyrighted software: the law permits downloads only with authorization or actual purchase.

The availability of pornographic or discriminatory materials has led to controversial discussions on the Internet censorship. The Internet as a whole, however, does not possess the same technology to implement censorship that centrally organized online services have at their disposal and practice. The US Communications Decency Act of 1995 attempted to make providers liable for the material transmitted over their networks. No simple technology exists to control individual sources. To avoid liability, providers had to make categorical decisions to exclude potential sources of liability. The decisions, of course, affected the general freedom to express opinions, especially when applied to newsgroups. The German multimedia law prescribes prosecution only for information suppliers, not for access providers.

A worldwide Internet also raises the question of how to classify obscenity that should carry a penalty. A previous decision of the US Supreme Court ruled that prevailing community standards provide the required guideline. How such a decision can apply throughout the world, however, remains questionable.

An enterprise must instruct its employees not to access problematic materials (based on copyright or obscenity issues) since criminal prosecution may result, particularly regarding child pornography. True professional use of the Internet for various business areas normally involves only the first two issues (the legal force of business deals and copyright infringement). The last point (censorship) raises ethical questions for each individual in our society.

2.4.4   Electronic commerce with the R/3 System

An enterprise that uses the SAP R/3 System to manage its many-sided tasks finds itself especially ready to take full advantages of the possibilities offered by high-quality electronic commerce. Electronic commerce includes the actual sale of goods and services on the Internet and the general economic use of the Internet for professional activity. Although the definition may seem somewhat loose, it has become quite common.

The ability of the SAP R/3 System to connect directly to the Internet by using various transactions and their business functions make the system particularly suitable for electronic commerce. Applications coupled to the Internet have a much greater meaning than WWW applications that operate in isolation. In addition to the advantages for general business activities noted above, connections beyond the previous borders of individual systems display some interesting characteristics;

- extending workflow to the customer;
- absolute currency of the data at all times;

- absolute availability of a productive system around the clock;

- specific treatment of individual customers;

- the ability to respond to external events more rapidly;

- integration of external events into internal processing;

- extending staff tasks to the end user.

The strategic considerations treated above defined various application areas and the user relationships required for any planned presence on the Internet. The present discussion of the Internet does not include an Intranet. The section on Intranets, below, treats the strategic considerations of opening an R/3 System to an Intranet in more detail. The application areas split into two large spheres (see following sections):

- sales and marketing plans;

- support and service plans.

These subject groups contain almost infinite application possibilities; this book can treat only some of them. No standard recipe for lucrative or useful applications exists. A presence on the Internet requires innovative thinking that considers the marginal factors of the enterprise:

- communications partners;

- geographic area of activity;

- type of goods or services;

- basis of its infrastructure.

A presence on the Internet automatically addresses a worldwide clientele. An enterprise must remember that a sudden, high demand for its products may well overwhelm its own production capacity. To do business on the Internet, some sort of infrastructure must exist to handle online payment (see Section 2.5) for example. In this case, the infrastructure consists of banks that accept Internet payments, clearing houses that transfer the payments and agencies that certify the identity of Internet users.

The type of goods or services offered still greatly influences any expected success. The very structure of the Internet community contributes this reality. The more clearly an enterprise can define and localize its intended clientele, the greater the chance of success. Past efforts to sell and support hardware and software on the Internet enjoyed particular success because Internet users logically made good customers for such products. These supplier/user relationships consist of three groups (see below):

- consumer-to-business;

- business-to-business;

- Intranet.

In the first group, consumers relate to the worldwide Internet community. In the other two groups, the profile of potential users remains well known. Such profiles belong to employees of the same company, business partners, or familiar customers. Many firms prefer a more secure path in the first step, and offer their services to the latter two groups. This approach has an advantage for R/3 System applications on the Internet. All expected users can work with the authorization concept of the system and the firm can tailor its offer to known users. The lack of an established anonymous Internet community (among households) provides another reason for concentrating on Intranet users or business partners in this first step. However, experts predict that the number of household users will grow significantly over the next few years.

The R/3 System Internet Application Components (IACs) contained in the standard system as of version 3.1 target either consumer-to-business, business-to-business, or Intranet applications. However, a firm may well apply some of these applications to more than one such relationship. One example might include a shopping catalogue that both anonymous Internet customers and business partners who process orders over a network connection would find useful.

The following criteria can serve as a rule of thumb to identify potential candidates for the use of Internet applications:

- Do some R/3 System applications promise greater usage through a mere simplification of significant SAPGUI applications? *Self-service* best describes such applications. Consider Intranet applications that perfectly link all employees with the Human Resources (HR) module to provide *employee self-service* (ESS).

- Do some applications gain a larger profile through an expansion of the local limits created by an internal R/3 System? The external sales force would benefit greatly from these applications.

- Would some relationships in the firm benefit from the automation provided by the WWW? Consider a distributed SD/MM scenario: an enterprise could work with two R/3 Systems coupled with a WWW application. The enterprise could purchase materials from another company and close the contract with the WWW application.

- What deficits and weaknesses exist in the communications within an enterprise? The structure of the Internet offers many-to-many communications, particularly among newsgroups.

- Can the WWW automate customer relations and make them more pleasant and efficient for both parties? Consider the ability to register for courses online and to check the status of the registration without having to call (all too often in vain). The training center at iXOS Software AG, IXTRAIN, already practices this method (*http://www.ixos.de/*).

The Internet presence of an enterprise always appears in the form of a central homepage that gathers all the services offered by the enterprise under one roof. A homepage includes both the Internet applications of an R/3 System and traditional WWW contents, thus creating a hybrid work.

The following two sections treat the essential characteristics of a central design for Internet applications. The subsequent section categorizes the applications according to the three user relationships noted above: consumer-to-business-, business-to-business- and Intranet.

Sales and Marketing Designs

Technology-based markets usually develop from the basic infrastructure to the necessary technological tools and finally, to the actual contents. A lack of payment systems that provides the infrastructure for electronic commerce illustrates the special problem that exists in the area of online sales of goods and services. Developments in the United States currently run about two years ahead of those in Germany, but even those developments do not fulfill the requirements for complete online commerce. The inability to guarantee the identity of a business partner displays yet another, equally important, deficit. The technology exists to provide digital certification, but such systems do not yet operate at enough sites.

Note the general distinction between the sale of goods distributed on the Internet itself (soft goods) and the distribution of normal goods (hard goods) by traditional means. Of course, the sale of soft goods tends to perform better on the Internet. Soft goods include all products stored in electronic form (programs, texts, music, images, and so on). The multimedia functions of the World Wide Web support a wide spectrum of products. Improved transmission performance on the Internet makes the sale of soft goods with this medium ever more attractive. Consider the future possibility of obtaining music from an online, on-demand CD service. Subscribers could access the material online and play it immediately.

Online sales can also support sales: it supplies the highest possible level of individual information on various products to customers. Another option provides information or services without cost on the network; advertising covers the costs. The German magazines *Focus* and *Der Spiegel* use this approach and earn considerable advertising revenue.

The design of online shopping applications can use the wide spectrum of multimedia abilities available on the Internet. A considered approach to the flow of the purchasing process itself, however, remains even more important. We would normally recommend provision of a virtual shopping cart that buyers can fill with goods. The actual purchase then takes place at the end of the process. Users should feel relaxed and unrushed, confronting the issue of payment as late as possible.

Enterprises that use the SD module from SAP will find this sort of application particularly appropriate. The Web page will contain the most up-to-date product information and permit immediate purchase.

Most enterprises first use the Internet as a marketing platform. The primary cause for this approach lies in the relatively easy and inexpensive implementation of marketing activities on the Internet. These activities also display interesting properties over and against traditional marketing. Previous marketing initiatives used the tools available: a unidirectional approach from the selling enterprise to potential customers, mostly in a one-to-many relationship. With these tools, marketing departments designed mail campaigns and television commercials or used other media. On the Internet, however, the users initiate the activity. They choose the enterprise's WWW page and inform themselves about its products or services. A marketing strategy for the Internet must adjust to these new possibilities and demands. Direct marketing (1:1 marketing) also plays a vital role in this context. An enterprise should strive to meet the individual interests of each traveler on the Information Highway. Marketing departments will find a user profile of those interested in the material most advantageous. The Internet itself can provide the desired information online and interactively. Obviously, such approaches drastically reduce marketing costs, since printing and mailing costs almost disappear.

An analysis of access to a Web site provides a particular advantage to those who make the site available. The Internet provides a significant amount of information about its anonymous users, without the users' awareness. This information includes the following points:

- the IP address of the visitor;

- the host name of the IP address;

- the time and length of the visit;

- the exact pages requested by the visitor;

- the page that provided a link to the current site;

- the visitor's e-mail address.

Only dishonest means, hacking, permit access to the last point and serve no purpose on the Internet. The etiquette observed on the Internet, 'netiquette,' forbids direct contact of Internet subscribers if previous visits to a Web site have revealed their e-mail addresses.

The information on the link that provided access to the site has more interest. Negotiations for advertising contracts can use this information to measure the effectiveness and value of advertising coverage.

Special procedures, 'cookies,' can legally store information at the user's site for later use (within a given period).

The evaluation of the HTML pages actually visited can reveal the popularity of products. Only an expensive market analysis can otherwise provide this information. Naturally, the unrepresentative population sample presented by Internet users creates some limitations.

In any case, marketing on the Internet offers a beneficial and reasonable supplement to traditional marketing design.

Support and Service Design

The search for profitable application areas on the Internet has often led to online support. Even successful products can raise questions about use or repair. Although particularly true of software, the same issues can affects other industries as well. Support requires tremendous resources in personnel and cost. Automated support services can noticeably reduce personnel costs and simultaneously serve customers better than a telephone call.

In fact, many problems solve themselves as soon as users describe the problem. Consider the following methods of support services on the Internet:

- frequently asked questions (FAQs): answers to common questions;

- online availability of guidelines, manuals and other materials;

- for software: availability of updates or new versions;

- structured forms for problem registration that simplify processing and permit rapid answers per e-mail;

- references to an order number to permit maintenance of a history.

Above all, the Internet distinguishes itself by its ability to communicate the existence of services. The Internet enables one-to-one, one-to-many or even many-to-many communication. The possibilities offered by this ability include employment or realty services. The users of employment services often find them more helpful than the usual advertisements in newspapers and magazines. Users can access them at any time, and they always offer current and long-distance information. The suppliers of these services no longer have to pay the high costs of print media. The relatively low cost of an online presence suffices.

Additional services might include general reservation and scheduling processes performed on line with a registration form or date book. Examples include theatre tickets or scheduling an appointment with an auto mechanic. Actual performance of the service takes place later.

Consumer-to-business (Internet)

This area displays the greatest challenges. In theory, an enterprise can strike the nail of a worldwide clientele with one hit of the hammer. The effort also manifests some problems. It requires security measures (such as firewalls) that prevent unauthorized access to the R/3 System and the internal network. It also requires the presence of an infrastructure to process Internet payments. All these measures depend upon the type of application. The measurable risks find their balance in the following list of ideas that borrow much from the idea of an electronic warehouse:

- The Internet makes products available beyond the confines of a particular region or internationally without additional expense to the manufacturer.

- Customers can view the online catalog of products in their own homes at any time. They can order products directly with an electronic shopping cart.

- The connection to an R/3 System permits cost and availability checks at any time.

- The Internet permits complete automation of contracts: from the order, to confirmation and, ultimately, to payment.

- Customers can check the status of the contract and delivery at any time in the R/3 System.

- The Internet can automate and intensify customer relations.

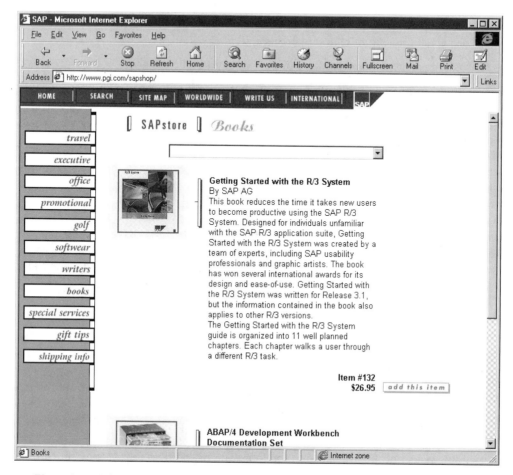

Figure 2.9   Sales with the R/3 System sales and distribution (SD) module on the Internet

Business-to-business (Internet/Extranet)

The Internet offers several interesting possibilities to manage business partners, dealers and distributors. The term Extranet defines Internet applications that make an internal application available to a closed, external group of users. The advantage of the Extranet involves familiarity with the expected users and the ability to grant users authorization to use particular applications. The benefits of Extranet applications thus apply to all participants and costs less than the use of other networks to accomplish similar tasks. Use of an Extranet can both automate and improve relationships between all participants. Consider the example of two enterprises, each of which uses an R/3 System. One enterprise orders and purchases its goods on the Internet from another enterprise. The ordering enterprise can process and make appropriate postings in its own R/3 System. Use of the Internet or an Extranet can thus optimize many dovetailed work processes in an extended logistics supply chain (see Chapter 1).

- Dealers can access their own specific price lists, containing current prices, at any time.

- The warehouse inventory always reflects up-to-the-minute numbers.

- The Internet can process special offers and complete orders directly in an R/3 System.

- Partners can query the status of their orders in the R/3 System.

- In a KANBAN environment, partners can see the KANBAN board and automatically trigger new deliveries in their own systems.

Intranet

The great Internet offensive frequently takes aim at the Intranet and considers it a playground for a company's first Internet experiences. Yet, an Intranet offers much greater potential than many realize. The section on e-mail already indicated the potential of electronic mail within a company, especially when compared to traditional office mail. Many enterprises already have an immense flow of information. Technical limitations limit access to certain documents to a few. An Intranet provides transparent access to important information beyond the boundaries of a department and a group. It also offers collective use of several functions. Consider a simple, yet effective example: online availability of all (public) information on employees, so that employees can learn each other's address, telephone number or special skills quickly. Like the Internet, an Intranet does not function as a centrally administered network, but lives in the 'contents' of many participants. Employees can create individual homepages, each offering important information for the enterprise. Telephone lists on paper belong to the past. The integration of an image archive, such as iXOS-ARCHIVE, allows established employees to recognize new colleagues from photographs.

The Internet offers completely new solutions for employees of large enterprises, especially when operating in several locations:

- Employees can post their own personal notices, such as vacation requests or address changes, in the R/3 System and set them on the way to further processing with R/3 Workflow.

- External staff can also see a list of available jobs.

- The ability to call certain *ad hoc* reports for management immediately and intuitively.

- Processing the supply orders of employees becomes much more simple and efficient.

- Forwarding, views and processing employment applications can take place on the screen.

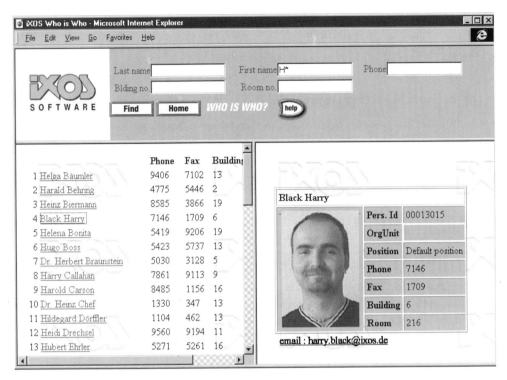

Figure 2.10   Searching for an employee with the HR module on an Intranet

According to Pincince *et al.* (1996), Intranets will replace proprietary Network Operating Systems (NOSs) in the future. An Intranet will expand beyond Web pages and include directory lists and e-mail in addition to file, print and network management. Connection to business systems such as SAP R/3 hones the additional potential of an Intranet.

Proprietary suppliers, such as Novell or Microsoft, run the risk of losing their market share. Simple connections to the outside enjoy the advantage. Such connections hope to enable the use of different applications from different suppliers. The goals remain twofold: greater independence and lower costs (compared to NOS).

2.4.5   Merchant systems

Merchant systems include solution designs provided by several manufacturers. The designs enable and simplify selling and buying goods on the World Wide Web. Merchant systems began as individual proprietary solutions, but soon entered the market as standard software. The same manufacturers also provide modular development environments to generate commercial web sites because the standard solutions alone often do not meet a customer's needs. The powerful commercialization of the Internet has created just as powerful growth in the number of merchant systems available. No one can offer a complete overview, but the following list includes the best-known standard solutions:

- Microsoft: Microsoft Merchant (*http://www.microsoft.com*);

- NetConsult Communications: Intershop Online (*http://www.intershop.de*);

- Netscape: Merchant Server (*http://home.nescape.com*).

The following supply development environments for merchant sites:

- Open Market (*http://www.openmarket.com*);

- Broadvision with One-To-One;

- Interworld Oasis (*http://www.interworld.com*);

- NetDynamics;

- NeXT WebObjects.

NetDynamics also offers Java functions with supplements for standard business applications (PeopleSoft, SAP R/3).

Merchant systems implement a *merchant site*, a WWW application that enables online ordering of products and processing of payments by using a product catalog or something similar. Merchant sites contain a variety of functions that permit comfortable and manageable ways of processing business on the Internet. These sites should display the following characteristics:

- sales offerings with a product catalog;

- multimedia attractions (audio, video);

- access control;

- ordering opportunities;

- support for and distinction between 'soft goods' and 'hard goods';

- payment on the Internet;

- creation and analysis of user profiles (for one-to-one relationships);

- integration of advertising campaigns;

- establishment of a shopping mall (integration of additional suppliers).

The design of merchant systems intends them for isolated use on a Web server, not for a 'direct' connection to production systems such as an R/3 System. However, merchant systems do include interfaces that provide connections to other systems. They usually provide integration by importing (batch input) productive data in their own transparent database. An API interface can also implement targeted access to external programs.

Under certain conditions, merchant systems offer an alternative to the solution presented in this book for creating an enterprise presence on the Internet. The primary condition includes the ability to integrate with an R/3 System over existing interfaces. Otherwise, two systems store the data; users would possess no guarantee of its currency. The following actions clarify the need for integration:

- access to current product data;

- availability of the products desired;

- clearing warehouse inventory;

- payment processing (including the order, accounting functions and payment posting).

The ongoing strategic cooperation between Microsoft and SAP-AG includes discussion of a connection between Microsoft Merchant and the R/3 System. The technical API interface would raise no difficulties and such a connection would find its best use in a retail business.

In a merchant site, the external side of the productive commercial and business system performs the heaviest work. Accordingly, developers speak of an *outside-in* design. Chapter 3 will compare the different methods of connecting a SAP R/3 System to the Internet and clarify the relationship between outside-in and inside-out (the ITS solution).

Merchant systems have the following principal advantages:

- availability of comprehensive functions;

- preparatory organization of the site that already includes integrated payment processing;

- ability to implement Internet projects rapidly.

These advantages apply only to an outside-in approach. The type of application can require a more comprehensive integration of a business system's processes. Control must remain, therefore, within the system itself. The more complex the context of a processing step, and the more intensively a business system such as the R/3 System handles the step (workflow), the more that developers should consider an inside-out design.

2.5   Payment procedures on the Internet

The commercialization of the Internet rises and falls with the availability of a functioning and comprehensive payment procedure. With the approach of procedures that manage national and international money transfers simply and inexpensively, an online presence for many business areas will soon become as indispensable as the fax machines currently in use.

Given the significant financial potential of a good and widely used payment procedure, the large number of recommended systems, all of which compete against each other, hardly comes as a surprise. The Internet will see the establishment of various payment procedures for different commercial areas, as in the real world. No one, for example, buys a newspaper with a credit card. In the end, only a few procedures will operate concurrently in the same market.

Consider the following items as criteria for acceptable and successful payment procedures on the Internet:

- ease of use and practicability;

- compatibility with the real world;

- internationalization;

- low operating costs;

- security;

- anonymity or authenticity.

Many of the competing designs address the critical question of security. The need to protect individuals from monetary loss takes on particular interest in this context.
Intriguingly, media coverage of this topic has focused on the same issue. However, the
special and most-often forgotten property of the Internet remains its ability to service an
international economic sphere without any limitations. A new payment procedure must
therefore approach this worldwide clientele universally. Credit cards already do so, but
no standard procedure to handle small amounts has established itself yet.

Whether an artificial, electronic currency, accepted only on the Internet as an electronic
traveler's check, will find acceptance remains questionable. Such a currency might even
come to exist as an independent form of cyber currency, which no one off the Internet
would accept. The credit card has established itself as the primary payment method on
the Internet for good reason, and secure protocols make it universally accepted. From the
beginning of human history until today, a society as a whole comes to accept a payment
method, whether the method involves seashells or glass beads.

Many procedures suffer from a particular handicap: their need for control instances
and clearing houses. The services performed by these institutions lead to relatively high
costs, costs incurred with every payment: the lower the amount, the higher the operating
costs. Demand remains high for a cost-effective mechanism to handle very small amounts,
or *micropayments*.

One essential requirement involves an anonymous payment procedure that permits the
customer to remain unknown to the dealer and the financial organization. Cash has this
character, and the Internet should come to possess a similar tool. This requirement, however, over conflicts with the need for security. The use of mathematical principles may
eventually guarantee parallel security and anonymity, as does the e-cash method developed by David Chaum, Holland's most famous cryptographer.

2.5.1   Encryption

Numerous mathematical algorithms exist that meet the principal demands of security,
integrity and anonymity of payments on the Internet. Another demand, authentication of
the participants in a given procedure, stands in direct opposition to the required
anonymity. The encryption methods described below display the maturity and security
demanded by this generation of computer systems. All relevant payment methods generally implement one or more of the following mathematical procedures:

- *Private Key Encryption (Symmetric Encryption Process)*
  Private Key corresponds to simple encryption with a password. The recipient must
  know the password of an encrypted message. Several suppliers offer the private key
  process: Digital Encryption Standard (DES), RC-4 by RSA and IDEA in Europe.

- *Public Key Encryption (Asymmetric Encryption Process)*
  RSA, the most important supplier, bases this process on modular arithmetic with prime numbers. (RSA is a cipher system developed by the mathematicians R. Rivest, A. Shamir and L. Adleman (Public Key Process). This method has become the standard for the encryption of confidential data. RSA Data Security, Inc., owns the marketing rights for the RSA algorithm. The process serves as the most important pillar of authentication efforts. Each partner receives a pair of keys: one public (known to all) and one private (known only to the user). Any message encrypted with one key requires the second key for decryption. Clever combinations of encryption can produce interesting effects, among them the Secure Electronic Transaction (SET) protocol used by MasterCard and VISA.

This cleverly designed method permits:

- A digital signature beneath a document with encryption by the private key. Others can use the public key to decrypt the correct authorship.

- Authentication of senders by using their public keys.

- Addressing a message to exactly one recipient by encrypting it with the recipient's public key. Only the private key can decrypt the message.

- *Secret sharing*
  Secret sharing requires the use of two or more keys for decryption. Banks and their safes use this principle: the safe will open only in the simultaneous presence of two keys. In the payment area, this method permits checking for double spending electronic money. Previously anonymous money reveals itself when someone tries to use it a second time, thus uncovering the swindler.

- *Secure Socket Layer/Secure HyperText Transfer Protocol (SSL/S-HTTP)*
  On the World Wide Web, simple encryption of the transmission path between the Web browser and the Web server permits a secure connection that can also meet the needs of sensitive financial transactions. Limited key length makes this method rather unpopular in Europe (see Section 2.6). In addition, the seller can see the customer's credit card information, opening the possibility of misuse.

- *Secure Hash*
  In some situations, encryption does not provide enough security. For example, consider the need to prove that an outgoing message and an incoming message are identical. Both a message digest, the unique depiction of a message on a unique bit sequence, and a checksum that uses a mathematical algorithm provide concrete correspondence between a bit sequence and a message. Any changes to the message appear when the recipient recreates the bit sequence for the file and compares the two sequences. If the sequences differ, so do the messages. The message received undergoes some sort of modification on its way to the recipient.

- *Blind Signatures*
  To spend circulating electronic money anonymously, and yet certify its validity, the bank using the funds gives them a blind signature: the bank does not know the recipient of the money. Along with secret sharing, this method can provide additional

protection against double spending and uncover the identity of the guilty party. If anyone tries to spend the money again, the bank recognizes its own signature and can initiate the appropriate account transfers.

A special problem exists when using the public key method. Someone must assign the pair of keys and guarantee their accuracy. Technically, a well-known and generally trust-worthy person or organization guarantees the genuineness of a set of public keys with a digital signature. Assignment and guarantee can take place within a *web-of-trust*: each participant in the transaction confirms the genuineness of the person or organization granting the keys only to those regarded as absolutely loyal. Another design, which fits better into the commercial use of the Internet, has a certificate authority assign the key pairs. On the Internet, these authorities have an authority similar to that of passport agencies. Demands for certificate authorities that cover large areas will grow in the future and possess a hierarchical structure. Users can well assume that the future will see government authorities involving themselves in this process.

2.5.2   Classification of the most important procedures

A systematic overview of the numerous payment procedures available on the Internet can reflect either traditional procedures or the particular demands of the Internet. The use of traditional methods provides the following classification:

- credit cards;
- debit cards;
- smart cards or chip cards;
- cash/E-cash;
- checks;
- customer accounts.

The Internet already possesses a means to process all these payment procedures. Customer accounts have provided the most secure method up to now. Customers have an account with the seller; the seller periodically withdraws the amount needed to cover the goods and services ordered. The procedure offers an advantage: it can accumulate even the smallest payments over a period and then post them with one transaction. The procedure also has a disadvantage: an enterprise must build up a set of regular customers . In this case, sellers must satisfy themselves with a rather small subset of customers, despite the large potential of the Internet community.

Classification of payment methods and procedures according to the particular applications provides a better overview, however. In this context, applications refer to the amounts of money involved. Regardless of their size, all amounts require handling.

- macropayments (over $10);
- small payments (under $10);
- micropayments (cents or fractions thereof).

Credit cards or electronic checks have long since established themselves as the preferred payment procedure for macropayments (at least in part). However, no such standard exists for a future, broadly based method of handling small payments or micropayments. The following lists the various procedures and their application.

Credit cards and secure electronic transaction (SET)

SET is a standard for processing credit card transactions on the Internet. All major credit card companies and numerous enterprises in the IT sector support SET and most suppliers of credit card solutions use it. SET offers a defined protocol that can apply (in various forms) to various payment procedures. Surprisingly, SET surpasses the level of security available for conventional credit card transactions by a significant margin. Possession of the credit card number and its expiration date by the seller has often displayed the weakness of the current system. The seller can easily misuse this information. SET uses two distinct information channels with three partners: the customer, the seller and the clearinghouse that checks, triggers and confirms the payments.

One information channel, visible only to the bank, contains only the payment information. The other channel carries business information for the seller. The seller receives a pledge for a future payment and the bank learns nothing about the actual purchase. SET uses a *dual signature*, a procedure based on public key. A certificate authority checks and guarantees the authenticity of the participating persons and organizations. Such a system offers customers secure knowledge that they deal with a real business, rather than a swindler masquerading as a business: the system prevents spoofing. In theory, the ideas and design of the SET standard can apply to other payment forms.

Electronic checks

For larger amounts, *electronic checks* provide a method comparable to credit cards. Electronic checks offer two advantages: the debit occurs immediately and the sellers may not have to pay the usual transaction fee for a credit card purchase. A digital signature provides the technical security for an electronic check. In the US, the following offer a payment procedure based on checks:

- Netcheque;

- CheckFree;

- NetChex;

- Cybercash.

Use of the European *EC Card* on the Internet poses its some difficulties. In principle, the EC Card uses transfers between accounts, similar to the check model. When used as a direct debit instrument, as widely practiced today by EC Direct, the EC Card fails because it must check a PIN in the user's own PC, a significant problem for security. Although a central instance might guarantee the PIN and identity of users, such a system would con-

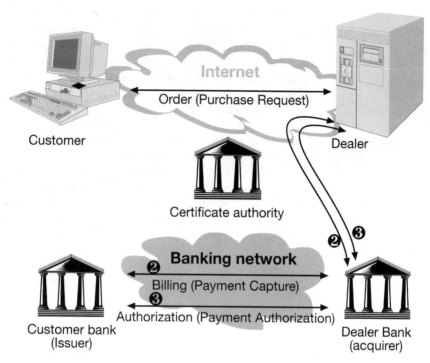

Figure 2.11   The most important phases of a purchase with Secure Electronic Transaction (SET)

tradict the current design concept of the card. When chip cards replace magnetic EC Cards, this idea might prove profitable, since encryption and control both take place in the card's microchip. Electronic chip cards used with the public key process would provide sufficient security.

Electronic cash

Electronic cash defines an electronic unit of value present in a storage medium. Users can transfer the units to others in exchange for goods or services. The discussion of electronic cash on the Internet has generated considerable excitement in the banking community. The commotion hardly comes as a surprise. Should electronic cash develop as a new currency, it promises change and the dangers that accompany any change. Until now, the transfers triggered by electronic checks or credit cards only modified the traditional means of monetary commerce, the method itself has remained in place. Electronic cash can create completely new conditions.

Physical measures against counterfeiting (watermarks, metallic threads) and its relatively short life have always provided a means to control and guarantee the economic security of cash. Its very form, however, makes reproducing electronic cash easy. No mechanism to prevent double spending yet exists.

Cash eventually returns to banks in rather short cycles, thus preventing separate and isolated circulation in closed circles, such as black markets. The danger of an electronic currency consists of this dangerous property: that money circulates in a closed circle of customers and suppliers on the Internet, a circle unbroken by any bank or outsider. Economic entities that run illegal and untaxed businesses could easily establish themselves. The high number of Internet users, spread throughout the world, makes the danger even larger. A trust center, through which each payment would flow, would provide a solution and control of the money flowing across the Internet.

The Internet poses another problem for the purchase of goods or services. Both generally exist in electronically reproducible versions, and the danger of unauthorized duplication always exists. The intellectual content of the goods, rather than representation in a file, reflects their actual value. Unofficial purchases of goods with counterfeit electronic money become difficult to identify and inspect, particularly by tax authorities.

To shorten the length of circulation, electronic money could also function as a claim or demand, similar to an electronic traveler's check. A customer receives electronic cash from a bank in exchange for real money. The customer exchanges the electronic cash with a seller in exchange for goods or services. The seller must then convert the electronic cash into real money at a bank. The bank can then realize a profit on the interest generated from the float.

Digicash, with its e-cash procedure, represents the best known exponent of this design. When used correctly, e-cash remains completely anonymous. Special mechanisms (secret sharing) prevent double spending with the same money. Digicash cooperates with several banks on various projects. In Germany, for example, it works with Deutsche Bank.

CyberCash offers a similar method in its payment procedure, CyberCoin. This money retains the proprietary character of the issuing bank and flows through a controlling payment gateway that maintains contact with the issuing bank over a normal banking network.

Smart cards or cards with microchips permit recharging against cash at bank terminals or telephone booths. Accordingly, some users call smart cards electronic wallets or purses. Mondex, a joint project of English banks, offers the best-known example. The wallets can contain only a limited amount of money. The microchip technology offers an advantageous method of preventing counterfeiting or copying – both remain next to impossible with this method. The use of smart cards on the Internet, however, displays the same problem of derailment into closed, unregulated circulation.

Electronic Cash offers a particularly good solution for the payment of smaller amounts of money. The use of an expensive trust center, however, may well endanger the usually low transaction fees.

Token-based procedures

For micropayments to become practicable, the transaction costs must reduce themselves to an acceptably low level. The costs of the good themselves often do not exceed fractions of a cent. Token-based designs seek to provide a practical solution here. This usage area includes the purchase of inexpensive services, such as the searching in a database, retrieval of information or reading online newspapers. Billing then rests upon measurements of actual use, rather than a flat fee. All current designs evidence the same weakness: practical usability. Although some interesting mathematical models exist, they still cannot provide universal implementation. The most important procedures include:

- Millicent
- PayMe
- Micromint
- Netcash.

In most cases, customers purchase tokens or coupons from a broker. Customers then use the tokens to purchase services from suppliers. However, only specific suppliers recognize the tokens' validity; customers cannot use the token everywhere.

Messaging systems

First Virtual Holdings has become known as the leading provider of messaging systems. The application area served by the company includes the sale of Info Goods, products the Internet can sell at advantageous prices. Customers who wish to purchase Info Goods from the suppliers who enjoy a partnership with First Virtual must first establish a virtual account with First Virtual. Charges appear periodically on the customer's credit card. With each purchase, however, no transmission of the credit card information takes place. Because a virtual PIN authorizes each purchase, this system requires no encryption – a unique feature.

Each purchase requires confirmation by e-mail. Any misuse of the customer's account becomes apparent immediately, so that either the customer or the company can cancel the purchase. In some cases, customers may have received the good before canceling the transaction. If that occurs, customers agree to delete the information and not use it.

Since each transaction costs the customer $0.29, the method applies best to products with a significantly higher value. First Virtual also encourages micromerchants to use its cumulative credit card system. After a 90-day security period, First Virtual transfers the collected receipts to the micromerchant's credit card account.

In addition to individual payment methods that represent exactly one payment, other methods use a strategy that seeks to function independently of concrete payments and a context for payment procedures in general. For such broadly based payment methods to achieve acceptance, they require not only a good procedure, but also the infrastructure required to bring all participants in Internet commerce into contact with each other. Since most procedures cannot operate without a bank, a tangled web of relationships can exist between customers, suppliers, banks, and in some cases, trust centers.

Trust center concepts

The American firm *CyberCash* has already used its trust center concept to create links with 80% of US banks, and currently has its eyes on the European market. CyberCash organizes processing according to various payment methods and integrates already established methods such as credit card payment (with the SET protocol) or the use of

CyberCoin, a procedure for electronic cash. CyberCoin also enables payments between individuals on the Internet, 'peer-to-peer', including indirect account transfers. The firm already uses or has plans to develop additional payment methods: electronic checks and payment by Smart Card, according to Mondex guidelines.

VeriFone has moved in a similar direction. It represents the most important supplier of traditional electronic payment procedures in the US; Hewlett Packard recently acquired the firm. This system, with its integration and provision of gateways that connect the Internet to closed banking networks will very likely find wide acceptance. Banks offer an advantage: traditional banking transactions can depict the financial transactions that occur on the Internet. Suppliers of CyberCash systems know that it and similar systems will eventually implement all relevant and accepted payment procedures. Parallel availability of various payment methods allows the customer to choose the most inexpensive. Customer accounts with CyberCash also permit other payment options, such as debit transactions.

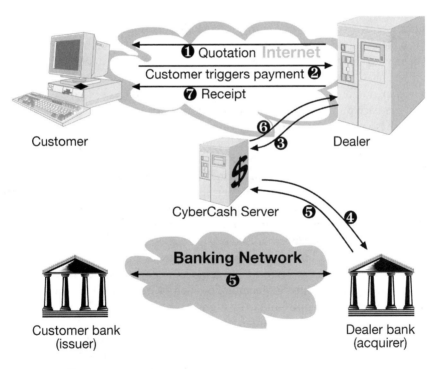

❸ Dealer redirects encrypted payment information
❹ CyberCash Server decrypts the information and
   redirects it to the bank
❺ Payment authorized
❻ Confirmation of payment to the dealer

Figure 2.12   The trust center concept from CyberCash

The CyberCash system contains several components:

- *Wallet*
  The wallet rests upon free software offered to the customer. It contains various pay-ment mechanisms: credit cards (from different suppliers), digital cash money and digital checks. Customers place their credit card information in the wallet. The system then encrypts and stores the data. When purchasing something, customers choose one payment method from the wallet with the 'pay' key. The credit data and the purchase data then go to the supplier with RSA encryption (1024 bits).

- *Secure Merchant Payment System (SMPS)*
  This software, installed at the supplier locations, connects vendors with the banking world and customers' electronic wallets. After receiving the encrypted payment and purchase data from customers, vendors add their own authorization and send it to the CyberCash payment gateway. The suppliers, however, never see the customer's data.

- *Payment Gateway*
  This server has connections to several banks along the general banking network, and triggers the actual payment. It decrypts the data sent by the vendor and forwards it to the bank. Once the bank has confirmed the payment, the server informs the vendor, who can then deliver the goods to the customer.

The financial institutions involved pay for the use of the services provided by the pay-ment gateway.

Today, connections to a commercial system, merchant systems or the R/3 System should integrate a payment system with long-term, constant interfaces: a system that can function internationally.

2.5.3   Integration options with the R/3 System

If desired, the payment methods and procedures for the Internet noted above require incorporation into an ALE/WEB application scenario along technical and organization lines. Technical integration depends upon the interface to the payment procedure under consideration. Rather than discussing any one particular payment method, this section will present only the most important contextual considerations. Each payment procedure requires contact (a connection) with a clearing or a gateway server. The server uses its connection with banks to check the creditworthiness of customers and to trigger the actual payment. This outline holds true for all traditional means of payment, including credit and debit cards. Development of other promising payment methods for the Internet continues to proceed. These methods rest upon the e-cash principle and allow payment to occur immediately. Electronic money (such as a Smart Card) can also permit direct exchange between vendor and customer, at least in some circumstances. A previous sec-tion noted the economic problems associated with such direct payments.

Figure 2.13 illustrates the traditional manner of ordering goods on the Internet. The scenario rests upon a known customer relationship, so that payment can occur with an invoice or COD.

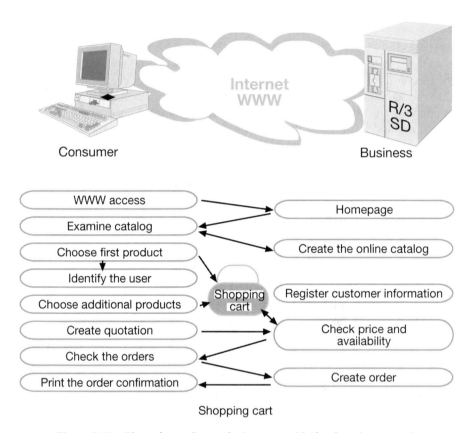

Figure 2.13   Flow of an order on the Internet with the shopping scenario

An expansion of the ALE/WEB shopping scenario to include processing Internet payments would bring some changes. After a display of the product catalog and a choice of desired products, the customer can no longer trigger creation of a sales order directly by selecting an 'ORDER' or 'PAY' button. The system must first check payment security for the customer, who usually has remained anonymous to this point. The system generates the order and triggers delivery only after it has received a payment guarantee or the actual payment. As a result, an R/3 System requires very tight coordination not only with the World Wide Web, but also with the appropriate payment system (CyberCash or VeriFone, for example). The event triggered by an incoming payment confirmation or the direct transfer of e-cash must then trigger additional events in the R/3 System. Users must separate authorization from final execution of payment.

If a merchant server that already offers integration with an Internet payment procedure implements the connection between an Internet application and an R/3 System, technical integration becomes simpler. In all cases, however, the need still exists to perform the work required to adjust the R/3 System to the payment procedure. Such adjustments might include, for example, all the processes defined in a Business Workflow.

Two different payment relationships exist:

- payments with indirect incoming payments (see Figure 2.14);
- payments with direct and immediate incoming payments (see Figure 2.15) and immediate posting of the financial transaction.

Payment with credit card, either over the Internet or over the counter (the traditional means) usually provides the customer with the desired goods as soon as the vendor receives the credit card information. The vendor's trust depends upon the guarantee of credit card organizations to pay for the goods, even for a stolen card used by someone other than the cardholder. The R/3 System can therefore create an order as soon as it has received the credit card information. The SET protocol determines the lawfulness of the transaction and the creditworthiness of the cardholder. A positive confirmation guarantees significantly higher security for the entire payment procedure. Above all, however, the confirmation protects the credit card organization that takes the risk.

Despite the payment guarantee (actual credit card payment can occur several weeks after the confirmation), an enterprise posts the payment only when it actually occurs. Figure 2.14 illustrates this procedure. After creating an order, the system runs through the various steps to create an invoice and an open customer account. The vendor can make an offsetting entry only after the bank has confirmed the receipt of the money in the vendor's account. The offsetting entry marks completion of the entire sales process.

The Internet's use of payment methods that permit the direct transfer of money from a customer to a vendor display somewhat different flows. Immediate money transfers mean that vendors have a payment as soon as the order takes place, so that they can deliver the goods immediately. This direct type of payment can work with various payment procedures:

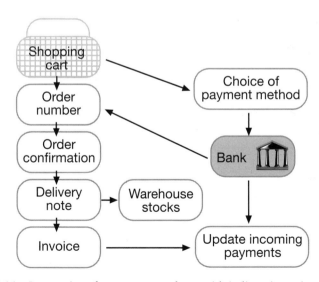

Figure 2.14   Integration of payment procedures with indirect incoming payments

- E-cash as developed by Digicash;

- electronic money as developed by CyberCoin or on Smart Cards (chip cards);

- direct transfers within a debit memo process, if a credit memo can result immediately.

Figure 2.15 illustrates that Smart Cards can initiate a direct transfer from the customer to the vendor, even if a clearing house becomes involved in the process. The vendor post any open items created immediately and deliver them to the customer. One area can create problems: many local laws require that financial transactions remain unclosed until the goods have reached the customer. For electronic products that the Internet itself can deliver, however, no such problem can arise, unlike the case of traditional deliveries.

The market for payment systems on the Internet changes constantly. Many firms hope to develop the payment system of the future. Market pressures will eventually bring some procedures to the fore and make electronic commerce realistically possible. Without a payment system, the Internet cannot support broadly based business activities. According to Weisman *et al.* (1996), systems based on credit cards and niche solutions will replace all other procedures over the long term.

As of release 4.0 of the R/3 System, *SAP Retail* manages credit card payments, installment payments and invoicing. The new component addresses not only the need to store the required credit card information, but also the entire flow and control of credit card transactions. The FI and CO application components contain extensions for financial accounting. SAP Retail orients itself especially toward EPOS (Electronic Point of Sale) systems and extends the supply chain to the end consumer. Besides processing technical finance questions, SAP Retail also manages questions of great significance in a modern vendor system. The areas, which cannot receive further treatment here, include inventory,

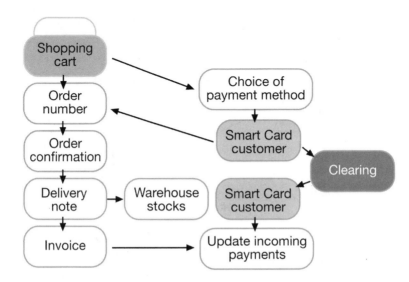

Figure 2.15   Integration of payment procedures with direct incoming payments

transport, merchandising, controlling, EDI and so on. The R/3 System itself, however, does not authorize credit card transaction and final payment instructions. It leaves such matters to its coupled payment system, such as CyberCash.

In the area of payment procedures for the Internet, the market will continue to change. At the same time, it will demand standardization, although it seems certain that several systems will establish themselves and operate in parallel. Expected developments in payment systems make it impossible for this section to offer any more than a flexible framework for further or deeper thoughts. The process required to establish online payment procedures for the Internet – especially for an R/3 System – remains complex and in flux.

2.6   Security components on the Internet

The security of enterprise data doubtlessly plays an ever more important role. The misuse of sensitive data can lead to immense economic damage, as seen in the controversy between General Motors and Volkswagen. Any discussion of protection for enterprise data must take place at all levels of the enterprise's interfaces that may pose a danger. The connection between a company and the Internet should not represent the first thoughts on security. The Internet simply serves as another interface that requires control. Section 2.2.4 briefly presented some aspect of security problems.

Figure 2.16 illustrates how security concerns constitute the greatest worry for enterprises considering use of the Internet. Such concerns focus primarily on business processes handled by the Internet.

According to Gartner Group (1995), the general concerns relate to the following:

- security of the networks in general;

- insecure service aspects;

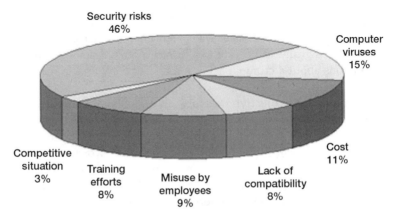

Figure 2.16   Concerns of system planners regarding the information highway
(Source: *CIO Magazine*, 1995)

- ease of infiltrating the Internet with fake messages (often from falsified sources);

- lack of new software for electronic commerce;

- expense required for secure operation;

- expenses and efforts required for main keys of encryption/decryption;

- computing power required for cryptography;

- insufficiently defined interfaces between Internet service providers and Electronic Data Interchange-Value Added Networks (EDI-VANs);

The specific security concerns relate to the following:

- security against unauthorized entry into corporate systems from the Internet;

- confidentiality of transmitted data;

- security of authenticating the sender;

- correctness/intactness of data;

- transaction security (that the data, e-mail for example, truly reached the intended recipient);

- security against importing computer viruses and Trojan horses;

- unauthorized export of data from the enterprise.

Experience has shown that most intruders come from within a company's own ranks. Companies generally know the thieves already: employees or business partners. Former employees pose a special risk: they know how to gain access to the system and they may still possess a valid authorization to do so. Although feared by many, hackers rarely break into internal networks. Because the damage caused by an intruder can reach considerable levels, security measures must exist to prevent loss.

A connection to the Internet increases the risk of a security breach caused by employees only because it provides a much easier way of storing the stolen data. Traditional thievery would require placing physical files into a briefcase. In a certain sense, the ease of theft reduces inhibitions about a criminal act as a thief can copy and transmit important data quite inconspicuously.

The consideration of protective measures in an isolated company network should become an issue long before connecting to the Internet and its potential risks. Simple and rarely changed user passwords reflect a frequent problem. Employees who use an easily guessed password can assume that others will find the passwords just as easy to discover.

The security designs required by the Internet supplement previous efforts; they do not provide a replacement. Guaranteed security arises only from a global design for the entire enterprise, a design that includes the Internet. Technical plans for and actual implementation of protective measures, such as firewalls, should develop within this context. Effective firewalls must protect against a particular person or event.

2.6.1   Security requirements

Security requirements include several areas, as described below. Each individual area demands attention, and each area should reach the security level determined by the security strategy of the enterprise.

Breaking into the local network or local computer

Carefully installed and maintained firewall systems provide extensive security against potential break-ins into a local network from the Internet. These systems monitor the network constantly and maintain a continuous log. The inability of a firewall to offer complete security, however, does not constitute the greatest security loophole. Rather, the greatest danger comes from unmonitored access to local networks via modems or other devices by employees – innocently or maliciously.

The installation and operation (administration) of firewalls demands special skills. In the next few years, the market will surely see special companies that provide these services as a form of outsourcing. A trustworthy Internet provider can also perform such services. The Internet Site Patrol design from BBN Planet offers a good example. The company provides customers with hardware and software, but monitoring and inspection of security issues takes place at the provider's site. Section 2.6.3 treats firewalls and filters.

Confidentiality of data

The use of cryptography and sufficiently long cipher keys provide high levels of security to maintain the confidentiality of data transmitted over the Internet. Practically nothing can break a good encryption process, such as RSA, with key lengths of 1024 bits – even with the computer capacity expected in the next ten years. High security for confidential data remains the essential precondition for the definitive commercialization of the Internet. This area includes the following problems:

- no current standard for the methods and their integration into Internet applications;

- import and export limitations on encryption methods and software components (especially from the US) as well as different legal situations in each country;

- handling the keys and a lack of key administration systems and trust centers;

- partially patented methods and their licensing agreements (for the RSA method in the US, for example). The US remains the trendsetter, as most software development for the Internet takes place there. Products could integrate the large number of defined methods that already exist as prototypes.

Export limitations place a handicap on the situation. Current American regulations permit only the export of key lengths of 40 bits (soon 56 bits). Key lengths of 40 to 56 bits do not satisfy security requirements, however. In the US, Netscape argues for a secure sockets layer (SSL) with a key length of 128 bits. The American export policy regarding message encryption shows no signs of change. Other firms move development of encryption software to other unregulated countries, as Sun Microsystems, for example, has done in Russia. American regulations do permit the export of encryption methods for special message types, such as financial transactions, with a predefined format and relatively short information records. SET, with 1024 bits, provides a good example. The need for secure international financial transactions emerges here as a significant issue.

Any security methods or procedures designed in the future (inkling the digital signature and authentication processes discussed below) will display the following properties:

- Only a few will establish themselves as standards or quasi-standards, so that the core products can support them all.

- Transparent integration into applications and sufficiently efficient performance can be achieved.

- Uniform installation is possible (beyond national borders).

- Administrative procedures and software for the keys are available.

Extensive integration of these methods into standard applications remains a task for the future. Processes for secure counting will play the forerunner's role (see Section 2.5.1). The new IP protocol 'Ipng' (also called 'Ipv6') already include special mechanisms for secure data transmission with encryption.

Intactness of data – digital signatures

Both documents and data can experience corruption during transmission over a network or later. Transmission failures and malicious intent can damage files. A checksum, delivered with the message, can verify the correctness or intactness of the data. Checksums are also called message digests (MDs) with *Secure Hash* (see Section 2.5.1). To provide high enough security, a checksum must have sufficient breadth. With a good digest method (that used to calculate the checksum), checksums of 128 bits and longer have proved themselves secure. MD2, MD3 and MD5 already operate as quasi standards, they function recommended standards in the US. Industry has shown little interest in the Digital Signature System (DSS), a standard developed by the US government. It assumes that DSS does not offer enough security since the government authorities can break it.

To avoid later changes to checksums, systems store them in encrypted form. The (public) key of the sender or recipient can then decrypt the checksum. Both Pretty Good Privacy (PGP) and Privacy Enhanced Mail (PEM) use this method. (PGP is a very popular shareware procedure developed by Phil Zimmermann. It works with a web-of-trust.) Integration of these processes into the applications available on the market, such as e-mail, FTP and the WWW, has yet to occur.

Authentication

Authentication provides unique identification of the sender, or author, of a given message or document. It also means a procedure to prove that transmission of the message or document took place under the correct name. To avoid falsified entry of this information, authentication systems encrypt it. Authors then use their (public) keys to inspect the information. The market offers various technical methods with differing formats and encryption processes. The principles developed for digital signatures can also find application here. Unfortunately, no standard with the appropriate recognition and spread yet exists, although one will soon appear.

As in the case of digital signatures, authentication requires administration of digital IDs, along with an instance that grants and registers the IDs. In the US, VeriSign (*http://www.verisign.com*) offers such a service with various ID classes and checks. A corresponding service does not exist in Europe, although the Internet can provide access to VeriSign from Europe.

Transaction security

Issues of transaction security generally lie outside the scope of Internet specification – the applications themselves must treat them. The Internet mail protocol, for example, lacks any confirmation of when the message arrived and when the recipient read it. Even in the payment area, where transaction security plays such a decisive role, the participating components must establish security measures. Simple applications can implement Java Applets. Leading German banks that offer Internet online banking use a Java Applet to execute account transfers. Future developments in transaction security will likely anchor themselves to higher protocols.

Users of R/3 Systems already enjoy the high level of transaction security offered by the system itself. The mechanisms that guarantee such security for a purely R/3 application with the SAPGUI can also apply to the Internet. The security at the application level in an R/3 System provides a great deal of protection. The installation of firewalls can and should greatly increase that protection.

Viruses

The danger of importing a virus depends primarily upon the type of virus, but the operating system and the application in use also play significant roles. The greatest danger posed by a virus affects DOS and Windows during the import of external programs, although damage can also occur when importing data or files. The dangers do not reach such high levels for mainframe systems, UNIX systems, MAC/OS and WindowsNT. Fewer viruses exist that attack those systems and the operating systems themselves offer better protection.

Virus scanning programs offer protection during imports of external programs and data, but the protection programs demand continual updates. Critical systems should forbid such imports entirely.

The following two sections treat various methods of encrypting the flow of data on the World Wide Web and the options available for erecting firewalls that limit access to internal networks.

2.6.2   Encryption on the World Wide Web

Various systems can encrypt data on the World Wide Web. Secure Socket Layer (SSL) works at the network level and can therefore serve several overlaid protocols, even when they primarily use HTTP and therefore the World Wide Web. The use of a Secure HTTP protocol (SHTTP) offers another option – an expansion of the HTTP standard based on messaging.

SSL Encryption

The Netscape browser and the corresponding Netscape servers have implemented SSL, although other manufacturers have so far failed to support it. SSL uses the RC4 encryption mechanism from RSA Data Security to guarantee the integrity of transmitted messages and the authenticity of client and servers.

Negotiations between the client and the server take place in a handshake procedure. Each partner authenticates itself to the other to transmit an encrypted message between the client and the server. A client, or its user, can use the server's certificate to see that the server truly functions as an online representative of the enterprise. The digital signature on the certificate makes the identification particularly apparent, as a certificate authority must issue the signature.

To receive an HTML page encrypted with SLL, users must enter a modified URL. Rather than entering the usual address, *http://www.ixos.de*, they must insert an 's' so that the address read *https://www.ixos.de*. The browser makes any use of SSL encryption immediately apparent with an intact key at the bottom of the screen and a blue line at the top of the window. Service providers can determine for themselves the business areas that remain accessible with or without encryption.

Over an SSL connection, the browser and server exchange encrypted data, such as credit card information. This procedure still does not provide complete security, as the vendor can still access the credit card information (see Section 2.5).

The SHTTP protocol

The SHTTP protocol, developed by Terisa Systems in the US, rests upon encryption mechanisms from RSA Data Security. Unlike SSL, this protocol operates independently of the browser and supports various methods of encryption, authentication and digital signatures. When establishing a connection, the client and server indicate the encryption method they wish to use, can use or must use. Negotiations can result in various combinations of security efforts: encryption, authentication and digital signatures. Depending on the application and the abilities of each communication partner, the system can use different types and levels of encryption.

SSL and SHTTP currently compete for domination of the World Wide Web. To provide safeguards for general communication over the Internet and to limit or prohibit access to internal enterprise networks, users must take additional steps. As noted, the authorization concept in the R/3 System contributes greatly to excluding unwelcome visitors at the application level. In addition, firewalls must provide additional protection at the network or protocol level.

2.6.3   Filters and firewalls

The treatment of Internet security in the media paints firewalls as the magic wand that keeps intruders at bay.

Creating and operating firewall systems, however, demands great effort. To provide a high level of security, it also presupposes a great deal of specialized knowledge. Firewalls also require constant monitoring and regular updating, particular when new methods of unauthorized access become apparent or new versions of the firewall software become available. The quality of a firewall depends not only upon the features of a given product, but also upon administration of the firewall. The administration, in turn, must orient itself toward an established security policy and/or strategy.

Every increase in security restrictions also results in a restriction or limitation of freedom of movement. Operation of a firewall complicates Internet access for all participants, even those with authorization. The required security checks can also slow the response time of the system.

A firewall can control access to available services and limit use to a discrete subset of users: it separates internal systems from external systems with a monitored entry point (gateway). Installation of a firewall limits network traffic in two directions, outside in and inside out. Firewalls can prohibit any implicitly or explicitly forbidden network traffic.

Firewall systems include the following distinct designs:

- packet-filter firewalls;

- application gateways.

Filters installed on a router normally regulate network traffic, but filter software products can also find use on a stand-alone computer. Filter-firewalls monitor network traffic by examining the incoming and outgoing IP packets. Whenever a packet breaks an established rule, the system breaks the connection. In general, filters define undesirable situations and permit all other automatically.

Routers establish direct IP-connections between two host systems. When installed on a router, filters exclude undesired services of other hosts or access to internal systems from these hosts.

Applications gateways examine the general flow of information or data at the application level, rather than checking the IP-packets. Application gateways permit concrete recording of all actions at the application level, such as file transfer over FTP. These gateways can also permit or forbid particular FTP commands. For example, they may prohibit an external user from writing a file to an internal computer with the PUT command.

Another option affects user authorization that takes place at the firewall level, rather than at the application level. A proxy-server can function as an application gateway. The proxy represents the entire corporate network to the Internet. External users see only the proxy that can execute additional monitored tasks within the corporate network. A proxy server must recognize any protocols that it may encounter.

Application gateways generally cost considerably more than other types of firewalls, such as routers. Nonetheless, they operate much more securely and effectively. Use of a router on its own cannot completely protect the complex communications flow of an enterprise, but a combination of router and application gateway can provide good protection.

An Internet provider or a monitoring center could also accomplish all these tasks. A center, operating a large number of such systems, could thrive economically, and offer monitoring services for firewalls around the clock, seven days a week.

Firewall systems themselves can operate at the customer site while a center monitors and loads them. Alternatively, the firewall system can operate at the provider's site and connect to the customer site over a secure standard line. The latter option permits better access by the control center in the event of problems.

Internet Site Patrol from BBN Plant serves as a good example and model for monitoring-center operation of a firewall. It offers the following services:

- Consultation on the creation and operation of a firewall system, including:
  - needs analysis;
  - definition of a security concept;
  - formulation of the security concept and training of customer employees.

The consulting issues do not depend upon where the firewall system operates (at the customer's or provider's site).

- providing a firewall system (rental);

- installation (at the customer site or at the provider site);

- operation, monitoring and maintenance;

- security audits.

Use of a web server does not always require installation of a firewall. For example, if a marketing plan places only statistical information about the enterprise on the World Wide Web, the internal network does not require any connections to the web server, thus avoiding any risk. In such a case, the web server would operate best as a completely isolated unit with Internet connections. However, if the system requires connections between the web server and the company network, the server should operate outside of the firewall and serve as the eye of a needle, guarding entry into the internal network.

The connection of an R/3 System to the Internet raises the question of required security measures to prevent intrusion into the company network and particularly into the R/3 System itself. In this case, too, firewalls can add extra security measures to those already present in the R/3 System. See Chapter 3 for more information on general security for R/3 Systems connected to the Internet and a discussion of the Internet Transaction Server (ITS).

2.7   A view toward the future

In a brief time, the Internet has developed into an extremely popular platform. What began as a military project progressed to use in universities and today functions in private, enterprise and commercial areas. The success of the Internet has occurred because of the victorious march of the World Wide Web and the Web's HTTP protocol. As such, the Internet has existed for quite some time, albeit with different protocols (e-mail with SMTP or FTP). Given its nature, the Internet continues to evolve. Its basis, the TCP/IP transfer protocol, has provided the foundation for a network structure that exists throughout the world. Many enterprises remain skeptical about the Internet. The press highlights scandalous events and misuse (hacking, pornography). The media pays little attention to successful and interesting business use of the Internet. What sort of future does the Internet have for global use in modern enterprises?

We recognize that widening the currently available bandwidth correlates to the increasing demands of multimedia applications and the large amounts of data that those applications transmit. In this situation, new bandwidths quickly become exhausted. Today we see common use of push mechanisms (the opposite of pull mechanisms). Push mechanisms constantly supply and burden the Internet with so much new information, that many information and new services transmit over special channels. Netscape has included *Netcaster* in its *Communicator* to allow offerings from these information services (such as PointCast). The increasing transmission of audio and video data also places a higher load on the Internet. We can only hope that available bandwidth increases at a higher proportion than the growing need for resources. A general, long-term improvement of capacity on the Internet would counter criticism based on slow response times. In this area, the US runs far ahead of Europe. The development of two classes of networks would enable enterprise use of one class and consumer use of the other.

The Internet will hardly degenerate into a toy. Although commercial use still requires broadly based billing procedures, considerable business potential remains untapped. Possibilities exist even beyond the use of enterprise connections; an extended supply chain that includes the Internet can easily become a reality (see Chapter 1).

The Internet as a worldwide network will truly accompany us into the next decade and beyond. The Internet will change and undergo improvements to improve and expand usage. These evolutionary changes will enable it to respond to business demands. Although the World Wide Web has become a synonym for the Internet, the Web merely reflects the Internet's best known protocol, HTTP, with HTML as its page-markup language. Should further developments replace the HTTP protocol, as HTTP replaced or overtook Gopher (see Section 2.2.1), the service or value-added service provided by the Internet will not change.

The following summarizes some of the changes that lie ahead (see Gartner Group, 1997):

The Internet Inter-Object Request Broker Protocol (IIOP), provides the design for a new protocol that, like HTTP, transfers data from servers to users. The newest version of Netscape Communicator already implements IIOP. Much like Microsoft's DCOM, IIOP will not replace HTTP, but expand access already present. IIOP focuses on expanding the area of status administration. HTTP will continue to access the vast majority of URLs.

HTML will soon appear in version 4 (see *http://www.w3.org/TR/PR-html40/*) and experience significant change. Recognized weaknesses in HTML have defined new derivatives of the *Standard Generalized Markup Language* (SGML), the Extensible Markup Language (XML) and the Resource Description Framework (RDF). XML provides a new method for the creation of tags in a standardized format. This method greatly improves search functions and indexing (see *http://www.w3c.com/*). RDF, a subset of XML, permits better processing of various data types. Most likely, however, more than 70% of all Web pages will continue to use HTML until 2002.

Various designs supplement the dynamic and multimedia properties missing in HTML: *Dynamic HTML* and Netscape's proprietary *Layer Technology*. Style-sheets, comparable to document templates in word processing, represent the most important innovation in Dynamic HTML. Style-sheets allow design of impressive Web pages in a short period: columns, text overlays, special graphic effects and animation no longer pose problems. Version 4.0 of the market-leading browsers, Netscape Communicator and Internet Explorer, will support Dynamic HTML. How much acceptance the comparable functions offered by Netscape's Layer Technology will find remains unclear.

Both the networks and the equipment used for communications and entertainment will likely merge in the long term. Telephony already displays serious activity on the Internet. All the large telecommunications entities currently plan to integrate telephony into the Internet. Users will find the lower fees for international conversations most attractive. The limited transmission capacity and the need for equipment with the corresponding functions (multiplex soundcards and telephone microphones) still present great difficulties. To enable equal use of various media, television and stereo units will also merge with computer hardware. These developments will become particularly evident in the end-consumer market. *Streaming Audio* and *Streaming Video* already display an additional level of integration. The insufficient bandwidth available today results in unacceptable quality for transmissions of live radio, individually selected CDs and videos. Users can already listen to selected excerpts of CDs without cost and then order the disk on the Internet (see *http://www.cdnow.com*). *Music on Demand* will offer yet another development: the ability of each user to listen to any desired CD at any time on the Internet.

The end-consumer market offers far more dramatic developments than that of enterprise communications. The driving force of the mass market, however, often creates an indication of the benefits available in business applications. Only these technologies enable SAP to design its business applications with Internet access: a revolutionary development. Up to now, the Internet has transmitted multimedia data created completely separately from any business context. Today, we can use existing business applications to access background data transparently. Different users on different networks and with different equipment can use application functions that become available to the users on a one-time basis. A business system can reap the benefits of the Internet and contribute to its professional quality simultaneously. Other manufacturers of standard business software have already moved in this direction or will likely do so.

Despite its massive popularity, the Internet remains nothing but a worldwide network structure that lives to enable many components to work together optimally. The Internet's greatest weakness also becomes apparent here: many developments depend upon each other. Research has already created many good designs for payment procedures. The designs find no implementation because of insufficient international regulation of identification methods (regulation needed to grant public keys, for example). The promises of electronic commerce, carried out on a large scale, cannot come to fruition without such regulations. More mature global cooperation forms the critical mass of the future of the Internet.

3 The SAP R/3 System and the Internet

The integration of SAP R/3 System business applications into the Internet represents not only a technological enhancement, but also a strategic opportunity for businesses that wish to participate in the globalization of markets. Chapter 1 treated the change in the meaning of an enterprise in detail. The Internet no longer functions as the long arm of an enterprise that acts globally. Rather, it seeks to integrate previously isolated areas within an enterprise. This description suits the extended supply chain aptly.

SAP recognized the strategic meaning of the Internet early and created its business Framework, a forward-looking system designed for maximum openness. Users no longer simply regard the R/3 System as a closed business-application system, but as a platform, one that integrates a heterogeneous landscape of varied hardware and software components. The opening to the Internet reflects a focus, albeit an essential one. The encapsulation of central and decisive business-application functions remains the core task of the R/3 System. That task aims at greater user utility in a variety of media and client/server application functions.

The central theme of this book presents alternative methods of connecting an R/3 System to the Internet. Users of R/3 Systems possess several options that differ depending upon the goals of each application. The principal concern lies in the Internet Transaction Server (ITS) that SAP provided in release 3.1. The ITS serves as the ideal foundation for the generation and use of applications on the Internet. Alongside the ITS, for example, other methods can use for example SAP Automation to provide remote control of R/3 System functions (see Section 3.6).

The Internet capabilities of the R/3 System enhance application functions already present and drive the internal development of yet more enhancements further. This situation affects SAP Business Workflow (see Section 3.3) in particular: only the Internet enables users to integrate the component into the entire business process and its corresponding workflow. The Internet also enables users to handle archived *business documents*. When combined with Business Workflow, the archiving feature creates new order of magnitude that increases the benefits of both the R/3 System and optical archiving. The ability of users at any Internet workstation to see and inspect documents will have positive effects on the applications themselves (see Section 3.4).

The Internet has also rekindled discussion of *Electronic Data Interchange* (EDI). Within the R/3 System, EDI plays a major role: many users have important EDI relationships with their vendors. How will the ability to place orders directly over the Internet in real-time affect EDI? Section 3.5 addresses this question.

The term *Web basis* refers to all the technical features offered by the HTTP protocol to connect an R/3 System to the Internet. Section 3.6 first compares basis technologies and then introduces SAP automation. The next section treats the Internet Transaction Server (ITS) in more detail.

The integration of transactions with the ITS highlights interesting aspects of the R/3 System and the Internet: the R/3 System still enjoys unique characteristics compared with other Enterprise Resource Planning (ERP) systems.

Discussions of integration between the World Wide Web and the R/3 System often raise the question of the Java programming language from Sun Microsystems. Can the SAPGUI function as a Java Applet for the Internet? Section 3.8 treats the significance of this design.

The following overview of the structure of the R/3 System provides a basis for evaluating the ability of the system to operate on the Internet.

3.1   Overview of the SAP R/3 System

The architecture and structure of an application system greatly influence the style and quality of the system's ability to communicate with the outside world. A connection to the Internet opens the door to additional possibilities, including the integration of other application systems in the office and back-office areas. Chapter 2 treated the options for integrating external applications over the World Wide Web (see Section 2.3.3). This chapter takes the next step: a consideration of the architecture or client/server technology of the R/3 System (see Buck-Emden and Galimow, 1996). That architecture has provided the basis for the success of the R/3 System and has enabled it to integrate Internet applications in a variety of ways. Section 3.6 details the different options available for connecting an R/3 System to the Internet.

Some discussions have focused critically on the suitability of the R/3 System for the future as well as the length and complexity of implementing the system (Cameron, 1996). The criticism has referred to the system's limited openness and associated isolation, including the following issues:

- A lack of market focus: 'the real action is outside the company.' The system integrates internal processes with each other and allows them to work together very well, but it does not integrate external processes.

- Developing Internet-oriented electronic commerce applications will rapidly replace the R/3 System.

- A lack of adaptability to developments in IT that enable new relationships with customers and go beyond the limits of EDI.

The modern architecture of the R/3 System allows the system to become 'Internet-ready' rather easily, and shows that the early decision for client/server computer pointed the way to the future. Today, development advances in flexible interfaces that can work on the Internet cast earlier criticism aside.

Client/server architecture alone does not bear full responsibility for these developments. The current situation requires standardization in the openness of applications in addition to the architectural setting. With its *Business Framework*, SAP offers a framework for the integrated use of business functions, even beyond the interfaces of the R/3 System itself (see Section 3.2). The strategic position of SAP and the availability of the right technologies and procedures have fulfilled the conditions noted by Forrester Research and silenced the resulting criticism. The innovation provided by SAP has produced system characteristics and application functions that SAP customers can soon put to productive, broad use. Europe remains hesitant about using Internet technology, although the technology stands at the ready. Experience has shown that the acceptance of new technologies always lags a few years behind their availability.

SAP R/3 stands well prepared for the modern communications age. It provides a solid foundation for the enhancement and further development of applications and interfaces that can meet the coming demands of electronic commerce and global inter-company relationships. The following presentation on the architecture of the SAP R/3 System provides an overview of the abilities the system on the Internet.

The Client/Server architecture of the R/3 System addresses the demands for enterprise-wide information management and runs contrary to the centrally oriented thinking of data processing departments. The integration of the R/3 system and its client/server architecture into the Internet will continue to consider the demands of enterprises for globalization and internationalization. The globe now repeats the same demands that enterprises previously made. It will become increasingly important for enterprises not only to optimize internal company processes, but also to make full use of the new possibilities offered by IT and to orient themselves to their customers.

The Internet makes the following requirements, already applicable as premises for the R/3 System, even more significant:

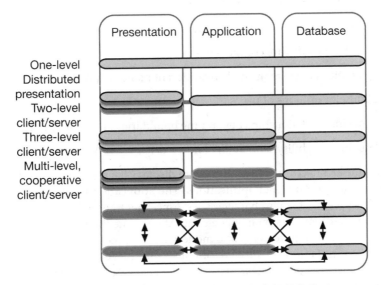

Figure 3.1   Client/server architecture of the R/3 System

- *Functional requirements:*
  - complete tracing of business processes: to consumers or business partners;
  - good operation of Internet applications with uniformly operable client software;
  - absolute currency of data at all times;
  - additional data and program integration with the use of universal browsers. Browsers now trend toward boarder functions, including universal viewers.
- *Technical requirements:*
  - portability of application software can become only more favorable;
  - standardization of the Internet provides a particularly open system architecture that permits excellent interaction with the R/3 System;
  - lower costs for expansion of the DP structure on the Internet, a public network;
  - direct transfer of the required and available scalability of the R/3 System to the Internet.

Constantly changing contextual conditions will make additional requirements, generally applicable to all current business systems, more indispensable. The contextual conditions arise from the globalization of IT applications and the increasing interaction of those applications:

- rapid development of new functions with a small risk of endangering existing processes;
- dynamic restructuring of existing systems;
- unlimited opportunities for maintenance and expansion;
- centralized and decentralized applications;
- simple reusability of software components;
- simple combinations of systems made by different manufacturers;
- good scalability for millions of users;
- end-to-end business relationships beyond the boundaries of an enterprise;
- unlimited quality, reliability, availability and security.

In many areas, the architecture of the R/3 System displays the essential properties required for efficient functions on Internet applications. The application level (or the application computer) offers several positive characteristics, especially transaction security with a roll-back function and efficient session management. At the same time, the Internet works as a catalyst to convert these requirements into modernizing business systems.

The R/3 System rests upon a software-oriented, multi-level client/server architecture. The system's three levels, *presentation, application* and *database,* provide an ideal design for connection to the Internet, a design that supports and uses the client/server concept of the R/3 System. For use on the Internet, this three-tier architecture can expand to multitier architecture. The expansion focuses on the additional possibilities offered by the presentation layer. Internet applications of an R/3 System merely reflect traditional R/3 System applications that use a Web browser rather than the SAPGUI. The division between the application and presentation layers becomes especially evident here: visualization occurs with HTML, but an actual R/3 function operates in the background.

Internationally recognized standards and open interfaces permit several types of connections between an R/3 System and the Internet. A particularly good option uses TCP/IP as a transport protocol. The Internet and the Internet Transaction Server (Presented in the next section) can access the application server of the R/3 System directly.

The R/3 System contains several interfaces that offer different connections to the Internet:

- Remote Function Call (RFC)

    - RFC permits the call of application functions from other computers.

- SAÏ Automation/Intelligent Terminal

    - SAP Automation permits direct use of SAPGUI functions from external programs.

- Screen interface of the SAP System

    - The dialog interface at the presentation level of the SAPGUI enables transparent access to the data flow to and from the R/3 application server. This interface is also known as the DIAG protocol, Dynamic Information and Action Gateway).

Section 3.6 discusses various designs for connecting an R/3 System to the Internet. Each of the designs rests upon one of these three interfaces. This section highlighted the architecture of the R/3 System and its capabilities for the Internet from a system viewpoint. Above all, however, the R/3 System distinguishes itself as comprehensive and efficient standard business software. The next section treats integration at the business level with the *Business Framework*.

3.2   The SAP Business Framework

Today, growing competition requires standard software to undergo increasingly rapid innovation cycles. To respond to the globalization of markets, standard software must operate with flexibility and integration while responding to the demands of external systems. Chapter 1 clarified the adjustments needed to deal with the changed context of a dynamic and global market both quickly and without interruption.

Business Framework architecture has the task of breaking new ground. This open, integrated and component-based architecture acts as the bridge between the ability to react to the market with maximum speed and the ability to react to individual requirements with the greatest flexibility. The architecture functions as a cloak that covers not only R/3 System applications themselves, but also the products and technologies of third parties. These high goals require the simplest upgrades and maintenance, improved interaction between the R/3 System and external, non-SAP systems together with improved, continual changes to the system as a whole. Such changes would prevent the need to implement a global release level throughout an enterprise over a weekend, for example. Applications that increasingly operate on global networks will demand such features.

The following provides an overview of some requirements:

Speed-to-market
- rapid application development without interrupted use;
- simplified reuse of components from various manufacturers;
- simplified cooperation with products from various manufacturers;
- improved adjustments to industry-specific solutions. ·

Flexibility
- dynamic adjustments to systems already implemented;
- choice of available components;
- simplified expansion with customer-specific functions;
- simple integration of new technologies.

The opening to the Internet clarifies the need for quickly developed applications, maximum interoperability and significant flexibility. From a functional viewpoint, Business Application Component Interfaces (BAPIs) play a major role in addressing these needs and have accelerated the overall development of the Business Framework. The interfaces of the Business Framework have not anchored themselves to the technological level of the system, but to business relationships. The relationships employ a semantic context to understand each other. Previous interfaces limited themselves to protocols, networks, objects, classes, distributed databases or the interaction of platform-dependent programming languages.

The Business Framework consists of several logically connected modules. Various new technologies, such as the *Business Information Warehouse or the Business Engineer* supplement the Business Framework. The Business Information Warehouse provides a general view of the flow in applications distributed throughout an enterprise. The R/3 Business Engineer is a knowledge-based configuration tool for the initial and continuing configuration of components in the Business Framework. The process level stands in the foreground of a number of distributed components.

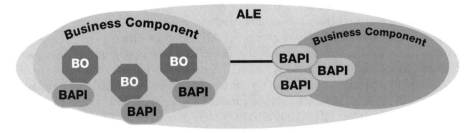

Figure 3.2   The core elements of the Business Framework

The Business Framework divides top-down into the following components:

- business components;

- business objects;

- BAPIs.

Business components define specific, encapsulated business functions that use a stable interface. The functions possess their own development and maintenance cycle and can run, at least partially, on different databases. Examples include the Business Engineer, Human Resources, Available-to-Promise or Product Data Management. Some business components cover several cross-application areas (HR, FI, and so on) of the R/3 System's core functions. Other components cover industry-specific components, Internet-relevant components, application modules (prepared by partners) or customer-specific components.

Business objects from form the core of SAP's object strategy. Release 3.0 contained over 170 business objects documented in the Business Object Repository. These business objects create stable definitions for units that exist in the real world, units such as 'customer' or 'invoice.' Using a semantic, business-oriented definition, business objects structure a stable and long-term interface to business components. The objects seek to operate independently of rapid changes to software implementation. Users can take advantage of business objects as required for their applications.

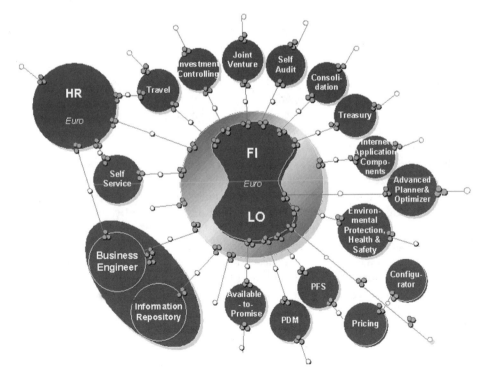

Figure 3.3   Division of an R/3 System into business components

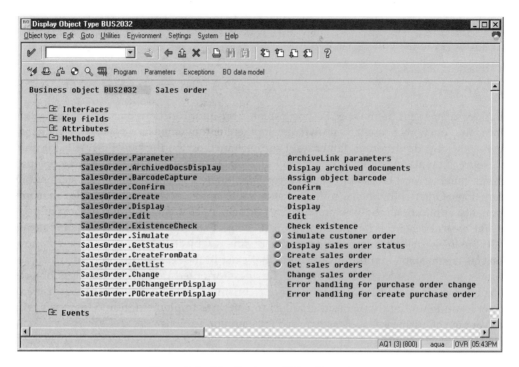

Figure 3.4   The Business Object Repository

A large number of ready-made BAPIs provide access to the business interface. The interface itself allows external applications to access the functions of an R/3 System transparently. (SAP already offers more than 150 defined BAPIs.) The Business Object Repository (BOR) administers the BAPIs along with business objects (BO), thus providing a better overview of the interfaces and the objects.

BAPIs are methods or functions assigned to exactly one business object. For example, the BAPI 'Employee.ChangeAddress' corresponds to the business object 'employee.' BAPIs play an important role in the creation of some Internet applications: they significantly reduce the complexity of such applications. Technically, BAPIs operate as RFC-enabled function modules. Chapter 4 treats the use of BAPIs in Internet applications.

The design of BAPIs provides obvious benefits. A BAPI captures a logical portion of application functions with a stable interface. It thus guarantees some release-independence and significantly reduces the efforts required for application development, as the BOR already contains the BAPIs. The benefits include the following:

- stable and public;

- simple, uncomplicated use;

- object-oriented capture of internal details;

- usable within various programming languages (ABAP, C, C++, Java, Visual Basic and so on);

- compatible with different communications technologies (COM/DCOM, CORBA and so on);

- available in different development environments (Visual Studio, Visual Age, Delphi and so on);

- support for the available interface;

- conformity with industry specifications (OAG and so on).

From the viewpoint of the application, several factors display the advantages of using BAPIs:

- simpler and easier use of the SAP R/3 System;

- universal access to business processes;

- rapid development of new application functions without interrupting productive time;

- simpler collaboration with other products;

- evolutionary introduction of new technology;

- stable and proven technology based on Internet application components;

- groups of BAPIs used together in a specific context: 'best business practice';

- independence from technical implementation of Internet application components;

- independent of releases.

SAP holds sovereignty in the creation of BAPIs. The firm makes every effort to provide ready-made BAPIs for all generally valid business processes. Nonetheless, a complete collection of BAPIs will take yet more time – an understandable situation.

A global consideration of all business components' available or planned, the interface technologies and the integration technologies reveals a wide frame for secure future development of the R/3 System. These components include the ability to use the Internet, ALE/WEB.

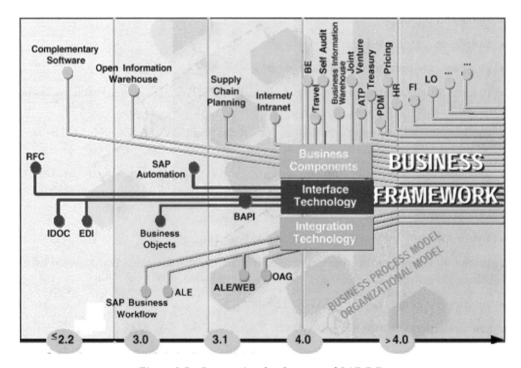

Figure 3.5   Integration development of SAP R/3

3.3   SAP Business Workflow and the Internet

The natural distribution of business processes beyond the limits of user departments highlights the need to optimize processes including the design and control of organization, throughput time and responsibility. Optimization reflects new technologies for handling activities. These new technologies require seamless integration between the processes and the activities, as well as between optical archiving, office applications and Internet technologies.

For the first time, with release 3.0 of the R/3 System, SAP Business Workflow provides a competitive, application-independent tool to process activities universally, efficiently and with controls. The following provides a brief overview of the use of Workflow in the context of the World Wide Web. See the official documentation for SAP Business Workflow for further information. Completely integrated in the R/3 System, SAP Business Workflow provides a solution it in its own right. It also offers an enhancement to the SAP-supplied software that can coordinate and control a customer-specific flow of business processes beyond the limits of isolated applications and workstations. Business Workflow functions as a technological conversion of *continuous business process engineering* because it enables dynamic adjustments to the system as a whole. Users can adjust business processes to changed contexts rapidly and without complication.

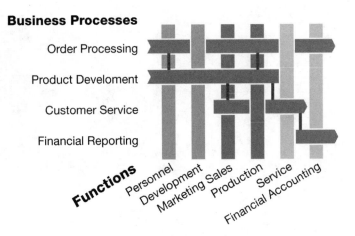

Business Processes

Order Processing

Product Develoment

Customer Service

Financial Reporting

Figure 3.6   Cross-application integration of SAP Business Workflow

Examples of application areas for Business Workflow include:

- posting incoming documents and releasing payments;
- writing credit memos;
- processing tasks;
- creating and changing master data;
- processing purchase orders;
- processing travel costs and calculations.

Workflow definitions reflect the design of application-specific and event-controlled process chains. The definition describes the active flow of data and control between the steps of a process. It also supplies each processing step with the necessary information. Each step produces calculated results that then influence the choice of additional steps. A Workflow Management System automatically controls the process or uses the integrated inbox to give control to a person responsible for further processing. The Workflow Management System can use the organizational and task structure from HR to allocate responsibilities dynamically at runtime. In this case, SAP offers use of the HR module free of charge. SAP highly recommends the definition of all users who participate in workflow within the organizational structures of the HR system.

Business processes always run with the *business documents* allocated to them, often a task in the form of a real document (letter, fax, e-mail, and so on). The documents mark the beginning of what can become a long process chain. In the past, staff evaluated documents and entered data into business application systems. File cabinets stored the originals for a while, until a dark and musty archive would take over the task. Later access to the documents proved slow and difficult. However, optical archiving of business documents (see Section 3.4) offers constant availability of the original documents, throughout the entire enterprise. When the design of a business process includes work-

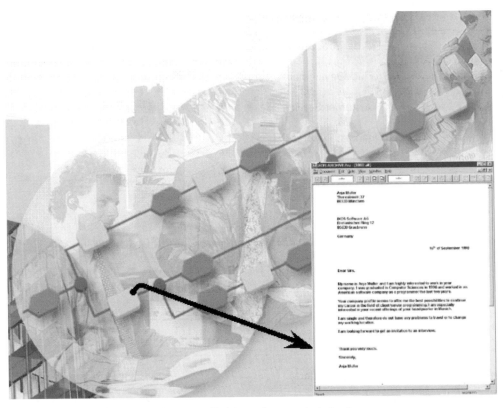

Figure 3.7   Allocation of business documents to business processes

flow, it seems particularly archaic to send required business documents (for invoice verification, for example) with interoffice mail, if the constraints of geography permit it at all.

A combination of the R/3 System, SAP Business Workflow and an optical archiving system can produce the maximum increase in efficiency. This scenario avoids the classic break in media, as all types of documents become available at the workstation and can become part of the electronic business flow seamlessly. A unified process can include incoming faxes, e-mail and letters along with outgoing SAP or Office documents – in effect, all business documents.

The cross-application properties of Workflow go beyond the use of an R/3 System and do not exclude external desktop programs or dealings not supported by computers. Employees linked to a Workflow definition enjoy a central role: they accompany the process and perform the required work. The suggestion might even arise to stretch the reach of existing systems as far as possible, integrating users across system boundaries to include those without access to the SAPGUI. Several of the application interfaces available allow the Internet or World Wide Web to play a special role. In addition, a connection between an R/3 System and the Internet in Business Workflow would allow sporadic use of the system within the enterprise as well as by vendors, customers and business partners (see Figure 3.8). The most important access options offered by workflow include the following:

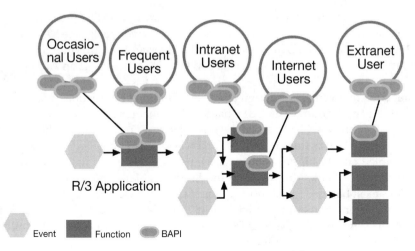

Figure 3.8   Expanded access to workflow

- inbox in the SAPGUI;

- SAPGUI in Java;

- integrated inbox as an Internet/Intranet application;

- MAPI-enabled clients;
  - MS Outlook;
  - MS Exchange client;
  - Lotus CC:Mail;

- forms;

- Lotus Notes (with open SAP Business Workflow interfaces).

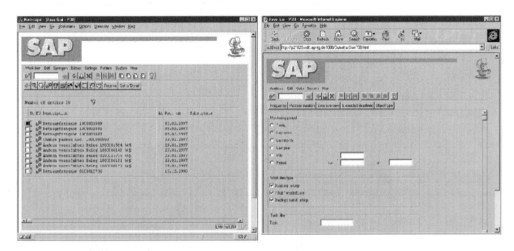

Figure 3.9   SAPGUI in Java as an integrated inbox and transaction system

The standard case involves the inbox integrated into the SAPGUI. From the inbox, Workflow calls the transactions required to perform a given task. The SAPGUI in Java extends the reach of standard functions onto the Internet with traditional R/3 System transactions. The only difference is that the SAPGUI in Java runs as an Applet in a Web browser (see Section 3.8).

The integrated inbox includes design as a special Internet transaction. As of release 3.1, a small, specific application exists (see Chapter 5) to enable reception of workflow messages over a Web browser. Unfortunately, however, only release 4.0 of the R/3 System permits starting the transactions necessary for a workflow directly from the inbox.

MAPI-enabled clients supply an alternative user interface in a network. The options available with MS Outlook, MS Exchange and Lotus CC:Mail come immediately to mind. These options exist because not all users employ the R/3 System's inbox. To allow all the employees of an enterprise to participate in Workflow, the integrated inbox in the Windows mail system offers a particularly good option. Users must become familiar with only a single system and can call the transactions required for a task automatically from these Windows clients.

Use of workflow over the World Wide Web will become more significant in the coming years. It offers the employees of an enterprise global access, more efficient processing

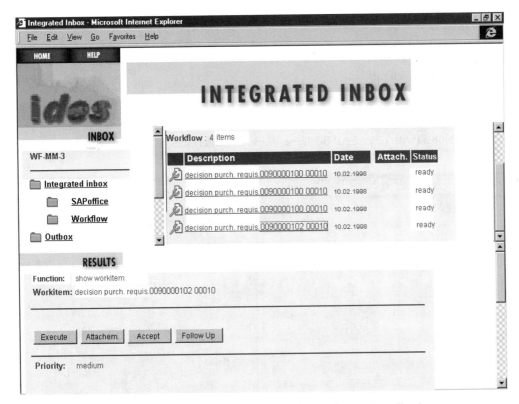

Figure 3.10   Inbox and selection of a task as an Internet application

because of better user leadership, improved self-service functions and a general higher quality of applications. The Gartner Group defines Web-capable workflow as follows:

- starting workflow on the Internet;

- tracing the work performed over the Internet;

- tracing the workflow history;

- responding to requests of other users.

From the viewpoints of both the enterprise and the application, the use of Web-based workflow offers a range of interesting advantages. The greatest advantage surely lies in the ability to integrate all participants in the value-creation process into the business process across the enterprise and the system.

The workflow can cover the entire enterprise and thus increase efficiency by a significant factor. Integration of all participants with a robust and simple application lowers overall administrative costs. Without special training, users integrated with workflow can access applications that lead users to a central distribution point for tasks. The use of a 'universal client,' the Web browser, simplifies use because of the high transparency it provides during access to heterogeneous processes and because of simple navigation. As before, trained staff can and will use the SAPGUI to access the overall workflow.

The integration of consumers and business partners into an R/3 System that workflow offers leads to completely new business possibilities. An externally activated workflow can start customer-specific processes within an enterprise. Take a service request as an example. Workflow can send the request to the person responsible automatically, or even accomplish the task itself by sending already-prepared electronic information to the requester. Staff can then spend their time on solving problems that truly require their assistance.

Consider another example from the Internet, that of an internal purchase-requisition. Usually employees themselves, rather than a supervisor, initiate the request for additional work materials. The supervisor simply fills the requisition. Nevertheless, cannot the employees themselves formulate the requisition rather than the supervisor? Special Internet applications can perform this task with an internal catalog of available materials. The request would automatically trigger a workflow with approval by the cost center as its first step. The supervisor or staff members responsible for approving the request can do so in the normal fashion with the SAPGUI. During the entire process, the requestor can follow the progress of the requisition, again, with a special Internet application. Approval of the request would automatically send the employee who initiated it an e-mail message.

A Business Workflow with associated Internet/Intranet applications can significantly improve all the activities and processes involved in hiring a new employee. The tasks can become daunting: checking the candidate's references and other information; finding space and materials for the new employee; and the document flow through various departments, such as personnel, security and health insurance. Such a workflow would not only free staff for other tasks, but also control and document the status of each step perfectly. Even the new employees can enjoy Business Workflow by watching the tasks executed on their behalf in the integrated inbox. Orientation of the new employees can take place rapidly.

Electronic commerce also suggests multiple scenarios. A purchase initiated within an electronic catalog can trigger an entire series of actions; SAP Business Workflow can regulate all the tasks. After registering the choice and order of the goods, the system determines the payment method and then automatically creates the purchase order that requests delivery of the goods. Depending upon the organization structure, the workflow also informs the shipping department and/or the warehouse of the impending delivery. Finally, the system assigns someone the task of packing and shipping the goods. In this scenario, employees perform actual tasks only at the end of the process. The system has automated the entire process: taking the order, creating the request and performing the availability check.

Release 4.0 includes new features to integrate Web-based SAP Business Workflow further into the world of R/3 System application optimally:

- HTML forms can start a workflow.

- Calls of Internet-capable transactions can come directly from the integrated inbox.

- Workflow Wizards permit rapid implementation of new workflow applications.

- Support for electronic forms for processing workflow.

- Availability of workflow-related process information with the Business Information Warehouse.

3.4   Optical archiving of business documents

Efficient use of an R/3 System requires the ability to access not only application data, but also original documents at any time, regardless of their actual physical location. The discussion of workflow in Section 3.3 has already clarified these requirements. Business documents trigger and accompany business processes. An order, for example, may trigger a business process that produces and requires other documents, such as an order confirmation, the delivery note and the invoice. Business documents can also include general documentation important for a production process, such as blueprints.

The global, enterprise-wide use of an R/3 System provides data to all users. Should not the same hold true for outgoing business documents? The question particularly affects any use of SAP Business Workflow, which becomes worth while only when its users can also process or display documents electronically at their workstations. The same applies to any scenario within the enterprise that requires access – across departments and desks – to any original documents linked to a business process. Quick and global access to electronic documents provides a particular advantage.

Access to documents over the Internet offers yet another level. Customers can view their invoices and delivery personnel can examine customer orders while on the road. Many enterprises do not yet recognize the potential of optical archiving.

Experience has proved the potential savings that use of an electronic archiving system provide. According to different characteristics, the research produced the following results display notable benefits:

- 0–90% reduction in processing time;

- 10–35% reduction of professional staff;

- 10–75% increase in productivity;

- 20–40% reduction (per unit) in processing costs;

- 30–50% savings in office space.

The introduction of an archiving system calculates a *return on investment* of one to two years.

SAP ArchiveLink serves as the interface between the R/3 System and the archive system, called a *business document system* in the following to reflect the totality of the overall system. The system uses it to store incoming and outgoing documents directly from the R/3 System. Business document systems, such as the market-leading *iXOS-ARCHIVE*, require certification for the interface to guarantee quality to SAP and its customers. (SAP AG and iXOS Software AG jointly developed and maintain the ArchiveLink interface.) The system can archive any type of document: incoming and outgoing business documents, faxes, multimedia files (sound, image, video and so on), and print lists from an R/3 System. It can also archive files from external systems with COLD (computer output on laser disk). The performance of a given optical business document system plays a central role here. ('Optical' because the system uses optical storage media, such as WORM or CD-ROM, to prevent later alteration of the original documents.) Not all manufacturers integrate the functions required by the ArchiveLink interface. The true benefits of a business document systems result from the integration of the archived documents into applications, the allocation of specific business processes to the documents and optimized access to the documents themselves.

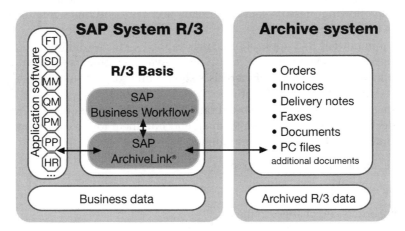

Figure 3.11   Integration of a business document system into an R/3 System

The use of ArchiveLink and a business document system provides the following benefits:

- Several persons in various locations can access the same documents simultaneously.

- Electronic availability reduces search and access times considerably. No one needs to look through a dusty basement. The R/3 System itself or its associated interfaces access the documents.

- The archive can contain incoming and outgoing documents of all types. The document types can include scanned paper documents as well as Office documents (MS Word, e-mail, and so on) and all multimedia formats (video, sound, and so on). Users can archive outgoing documents directly from the R/3 System (invoices, print lists).

- Electronic availability eliminates the media break when using an R/3 System.

- Optical storage media prevent changing the archived documents. This feature builds a foundation for accounting according to generally accepted legal and professional standards.

- Document display functions independently of the release level, since application-independent formats (OTF, FAX, PDF, and RTF) store the documents.

- Electronic availability provides numerous organizational advantages, lower storage costs and better security.

- SAP Business Workflow reaches its full potential only with an integrated business document system that enables a unified and coherent (without media breaks) processing of business tasks.

- Internet applications can create documents virtually. The system can archive the invoice from an online sale and send it to the customer over the Internet.

This section does not require a discussion of the actual process of archiving (early, simultaneous or late). The Homepage of iXOS Software AG (*http://www.ixos.de*) provides a good overview of the process and a detailed description of document archiving with a SAP R/3 System. The following presents some exemplary scenarios and highlights the potentials involved in using the Internet.

The most important R/3 applications, such as SD, FI, HR, MM, PM, PP, PA and QM, already support various methods of archiving relevant documents – depending on the version of the R/3 System in use. Enterprises should first consider the archiving scenario that promises the best cost–benefit ratio.

Processing sales with Sales & Distribution (SD) typically creates several documents. A business document system can store them all and link them to the corresponding documents records in the R/3 System. For example:

- incoming inquiries and changes to them;

- outgoing quotations;

- incoming orders and changes to them;

- outgoing order confirmations.

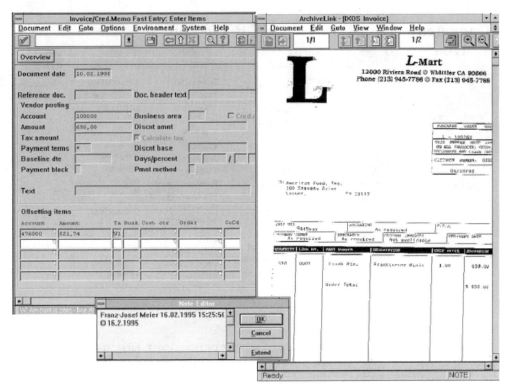

Figure 3.12   Linkage between business processes and a business document

Since a document always contains hard links to a document type in the R/3 System, users can include the documents in SAP Business Workflow and display them if required. For example, if an invoice requires verification, a request to do so appears in the integrated inbox of the person responsible for the verification. That person can display the invoice and the document contained in the R/3 System with a click of the mouse and then compare the two. Normally, a special viewer (delivered with the archiving system) displays documents, but the R/3 System also contains its own simple viewer.

The desire to display documents over the Internet increases continuously. This desire applies particularly to enterprises that use SAP Business Workflow globally. Such installations include users on the Internet, an Intranet and an Extranet. The ability to display documents in the most varied Internet applications strikes many users as interesting and useful. For an example, see the display of documents within a document flow triggered by an application, as described in Chapter 6.

Until recently, however, Web browsers could display images only in GIF or JPG. Browsers could not display the formats present in the business document systems (OTF, FAX, and RTF). Besides installing a browser, users also had to install a special image viewer. Definition of the viewer as a 'helper application' enables the browser to start the right application for viewing the image.

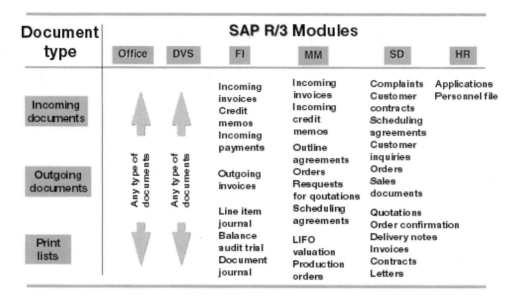

Figure 3.13   A selection of supported document types

To employ the browser itself as a viewer, several options exist. First, users can install a specially developed component, a plug-in, to enhance the browser with an added function. Second, users can load a Java Applet when they wish to display an image – the Applet then provides the additional functions to the browser. As a third option, the system can convert the original documents into GIF of JPG format at runtime. Additionally, ActiveX can display images on Windows platforms, but only with the Internet Explorer from Microsoft.

Until recently, only special programs enabled an Internet connection to a business document system and its information. The systems themselves offered the function. Only iXOS-Archive solves this problem in the context of a SAP R/3 System. The future will bring a standardized access mechanism. Today, HTTP interfaces to business document systems have established a new standard for easy access to business documents over the World Wide Web.

3.5   EDI and the Internet

Electronic Data Interchange (EDI) still contributes greatly to the automation of cross-enterprise and cross-system business processes. EDI has already optimized the daily exchange of business messages, particularly in industries with intensive relationships to supplies, such as the automobile industry. An EDI message usually replaces an action formerly performed with paper, a customer order or a supplier's invoice, for example. EDI offers a substantial benefit: since both partners communicate with EDI, their application systems can communicate with each other asynchronously, eliminating the need to enter data twice.

The success of the Internet has raised the question of whether and in what form it can become a replacement for EDI. To clarify the question, the following presents the basic concepts of EDI based on current options in R/3 System.

SAP delivers the interface for EDI under the name an Intermediate Document (IDoc). IDocs prepare outgoing messages from applications and prepare incoming messages for further processing by applications. Third-party manufactures offer the conversion and communications software for EDI, usually called EDI sub-systems. Both officially certified and uncertified EDI sub-systems can use the open IDoc interface.

Within the SAP system environment, the use of SAP Business Workflow offers yet another form of integration. Business Workflow can handle unexpected exceptions and errors by sending a message to an integrated inbox. The user must then react to the message. The EDI messages supported by SAP correspond to existing standards (ANSI X.12 EDIFACT) and available only within certain release levels. Industry-specific standards also exist, such as VDA/ODETTE in the automobile industry. Table 3.1 organizes messages supported by IDocs according to module.

In addition to a point-to-point connection (in a fixed vendor relationship, for example), EDI users can also contract with special *value-added networks* (VANs). These services guarantee complete security for functions and data, an important consideration for most EDI relationships. VANs, however, remain rather expensive. The contractual obligations between the parties make it difficult to change services after the initial selection of a network. The direct and cross-enterprise options for electronic connections over the Internet raise the question of how the Internet might replace EDI and the advantages/disadvantages of each method.

Table 3.1   EDI messages supported by IDocs in the R/3 System

Module	Outgoing	Incoming
SD	Invoice Quotation Order confirmation Confirmation of changed orders Delivery note	Forecast delivery schedule Inquiry Orders and changes to them Warehouse delivery note JIT delivery schedule

MM	Forecast delivery schedule
	Inquiry
	Orders and changes to them
	JIT delivery schedule/Forecast
	  delivery schedule
		Invoice (order-related)
		Order confirmation
		  (with and without changes)
		Delivery note
		Changes to orders (triggered by vendors)

FI	Payment advice	Invoice Payment advice Lock box
General		Text message

Table 3.2   Overview of various EDI replacement options
(Source: Seeburger Unternehmensberatung GmbH)

	Standard EDI	*Internet as Transmission Medium*	*Internet Applications*
Volume of Data	High	Medium	Low
Type of Business Transaction	Repetitive, standard	Repetitive, standard	Alternatives allowed, interactive
Security	Industry-specific communications protocols; Store-and-forward principle	Supplementary encryption/ Electronic signature	Supplementary encryption/Electronic signature
Communication	Point-to-point X.400 mailbox systems	Mail or FTP	HTML pages
Data contents	Any structures	Any structures	HTML pages
Application integration:			
Sender	High; completely automated flow	Automatic/manual	Created manually
Recipient	Completely automated flow	Automatic/manual	Automatic/manual
SAP interface	EDIFACT, VDA ... IDOC/RFC	EDIFACT, VDA ... IDOC/RFC	BAPI

The Internet can transmit business messages in two different ways. According to one option, it can send traditional EDI messages that follow an EDI standard. The very structure of the Internet as a public network, however, means that it cannot guarantee 100% availability. Criticism of this option focuses on the general lack of security on the Internet. Privacy plays an important role in critical and confidential commercial information. Use of the Internet in this context requires additional security measures for encryption and authentication. The distribution of EDI messages over unknown nodes on the Internet places the information at risk, despite all the security measures. This danger does not exist in point-to-point communications.

The second option transmits business messages with special Internet applications, such as those from SAP. A special Internet application can place an order with a vendor, for example. The vendor's system would immediately record the order as a new business process, such as the IAC 'Sales Order Creation' (see Chapter 5). Over the World Wide Web, the ordering party must start the Internet application of the vendor for each order. The type of application used allows the vendor to limit access to specific customers and even then would require supplemental authentication. Note that this procedure represents not only a changed form of EDI, but also manner of transacting cross-enterprise and cross-system business activities.

As an alternative, transmission of business messages can continue with standardized EDI messages, but only after completing an HTML form. In this case, the Internet application has no connection to an R/3 System. The R/3 System merely stores the transmitted EDI document as an IDoc. Frequent messages with high volumes of data do not seem appropriate for Internet applications. They require manual entry with the browser and do not link the business application systems of all participants. An optimized supply chain should avoid double entries: an internal purchase order (PO) should not require entering an inquiry in the vendor's system. This alternative attracts small users who cannot afford (but do want to purchase) expensive EDI systems. It allows such users to exchange standardized business messages with other enterprises. The use of the Internet to exchange a low volume of EDI messages between two different business application systems can function just as well as the use of VANs do for frequent, high-volume business activities.

3.6   Internet connections to an R/3 System

As in the case of the interfaces treated above, three different approaches can connect Internet applications to an R/3 System. The overview given in Figure 3.14 shows a schematic overview of the three methods.

The first method, portrayed at the top of the illustration, implements the connection between an R/3 System and the Internet as available from release 3.1 onward: integrated *ALE/WEB technology*. The *Internet Transaction Server* (ITS) provides access to the functions of the R/3 System, and the communications channel of the SAPGUI effects the actual connection to the R/3 application server. This design uses the name *SAP Web Basis*. The ITS simulates the SAPGUI expected by the application server. Simultaneously, it also serves as a gateway for conversion of HTML and as the interface to the Web server.

The remaining two designs also open the functions of an R/3 System to access on the Internet. The middle section of the illustration sketches a connection with *SAP Automation*. This design, also called *Intelligent Terminal*, enables direct communications between external applications and the SAPGUI : (four-tier architecture). This design makes available all the data of the SAPGUI to an external application.

The third method, shown in the lower portion of the illustration, symbolizes electronic commerce applications that access the functions and data of an R/3 System with *Remote Function Calls* (RFC). The RFCs, written in programming languages such as Visual Basic, Java, C, or C++, represent applications that operate outside of the R/3 System.

The designs of all these solutions permit access to standard business transactions with open BAPIs (if already available for a specific business case the application problem already contains them). The BAPIs play a central role, beyond the Internet applications themselves, as open and standard interfaces. New applications can couple so loosely with the R/3 System that the system's kernel requires no changes for newly developed applications. When using BAPIs, Internet applications take the forefront and clarify the enormous need for standard business interfaces. BAPIs possess general validity; future versions of the R/3 System will implement business processes by using BAPIs. ALE/WEB is the general term for communications on the Internet by using interfaces to an R/3 System.

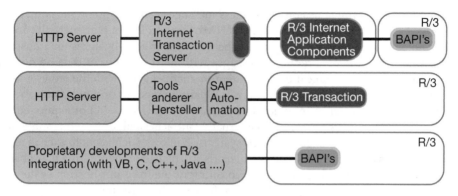

Figure 3.14   *Alternative methods of connecting an R/3 System to the Internet*

All three designs in figure 3.14 use different strategies to their individual usage areas, but with a common goal: availability of R/3 functions on the Internet.

The complexity of the usage area of the desired R/3 Internet applications and the related level of integration in the R/3 System differentiate these usage areas. The first design, the ITS, permits or automatically enables broad-based use of the R/3 System, including its mechanisms for transaction security, access security and scalability. The other two designs, however, require separate implementation of these mechanisms, as far as

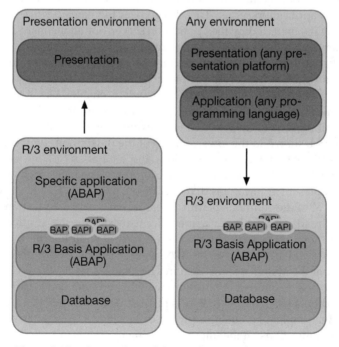

Figure 3.15   *Comparison of the inside-out and outside-in designs*

required or desired. This distinction leads to the terms *inside-out* and *outside-in*. From the perspective of the R/3 System, the distinctions show the location of the application logic that controls the BAPIs in use. If the application remains in the R/3 System as an ABAP program, designers use the inside-out method. If the application logic rests outside of the R/3 System, in a Visual Basic application, for example, the outside-in method applies.

Sections 3.6.1 and 3.6.2 treat the two designs in more detail. Each specific usage area justifies use of one of the two designs.

Because the design with the *Internet Transaction Server* has functions close to the R/3 kernel and has its own advantages, SAP prefers it above other designs. Primarily for this reason, SAP has integrated and delivered the Internet Transaction Server as the preferred solution for Internet applications as of release 3.1.

Access with RFC and the use of the functions found in the outside-in design use broad-based application logic. The logic resides outside of the R/3 System despite the use of any BAPIs present. The principal problem evidenced here reflects the doubled application development on two different systems.

In the US, users prefer designs with SAP Automation. In other areas, users tend toward the ITS. The reason for each preference does not arise from a conviction that one design offers a better technical solution that the other. The ITS design requires a programmer proficient in ABAP who also understands the World Wide Web. Obviously, the US has more Visual Basic programmers than specialists in ABAP.

The actual interface to an R/3 System has a business-oriented nature best embodied in BAPIs, despite all the technical access and integration options shown in Figure 3.16. Clearly, then, a correct understand of the R/3 System does not see it as a closed business application system, but one that integrates the orderly interaction of numerous internal and external application. The communications interfaces include the following base technologies:

- HTTP;

- JAVA;

- COM/DCOM;

- CORBA.

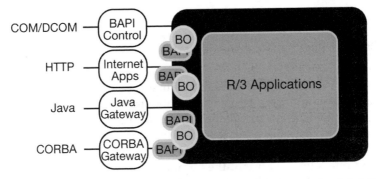

Figure 3.16   Technologically independent access to the business processes of an R/3 System

Release 4.0 contains all the technologies, including the *DCOM Component Connector*; earlier releases contained only some. As DCOM developments apply to Windows platforms, DCOM CORBA addresses UNIX systems. HTTP, the ITS and the JAVA SAPGUI use the inside-out design. The other technologies use outside-in, since they use the BAPIs that they require from the R/3 System (with RFC) and keep further application logic outside of the R/3 System. The following sections describe the inside-out and outside-in designs in more detail and present several options for their use. They will not treat the internal processes used by external applications to access and R/3 System with RFC; the publications available for each programming language provide any information required. The remaining chapters of this book deal with an overview of the SAP Automation design. They then describe the Internet Transaction Server along with its architecture and possible uses. Finally, they focus on standard applications and programming new *Internet application components* (IACs).

3.6.1   Inside-Out

The Internet Transaction Server covers one of the two inside-out designs. The application logic remains completely in the R/3 System while the presentation level operates outside. The other design involves use of the JAVA SAPGUI, and has a completely different goal (see Section 3.8). The currently active transaction in the R/3 System regulates program flow completely and controls the mechanisms that ensure transaction security (session management, roll back and so on).

The Internet Transaction Server expands the three-tier architecture of the R/3 System to a fourth tier, one that implements the connection to the Internet technically. The system now operates with multi-tier architecture, as indicated in Figure 3.17.

The multi-tier architecture of an R/3 System connected to the Internet provides the scalability required by the Internet. Its very design enables it to process several Internet transactions simultaneously.

This solution, integrated into the system as of release 3.1, offers the advantages of all the mechanisms for secure transactions already present in the R/3 System:

- transaction security;

- access security;

- session management;

- scalability.

Access over the Internet increases the need for such mechanisms. Once the system opens itself to access by partly unknown user groups, these mechanisms protect against unauthorized use (access security). They also guarantee the stability and quality of the connection, which also guarantees the integrity of the data (transaction security). On the Internet, scalability, the ability to guarantee a response time for a group of users of unknown numbers trying to access the system simultaneously, plays an especially crucial role.

ALE/WEB offers implicit use of the authorization concept of the R/3 System (see Section 3.9). Because ALE/WEB operates with a traditional R/3 session, (even if written

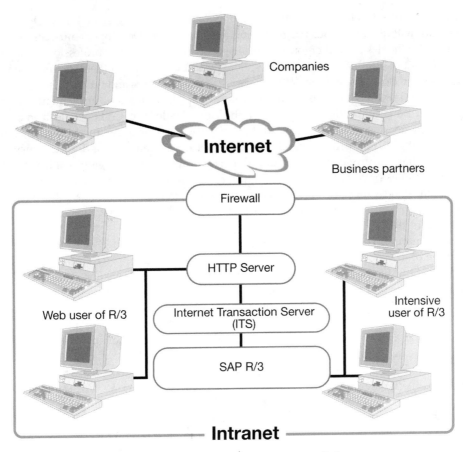

Figure 3.17   Internet architecture in an R/3 System

specifically for Internet applications), it offers the required transaction security automatically. The Internet Transaction Server expands the reach of transactions in and R/3 System to include the Web browser. Only such a design guarantees that the system can complete or cancel (roll back) transactions triggered on the Internet just as it does at the local R/3 workstation.

The user load expected on the Internet is difficult to estimate. If too many users make it impossible to process inquiries, a vendor cannot count on the understanding of dissatisfied users. External users may well turn to another sources and internal users may well refuse to accept the system. The scalability already present in the R/3 System comes completely to the fore on the Internet. In addition, the use of several Web servers also enables scalability for Internet sites.

Application developers enjoy another advantage. They can still work within the familiar SAP development environment. They can apply already well-known tools (such as the ABAP Debugger) to the development Internet transactions. Developers familiar with ABAP will require little extra training. This heterogeneous development environment also places new demands on developers. In particular, they require Internet-specific knowledge. They must work with the numerous programming tools of HTML. Developers must also have a command of the design and ergonomic principles demanded for the professional and successful layout of graphical user interfaces. One person rarely has all these abilities. Success depends upon close cooperation between various team members and their skills.

The design of the ITS focuses on R/3 Internet applications that implement uniform application scenarios of the R/3 System on the World Wide Web. Consider electronic commerce as a good example, it can contain significant workflow relationships. After examining the current product catalog, an Internet user receives an individual customer quotation that, in turn, can trigger an order. The order becomes legally valid when the customer makes payment online or can at least guarantee payment. The scenario then delivers the goods, and the seller must then replenish warehouse supplies. If the customer pays online or with an Internet payment procedure, the seller may post the incoming receipts directly.

This scenario involves several modules of the R/3 System. An R/3 session guarantees execution of the application steps in the defined order, just as it does for uniform processing throughout the process chain. The security aspects noted above come into play here. The most important challenge remains building a bridge over the Web's lack of status (statelessness) during any interaction between the R/3 System and the Internet. The same bridge must guarantee the completeness and accuracy of transactions in a traditional R/3 session. *Internet Application Components (IACs)* implement the actual application logic (see Chapter 4). The IACs include the application logic with the R/3 System and the HTML modules on the Web server. IACs usually rest upon open *Business Application Programming Interfaces* (BAPIs) that now find optimal use in Internet applications. IACs can also work without BAPIs, however. BAPIs (see Section 3.2) enable quick and simple integration of business logic even to the inexperienced R/3 developer.

The split between the application logic of business processes (in ABAP/4) and the implementation logic of the World Wide Web (HTML) places more demands on the integrating elements of the R/3 System, even beyond its original application design. The application design thus remains in the R/3 System. R/3 Internet architecture completely separates the design process of the user interface for the WWW applications from the R/3 Internet applications written in ABAP. Design changes that affect only appearance do not require changes in the application development within the R/3 System.

Chapter 4 provides a more detailed presentation of ITS technology. Chapter 7 treats the programming and organization of R/3 Internet applications.

3.6.2 Outside-in

In theory, outside-in design means the integration of any external application with an R/3 System. A great deal of freedom of choice therefore exists among new applications in the following areas:

- runtime environment (Microsoft, IBM, HAHT and so on);

- development environment (MS Visual InterDev, Visual Age, HAHT and so on);

- programming languages (C, C++, Delphi, Java, Visual Basic and so on);

- presentation platform (Web, Kiosk and so on).

The tools available to develop new application components reflect equal variation, and continue to grow. Some of the more familiar tools include:

- MS Visual Studio;

- IBM VisualAge;

- Netdynamics (with WebExtend for SAP R/3, it also integrates SAP Automation);

- WebObjects (with Advis Mantle);

- Borland Delphi/Connect for SAP.

The number of options available and the desire to use traditional means to access the application logic of an R/3 System can easily lead to confusion. Developers can tailor the types of applications to the graphic elements of a modern graphical user interface. Those interfaces will strike sporadic users as having nothing in common with the seemingly dull appearance of the SAPGUI application interface.

Note, however, that the transaction grasp of applications lying outside the R/3 System often does not provide the required breadth. A dedicated RFC (in the best case with a BAPI) can record only a moment. If a developer wishes to present an order catalog, for example, the R/3 System itself can generate the catalog with a function call. Of course, the contents of a catalog rarely change at runtime. To execute an order, the developer must ensure that the system can perform all the required steps and that, if necessary, it can cancel (roll back) steps already taken. In addition, the outside-in design does not permit several users to inquire about validity simultaneously, since each order changes warehouse stock. Only access managed by monitored R/3 transactions and session management permits the R/3 System to respond consistently to inquiries from any number of Internet users. The type of application, and its complexity, very much determines the correct approach: outside-in or inside-out.

An RFC, managed in various ways, provides integration of the BAPIs. COM/DCOM offers perhaps the most important aspect of integration for Windows platforms. A *BAPI*

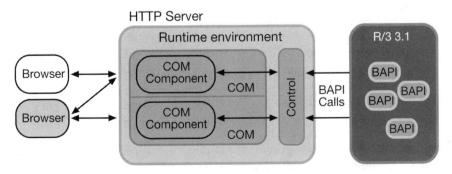

Figure 3.18   Calling a BAPI with COM/DCOM

Control integrated into the external application control the BAPI calls. The *DCOM Component Connector*, available in the R/3 System itself, represents an additional development.

In any case, the BAPIs remain in the R/3 System. The external application system contains only their definitions. At runtime, the external system calls the appropriate BAPI directly from within the R/3 System and integrates it transparently into the application logic of the external program.

In an outside-in approach, scaling occurs primarily by duplicating the Web server platform contained in the runtime environment of the external application. The R/3 System experiences only sporadic load and no session takes place with it. The R/3 System merely receives individual requests, such as BAPI calls, from the external application. The external application itself experiences the load. The R/3 System of course, can reflect scaling as usual, if required.

Function calls with RFC

The *outside-in principle* implements access to the functions of an R/3 System with *Remote Function Call* (RFC). An external, independent system briefly uses the functions of an R/3 System with an RFC system call. Control remains with the external system that triggered the RFC.

The RFC interface allows function calls beyond the limits of computers or systems. These situations can exist between two SAP systems (R/3 or R/2), or between a SAP system and a non-SAP system. To call a function module with RFC, the function library must contain a definition of the module that indicates readiness for RFC. The BAPIs noted above contain such definitions.

The RCF interface can also access RFC modules from within ABAP programs with CALL FUNCTION...DESTINATION, just as RFC-API does from within non-SAP programs. RFC-API, for example, reflects a specific program interface that allows C programs, for example, to use RFC calls. R/2 or R/3 programs can also employ RFC-API to use functions of external programs.

RFC thus permits any external WWW applications to make contact with the function library of the R/3 System. Unlike the case of ALE/WEB, an R/3 session does not manage this one-time contact. Accordingly, the mechanisms for transaction security, scalability and access protection require additional implementation.

RFC offers a special advantage when the type of Internet application does not make any special use of R/3 System services. This case applies to relatively self-contained Internet applications that demand only sporadic or detached actions within the R/3 System. An example might include a marketing strategy that includes the visual availability of product information, but without any coupled ability to process an order within an R/3 System.

One of the major advantages offered by outside-in lies in its ability to integrate heterogeneous sources (such as databases and so on) that reside outside of the R/3 system. The inside-out and outside-in approaches in any company should always coexist to address all the different needs for the required applications.

As soon as RFC access fails to provide the required transaction security, scalability or access protection, designers should consider the inside-out approach, especially if they do not wish to implement any supplementary security mechanisms.

3.6.3   SAP Automation

SAP Automation offers a special form of the *outside-in approach*. External systems use the programming interface of the SAPGUI to employ the desired functions of the R/3 System. *Intelligent Terminal* is another name for SAP Automation. SAP Automation arose from the general need to give users access to other application interfaces, in addition to the SAPGUI. The need to provide an intuitive user interface for untrained users forms the background to SAP Automation. The hypertext technology of the World Wide Web solved the same problem marvellously and contributed greatly to the success of the Web.

The RFC interface was a precursor to SAP automation that used OLE automation, which permitted access to the R/3 System with desktop PCs. Compared to SAP Automation, however, RFC has the following disadvantages:

- Only direct interaction with the SAPGUI presents the full range of basic business rules of the R/3 System. The API does not.

- To access the desired data with RFC, the user must know ABAP.

The use of SAP Automation requires no special knowledge of ABAP programming or internal business rules. SAP Automation accesses existing application only abstractly, and primarily generates a new user interface. The availability of these interfaces on the World Wide Web clarifies the integration level of SAP Automation particularly well.

One disadvantage: SAP Automation can access only existing transactions. However, if the ABAP program required additional changes, the advantages of abstraction became lost. SAP Automation therefore offers a supplementary procedure to make ABAP applications available over a new and simplified user interface.

In a Windows system, the SAPGUI normally consists of two components:

- SAPGUI.EXE;

- FRONT.EXE.

In SAP Automation, ITSGUI.DLL replaces SAPGUI.EXE. The MERLIN.DLL library contains a C-API interface that that makes screen contents available with data structures and function calls. Two additional interfaces also play an important role: the OLE Automation Server (used with a Windows client programmed in Visual Basic) and a terminal server that creates connections between heterogeneous systems.

Above all, SAP Automation provides a simplified interface for applications on the World Wide Web when existing applications require only minor changes, rather than wide-ranging modification. It has an advantage over RFC. SAP Automation requires changes at the API level of the SAPGUI, while RFC demands work at the level of function modules. SAP Automation becomes most valuable within an entire outside-in design. Such an approach enriches the stand-alone development environment of the World Wide Web with elements from R/3 applications, without having to use RFCs.

Employee self services

For internal users of HR functions, SAP provides a ready-made collection of *Employee Self Services* (ESSs). The services enable employees to manage by themselves a great many administrative tasks that affect them. The use of intuitive interfaces similar to the World Wide Web enables for the first time, employees to post data about themselves securely. With ESS, SAP delivers ready-made applications in the context of specific tools and a development environment that lean on SAP Automation. SAP aims at a complete solution that enables users to take advantage of an existing Intranet infrastructure without additional training. The technology for ESS applications arises from the use of *HAHTsite* and uses the functions of SAP Automation (from HAHT Software, Inc., Raleigh, NC). HAHTsite has a development environment similar to Visual Basic for programming Web-based applications. These ready-made applications operate similarly to IACs for the ITS. Visually, nothing differentiates IACs and ESS applications at first glance. Both application types run within a Web browser and have similar characteristics. Behind both, however, lies a completely different technology (inside-out vs. outside-in).

The following lists some of the applications available for ESS:

- *Managing Personal Information*
  Employees can often administer their own personal data better than the HR department, especially because the data changes frequently (address, for example).

- *Banking Information*
  Employees can change their own account information.

- *Time Recording (Time Entry & Time Off)*
  The feature includes time recording, verification and the entry of sick days and vacation days.

- *Purchase Requisition*
  Employees can complete a PR with or without an online catalog.

- *Employment and Salary Verification*
  Employees can enter the address of banks or other financial institutions and have the company send required reports by mail or fax.

- *Training and Event Management*
  To attain a better overview, employees can see the training schedule and learn of prerequisites. If required, online booking can also apply here.

- *Benefits Inquiries and Open Enrollment*
  Employees can inquire about or claim social service benefits.

- *SAP Business Workflow: (Form-based Workflow)*
  Employees can process work items from a workflow in the Web browser.

- *Receipt Entry*
  Employees can enter the required data for receipts in an Excel spreadsheet offline, and later transfer the data to the R/3 System with an online connection.

- *Travel Expenses*
  Employees can calculate travel costs offline in an Excel spreadsheet and later transfer the data to the R/3 System with an online connection.

- *New Employee Event*
  New employees can enter personal data themselves.

- *Electronic Paystub*
  Employees often require specific information for personal reasons such as a credit check or tax information. They can simply call the information from the system.

- *Employee Directory*
  Employees can access current public information about colleagues directly from the HR module of the R/3 System.

- *Change Password*
  Employees can change their own passwords and spare MIS the effort.

Consult SAP documentation for a detailed description of ESS components.

Besides an R/3 System (release 3.0D and later), ESS also requires a Web server that runs on a Microsoft Windows NT platform. The Web server itself can be a Microsoft Information Server or a Netscape Enterprise Server. Since the applications reflect development under HAHTsite (see *http://www.haht.com*), the runtime environment requires a HAHTsite Engine 2.0. The Web server must also have installed versions of Microsoft Office 97 and Visual Basic (version 5.0 and above).

Almost exclusively, the user requires systems delivered with a Web browser (Netscape Navigator 3.0 + and Microsoft Internet Explorer 3.02 +). To enter travel costs, they also require Microsoft Excel 97.

Web applications implement ESS. Those applications have JavaScript on the client side and a language compatible with Visual Basic on the server side. Microsoft COM/DCOM provides access to business objects on the server side. The R/3 System uses BAPIs for this access. Theoretically, any common *Web authoring tools* can produce ESS applications. In particular, SAP supports the entire palette of Internet development tools from Microsoft so customers can cover the leading technologies well. In the middleware area, these tools include Microsoft Transaction Server, Message Queuing Server, Directory Services and the use of available security mechanisms.

Interactive Voice Response (IVR) provides yet another means of access to an R/3 System with SAP Automation. IVR enables operation of some applications from a telephone (standard or mobile).

Releases of the R/3 System later than 4.5 will make all these ready-made ESS applications available with ITS technology.

3.7   Integrating business processes

The ability to make R/3 transactions usable over the Internet provides yet another enhancement to the R/3 System: an expansion of the enterprise's area of economic activity and the radius of its workflow. Chapter 2 provided an example of integration payment procedures into an R/3 System.

From a global economic and political perspective, these opportunities present an interesting development. Past developments already show formerly isolated, national enterprises changing step by step into ever more complex corporations and finally into global enterprises (see Chapter 1). Business integration beyond the borders (and limits) of countries and enterprises defines the next step. Internet users will hardly concern themselves with the actual location of the enterprise they encounter on the World Wide Web. Competition between enterprises will no longer recognize any geographic or political borders. Rather, enterprises will meet within a global online market. In many cases, location alone will not satisfy the need for diversification within an enterprise.

The integration of business transactions also has meaning for the Internet itself. The development of the integration of business contents into the Internet results in the tendency shown in Figure 3.19.

The Internet's first level of integration included the presentation of multimedia content that users could call if desired. This level offered no interaction with systems. A mass mailing of marketing brochures functioned similarly.

Users find it difficult to examine a large number of static WWW pages and find waiting for them to download even more difficult. HTML pages claim to provide the most current information. In this area, it becomes possible to separate the data from the presentation level as has long occurred in traditional data processing.

The next integration phase or step created the opportunity to link real and maintained data interactively in the static HTML pages by integrating databases. Numerous solutions exist today that integrate databases into WWW pages, including all the leading database manufacturers.

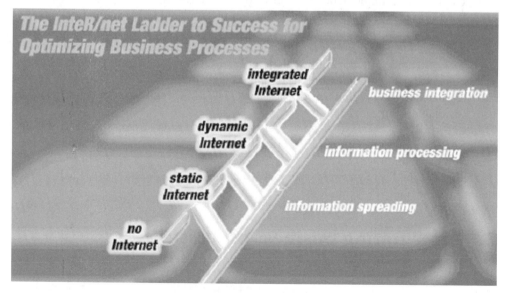

Figure 3.19   Integrating business functions on the Internet

The data processing needs of an enterprise do not limit themselves to storage of enterprise data, but require intelligent access to data as transactions. The requirements here go beyond entering data into a database table or extracting data from it.

The title of Figure 3.19, *Ladder of Success*, takes its name from the next step. This phase sees the ability to access data from an R/3 System as easily on the Internet as users already do at normal R/3 workstations. Access takes places with business transactions: defined business processes that make use of extant data and create new data. Dynamic pricing provides a good example. A known user receives a special price calculation that leads to a quotation of an individual price never before fixed to the goods.

The goal remains the use of extant transactions or transaction integrated into an existing system landscape. It does not include placing new ones on the WWW and using new transactions in isolation. The use of complete transactions does not necessarily decide the matter. Encapsulated access to specific business processes with BAPIs identifies the decisive factor.

An Internet connection to an R/3 System may well require a first step that seamlessly transfers the range of transactions and the foundational business processes of a standard business system to the Internet. In reality, not only does the Internet make a valuable contribution to the value of the SAP R/3 System, but also makes just as valuable a contribution to business by providing a new quality of valuable usability. The enterprise itself can thus extend the chain of created value and stretch it to include consumers.

This ability produces an integrated information and process flow that extends the supply chain to consumers and optimally integrates their demands into the enterprise's planning. Equally valuable new possibilities will open to employees, when they can perform their own administrative tasks over a simply operated system.

3.8   Frontends: SAPGUI; JAVA SAPGUI or Browser

A Web browser and the SAPGUI both function according to the principles of client/server technology. Both operate as clients 'served' by the server. The integration with the Internet as well as the platform and operating system independence offered by the Java programming language from SUN Microsystems have made headlines throughout the world. Java has also enabled a new part of the R/3 System, the JAVA SAPGUI. SAP includes the Java-SAPGUI as part of the standard R/3 System as of release 4.0.

Each of these three designs (Web-Browser, SAPGUI, and JAVA SAPGUI) targets a different goal. Transaction retrieval on the Internet over a Web browser includes the following essential points:

- presentation of dedicated business processes for the target application over the Internet;

- simple access for inexperienced users;

- expansion of the enterprise's area of activity beyond the limits of geography and the platform used.

The essence of a Web browser relates to providing implicit access to selected transactions of the R/3 System to a previously unreached (for geographic or other complex reasons) group of users. The new self-service functions enable even untrained users to use specific applications. Sporadic users with very specific tasks to perform will find these functions particularly helpful. A connection with Human Resources (HR) provides numerous examples of applications on the Internet.

The other two designs differ from the goals of the Web browser considerably. Although the typical SAPGUI can connect to an R/3 application server over a great distance with TCP/IP, the connection offers an inexperienced user little added value because the user model has not changed. Internet applications seek to provide exactly that type of value.

The same holds true for the JAVA SAPGUI. The Java version aims at a tactical target: to save the expenses of installing a client. A Java-enabled browser can access the JAVA SAPGUI directly from a central SAPGUI server at the time of use. Global access saves the expense of installing a client and users always work with the most current version. The JAVA SAPGUI can also accept later changes and better reflect customer-specific needs. Since the JAVA SAPGUI runs in Applet mode within the browser, it offers its services independently of any platform. The installation of new software can often require a great deal of time and money. This age of networked enterprises no longer recognizes geographical boundaries within a global enterprise structure. Installation of several thousand clients can last for months. However, the similarity between the JAVA SAPGUI and the traditional SAPGUI means that users do not find the reduced complexity and self-service characteristics they expect from Internet applications. Only users trained in the operation of the SAPGUI can use its Java counterpart.

3.9   Security for the R/3 System

The factors that provide security for the Internet in general (see Section 2.6.1) also apply to the security of an R/3 System. This section treats the general security criteria of the R/3 System (see Chapter 5 for the additional or specific measures required by the ITS solution):

- confidentiality of transferred data;

- security for authentication of the sender;

- authorization;

- accuracy/intactness of data;

- transaction security.

Closed systems and networks usually require similar security measured as global and open systems. An enterprise can also assume that an enemy or danger hides within its own ranks. Closed systems have advantages: an overview of users and a lack of anonymity among users. Any opening of this closed system increases the range of possible security breaches and demands stricter procedures. The growth of networks adds weight to the security of applications.

Users increasingly encounter client/server communication between the SAPGUI and the R/3 System over Wide Area Networks (WANs). Telecommuting and remote sites use modem connections to access an R/3 System from any location. In such cases, confidentiality and intactness of data are absolute necessities. Critical connections over open networks require encryption on the leg between the SAPGUI and the application server.

As of version 3.1G, SAP and SECUDE GmbH developed a special security solution for the R/3 System. The solution uses a public key to encrypt user authentication between users, SAPRouters and R/3 application servers. The solution does not encrypt the data itself. The components thus exchange digital signatures with each other, signatures provided by a certificate authority. The asymmetric encryption takes place with RSA; symmetric algorithms include DES, Triple DES or IDEA. The Secure Single SignOn procedure establishes a single secure connection at the start of the session. This process requires expense in maintaining the security infrastructure, especially during assignment of the key-pairs that a specific SECUDE module handles.

The authorization concept of SAP R/3 contributes to general efforts at authorization and authentication. The authorization concept becomes useful only after correct installation. Administrators must also critically inspect and maintain authorizations granted to current users. As the section on Internet security made clear, security hardly constitutes a purely technical subject. Rather, it demands a great deal of administrative and organizational efforts. To prohibit inappropriate access to the internal system at the system and application level, the authorization concept can also apply to open networks.

Transaction security constitutes a central task of the R/3 System. The system must guarantee that critical actions, often dependent upon each other, take place as units or not at all. The roll-back feature holds responsibility for an orderly cancellation of any corruption in the system. The use of SAP R/3 over open networks can also use this feature. For ALE/WEB, for example, the ITS performs this task. In case of a sudden termination of an R/3 session (leaving the Web browser, selecting the cancel key) the ITS must ensure that the R/3 System remains stable.

The above fulfills all the essential security criteria. Any opening of an R/3 System to the Internet requires additional stringent security measures. The security concepts build on the procedures noted in Section 2.6, and receive additional treatment in Chapter 4, along with the ITS solution.

4 Structure and use of the ITS

Early on, the strategic significance of the Internet for enterprises inspired SAP to consider high-end designs that would provide secure and efficient connections between an R/3 System and the Internet. The *inside-out* design of the Internet Transaction Server shows the success of this consideration. The ITS offers direct Internet access to and use of the high performance features of R/3 System architecture. Chapter 3 introduced two different designs: *inside-out* and *outside-in*.

The standard R/3 System includes delivery of the Internet Transaction Server, a component that serves as an essential module of the technologies that open the R/3 System and enables its use in business across different platforms and systems. The following section introduces the Internet Transaction Server in detail as well as some basics regarding its use. Later sections present the applications, IACs, provided by SAP for the Internet Transaction Server. Programming guidelines provide many examples for individual programming of personal applications.

4.1 Design requirements

The Internet Transaction Server and its functional principles reflect the functional requirements and performance characteristics that must exist to open R/3 System transactions. Because the application logic remains within the R/3 System itself, design follows the inside-out method. SAP also considered an outside-in design with RFC access to BAPIs or function modules. However, the primary desire – to make complete R/3 System transactions with all the benefits of high-end performance available on the Internet – moved SAP to develop the inside-out design.

The elements that contributed to the current success of the R/3 System required transfer to a new presentation interface for the Internet. The overall concept, therefore, reflected the principles of *multi-tier architecture* that enables consideration of a multiplicity of presentation levels beyond the database and application level – especially the Internet. High-end integration of this new user interface, the World Wide Web, required the following elements in particular:

- *A common, stable basis for all R/3 System applications*
  Internet transactions should not exist apart from actual R/3 System transactions. Internet transactions must also use the advantages offered by a stable and proven platform for business transactions. The advantages include not only the platform for the runtime system, but also the development environment. Especially here, the R/3 System has undergone valuable improvements over time that have equipped it with a

high-quality development environment. The transport system, in particular, has proved itself as a basic element for porting existing applications in new versions of the system. Administrators, however, must check external applications (such as Visual Basic) for correct functions when they update the R/3 System. The use of BAPIs generally ensures release-independence.

- *Security and scalability*
  The requirements that apply to traditional R/3 System transaction should also apply to Internet applications, especially for security and the guaranteed performance of the dialog system. The R/3 System integrates numerous mechanisms to protect against unauthorized access to sensitive data (user management, for example). The system also offers additional procedures to ensure maximum availability and correct execution of the applications (the rollback, for example). Flexible scalability, provided by the client/server structure of the R/3 System architecture, can manage very high numbers of users and permit continual expansion of the system without interrupting running processes. The Internet, which frequently displays several million daily accesses to popular sites, makes this requirement particularly important.

- *Up-to-date information*
  At runtime, an R/3 System takes information dynamically not only from the database, but also from the application system. Consider a customer-specific price that the system calculates online at runtime based on a discount record in the database. In this case, the information reflects absolute currency. An Internet application must offer the same level of currency, and therefore demands direct integration with the processes and corresponding data of an R/3 System. The system must dynamically create the HTML files whenever a user requests them and must take online data directly from the R/3 System at runtime. Separation of the application logic from the presentation level means that the IACs contain no application data in static HTML files. The IACs must generate the files with active business processes based upon data from the database on the fly. Today's Web applications generally have no direct link to the application data of business systems and therefore do not supply completely consistent data.

- *Separation of presentation and application logic*
  The demands of software engineering cause today's software system to separate the presentation level from the application logic upon which it rests whenever possible. The same holds true on the Internet. HTML pages should therefore contain no application logic, but only information on appearance (graphics, layout and so on). Internet application components meet these requirements, since the HTML templates on the Web server contain only layout information. The transactions remain in the R/3 System.

- *Compatibility with all standard Web browsers*
  Support of all leading Web browsers forms another crucial requirement. Developers cannot assume that all Internet users employ the same Web browser, although they can do so on an internal enterprise network (Intranet). The ITS itself offers the preconditions for interaction with all current Web browsers. The Internet Application Components supplied by SAP meet all requirements based upon a lowest common

denominator, so that the components can support all well-known Web browsers. In customizing, of course, developers remain free to make individual and proprietary additions to the components.

- *Support for leading Web servers*
  The Internet has long since become the norm in many enterprises, either as Intranet, Extranet or specifically as the Internet. Accordingly, the ITS must support the most important Web servers already in use at enterprises. The ITS must also consider both WindowsNT and UNIX. The architecture of the ITS must mesh seamlessly with the existing infrastructure (webroot, file system, and Web organization), to permit easy consistency and integration between existing Web pages and the applications of the ITS. The ITS provides the basis to meet these requirements.

The following section introduces the ITS in more detail. The architecture of the ITS reflects the requirements listed above.

4.2   Architecture of the ITS

Development of the Internet Transaction Server (ITS) targeted linking an R/3 System to the World Wide Web or with Web servers and Web browsers. The ITS serves as the link between both systems or as a gateway that adjusts the different communications protocols and data formats of the R/3 System and the Internet to each other. Two very different worlds meet here, since the lack of status that characterizes the World Wide Web cannot join a transaction-oriented application system such as the R/3 System without additional work. The problems created by this lack of status on the Internet have already triggered suggestions for improvements to the protocols currently in use (see Section 2.7).

The ITS aims at the transaction parenthesis of the R/3 System over the Internet. It seeks to include the Web browser at a workstation and to guarantee complete application functions. The workstation should provide such secure and complete use of special R/3 transactions as does the normal SAPGUI. In principle, only the presentation interface to the user should change: rather than as a screen in the SAPGUI, it should contain HTML definitions.

A user on the World Wide Web can use a link within a specific HTML page to start an Internet transaction in an R/3 System. The Web server transfers the request directly to the ITS, which then establishes a concrete connection to a pre-defined R/3 System to start the requested transaction. The DIAG communications channel (Dynamic Information and Actions Gateway) implements the connection between the ITS and the R/3 System. The ITS behaves as though it were several traditional SAPGUIs connected to the R/3 application server. The ITS then packages the data returned by the R/3 System into HTML and sends back to the Web server, which then displays it in the Web browser. With each additional user action, the transaction running in the R/3 System completes another step in the application. The data required to control the R/3 application comes from field contents in the HTML forms completed or selected by the user. The ITS transfers this data into the defined screen fields of the R/3 transaction.

The special requirements of the HTML presentation interface make it impossible to execute all ABAP transactions on the World Wide Web without additional adjustments. These

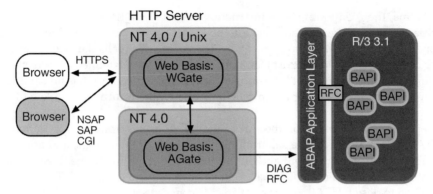

Figure 4.1   The Architecture of the Internet Transaction Server

special requirements include the appearance of the user interface and the authorization concept intended for implementation (see Section 4.4.3). For Internet transactions, we also recommend the use of BAPIs since they provide release-independence and better opportunities to maintain the application. Internet applications intended for the ITS that consist of ABAP transactions and the corresponding HTML templates are known as Internet Application Components (IACs).

In addition to the actual data exchange, the ITS also manages a series of administrative tasks, such as session management (to administer various system resources) and login management.

The ITS consists of two separable components, each of which can run on a different computer: the Application Gateway (AGate) and the Web Gateway (WGate). A TCP/IP connection must exist between the two gateways. The WGate creates the interface to the Web server and can load as a dynamic component (Dynamic Link Library, or DLL) at runtime. The DLLs (WGate.dll) exist for Windows NT 4.0 only on the Netscape Server and the Microsoft Information Server. In any case, however, a properly prepared CGI interface enables communications with any Web server. In general, however, CGI programs display poorer performance values than dynamic libraries. Specific WGates exist for special UNIX platforms.

The AGate (AGate.exe) uses the DIAG protocol to create the interface to the R/3 application server and currently exists for Windows NT only from version 4.0. The AGate and the WGate communicate with each other over the TCP/IP protocol and therefore can run on different hardware platforms. This situation can become necessary when security mechanisms (firewalls) run on UNIX Web servers, or when scalability requires a distributed system.

The HTML templates, along with the actual ABAP transaction, form the Internet Application Components. HTML templates generate the complete HTML pages as seen by users. At runtime, the system inserts current data from the R/3 transaction into placeholders in the template. To describe the placeholders, SAP uses its own language that the ITS can interpret and which works only with the ITS: HTML[Business] (this is the proper name assigned by SAP). This language serves only to place online data from an R/3 System into templates. It cannot implement application logic. Consequently, the application logic remains in the R/3 System.

At runtime, the AGate translates instructions into HTML files with backticks (`) or {Server}-tags that it recognizes and include the HTML[Business] statements. The statements target specific screens within the application. The AGate then calls data from the screen fields. Exactly one HTML page exists for a defined screen (or its defined subscreens). The screen functions like a transport interface and its optical appearance has no significance whatsoever. After translation of the instructions, the AGate returns a completed HTML page to the Web server.

The separation of templates on the side of the HTML pages from the application logic of the R/3 System also creates a separation between presentation logic and application logic. HTML[Business] sets only input and output fields and their order. The R/3 transaction itself continues to maintain the fields. Developers can use any common HTML programming method to design HTML pages and can create an especially individual appearance.

The architecture of the ITS displays some advantages over other methods of integrating the Internet with an R/3 System:

- *Integration: Accessing the Strength of the R/3 System*
  The ITS allows, for the first time, a direct opening of R/3 transactions to the Internet. Although Internet applications require new programs, the programs nonetheless use the proven, uniform development environment (implementation, test, debugging) of the R/3 System. Developers can also automatically use the multilingual capabilities of the R/3 System.

- *Transaction-oriented*
  The process does not involve mere data transfer to an external application because the application, as before, runs in the R/3 System. Internet applications therefore display the same qualities as do normal R/3 applications. An integrated rollback procedure guarantees orderly execution or cancellation of a request should the transmission fail.

- *Dynamic and in real time*
  Direct access to live data in the R/3 System means that any request data remains completely up-to-date.

- *Secure*
  The R/3 System contains security mechanisms to prohibit unauthorized access to data. These features include user administration and access rights. Internet applications can also use these mechanisms.

- *Easily maintained*
  Maintenance of distributed applications on various platforms quickly become burdensome. Frequently the connections between changes made to one system and the effects on another system become apparent only at runtime, when an error occurs. The ITS permits central control of maintenance and updates with the R/3 System. The use of test systems and production systems provide optimal preparation of applications. The use of BAPIs and their fixed interfaces ensures release-independence and integrates new features (such as new error messages) automatically. If data within the R/3 System changes (product illustrations, for example), the system's dynamic integration automatically updates the data in the applications at runtime.

User-friendly maintenance rests upon SAP's delivery of standard applications that the system itself updates at each release upgrade at each customer site and that use the SAP infrastructure.

4.2.1   The Web Gateway (WGate)

The WGate forms the link for the transfer of HTTP requests from the Web server to the AGate and for HTTP responses from the AGate back to the Web server. The WGate always functions as an abstract interface to various Web servers. The interface, for example, might connect to a CGI interface that starts an individual process for each query. The open interface permits addressing any Web server. In addition, adapted WGate modules for some Web servers have WGate modules that communicate with the Web server over an API interface. Since each Web server has its own API interface, SAP supports on the leading Web servers:

- Microsoft Internet Information Server (IIS) with the ISAPI interface;

- various Netscape servers with the NSAPI interface.

Each Web server starts the appropriate WGate.dll (Dynamic Link Library) when the server itself starts or with an appropriate query from the Internet. The Web server creates an additional *thread* (*thread* can be understood as a subprocess controlled completely by a transferred process. In this case, the AGate controls several threads simultaneously) that ends upon completion of processing of the query. Threads enable simultaneous processing of several queries and permit better control of system resources. Individual Web servers can limit the number of available threads. In addition to the two Web servers noted above (which run on Windows NT above version 4.0), SAP supports selected UNIX platforms. SAP documentation offers information on concrete options.

Besides the interface to the Web server, the connection to the AGate also plays a crucial role. A TCP/IP connection exchanges data bidirectionally, if necessary even between various computer systems:

- The system redirects the data and parameters of queries made on the World Wide Web to the AGate in a compatible form. The first call of a new session creates a new session in the ITS and, therefore, a new transaction in the R/3 System. During data transfer, the system stores the data in the context data structures of the AGate, which then makes the ITS accessible to the transactions or which requires control of the session.

- The AGate returns requested HTML pages to the WGate with the proper formatting. The system then makes them available to the Web server immediately.

The AGate takes over the essential tasks of managing an R/3 session. The following section treats this issue in detail. The separation between the AGate and the WGate offers a decided advantage, as the AGate service maintains its independence from the Web server in use only in the manner of use. In the context of scaling, various Web servers and their WGates can communicate with a single AGate. Technical security reasons also speak for a separation of the Web server platform from the AGate.

4.2.2   The Application Gateway (AGate)

The AGate serves as the heart of the ITS. Expansion of the transaction parenthesis to the Internet requires mechanisms that guarantee a performance-oriented, secure and function-rich manner of working with R/3 transactions, even for several users simultaneously. The AGate includes the means needed to meet the requirements and possesses an extremely complex internal structure. This section treats the most important elements and tasks from the viewpoint of the user.

A *mapping manager* controls the AGate itself. The mapping manager can handle multiple threads: it therefore records and processes multiple queries of a WGAte. A dispatcher thread divides the available threads for further processing. The entry in the system settings of the NT registry determines how many threads can remain open at any given time. The NT registry also controls memory management. Administration of threads remains elementary, and reflects influences from the following mechanisms:

- *Timeout mechanism*
  The service description of an Internet application sets a maximum timeout. If the user exceeds this limit between two given actions, the threads become idle and terminate the transaction. The unpredictability of user behavior on the World Wide Web makes this procedure necessary. Users can use the browser's back button to leave a transaction before completing it or select a different link of related or different interest. The length of the timeout should consider the type of application, as some applications require more time between user input (during online shopping, for example). The start of a new thread can also cause cutting other threads that the user may not have used for a considerable period. If the system has already allocated all available threads and all threads remain active, the system will reject any new query.

- *The dispatcher*
  The AGate Dispatcher organizes queries from the World Wide Web and the work threads of the WGate. It performs this task in a manner similar to the allocation of normal R/3 statements to the running processes of the R/3 application server. The system uses session identification to determine if it should start a new session. Threads, however, do not have static links to a particular user session.

The AGate itself forms the interface between the WGate and the R/3 System. The AGate can run on Windows NT platforms as of version 4.0 and communicates with the WGate over a TCP/IP connection. It uses the DIAG protocol to connect to the R/3 System and behaves like a SAPGUI with the application server.

From the user's viewpoint, the most important tasks of the AGate include the following:

Service management

Service descriptions contain important information that the system requires to start IACs. A special services directory stores the service files that belong to a particular IAC. In addition to the specific service descriptions, a global service also exists. The system reads the global service and, if necessary, rewrites its individual definitions with those of the specific service file. The service concept serves to assign the following characteristics before the start of the individual IACs:

- *~appserver or ~messageserver*
  The name of the R/3 System or message server on which the transaction runs. If an entry for the message server exists, that server regulates allocation to the intended application server.

- *~transaction*
  The R/3 transaction that is to start.

If the service does not define the following *optional* entries, the system requests user input.

- *~login*
  The user name of the R/3 user

- *~password*
  The user's password. The system can also store an encrypted (DES) form of the password.

- *~client*
  The client under which the login takes place.

- *~language*
  The login language in the R/3 System. The system displays all messages, field contents and descriptions on the screen in this language (if the language is maintained). Users can also access other language resources to select a language.

Additional *optional* parameters include:

- *~theme*
  This entry allows selection of the desired version of the HTML template. Several service descriptions that differ only for this entry enable the same transaction to appear with a completely different design or layout.

- *~timeout*
  An interactive session ends after this time has elapsed. The default value equals 60 minutes.

Login and user management

The AGate uses the entries for user and password in the service description to execute a login procedure to the R/3 System automatically. If the entries do not exist in the description, the system requests them from the user when it starts the IAC. The login procedure takes place transparently when the entries exist. Internet users therefore have the impression that they operate an R/3 application without having logged on or they fail to notice that they work anonymously in an R/3 System.

Developers will often find it advantageous to define a generic Web user as an R/3 user with quite limited access rights. However, some applications may benefit from individual logins by different users so that their authorization profiles can control the application exactly. Restrictive programming can limit the options available to a Web user to a specific application. Once a user has logged on anonymously, the system can request a specific Web user ID at runtime and check it according to specific applications, such as particular

BAPIs. This procedure applies to some of the IACs delivered by SAP, especially for the job application process. The system can also generate a Web user at runtime and send a message that contains the ID to the user. Should applicants later query the status of their job applications, they can enter the ID to gain access to the information.

On an *Intranet*, the system can use the normal R/3 login procedure to check authorizations because R/3 users already exist. If, however, the system should address 'unknown' user groups, as on the *Internet*, the login must take place for a generic R/3 user. This approach can also apply to many Intranet applications that offer unspecific services, such as an employee catalog. Application-oriented authorization checks with BAPIs can supply additional legitimization with a generic login.

Session management

The start of an IAC establishes an R/3 session. All further actions of the user run within this session. As usual, the R/3 System holds the user context of a session. The connection breaks only when the user formally logs off or when a timeout occurs.

Accordingly, the AGate Session Manager holds responsibility only for the initial login to the R/3 System (Login Management) and for the establishment of the session that corresponds to the login. The Session State remains important for the control of a session, the allocation of the correct HTML pages to a session and for correct conditions in the flow. The Session State enables resynchronization of conditions on the Web and the corresponding R/3 transaction. The Session State is required because the user can select the browser's back button to select an older HTML file and execute additional actions from within that file.

HTML^{Business} interpreter

In addition to transferring information from the Web into the R/3 System, a central task of the AGate involves placing real R/3 data into HTML templates. Both activities use specific context fields contained in the ITS. Equivalent names enable the allocation of information from HTML files to screen fields and vice versa. The HTML^{Business} language prepares HTML templates so that at runtime the AGate can compare the field names (input and output fields) in the template with those of the screen and can transfer the appropriate data. The process generates a pure HTML file that any normal Web browser can display. The section on programming guidelines provides explicit information on how HTML^{Business} works.

4.3   Function and application principles

Correct programming of IACs alone does not provide an enterprise with successful use of ITS technology. Users must understand and observe additional principles. The separation of the presentation and application levels in IACs open an entire series of interesting possibilities that can apply to various user interfaces for a single application. An examination of the precise flow of a dialog-based application will also clarify the correct use of the special characteristics of an Internet-based application.

The much-discussed topics of security and scalability of business systems on the Internet also demand examination if the applications will find productive use and acceptance among users. The following sections will address these topics in detail.

4.3.1   Separation of presentation and business logic

The ability to separate actual R/3 transactions running in the background from the final appearance of those transactions in a Web browser defines one of the most important characteristics of Internet application components. Within this context, developers speak of *topic independence*. Software development offers the advantage that developers must pay attention to only the available interface when designing the presentation level. IACs, however, permit the simultaneous and parallel definition of multiple presentation levels for a single transaction in the R/3 System. Consequently, one transaction can run multiple times on R/3 application server and several versions that differ in appearance (to the user) can exist in parallel. Several examples of applications exist. Developers can observe the design guidelines of various branches of the enterprise. In addition, the system can supply different groups of customers with the same transaction yet tailor the design to the requirements of each user (age, gender, country-specific criteria and so on). Individual possibilities for design encompass the full spectrum of options available for the design of HTML pages. The possibility also exists to place the fields of an R/3 transaction differently in each version or to suppress them entirely. During installation of the ITS over 38 IACs become available. If customers wish a design that differs from the one offered by SAP, they can change, adjust or create a new format at any time.

Since the ITS operates with the inside-out concept to access R/3 functions completely, the IACs automatically enjoy *language independence*. As long as the system administrators

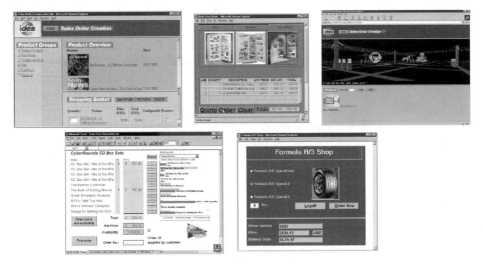

Figure 4.2   Various technologies access the same R/3 application (from above left to below right): HTML, Java, VRML, Excel, and ActiveX)

have maintained a given R/3 transaction with the appropriate languages, users themselves can select a desired language at runtime. In the R/3 System, this option comes into play at login (login language). Internet users would use predefined links to start the transaction in the selected language. The ITS supports both options. In addition to using the multilingual capabilities of the R/3 System directly, different HTML templates at the presentation level can also define various languages. The following section introduces the technical aspects of implementing topic and language independence.

Three different options exist to define language independence. These settings also affect topic independence.

- *Using the language independence of the R/3 System*
  The simplest method of implementing language independence involves using the language information already contained in the R/3 System. The system displays language-dependent text based on the language indicated at login. Proper maintenance of the desired linguistic elements in the system offers the only precondition. The HTML template can then refer directly to language-dependent text elements. For example, developers can use 'text-posnr.label' with the label attribute in the HTML template to address language-dependent field names. Since the screen cannot always display all the language-dependent text information, additional procedures exist to control the output of languages.

- *Using language or topic-specific templates*
  A group of HTML templates is created for each language or design variant. To distinguish the language versions, a special naming environment with a language ID automatically indicates to the system that it should use the HTML template associated with the login language. The naming convention, <modulepool>_<screennumber>_<language>.html, can, for example, lead to SAPVW01_1000_D.html. The system stores all HTML templates in the same directory or in specific topic-oriented subdirectories. The service that starts the transaction in the ITS identifies the main directory.

  To design different presentation versions (topic independence), the system must store the individual variants in their own directories. The variants must indicate the corresponding services, which also bear the name of the directory. The various service files will then always start the same R/3 transaction, so that only the presentation level must contain different versions to support a different language or layout. The name of each service can include the design variant (VW01_ixos or VW01_sap, for example). The disadvantage of this procedure involves the necessity of maintaining each different HTML template for each different topic individually when a general change takes place. Although the ITS offers this option, the disadvantages far outweigh the advantages, and we do not recommend it.

- *Using language resources*
  An additional means of controlling language output involves linking all language-dependent texts and graphics (radio and push buttons, for example) to variables in the HTML templates and allowing definition of the variables at runtime. To do so, define language-dependent resource files for each language desired. The resource files replace the variables with the current values: an ID or the filename of the graphic. The direc-

tory that stores the resource files also stores the HTML templates themselves. The use of language resources prohibits the simultaneous use of language-dependent templates. The use of language resources allows developers to encapsulate the presentation logic of the HTML templates further, as the HTML templates no longer directly identify any hard-coded information (text, images, and so on). The Web Studio used to program HTML templates, supports administration of the language information in the language resource files. The customer can thus choose between an external translation and an R/3-internal translation.

The ITS can also use National Language Support (NLS) of the R/3 System with the Unicode Character Set (ISO 10646) as used under Windows NT 4.0. For communication with the Web server or the R/3 System, conversions into the Multi-Byte Character Set (MBCS) take place. Conversion can also interpret and process national character sets (MBCS and UNICODE) or permit use of languages such as Latin-1 and Shift-Jis with the code pages available in the R/3 System.

4.3.2   Dialog-controlled business transactions

The special aspect of Internet transactions involves their use of a dialog-controlled process that serves and controls a real R/3 transaction in an R/3 System by using user interaction from within a Web browser. The Internet Transaction Server and the R/3 System do not regard the flow of an Internet user's session and the interaction with the Web server as trivial. The flow of the R/3 transaction in the R/3 System must agree completely with the visual display in the user's Web browser. In addition to correct synchronization, the system also requires other actions, such as user login to the R/3 System, session management and a correct end to the session. Figure 4.3 shows the schematic flow of an Internet session. Synchronization of the status in the Web browser and of the transaction in the R/3 System plays a pivotal role. The Web user can leave the current HTML page at any time with the back button or enter a new URL. This ability also allows the user to display an older page from the ITS in the browser and select a link from it. However, the condition of the transaction in the R/3 System may no longer function or the session may have already ended. Dynamic URLs that operate behind the links of the HTML page can regulate and control execution of steps in the correct order. In this case, the URL contains status information that the AGate evaluates to equalize the status of the transaction and the correct status of the HTML page. Should a conflict occur, the AGate attempts to create a synchronized condition transparently to the user.

Context fields in the AGate temporarily store the data exchanged between the ITS and the R/3 System. The system stores global data relating to the session for the entire length of the transaction. The context contains the following:

- information on the service (~timeout, ~transaction, ~URLWgate, and so on);

- user requests (~OKCode, filled field values from the HTML form);

- responses of the R/3 System (current values of the screen fields).

Table 4.1 shows the flow of an ITS session in detail; Figure 4.3 shows the general flow of the steps.

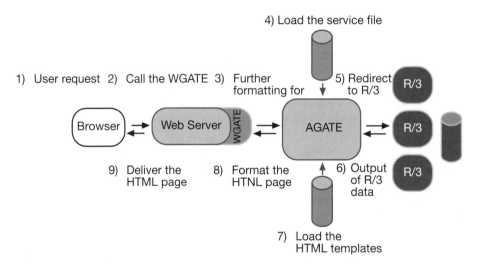

Figure 4.3   Typical flow of a query in an ITS session

The flow of an R/3 transaction follows the usual principles of flow control in ABAP programming (PB, PAI and so on). User interaction with selection options maintains the dialog and exchanges data between the Web browser and the R/3 transaction via the ITS context. If the transaction ends incorrectly and produces an inconsistent condition (for example, after an interrupted transfer), the system returns everything to its original condition with a rollback. This feature protects against processing incorrect orders on the Internet, for example.

4.3.3   Security considerations

An enterprise must take the security of an R/3 System seriously. In addition to data security (protection from lost data), the Internet requires access security and protection from unauthorized entry into the internal network. Opening an R/3 System to the Internet carries increased security risks unless administrators act to enhance security.

Complete use of the R/3 System can apply all the protection mechanisms available to the system to the security of Internet transactions and applications. Such measures include two special features, user management and login management. Additional mechanisms provide explicit protection from breaking into an internal network from the Internet. Special firewalls provide an excellent example. To preserve the confidentiality of enterprise data that travels along a public network, administrators should use special encryption procedures.

User authentication

Within an enterprise, the authorization concept protects against unauthorized access to data in an R/3 System. Transactions permit only the processing steps defined in the

Table 4.1   Example of the flow of an ITS request

Step	Action
1	The user employs a Web browser to select an HTML page that contains a link to call the desired IAC.
2	The URL, for example *http://myserver/scripts/wgate/PV0I/!?~language=D&~theme=69*, triggers the start of the R/3 transaction. The example also sets the language and the topic in the call, thus overwriting the entries contained in the service.
3	The AGate identifies the service (here PV0I) and interprets the service description. Login occurs and the system starts the transaction identified in the service file on the R/3 application server.
4	The system transmits the first screen to the AGate via the DIAG channel. The AGate stores the required context fields in the ITS after Process Before Output (PBO).
5	Naming the corresponding HTML templates allows the ITS to insert the screen data into the correct templates. The system processes commands written in HTML^{Business} and employs the context information.
6	The AGate transmits the completed HTML page to the WGate, which returns the page to the user's Web browser via the Web server.
7	The user performs additional actions: filling out form fields or selecting other options. Each Submit reestablishes contact with the AGate and stores the transmitted data in the context of the ITS. Each OK code switches to the transaction in the R/3 System. After Process After Input (PAI) the system transmits the data from the ITS context into the R/3 application. This step clears the context.
8	All further actions follow the flow given above.
9	The session remains active until a timeout occurs or the user ends it by selecting a button. In both cases, the R/3 System receives an EXIT code. The service description can specify the HTML page the system sends to the browser after the transaction ends.

authorization profiles of the user. Internet applications can use the same authorization concept. In addition to any defined R/3 users, the system can also define application-specific users controlled by the application, rather than by the R/3 Basis system. This ability produces the following three usage variants:

- *Authentication with generic Web users*
  This user type requires definition of a normal R/3 user; the system then permits this defined user for anonymous logins of any Internet user. The appropriate service stores the generic R/3 user and password, so that the login procedure occurs completely transparently to the Internet user. This type of login applies best to situations that require read-only authorization, such as catalog display. The authorization profile of the anonymous R/3 user must therefore contain as few writes as possible.

- *Authentication with dedicated R/3 users*
  If the service description contains no user entries, the ITS requests login information from the user with a system template at the start of the IAC. After successful entry, the user can

use the transaction according to the authorization profile. Application areas for this type of authentication include HR and applications that process personal travel costs. Privacy considerations require that users may display only individual, personal data.

- *Authentication with application-dependent users*
  The process relies upon a login by a generic R/3 user, since an R/3 transaction can start only with a specific user. If a general Internet application executes user-specific actions, the system requires a user controlled by the application. Specific processing steps can require the presence of such a user. For example, online job applications can require assignment of an applicant number and password, so that the applicant can later check the status of the application. The application itself checks the authorization, so that application programming must prevent unauthorized access. If the system uses BAPIs, application developers must ensure that the application transfers the user name and password to the BAPI. The BAPI then executes the check.

Developers must ensure that the user name and password never appear as call parameters in the URL itself. Otherwise, everyone can read them. The service description should always contain an encrypted version of the user's password. The Web Studio offers an explicit DES encryption for this task.

On the Internet, repeated logins with an R/3 user during extended operation of IACs becomes burdensome. Version 2.0 of the ITS therefore introduced a login context valid for all services than can be called from the same workstation. Previous versions of the ITS did not offer this feature. For security reasons, the system creates the login context only for logins created interactively with a login template (mask). This feature ensures that other IACs that require interactive login automatically have transparent access to the information.

The login context remains valid until the start of a service with its own user login or a timeout occurs in the login context. The Global.srvc (~userTimeout) can set the timeout. In either case, however, the system requires a new login. A logoff command can indicate the end of a session to the ITS, which then ends the login context immediately:

```
http://www.yourserver.com/scripts/wgate.dll?~Command=Logoff
```

The SAP license model distinguishes between use of each authentication method. It recognizes the difference between known Intranet users with access to the R/3 System and anonymous users. Whether an Intranet user operates with an IAC or some other technology of the R/3 System has no major significance. The calculation of license costs for anonymous users depends on the number of simultaneously available sessions and channels open between the ITS and the application server.

Firewalls and encryption

After performance on the part of the R/3 System of all the measures necessary to prevent unauthorized access to system data, developers must make the ITS network itself secure. These steps prevent unauthorized entry from the Web server to the enterprise's Intranet, especially to the R/3 application server and its data at the network level. Firewalls installed in each enterprise provide the first line of defense. Firewalls should stand in every case where the Web server opens to the Internet unless the server operates in isolation from the Intranet. When connected to an R/3 System, however, the Web server must have a connection to the Intranet.

The architecture of the ITS permits erection of firewalls at two special places. The AGate and WGate, however, must operate on two different platforms. Although the technical possibility of running both processes on one system exists, security considerations require separate installation. This requirement also offers advantages for scaling the system later.

The first firewall must stand directly in front of the Web server so that it can record requests from the HTTP port on the Web server. Typically, port 90 fulfills this function, but another port may serve. This installation rejects all other Internet services (FTP, Telnet and so on). Special recording methods that use log files can monitor access. Monitoring permits early discovery of entry attempts so that the administrators can take defensive measures early. It also provides a good overview of usage statistics. Log files usually contain the IP number of the visitor, the name of the accessed HTML files and the frequency of access.

A second firewall protects the exchange of data between the WGate and the AGate. The configuration of the firewall allows only the protocols to travel between the two processors. This configuration prohibits uncontrolled access to the critical processes of the AGate. The firewall requires separate installation of the WGate and AGate on two different computers. The service descriptions, in particular, must have very special protection from uncontrolled access because they contain extensive information on the system.

As a second security option, developers can encrypt transmission between the AGate and the R/3 application computer and limit it to the DIAG and the RFC channel. We rec-

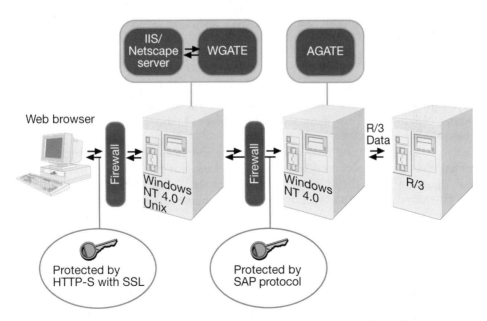

Figure 4.4   Network security provided by the ITS with firewalls

ommend the use of firewalls most emphatically. Unless administrators maintain the authorization concept properly, however, firewalls will not protect against improper entry into the system. Use of a dedicated R/3 System for the Web can also protect the actual R/3 System used for mission-critical applications. The installation of an additional firewall between the two systems limits RFC communications between the two systems. The database of the mission-critical R/3 then stores the actual application data, which supplies even better protection. Because guaranteed availability of the R/3 System reflects an essential reason for such a division, the following section on scaling will treat Mission-Critical R/3 in more detail.

Transmission of confidential data on the public Internet takes place over unknown paths and nodes that no one can monitor or control. In theory, someone can eavesdrop on the data at any point along the transmission route. To prevent this problem, we recommend encryption of the transmissions between the Web browser and the Web server with the SSL protocol (Secure Socket Layer, see Chapter 2). On the one hand, the protocol provides actual encryption of the data (confidentiality). On the other hand, it monitors the accuracy of the data (integrity) and offers the possibility of authentication. Distributed certificates, assigned by certificate centers, trigger the authentication. A Web server can use the SSL protocol only when it possesses such a certificate. In the past, browsers did not possess individual certificates for each user: SSL-capable browsers contain a generic certificate. The URL *https://...* can request the SSL protocol from the server.

Questions relating to the security of an R/3 System do not appear first when the system opens itself to the Internet. Enterprises should produce a security policy with clear designs long before considering a presence on the Internet. Expansion into the world of the Internet does not raise any essentially new issues, but simply opens the system to a new group of users. In addition to preventing entry into an internal network, security measures should also protect R/3 functions from unauthorized use.

4.3.4   Scalability

Maintaining the performance characteristics of the existing R/3 reflects a decisive element of successful use of the ITS. The new applications will place additional load on the R/3 System, which may not provide unsatisfactory response time for normal operations or for the new applications.

Early in the design phase, developers must pay special attention to the amount of data expected in the new applications and prepare measures for dynamic or planned scaling to expand the capacity of the overall system seamlessly. The multi-tier architecture of the R/3 System and use of the ITS provide a very good basis for scaling the individual system components.

The mission-critical R/3 system

The design of a separated Web R/3 System and a Mission-Critical R/3 System noted in the previous section attempts to forbid any overload of the productive R/3 System. The actual Internet transactions run on the Web R/3 System and make contact with the Mission-Critical R/3 System when they must read data from, change data on or insert

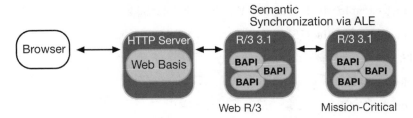

Figure 4.5   Use of a mission-critical R/3 System

data into the productive system. ALE provides the connection between the two systems. Such a design limits the load of several simultaneous sessions to the Web R/3 System and should that system fail, the Mission-Critical R/3 System suffers no ill effects. Developers should assume the probability of an overload whenever the R/3 System opens to the Internet and no one can estimate the number of expected users exactly. The previous section presented the supplemental security aspects of a separated R/3 System.

Benchmarks and determination of hardware requirements

The standard benchmarks offered by SAP can calculate the exact numbers needed to determine the correct hardware for the ITS. The equipment for the Web server platform, including the WGate, plays a less important role than the AGate platform and the R/3 application server.

SAP's Standard Benchmark, K1, rests upon the IAC of an electronic sales catalog (sales order creation). Simulations of typical user behavior with catalog browsers and order creation as well as a fixed load permit calculation of exact numbers for the load on the computers are tested. The numbers indicate if any hardware upgrades will become necessary.

The standard benchmark, however, provides values only for the one IAC (sales order creation), and therefore offers only an approximation of the values for other IACs that customer would actually use. Individual determination of the benchmark for use with any IAC requires a supplemental benchmark tool from iXOS Software.

A typical K1 benchmark executed by SAP on a 4-way Pentium Pro System from NCR produced the following values (certificate number: 1999801):

- number of benchmark users: 170 ITS (Internet Transaction Server);

- average response time for each request: 1.35 s;

- throughput:
    - Internet orders processed per hour: 1440
    - Hits/h: 148,000
    - Hits/s: 41;

- average database response time (dia/upd): 0.202 sec / 0.121 sec;

- CPU load on the R/3 server: 43%;

- CPU load on the ITS server: 96%;

- operating system for the R/3 server: Windows NT 4.0 SP3;

- operating system for the ITS server: Windows NT 4.0 SP3;

- RDBMS: Oracle 7.3.3;

- R/3 Release: 3.1 G;

- disk capacity: 32 GB.

  System configuration included the following:

- one R/3 application server:
  - SNI Primergy 769/560, 4-processor Pentium Pro 200 MHz
  - 512 KB L2 Cache, 1 GB main memory;

- one Internet transaction server:
  - NCR Worldmark Model 4300, 4-processor Pentium Pro 200 MHz;

- 1 MB L2 Cache, 2 GB main memory.

These numbers do not apply to the ITS version 2.0, which has already produced better results. The measurements show quite exactly how close the system comes to the load limit and whether the ITS computer will require any new hardware. The capacity of the processor and the main memory available play particularly crucial roles. The critical size of an ITS stress test remains the amount of hits and orders estimated originally. The value of this parameter critically affects the results of the benchmark. The load on the AGate primarily depends upon the number of simultaneous users or upon the number of requests the users generate. We therefore recommend erring on the side of caution: a large estimate and higher access rates. Good scaling and correct choice of hardware can improve the performance of the overall system. The following section discusses the options for scaling.

Scaling

Multi-tier architecture allows the R/3 System and the ITS great flexibility in scaling the system to meet the demands placed on the system as well as possible. The R/3 System itself contains a design well suited for operations with a large number of concurrent users. The design owes much to the client/server concept (see Chapter 2).

Scaling procedures that supplement those present in a traditional R/3 System can also apply to the ITS environment. The following system units stand at the ready for scaling efforts:

- Web server and WGate;

- AGate;

- R/3 System.

A clever enough combination of these elements can result in almost any level of scaling, at least in theory. The HTML links that start various transactions can point to HTML pages

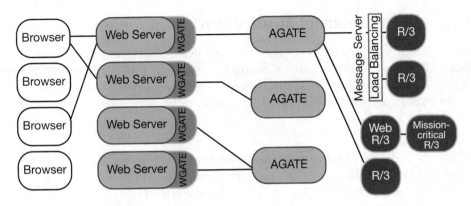

Figure 4.6 Scalability of the ITS and the R/3 System

on different Web servers, thus distributing the load on the Web server and the WGate. A WGate can address several AGate instances. An AGate can communicate with several R/3 Systems or connect to a previously underutilized R/3 System in the context of *load balancing*. The use of the DIAG communication channel provides the essential basis for good scalability of the ITS. The AGate relates to the R/3 System like a SAPGUI and offers the complete range of scalability options available in the R/3 System to the ITS.

4.4 Internet Application Components (IAC)

An Internet Application Component (IAC) defines a complete Internet application consisting of an actual transaction from the R/3 System and the corresponding HTML templates of the AGate. IACs also include the service descriptions required to start the components.

To run on a Web browser, the R/3 transaction must fulfill certain requirements (see Section 4.4.4). A special R/3 transaction created for the Internet, usually implements business processes, such as order creation, with *Business Application Programming Interfaces* (BAPIs). Section 4.4.5 introduces the BAPI concept. Although not mandatory, the use of BAPIs displays significant advantages for easy maintenance because of the release-independence of the BAPI interface. In place of BAPIs, developers might also use traditional function modules.

HTML templates consist of normal HTML statements and HTML[Business] statements. As delivered by SAP, IACs consist of HTML templates that contain only standard HTML statements. Any desired supplements, such as plug-ins, Java, ActiveX, JavaScript and so on, can enrich the templates further.

Since the ITS connects to the R/3 System with the DIAG communication channel, the system can exchange only information contained as fields and field values on the screen. Exactly one HTML template exists for each screen: it enables data exchange between the screen and the HTML template because of equivalent names in each.

4.4.1   Using Internet application components

What must an enterprise do to prepare for productive use of ITS technology and its IACs? This section presents the essential elements to consider or produce, how to use existing IACs and the preconditions that must exist to develop new IACs.

The most important condition for the use of ITS technology remains an R/3 System at release level 3.1G or above.

- *Infrastructure*
  Installation of the ITS presumes the presence of a Web server that already forms an integrated part of the enterprise's network. Enterprises that already use an R/3 System already possess a well-functioning TCP/IP network or one that simply requires expansion. The ITS can use existing Web servers, as long as they meet the requirements of the WGate. The WGate does not demand the full capacity of the Web server. Rather, it integrates itself transparently into the server's current tasks. An opening to the global Internet demands the appropriate security measures, particularly firewalls.

- *Expertise*
  Management and understanding of new technology requires a minimum level of expertise that can come from training or consulting. SAP offers special courses on programming and using the ITS. An overview of the technology often provides a sufficient understanding of the applicable process model. Since customers must check their requirements against the ability to implement them, such knowledge plays an important role. An understanding of the technology opens the customer to a new range of possibilities unthinkable in the past. Customers must ask informed questions about the potential benefits of the desired application.

- *Developing Internet application components*
  Before developing any new applications, customer should check the standard IACs delivered with the R/3 System to see if they can provide the desired functions. The standard IACs often prove sufficient, even if they do not always meet all the customer-specific requirements. If the standard IACs prove unsatisfactory, customers must develop new ones. Sections 4.4.2 and 4.4.3 discuss adjusting existing IACs and developing new components. Besides developing customer-specific IACs, developers can also make the existing R/3 environments usable with the ITS. Section 4.4.4 discusses the conditions that apply to existing transactions. Existing transactions can use release 3.0D without additional support from SAP.

- *Benchmarking/hardware requirements*
  Successful use of the applications requires correct dimensioning of the hardware used by the ITS. Developers must calculate the expected load and plan any required scaling. Section 4.3.4 presents this issue in detail.

4.4.2   Developing new IACs

The programming guidelines in the book provide details on actual development. What constitutes the development environment of IAC developers and what preconditions must the developers meet?

Development of IACs takes place in a homogenous environment, the R/3 System. The environment uses the familiar methods and tools of R/3 development: the Development Workbench. The Data Dictionary of the R/3 System serves to provide consistent definition of data. Development and testing of an IAC occurs completely within the R/3 System. Clearly, an experienced ABAP/4 developer can handle the ITS. Separation of the application and presentation logic permits definition of HTML templates outside the R/3 System through use of the SAP@Web Studio. The studio demands additional expertise, not normally in the possession of an ABAP/4 developer, to program with HTML and HTML[Business] as well as operation of the SAP@Web Studio (see programming guidelines). The *check-in* and *check-out* features of the R/3 Correction and Transport System (CTS) can manage maintenance and operation of HTML templates, even those processed externally.

The same person should program both the ABAP transactions and the preparation of the HTML templates. Large projects should always distribute the development of new screen and any associated HTML pages to the same person. The process model in Figure 4.8 clarifies this requirement, as it shows a very iterative development process. After creation of raw HTML templates, someone must provide the visual design. The Web designer usually performs this task by applying conventions from the World Wide Web to provide the HTML page with the correct corporate design. The designer then inserts the completed graphics into the proper place in the HTML template and controls the overall appearance of the new IAC. At best, designers should have some knowledge of HTML, so that they can work closely with developers. Figure 4.7 illustrates the schematic distribution of tasks between developers and designers.

The process model in Figure 4.8 indicates an additional iterative process. The first iteration should already include some 80% of application development in ABAP/4. The remaining 20% consist of changes or additions to the HTML template that remained unplanned during the design phase or became necessary during development.

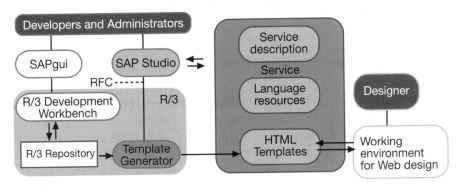

Figure 4.7 Distribution of tasks between developers and designers

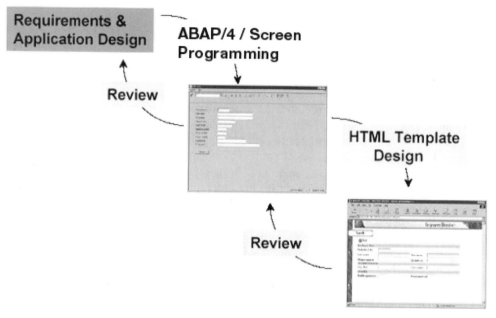

Figure 4.8   *Process model for IAC software development*

The development environment includes the following components:

- The SAP development environment with the Development Workbench;

- SAP@Web Studio;

- the correction and transport system.

4.4.3   Adjusting standard IACs

SAP supports changes to the IACs included in delivery of the standard R/3 System. If required, special requests from customers can change the following:

- design;

- presentation logic;

- application logic.

Changes to the application logic in an ABAP program demand the most effort. If possible, developers should avoid such changes. It will often prove sufficient to redefine the allocation of fields, or to insert fields into or delete fields from the HTML template. If the screen, rather than the HTML template (as delivered), already contains definitions for new fields, inserting new fields poses no difficulties. The development presentation logic as such can also change and can use additional methods for HTML design. The tools of HTML[Business] and HTML (with extensions) can execute any needed changes. Chapter 8 provides details on the new possibilities to expand the design options of normal HTML files. Changes to HTML templates and their presentation logic demand knowledge of HTML and HTML[Business], but do not require excessive effort.

The simplest way to adjust an IAC as delivered involves exchanging the graphics already integrated into the HTML templates. The standard design offers options for simple changes that do not require the work of a professional Web graphic artist. The following principles apply:

- Transparent graphical interface elements permit simple replacement of the background.

- HTML table enable changing table colors and borders.

- General switches such as *Home*, *Help*, *Title* and *Logo* are organized to save space.

- The colors used are basically neutral and comfortable.

- Font options for color, type and size can be changed at will.

- The standard size of the HTML template fits screen with a resolution of 800×600 pixels.

The definition of a new, individual *topic* can supply the standard HTML templates with a new, individual graphic. Users can exchange the following basic graphic elements:

- background images;

- buttons;

- titles;

- images.

In the simplest case, the system does not store changed HTML templates, but new graphics that use the same name as the old graphics.

Customers often display dissatisfaction with the exchange of basic graphical elements because they want a more individual design that can often result in a completely changed layout. Figure 4.9 provides an overview of the various presentation forms available for an IAC that has undergone extensive design changes. The effort spent on these changes by a Web designer can become considerable.

4.4.4 Requirements for R/3 transactions

Transactions that will run on the Internet with the ITS must fulfill very special conditions. Normal R/3 transactions cannot generally integrate themselves into an IAC without additional efforts. The inability to use existing transactions 'as is' and the need to develop specific transactions for the Internet, even if the new transactions can make some use of existing programs, may well seem annoying. Only new applications, however, can fulfill the special considerations that apply to the requirements of program flow on the Internet.

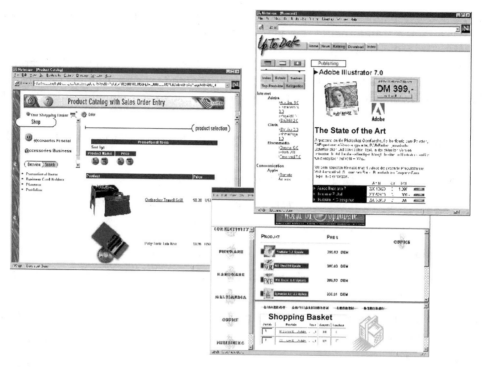

Figure 4.9   Graphic adjustment of standard IACs

The characteristics of the World Wide Web make it impossible to support all the screen characteristics of normal R/3 transaction. Application programming must therefore omit the following:

- menu bar;

- tool bar;

- popups (for warnings or messages);

- F1 Help, F4 selection help/matchcodes;

- table widget.

Special programming techniques can remedy some of these deficiencies (see programming guidelines). Special instructions can recreate and implement help for selections. Although special HTML input fields can simulate selection fields and buttons, the transaction must capture them specifically. In general, the system cannot display popups. Should popups appear during a user session, the ITS automatically suppresses them.

Application development of R/3 transactions intended for use within IACs orients itself toward different considerations for the design of the screen. Except for tests and debugging, such transactions never appear in a SAPGUI. Field values on the screen can control the presentation logic on the HTML template. The screen must display these fields in their proper positions since the system can send only information contained in screen fields to the AGate. Therefore, a screen may appear only as a collection of fields.

Frames reflect yet another special feature of the World Wide Web. Frames divide the browser window into several window areas (frames). An HTML file defines the frame structure for the entire window, and additional HTML files fill each window area.

Depending upon the application, frames can simplify operations, as they provide a better overview of the user's location within the HTML application. For example, selection menus might remain in their own frames while an additional frame displays the selected contents. Implementation of frames requires definition of several subscreens in the context of the dynamic program (dynpro) that controls screens for the R/3 transaction. The system assigns a specific HTML template to these subscreens at runtime, and can later load new HTML templates for the changing subscreens.

Remember, however, that frames can fill a screen very quickly, especially with a maximum resolution of 800×600 pixels. Users may have to scroll within the individual frames to display the information they seek. In such cases, developers should avoid frame structures, despite their popularity in many Web pages.

4.4.5   Using BAPIs

Chapter 3.2 introduces *Business Application Programming Interfaces* (BAPIs) and their place in the design of the Business Framework in detail. BAPIs represent a business interface in the R/3 System and became available with release 3.1. They offer simpler application development and standard access to the business processes of the R/3 System. BAPIs have proved themselves as the ideal design for a standardized opening of the R/3 System by using business interfaces. New Internet technology that demanded rapid application development triggered the design of BAPIs.

Not only R/3 transactions designed for the ITS and the Internet can access BAPIs, but any RFC-enabled communications path can do the same:

- with programming languages such as ABAP Objects, C, C++, Java, Visual Basic, and so on;

- with various communications technologies, such as COM/DCOM, CORBA and so on;

- within development environments such as Visual Studio, Visual Age, Delphi, and so on.

A design that features worldwide standardization of business interfaces along the lines of BAPIs has found some interest. The suggestion first arose in the Internet Engineering Task Force (IETF). General availability of such a business interface would produce some interesting scenarios:

- Different business systems could communicate over the interface directly.

- Once developed, an application could use the defined interface to make contact with any business system.

From the technical viewpoint, a BAPI functions like an RFC-enabled function module defined as a method of a business object within the Business Object Repository (BOR). Actual R/3 transactions use BAPIs much as they use function modules. BAPIs differ from function modules in only a few, formal respects:

- The interface has the definition of an input/output parameter and remains constant over several versions of the R/3 System.

- One specific function within a business process sets the task description of a BAPI.

- Performance of the task generally takes place in a stateless manner. Applications that follow the outside-in approach find this point particularly important.

- The BOR contains a definition of the BAPI as a method of a business object.

- Special error handling: the system captures all exceptions and returns them with a return code (SY-SUBRC). This process suppresses automatic popups or incoming dialogs. The application must handle possible errors explicitly.

The description of outside-in approaches in section 3.6.2 shows how, for example, how external applications can integrate BAPIs with COM/DCOM.

During development of IACs (and therefore new R/3 transactions), the amount of expected development effort and later maintenance needs for the IAC determine the need for a BAPI. The use of BAPIs guarantees a certain level of release-independence, since the interface remains frozen over several release changes. Accordingly, developers should search for usable BAPIs early in the development process. Individual customers cannot develop or maintain BAPIs; SAP reserves these tasks to itself.

Transaction SW02 searches the BOR of an R/3 System for appropriate BAPIs. Users must select the corresponding business object (such as 'employee') that then displays the available methods or BAPIs ('Employee.ChangeAddress'). The BOR uses special identification, different from that of other methods, to mark a BAPI. Transaction SE37 displays the source code of a BAPI within the ABAP/4 Development Workbench.

The naming environment of a BAPI uses the convention BAPI_{object_name}_{method_name}. For example:

```
_BAPI_ Employee_ChangeAddress
```

Two types of BAPIs exist: those that write and those that only read. Writing BAPIs, particularly, display the significance of statelessness. After it executes the BAPI, the system reaches a consistent condition. If an error appears during execution of a BAPI, a rollback returns the R/3 System to a consistent exit condition. Statelessness makes clear that a BAPI executes a clearly defined, elementary business process.

4.4.6   The WebRFC gateway interface

The WebRFC Interface supplements the concept for Internet applications that use R/3 functions. It provides a defined interface based upon Remote Function Call (RFC). Use of the WebRFC Gateway Interface allows users to omit programming Web access to an R/3

System with another programming language. Such programming would normally occur with a CGI script and applies to ABAP developers, who otherwise would have to work in languages such as C or C++.

A WebRFC application consists of a collection of ABAP/4 modules, all of which have a standard interface and permit access from a Web browser with a particular URL. In addition to specially developed application modules, any desired RFC-enabled function modules could use the WebRFC Gateway on the Internet. To do so, the call of a conversion module must first adjust dynamically to the standardized interface of the function module. The traditional RFC interface of the R/3 System cannot call WebRFC applications because it does not support certain parameter functions (*Changing-Parameter*).

With its RFC channel to the R/3 application server, the ITS uses the functions of the WebRFC Gateway Interface. A Dynamic Link Library (DLL) implements the WebRFC Gateway Interface on the Web server and is delivered with the ITS. An Internet application that uses the WebRFC to access an R/3 System normally uses a fixed function module for entry to the system. The function module then enables further access to other function modules with dynamically generated links in the HTML files. When calling a function module, users can also enter numerous parameters, which the system then stores in an internal table. One parameter specifies the name of the function module being called, and is therefore a mandatory entry. The ITS returns the results of a function module as a complete HTML page or as binary data (such as images) to the Web browser. RFC calls with the ITS have a special advantage: unlike direct RFC calls, the ITS can automatically distribute load.

The following summarizes the functions of the WebRFC Interface:

- simple programming with function modules;

- support of MIME types (for images, for example);

- enablement of simultaneous connections to several R/3 and R/2 System in one Web session;

- authorization of R/3 users;

- central administration of Web objects in the R/3 System (CTS);

- generation of HTML pages and support of templates lies completely in the R/3 System.

Specially prepared function modules can also call reports from the R/3 System, a process known as *SAP Web Reporting*. Reports include the following:

- complete reports that return dynamically generated results in HTML files to the Web browser (with `WWW_GET_REPORT`);

- selection from a list of available reports (with `WWW_GET_SELSCREEN`);

- display of a hierarchical report tree with a Web Reporting browser (with `WWW_GET_TREE_LIST`)

Integration of dialog mechanisms also enables interactive reporting, although with some limitations. Users and managers alike will find the use of Web reporting very interesting, since they would not normally have access to a SAPGUI. These reports provide a simple and quick way to receive important numerical data that an enterprise requires for decisions every day. The external sales force will find this feature particularly helpful. To provide security for restricted access to sensitive data, the same mechanisms for security and authentication that apply to the ITS apply here also. To execute a report, the user must have the appropriate rights (*Submit Authority*).

5 Standard Internet application components (IACs) for the SAP R/3 System

The technology of the Internet Transaction Server and the advantages it offers for connections to the Internet first become evident with R/3-based Internet applications. As of version 3.1G of the R/3 System, SAP delivers *Internet Application Components* (IACs) with the R/3 System. Customers can use these applications as soon as they have installed the R/3 System. With these applications, the users employ the Internet to process business transactions within an enterprise and beyond its borders. The applications make the most varied information available to a wide range of users. The applications simplify communications within an enterprise and with customers, vendors and so on. This chapter provides an overview of the IACs delivered with the R/3 System.

5.1 Overview

With delivery of version 4.0, the R/3 System contains 35 Internet applications from logistics, human resources and financial accounting. Customers receive an Internet-ready R/3 System that they can use immediately. The applications implement comfortable and easily operated access to traditional transactions over the Web. The applications simplify functions and present them accordingly. A wide range of users thus has access to the information in an R/3 System for the first time in a simplified form.

The Internet applications cover the functions most frequently requested by customers. These IACs provide a basis that customers can change or expand with customer-specific developments and supplements.

5.1.1 Advantages of R/3 Internet applications

Internet applications and standard transactions in the R/3 System differ from each other in two important respects: the complexity of the application and the appearance of the user interface. The standard applications of the R/3 System display great power that covers a wide range of requirements. The complexity of the applications mirrors the varied requirements, so that operation requires numerous input parameters. Novice users without some knowledge normally require training to operate the system. Occasional users, such as managers, need to become familiar with the applications before they can work with them.

Internet applications target a different goal. Internet users and the community they form rarely confront an R/3 System. They find no route through the system's terminology. To reach these users, IACs present an R/3 interface that presents to users familiar with a Web browser no difficulty in executing functions in R/3 applications. The Internet applications extend users to include customers, potential clients, vendors, business partners and all employees. An effective design and a clear presentation both form absolute preconditions for meeting the goals of these applications.

The Internet itself profits from IACs and becomes increasingly attractive to business purposes. The origins of the Internet reflected a desire to transmit information as platform-independent documents. As it became more popular, however, Internet users clamored for interactive applications. Various interfaces and supplemental programs therefore implemented interaction with special, isolated Web applications. Enterprises then faced the need to operate several systems and to administer redundant data. Only a direct connection between the Internet and a productive business system, such as the R/3 System, can provide efficient interaction with a wider range of users. Such a solution eliminates maintenance of multiple systems and data redundancy, with the related danger of inconsistency.

Linking the Internet and an R/3 System offers decided advantages to both end users and those that operate the systems. As a global network, the Internet has no limited hours of operation. No national borders confine it. The Internet remains available to every user around the clock, 365 days a year and throughout the entire world. An Internet browser can execute applications for orders, complaints, service calls and so on. Browsers offer the user simple and intuitive navigation, an easily understood overview of information as well as a comfortable user interface. These features enable the user to operate a business application easily. The multimedia interface can present information with graphics, video, sound and so on.

The enterprise sees the advantage of IACs in the cost-effective implementation of business processes on the Internet. Direct links between the enterprise and its customers or vendors now exist. Rapid data creation by customers or suppliers accelerates processing significantly. These applications generally do not require lengthy and expensive training because of the intuitive, self-explanatory structure of the IACs. Even within an enterprise, this solution provides effective execution of common tasks, such as internal order processing, to inexperienced users.

5.1.2 Classification of the applications

All R/3 Internet applications use the basic technology of the *Internet Transaction Server*. Usage areas provide a solid foundation for classification of these applications. One distinction reflects applications executed only on the local network of an enterprise (*Intranet*), such as an electronic telephone book for internal offices, and applications used beyond the confines of the enterprise. The latter category also subdivides into two areas: *consumer-to-business and business-to-business*. Business-to-business means the exclusive interaction between business partners. For example, an enterprise might query the material levels available at a vendor if it has the proper authorization to do so. In this case, the query takes place over an Extranet. These applications exclude the broader Internet community. The consumer-to-business area provides use of applications without additional limitations. These applications fall into the general category of Internet applications. The entire Internet community can use the applications that address every potential customer, private as well as other businesses.

An enterprise may not always find it possible to allocate a given scenario to one of these areas. A product catalog, for example, should appear on both the Internet and the Extranet. The type of goods often serves as one aid to correct classification, although the type of goods exists independently of the application. Accordingly, we have classified the scenarios described in this section according to their topical relation to the following:

- electronic retailing;

- purchasing;

- customer service;

- employee self-service;

- internal services.

Most of the IACs described here are implemented as an R/3 transaction. Each HTML page therefore refers to a screen mask of the transaction. Two applications use the WebRFC Gateway, described in more detail in Section 4.4.6 (WebRFC Gateway). The applications that use the WebRFC Gateway execute function modules or reports, rather than transactions, in the R/3 System.

The applications in the above categories limit themselves to interaction between a user and an R/3 System. Automation and expansion of the supply chain, however, make additional demands for the distribution of applications across several business systems. For example, a request for supplies from an employee affects the in-house R/3 System; the order created by the request affects the vendor's R/3 System. Section 5.8 examines the meaning of distributed business applications in the context of the business-to-business category and provides a concrete example.

5.1.3   Setup and installation

The use of transactions requires only settings in customizing as long as the functions of the applications will not expand. The descriptions of the individual IACs display any settings required. Administrators must install the ITS before setting up the Internet applications. During ITS installation, the system sets up all additional components of the IACs, such as HTML templates and services , that must be stored outside the R/3 System. To start an application, the Web server should have an HTML file containing the references needed to start the IACs. If the local system will use all the application components, administrators can also use the Web page prepared by SAP that contains the links, subdivided into five groups, needed to start IACs. Web pages at most enterprises have a uniform appearance. In this case, paste the links into the layout as appropriate.

Section 4.3.3 on security treated the various methods of logging in to an R/3 System with IACs. Some Internet applications require storage of a default R/3 identification (with a password) in the service description. However, for security reasons, administrators should limit the rights granted to the users of the applications. For Intranet applications, administrators might find it advantageous to give every user an R/3 login, as individual employees can possess different authorizations/rights.

5.1.4   Preallocating values

Internet applications permit processing business events in an R/3 System. To simplify operation, some components contain preallocated values. For example, the creation of an order requires entry of the organizational unit and plant. Internet users, however, will not have the required information.

Preallocation of values can follow one of two paths. A direct, unconditional allocation of values in the program text constitutes the simplest path. Only a change to the program text itself can reset the values. Allocation of user defaults in the user profile of the R/3 login offers a more elegant route. The master record of an R/3 user can contain parameters with various values. The transaction queries and sets up the parameters. For example, if all orders on the Internet have distribution channel 01 and organizational unit 0001, the preallocated values for the R/3 user reflect these settings. This user thus performs all Internet orders. Administrators can define special business partners, who also enter orders over the Internet, as additional users with different parameters. If the transaction of an IAC requires preallocated values, the following description contains the needed entries.

5.1.5   Authorization check

An R/3 System contains a great deal of confidential information that should not become available to every employee, let alone to the entire Internet community. Depending upon an application and the information it contains, the system requires execution of authorization checks. As explained in Section 4.3.3, Internet connections to an R/3 System permit multiple authorization checks. The simplest means of limiting rights involves assigning an R/3 login and setting an individual authorization for the user. In critical applications, users must enter their specific identification when they log in the System. An authorization allows users to execute the functions of the IAC completely, in a limited manner, or not at all. Scenarios executed only within an enterprise would use this method, as each employee can have an individual R/3 login .

This approach, however, can hardly apply to the entire Internet community. Accordingly, Internet and Extranet applications require special R/3 identification, stored in the service description for the applications. The description of the IACs should indicate all the authorizations required for the application. Users then log in to the R/3 System with this special identification, although they do so implicitly, as the system transmits the information transparently and automatically. Only persons duly authorized and known to the R/3 System may perform actual postings within the system. As an example, consider an order: only customers for whom a customer master record already exists may create the order. Accordingly, the system must perform an authorization check here. It does not check the authorization of the R/3 login , but the existence and identity of a customer. The R/3 System must contain an *Internet User* that allocates a password to an existing customer master record. In addition to customers, other persons, such as vendors, may also require such identification. Transaction SU05 creates identification for multiple persons.

Maintaining Internet users: transaction SU05

Version 3.1G of the R/3 System includes delivery of transaction SU05, which maintains Internet users (select `Tools | Administration | User Maintenance | Internet User`). The master records in the R/3 System provide the basis for the identifications. A customer can receive an allocated identification only if the appropriate customer master record already exists.

The following required steps set up an Internet user:

- *User ID and the Object Type*
  During creation of a master record, the R/3 System assigns a unique number that identifies a person, organization, company and so on. To create an Internet user for that person (organization, etc), the system also requires the user type, such as `KNA1` for customer or `LFA1` for vendor, in addition to the previously mentioned ID. The IACs also use the types given in Table 5.1. Table TOJTB contains additional user types.

Table 5.1   Types of Internet users

Type	Description
BUS1007	Customer
BUS1008	Vendor
BUS1006001	Employee of a business partner
APPLICANT	Applicant
PDOTYPE_PT	Participant

- *Generating the user*
  If it finds a correct user ID, the system initializes the Internet user. It inserts an additional entry into table `BAPIUSW01`. In addition to the user IDs, the table contains the corresponding passwords assigned by the system automatically during initialization. All authorization checks of Internet IDs test for the correct password.

- *Changing a password*
  The password generated by the system consists of a random combination of letters and numbers. The system allows direct changes to the password.

Creation of master records and Internet users directly within an Internet application can offer some benefits in certain cases. The IAC *Online Store*, for example, permits customers to generate their own master record and Internet users. Customers previously unknown to the system can thus enter an order.

The system provides the following functions to administer identifications:

- *Locking and unlocking an identification*
  If administrators wish to remove authorization to execute specific applications from any users, they can use this transaction to lock users and later unlock them.

- *Deleting an identification*
  The system also permits complete deletion of identification. It leaves the master record untouched, but deletes the entry in table `BAPIUSW01`.

5.1.6   Modification of IACs

As delivered, IACs offer a first foundation for handling R/3-based business processes on the Internet. However, enterprises usually change and adjust the foundation, or even supplement it with new applications. Chapter 7 on programming guidelines describes the development of such applications.

Modification of a standard IAC usually involves the layout of the HTML page so that the page reflects the corporate design of the enterprise. Developers can not only change the appearance of the page, but also expand its functions. Changes to Internet applications affect two areas:

- *Changing the layout*
  An enterprise usually has a uniform layout for its own Web pages, and must adjust the standard IACs to fit corporate design. Changes here involve graphics, logos and colors in the HTML templates. The basic structure of the application, however, remains unchanged unless the corresponding transaction reflects changes.

- *Inserting functions*
  To insert additional functions, customers must modify the ABAP/4 code of the application. The description of the IAC also includes the module pool or function group for a transaction. Customers must never attempt to modify SAP objects. An update to a new release level of the R/3 System overwrites all changes. Accordingly, customers should first copy the complete transaction (including templates). Development takes place in the customer's naming environment ; future versions will not change or overwrite it. If the intended changes affect both the structure and output of the transaction, the templates must also contain the changes.

If the changes modify the essence of the original transaction, customers should set up a new service. A new service can also handle the most varied uses of the same transaction, when two different groups with different R/3 user parameters use the same application. The service description stores the R/3 login.

In the R/3 System, the Correction and Transport System (CTS) administers the ABAP/4 program texts for a transaction. The CTS excludes the external objects of an IAC, but the studio in the R/3 System can check any external objects in and out (see Section 7.7.1, Check In/Check Out). The following transactions provide additional administrative tasks:

- *Maintenance of source control objects: transaction SIAC*
  This transaction gives a developer access to the source control of ITS objects. Developers can attach a correction request in the R/3 System to ITS components. Section 7.8 provides a detailed description of this transaction.

- *Maintenance of Web objects: transaction SMW0*
  Transaction SMW0 maintains all objects not maintained by transaction SIAC. This situation affects Web objects and HTML templates required for Web reporting. Online documentation provides a detailed description of the transaction.

5.1.7   Comments

The following scenario descriptions divide into two categories: a descriptive section and a technical section. The first section explains the scenario and the prerequisites for users, such as user identification or the knowledge required by the application. The second section lists the IAC components, the authorizations required by the R/3 user, the comparisons with the traditional R/3 transaction (if available) and the interfaces used by the module. The descriptive section briefly presents the business background, but without detail. The online documentation provides more details. In principle, a wide range of users should not require any special knowledge. Nonetheless, some IACs limit themselves to users with special knowledge of a certain topic, who can operate an IAC, but not the R/3 System. This situation applies to Intranet applications in particular, which sometimes presume specialized knowledge of the application area.

An enterprise can decide for itself which applications run on the Internet, an Extranet or an Intranet. Applications designed for an Intranet can also run on the Internet. In principle, all Internet applications can have an R/3 login stored in the service. The descriptions of the IACs, however, assume logical allocation of the areas most appropriate to each application and the applications that require a specific login.

The ITS runs with version 3.0D (and higher) of the R/3 System. We recommend against transporting the Internet applications of a 3.1G or 4.0 system into a system running versions 3.0D. These applications rest upon BAPIs in version 3.1G of the R/3 System. This means that transport must include all the required BAPIs, structures and data elements. Such a transport would require tremendous effort.

SAP has made a demo system (*Customer and Partner System* or *CPS*) available to all interested customers and partners. The demo permits execution and trial of current scenarios. SAP can provide additional information on the CPS.

Should an enterprise wish to test the scenarios on its own R/3 System, it can use the *International Demonstrating and Education System* (IDES) client from SAP. IDES already contains all the settings for a model company as well as data. Therefore, for an initial look, a copy of the firm's own data from a productive R/3 System is not required.

5.2   Internet applications: deliverables

Version 3.1H of the R/3 System contains a foundation of 28 Internet applications. Version 4.0 expands the Internet packet with six additional scenarios. Given the popularity of Internet applications, customers can expect SAP to provide even more applications in later versions.

Figure 5.1   Grouping of IAC scenarios

Table 5.2 provides an overview of all the scenarios described in later sections.

5.3   Electronic retailing

The Internet opens a completely new and very efficient distribution channel to suppliers of goods and services. The Internet's worldwide availability and rapidly growing number of users offer suppliers the opportunity to address a large number of potential customers. The Internet allows suppliers to present multimedia information on their products at an effective cost. Companies can accept orders from customers automatically and can directly address both end consumers (customer-to-business) as well as familiar business customers (business-to-business).

A presence on the Internet provides distinct advantages to both the supplier and the cus- tomer. Customers have detailed information on the currently available products of various companies. They can access the information at any time and compare prices. Customers can request an individual price and receive discounts and a credit rating. Once the system has checked availability of the goods and set a delivery data (all online), customers can adjust their orders accordingly. Conversion to an actual sale requires neither a telephone call nor a fax. Customers can query the status of an order and follow its progress. Suppliers have a

Table 5.2   Standard R/3 Internet application of components

Application	Module	Users
Electronic retailing		
Product catalog	LO	Internet
Online store	LO	Internet
Sales order creation	SD	Internet
Sales order status	SD	Internet
Availability check	SD	Extranet
Customer account information	FI	Internet/Extranet
Customer service		
Quality certificates	QM	Extranet
Quality notification	QM	Internet/Extranet
Service notification	PM	Internet/Extranet
Measurement and counter readings	PM	Intranet/Extranet
KANBAN	PP	Extranet
Consignment stocks status	MM	Extranet
Purchasing		
Requirement request	MM	Intranet
Requirement request status	MM	Intranet
Collective release of purchase requisitions	MM	Intranet
Collective release of orders	MM	Intranet
Collective release of service entry sheets	MM	Intranet
Employee self-service		
Employee directory (who's who)	PA	Intranet
Calendar of events	PD	Intranet/Internet
Booking attendance	PD	Intranet
Booked events	PD	Intranet/Internet
Canceling attendance	PD	Intranet
Employment opportunities	PA	Internet
Application status	PA	Internet
Time reporting	PA	Intranet
Internal services		
Integrated inbox	BC	Intranet
Workflow status	BC	Intranet
Internal activity allocation	CO	Intranet
Internal price list	CO	Intranet
Project data confirmation	PS	Intranet
Project documents	PS	Intranet
Asset information	FI	Intranet
Web-reporting browser	—	Intranet
Distributed business application		
Procurement via Catalogs	MM/SD	Intranet/Extranet

tool that remains available around the clock around the world, and can aim at higher revenues. Suppliers receive an order upon creation online and can react to customer needs quickly. The use of this modern medium improves corporate image among private customers and targets new customer groups. Sales processing on the Internet opens the opportunities to become familiar with customers and to treat them individually.

The scenarios presented here form a basis for processing online orders:

Table 5.3   R/3 Internet applications for electronic retailing

Scenario	Description
Product Catalog	Presentation of products from various catalogs
Online Store	Ordering products from catalogs
Order Creation	Presentation of products and processing of customer orders
Order Status	Checking the current status of a customer order
Availability Check	Checking the availability of a particular product
Customer Account Information	Checking open items, account balances and general customer data

5.3.1   Product catalog

Its multimedia capabilities make the Internet an ideal tool for an enterprise that wishes to present itself to the public. The enterprise can provide information (such as strategies) and display its products in a catalog. Product catalogs advertise and support sales because they provide customers with all the important information they need to make a purchase. Electronic advertising has an obvious advantage: it does not require any printing onto expensive paper or CDs. The company can also change its offerings easily and rapidly, and correct errors immediately. The Internet also permits use of additional media, such as images, sound or video. An enterprise can distribute this information at price-effective rates.

The *Product Catalog* Internet Application presents the offerings of a supplier simply and efficiently on the Internet. It forms the basis for and functions as a constitutive element of the *Online Store* Internet Application, described in Section 5.3.2.

Data recorded with the Product Catalog application component of the R/3 System provides the base for this IACs. The functions of the Product Catalog enable the storage, retrieval and administration of all the data required to produce catalogs in any medium. A product catalog maintained in the R/3 System provides the basis not only for an Internet catalog, but also for print and CDROM catalogs. This R/3 application component also sets the structure of the Internet product catalog. You can also define variants of the catalog to set the language used in texts and the currency used for prices. When an IAC displays such a variant, the system displays only the appropriate language and currency. Since the IACs retrieve the information, particularly the prices, directly from the R/3 System, users always see up-to-date information.

An enterprise can use its Internet product catalog for varied target groups and purposes:

- Mail order for wholesalers (such as an Internet Catalog for retailers).

- Shipping industry.

- A multimedia kiosk at branch points of sale. Sales staff could use the product catalog to inform customers about products unavailable in the local warehouse but that they can order.

This method offers two essential advantages: the currency of the information and its global availability. An Internet product catalog can remain up to date even without additional production efforts, and offers itself without limitation to a large group of potential readers.

Figure 5.2   IAC Product Catalog

Preconditions

A wide audience should have access to product catalogs. Accordingly, the system does not support identification for catalog information.

Flow

A private individual wishes to purchase a new printer. This customer uses the Web to retrieve information on models from various manufacturers and to compare prices. When the customer finds an enterprise that uses the *Product Catalog* IAC, the following takes place:

- *Starting the application*
  If the Internet application is called only by the service name (*http://...wgate.dll/WW10/!*), a page appears that displays an overview of all the product catalogs and their variants in the R/3 System. The customer can then select a variant. The is feature permits the combination of catalogs from various suppliers into a virtual shopping mall .

  The supplier of the service, however, can limit display to a specific product catalog on the firm's home page. The supplier simply needs to expand the URL in the hyperlink to include the product catalog and its variants. See the section on default settings for additional information.

- *Selecting a shop*
  The system divides the product catalog into various *Shops*, corresponding to departments in a traditional store. A computer catalog, for example, might contain shops for *Hardware* and *Software*, each with its own text, images and sound.

- *Navigation within a shop*
  Numerous navigation options confront a customer within a shop. The left window displays an overview of products arranged into product groups and offered for sale. A hardware shop, for example, might contain the product groups *Personal computers* and *accessories*, while the accessories shop would contain product groups for *Printers*, *Scanners* and *Disk drives*.

  The same window permits the user to search according to product name and/or price intervals.

  The system always displays the navigation window within a shop: the customer can always use a button to switch from the overview of product groups to searching for a specific product. Arrow keys permit the customer to switch between the various shops.

- *Selecting a product*
  When the customer selects a product group (such as *Personal Computers* in the above example), the right window displays the articles belonging to the product group. This area also displays the articles found by a search within the shop. The list contains a short description of the product (image and description) and its price. Articles with varying prices for different characteristics (color or size, for example), the system displays the lowest price as a *price from*. The application can sort a product list according to product description and price.

- *Detailed view of a product*
  From within a product list, users can branch to a detailed view that includes a long text, image and sound. If articles have variants, the system displays selection boxes. If the variants themselves have different characteristics (such a color and size), the system can also display one or more selection boxes (one for each characteristic), depending on the availability of the variants and the settings made by the user. If the article forms a package or set, the system permits the customer to retrieve product information on the individual components and the set as a whole.

Technical information

Table 5.4   Technical Information for the IAC Product Catalog

Service	Users	Transaction	Development class	Module pool	Function group
WW10	Internet, Extranet	WW10	WWMB	SAPMWWMJ	

Default settings

This Internet application uses data recorded by the Product Catalog application component of the R/3 System.

The layout area hierarchy of the R/3 Product Catalog sets the division of the Internet product catalog into shops and product groups as follows:

- First level layout areas appear as shops.

- Layout areas below a shop node appear as product groups within a shop.

Accordingly, any R/3 Product Catalog used by an IAC must have at least two layout areas: an upper level for shops and a lower level for product groups. Performance and ergonomic considerations dictate that a layout area hierarchy should consist of a maximum of four levels, and that a layout area should contain a maximum of 30 articles.

If the enterprise uses images or sound data with the shops, settings in R/3 Customizing must tell the system where it can find the data. To make the appropriate settings in Customizing for document administration, select (`Cross-Application Components | Document Management System | General Data`). To make the appropriate setting in Customizing for logistics, select (`Logistics – General | Logistics Basic Data: Product Catalog | Internet Application Component`).

As a rule, an enterprise defines several different catalogs. The call of an Internet application can specify a particular catalog. In this case, the URL would appear as follows:

```
http://...wgate.dll/WW10/!?~OkCode=OK&CATALOG=<catalog>&
VARIANT=<variant>
```

In the example, `<catalog>` defines the product catalog and `<variant>` defines the variant. The URL can not only specify the login language and the login user, but also the language and currency used to display the Internet catalog. The definition of the login user can also provide a county-specific date and price format.

Authorizations

All Internet users should have access to the information contained in product catalogs. Accordingly, the system does not require any special authorizations.

Interfaces

Table 5.5   Interfaces used in the IAC Product Catalog

Interface	Description
BAPI_ADV_MED_GET_ITEMS	Determines the items in a product catalog
BAPI_ADV_MED_GET_LAYOBJ_DOCS	Determines documents for a layout area
BAPI_ADV_MED_GET_LAYOBJ_DESCR	Determines long text for a layout area
BAPI_ADV_MED_GET_LAYOUT	Determines the layout for a product catalog
BAPI_ADV_MED_GET_LIST	Determines the list for the product catalog
BAPI_ADV_MED_GET_PRICES	Determines prices for items in the product catalog
BAPI_ADV_MED_GET_VARIANT_LIST	Determines variants of the product catalog
BAPI_MATERIAL_GETCOMPONENTS	Breaks down structured articles
BAPI_MATERIAL_GETCHARMERCHHIER	Determines the characteristics of an article with variants

5.3.2   Online store

The electronic catalog presented above provides much more up-to-date information and requires far less effort and resources than a printed catalog. In addition to the currency of its information, however, the Internet also offers the advantage of interaction with customers. Interaction opens a wider and more price-effective distribution channel to an enterprise. A firm can accept customer orders at any time; telephone calls or faxes are no longer necessary.

The *Online Store* Internet application builds upon the *Product Catalog* IAC. It offers the opportunity to create customer data, enter orders and accept payment by credit card (see Section 2.5 for more information on credit card payments). During entry of orders, users enjoy all the common functions of the R/3 System: current pricing data, consideration of volume-based rebates and other discounts, availability check and the immediate determination of the earliest possible delivery date. Regulations on permissible opening hours no longer apply to the suppliers of these services. Since the customer creates the order directly in the R/3 System, the enterprise can react to it far more quickly.

Customers enjoy comfortable and exciting shopping: rapid searches for products and information, direct purchasing decisions around the clock and knowing when the goods will arrive.

Preconditions

Since this application enjoys wide availability, it does not require any special preconditions. If the enterprise already counts the user among its customers, the user needs a customer number or e-mail address (depending on the desires of the supplier) and a password. The IAC permits creation of a customer master for new customers.

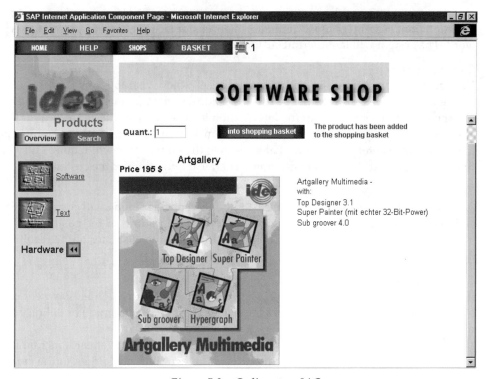

Figure 5.3   Online store IAC

Flow

After customers have decided on a particular product from the product catalog, they enter an order for the item. The first steps of this scenario reflect those of the product catalog. The following presents a brief description of these steps (see the description of the *Product Catalog* IAC for a more detailed description):

- selecting a catalog (in a mall);

- selecting a shop or layout area;

- possible selection of a department or a subordinate layout area;

- selecting a product.

- *Filling a virtual shopping cart*
  Once customers decide on a product and wish to order it, they place it in a virtual shopping cart. The shopping cart consists of a list of all the products that the customer has chosen so far to belong to the order. The SHOPPING CART pushbutton in the application displays a list of all the goods contained in the cart. To change or cancel a selection, customers mark the item in the list and then delete or change it. After selecting all their goods, customers can request quotation by selecting the pushbutton in the virtual shopping cart. Calculation of the quotation considers individual

customer conditions, such as customer-specific discounts. To place an order based on the quotation, customers must first enter their customer number and personal password. The system will later permit customers to change an existing password.

- *Creating a customer*
  New customers must register with the enterprise if they wish to receive a quotation. The registration process records a customer's address data (name, street, city, and so on) and e-mail. The system uses the information to create an R/3 master record for the customer and assigns a customer number. Immediately afterward, the system asks the customer to enter a password. Later visits to the online store will require entry of the same password. The system can now generate a quotation for the customer.

- *Generating a quotation*
  After successful identification of the customer and consideration of all customer-specific requirements, the system can generate a price quotation for the customer. The system checks current product availability and notifies the customer of the resulting delivery date.

- *Creating an order*
  If customers agree with the quotation, they can convert it into an order. Payment can occur in one of two ways: based upon an invoice (sent by regular mail) or online payment with a credit card.
  Customers who choose the second option must enter the type of card, its number and its expiry date. The owner of an online store can limit customers to the credit cards that the company supports. The owner can also check the accuracy and validity of the credit card number. The R/3 System can accept authorization for the sale amount from an (external) clearing house.
  To assuage a customer's concerns about security and privacy, the online store of the future will offer an interface that implements the SSL or SET method of secure data transmission for credit card payments (see Section 2.5).
  Before customers confirm the final purchase, they can inspect the delivery address stored in the system. If the address has changed, the system offers customers an opportunity to correct it.
  Once customers have ordered goods, they receive a notification that includes information on the product (product name, quantity and availability) and the order number generated online in the R/3 System. Customers can use the number later to access the *Sales order status* IAC to see how many or which articles the vendor has prepared for shipping or has already shipped.

Technical information

Table 5.6   Technical Information for the Online Store IAC

Service	Users	Transaction	Development class	Module pool	Function group
WW20	Internet, Extranet	WW20	WWMB	SAPMWWMJ	

Default settings

Maintenance of the catalog must be complete. When users register themselves as customers in the online store, the R/3 System creates a customer master record. To do so, the system takes the following (required) parameters from the basic data in the product catalog: *sales organization, distribution channel, division*, and *reference customer*. The system also takes the data for *language* and *currency* from the product catalog variant.

   If a customer enters an order, the R/3 System creates an order that requires certain parameters. The system again takes the *sales organization, distribution channel* and *division* from the basic data in the product catalog. The system fills the *order type* with the value of the AAT parameter from the fixed values for the user. If the parameter setting is empty, the system uses order type TA (standard order).

Authorizations

If the R/3 System creates a customer with this IAC, the R/3 login used must possess an authorization profile of *V_Verkauf*. If the system allocates a password to a customer with transaction SU05, an entry for object type KNA1 must also exist. To generate an order, the R/3 user must have all authorization rights for the object class *sales*.

Interfaces

In addition to the interfaces listed for the product catalog, the online store application also requires the interfaces given in Table 5.7.

Table 5.7   Interfaces used in the Online Store IAC

Interface	Description
BAPI_AD_ME_GET_SALES_AREA	Determines the sales area for a product catalog
BAPI_SALESORDER_SIMULATE	Simulates a customer order for a quotation
BAPI_SALESORDER_CREATEFROMDATA	Creates a customer order
BAPI_CUSTOMER_CREATEPWREG	Creates an entry for a customer password
BAPI_CUSTOMER_INITPASSWORD	Initializes the customer password
BAPI_CUSTOMER_CREATEFROMDATA	Generates an R/3 customer
BAPI_CUSTOMER_CHANGEFROMDATA	Changes the data of an R/3 customer
BAPI_CUSTOMER_GETDETAIL	Reads the data of an R/3 customer
BAPI_CUSTOMER_SEARCH	Determines the customer number from an e-mail address
BAPI_CUSTOMER_CHECKPASSWORD	Checks the customer password
BAPI_CUSTOMER_CHANGEPASSWORD	Changes the customer password

5.3.3   Sales order creation

Electronic commerce has developed several solution designs to create customer orders on the Web. If external systems produce the order, rather than the productive business systems that process other customer information and orders, an enterprise can expend a great deal of extra effort. The enterprise must store customer data twice and transfer orders, leading to unnecessary data redundancy.

Use of the *Sales Order Creation* IAC to create and process orders on the Internet involves much less effort and operates much more simply. Much like the product catalog, the application presents all the company's products on the Web. The R/3 System, however, bases product catalogs on elements of planning for advertising. The enterprise must maintain all its products in the appropriate catalog. This application bases its presentation of products directly on the product groups present in the R/3 System and a list of the products contained in the product groups. This application offers the same advantages offered by a Web presence described in the *Product Catalog* IAC: currency, depictions with images or sound, constant availability and so on. Customers can directly enter orders that immediately become available in the R/3 System as customer orders. Doubled storage of data is no longer necessary. Direct order generation permits the vendor to react quickly. This IAC also permits the customer to assemble goods from individual components (a PC, for example). In

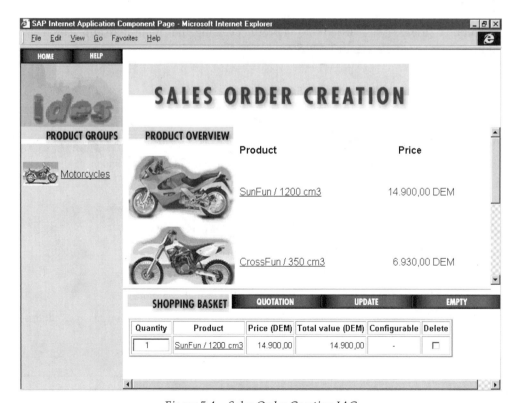

Figure 5.4   Sales Order Creation IAC

this case, the vendor simply must maintain the appropriate materials so that the system can use the SAP Configurator to configure them. In addition to creating a new customer, this IAC permits payment of the selected goods with an invoice or a credit card (see Section 2.5).

Preconditions

This application can create orders only when the R/3 System recognizes the user as a customer. If the user is already a customer, the system requires a password (type: KNA1 (customer)) in addition to the customer number. The customer parameters must agree with the used R/3 login . For example, if the customer belongs to sales organization 0001 and the R/3 user for executing this application belongs to sales organization 0010, the R/3 System will not accept the customer. This IAC permits creation of a customer master record for new customers.

Flow

An enterprise procures its data processing equipment from a specific manufacturer. When they order a new computer, the responsible employees of the enterprise wish to learn about the manufacturer's newest products. They scroll through the products of a specific product group:

- *Selecting a product group*
  After it loads, the application immediately lists all released product groups in the left window. Selection of a product group lists all the products belonging to the group in the upper right window.

- *Selecting a product*
  If images are available, the IAC presents them for each product and lists prices. Selection of a product triggers display of all the product information contained in the R/3 System. If the product does not require configuration, the user can enter the quantity and use the Add pushbutton to place the item in the virtual shopping cart.

- *Configuration*
  If a product requires configuration, the system lists all the corresponding components. As an example, consider a PC that can consist of a monitor, hard drive, processor, motherboard, memory and so on. The customer must specify a value for each component. The SAP Configurator 'assembles' the unit. Dependencies can exist between the various components, if they are maintained in the R/3 System. For example, some processors may be compatible only with certain motherboards. Configuration checks for these dependencies. The checks ensure that the company can deliver the product as selected.

- *Adding an item to the virtual shopping cart*
  Customers must identify themselves to the R/3 System with a customer number and password before they can place items in the virtual shopping cart. The system first queries users if they are already customers. If they answer yes, they must then enter their customer numbers and passwords. To change a password, should customers desire to change an initial password, for example, they can use the CHANGE PASSWORD pushbutton. If the user is a new customer, the IAC can create a new customer in the R/3 System. The system displays an entry template for different data, such as name,

address, e-mail and so on. New customers receive a customer number along with a password that they can change immediately. Afterward, customers place the selected product in the shopping cart and can add items from the same product group or other groups to the shopping cart. The system checks the password only once.

- *Generating a quotation*
  Once customers have made their selections, they request a quotation based on the product list. The system generates the quotation based on normal pricing. If a given customer usually receives a discount or if the product has a certain price scaling, the system considers it when calculating the price. To avoid generating multiple quotations needlessly, the system simulates the generation of a quotation to perform pricing. This method does not store a concrete quotation in the R/3 System.

- *Creating an order*
  If the customer accepts the quotation, the Order pushbutton creates a concrete order. At this point, the system has already queried the customer about the preferred method of payment. The customer can choose to pay the amount from an invoice or with a credit card. Payment by credit card requires entry of the card's type, number and expiration date. The mechanism for this type of payment corresponds to that used by the *Online Store* IAC. See Sections 5.3.2 and 2.5 for further information. The R/3 System then generates an order number and displays it in a new window. The customer should note the order number, as any later query of the order's status requires entry of the order number.

Technical information

Table 5.8   Technical information for the Sales Order Creation IAC

Service	Users	Transaction	Development class	Module pool	Function group
VW 01	Internet, Intranet	VW01	VAW	SAPMV45W	

Default settings

Creation of a customer order in the R/3 System requires entry of various parameter values. The system takes these values from the suggested parameters in the R/3 user settings . The values include the parameters given in Table 5.9.

Table 5.9   User default values for the Sales Order Creation IAC

Parameter	Value (default)	Description
AAT	TA	Order type
VKO	0001	Sales organization
VTW	01	Distribution channel
SPA	01	Division

If the R/3 system has not stored any parameter values for the R/3 user, it takes the default values listed above. The system can display product groups only if they have been released concretely for the Internet. To release a product group, go to the Customizing of product groups and set its authorization to WWW .

Authorizations

To generate an order, the R/3 user of this application must have all authorization rights for the object class *sales*.

Interfaces

Table 5.10   *Interfaces used in the Sales Order Creation IAC*

Interface	Description
BAPI_CUSTOMERORDER_SIMULATE	Simulates a customer order for a quotation
BAPI_CUSTOMERORDER_CREATE	Creates a customer order
BAPI_CUSTOMER_CREATE_PW_REG	Creates an entry for a customer password
BAPI_CUSTOMER_INITPASSWORT	Initializes the customer password
BAPI_CUSTOMER_CHECKPASSWORD	Checks the customer password
BAPI_CUSTOMER_CHANGEPASSWORT	Changes the customer password
SD_MATERIALS_FOR_GROUP_WWW	Materials of the material group for the WWW
SD_MATERIAL_DETAIL_WWW	Detailed data on the material for the WWW

5.3.4   Sales order status

Previously, a customer who desired information on an order had to ask for it by telephone or fax.

The *Sales Order Status* Internet Application provides a much more elegant method. This application offers information on the processing of a given order at any time and from any computer with access to the Internet. The status can indicate if the product has already been shipped. This application gives the customer the ability to observe the processing status of an order and lifts the burden of constant inquires from the enterprise.

Preconditions

To execute this Internet application, the customer must have already placed an order. The customer also requires a customer number and password (type: KNA1 (customer)).

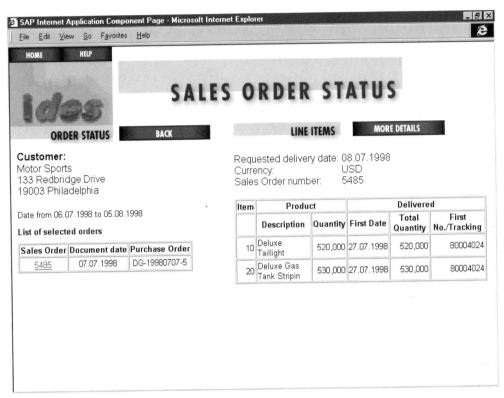

Figure 5.5   Sales Order Status IAC

Flow

The customer has used the previous Internet application to order a product. The enterprise, however, has not yet reacted to the customer's order. The customer now wishes to query the status of the order:

- *Login by the customer*
  This scenario allows customers to check the status of their own orders. Users must therefore identify themselves on the first screen by customer number and password. If a customer has placed several orders, the system can use this page to limit the orders displayed by order number, order date, article number or material number.

- *Selecting an order*
  If the customer has not selected any limitation on the first page, the next page displays a list of all orders associated with the customer in the left window. The customer can select an order. The system then displays the status of the order in the right window.

- *Status display*
  The status overview contains a description of the individual items and the following additional information:

- The quantity of the product available on the desired delivery date

- The number of articles the shipping department has already started to process

- *Displaying detailed information*
  The detail view provides the user with additional status information. In addition to the data noted above, this display shows the confirmed quantities as of a specific date.

Technical information

Table 5.11   Technical information for the Sales Order Status IAC

Service	Users	Transaction	Development class	Module pool	Function group
VW10	Internet, Intranet	VW10	VAW	SAPMV45X	

Default settings

The system does not require any additional settings.

Authorizations

The R/3 user must possess authorization for sales. If various types of orders remain hidden for the customer, the authorization should be limited accordingly.

Interfaces

Table 5.12   Interfaces used in the Sales Order Status IAC

Interface	Description
BAPI_CUSTOMER_GET_STATUS	Determines the customer order status
BAPI_CUSTOMERORDER_GETLIST	Determines all the orders for a customer
BAPI_CUSTOMER_CHECKPASSWORD	Checks the customer's password

5.3.5   Availability check

Many customers make purchasing decisions based upon the availability of the desired material. Sales employees can promise a reliable delivery date to customers only when they have access to the current availability of a product.

The Internet application *Availability Check* provides a simple and understandable overview of product availability. Both suppliers and customers can use this scenario. Customers can query the supplier about the availability of a specific material, without having to contact the sales department directly. The supplier/vendor of the company that serves this application can query the company's availability of sufficient stock and use this information to prepare for a new order from that company.

This scenario determines the availability of a specific material. If a user queries the availability of 100 pieces of a material, for example, the system first determines and displays the inventory level. If the manufacturer has too little of the material, the system determines when the remaining will become available. The application also enables presentation of the material in multimedia: images, video and so on.

Note: This is the only IAC that use Java technology. Clearly, all Internet applications can use Java Applets.

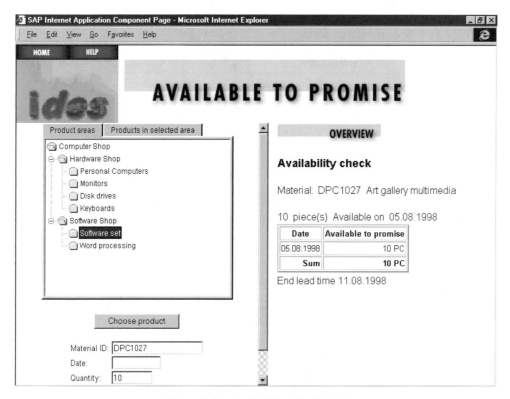

Figure 5.6   Availability Check IAC

Preconditions

To display materials, this application uses a Java Applet. The Internet browser must therefore support Java and its execution.

Only customers and vendors known to the R/3 System can use the availability check. The first page requests the customer or vendor number and the password. To assign Internet users with transaction SU05, the customer user identification requires object type KNA1 (customer); the vendor user identification requires object type BUS1008 (vendor).

Flow

As part of an expansion effort, a training enterprise plans for new training rooms. Planning depends on the availability of new computers, monitors and so on. Training cannot take place without the required equipment. The enterprise procures all its DP systems from a firm that uses the IAC to check availability:

- *Login by the user*
  Only specific persons have access to the availability check. The first page involves the identification of the customer or vendor.

- *Selecting a product*
  The next page uses a graphical user interface, a Java Applet, to present the list of products. If users know the material number, they can enter it directly. If they do not know the number, the Java Applet offers a search function. The search can take place in one of two ways: navigation within a tree structure that contains various product groups, or a text search. The text search requires entry of the product name only. At first, navigation offers only product groups for selection, but after selection, it lists all the products contained in the product group. After the user has selected a product and entered the desired quantity and delivery date, the system starts the availability check. The text search also supports a generic search, permitting users to enter wildcards (*) instead of the entire product name.

- *Availability information*
  The right window displays the availability. If the desired quantity is unavailable on the desired delivery date, the system displays the quantity available immediately and a date for delivery of the remaining material. If the user has not entered a date, the system determines future availability based upon the current date. If the user has not entered a quantity, the system displays the quantity available.
  Note: The system outputs the data on which the material becomes available, rather than a delivery date. The delivery date function is not active on the Internet.

Technical information

Table 5.13   Technical information for the Availability Check IAC

Service	Users	Transaction	Development class	Module pool	Function group
CKAV	Internet, Extranet	CKAV	MDW1	SAPMAVCK	W61V

Default settings

The Java Applet used in the application displays the product group in a tree structure. However, the Applet receives this information from a file stored on the Web server, rather than directly from the R/3 System. Report PCATALOG generates the file by extracting the required data from the advertising catalog. Administrators must then copy the file to the Web server.

The R/3 System outputs availability information according to a check scope. The checking group and checking rule A determine the scope of the check. See the documentation on the function module `BAPI_MATERIAL_AVAILABILITY` for information on how to use a special checking rule.

The availability information depends upon the plant of the material. The system determines the plant from R/3 default values of the user.

Authorizations

The application requires no additional authorizations.

Interfaces

Table 5.14   Interfaces used in the Availability Check IAC

Interface	Description
BAPI_MATERIAL_AVAILABILITY	Checks the availability of the material
MATERIAL_UNIT_CONVERSION	Material-specific conversion of measurement units
MATERIAL_LESEN	Reads the material master

Table 5.14 does not list all the BAPIs required to identify the customer: see the interfaces for the *Sales Order Creation* IAC.

5.3.6   Customer account information

In critical situations, customers with several orders from one enterprise often wish to inquire about specific information. Until recently, obtaining the desired information required several telephone calls or involved correspondence. With the Internet application for *Customer Account Information,* an enterprise makes customer data available to the customers. The customer can request and check account balances, line items, open items or master data.

If an enterprise has received a payment from a customer and cannot assign it to an invoice, the enterprise asks the customer to clarify the situation. The customer uses this IAC to check the line items and discover the required information on the invoice. The customer can then send the invoice number in an e-mail message. Customers can also research missing payments exactly.

This application permits only the display of information; it does not support data entry. If customers discover errors, they can contact the enterprise with e-mail.

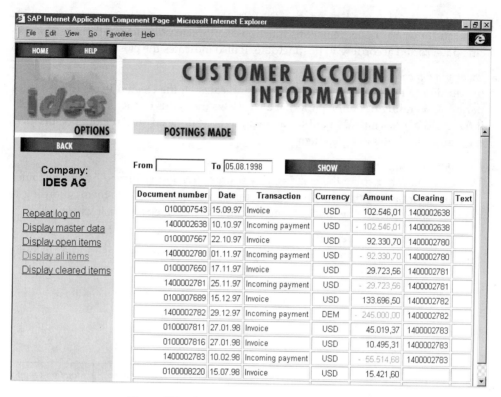

Figure 5.7 Customer Account Information IAC

Preconditions

The application provides customer account information only to authorized customers. It requires a customer number and a password (type: BUS1007 (customer)).

Flow

A customer has placed several orders with an enterprise. To see the open items and an the current account status, the customer starts the Customer Account Information IAC:

- *Login by the user*
  Since the application permits inquiries on the account status only to authorized customers, the user must first provide a customer number and password for identification. The customer can then select one of the following displays:

- *Displaying master data*
  This function displays the customer's address, contact person, Internet address, bank accounts and so on . It does not display internal information such as payment blocking indicators and so on.

- *Displaying open items*
  If the customer has open items, this function displays an overview of them as of a specific date, sorted according to posting date. It also indicates the closing balance.

- *Displaying line items*
  In addition to the open items, this display indicates all the cleared items for a specific period. Depending upon the period, it also shows the status of each item. For example, if the customer has already paid for an item, but has done so after the period specified, the display indicates an open item.

- *Displaying clearing procedures*
  This function can display the clearing procedures already performed by the customer. By entering a period, the system displays the procedures and sorts them according to clearing document number and posting date. It also indicates the closing balance.

- *Displaying the account statement*
  This functions displays the account statement, including all postings for the customer account, sorted according to posting date, and the end closing balance.

Technical information

Table 5.15   Technical information for the Customer Account Information IAC

Service	Users	Transaction	Development class	Module pool	Function group
IKA1	Internet, Extranet	IKA1	FIW	SAPRFIKA	

Default settings

This application requires Customizing entries in the customer's FI module. The first step creates a user for a person in charge. The second step creates an identification code for the person in charge by making the appropriate entry in Customizing for customer accounting. The third step enters the newly created user as an SAP office user. Finally, the identification code for the person in charge is entered in the customer's master data under correspondence.

Authorizations

The R/3 login requires no additional authorizations.

Interfaces

Table 5.16   *Interfaces used in the Customer Account Information IAC*

Interface	Description
BAPI_DEBITOR_CHANGEPASSWORD	Changes the customer password
BAPI_DEBITOR_CREATE_PW_REG	Creates an entry for a customer password
BAPI_DEBITOR_INITPASSWORD	Initializes the customer password
BAPI_DEBITOR_CHECKPASSWORD	Checks the customer password
GET_CLEARED_ITEMS	Determines the cleared items for a payment document

5.4   Purchasing

When a company purchases goods for internal use, several persons participate in the process: employees who make their needs known, managers who must approve a request and employees who direct the order to a supplier. Rapid processing of an order demands an efficient system.

The Internet applications delivered by SAP support purchasing. The applications include the creation and release of purchase requisitions. Employees can enter their own requisitions directly into the R/3 System. Accordingly, these applications run only on the Intranet:

Table 5.17   *R/3 Internet Applications for Purchasing*

Scenario	Description
Requirement Request	Creates the purchase requisition
Requirement Request status	Checks the processing status of a purchase requisition
Collective Release of Purchase Requisitions	Lists all the purchase requisitions to be released and their release
Collective Release of Orders	Lists all the orders to be released and their release
Collective Release of Service Entry Sheets	Lists all the service entry sheets to be released

5.4.1   Requirement request

A requirement request for working materials and tools often produces a great deal of bureaucratic activity, as many people must become involved in the process. For example, if a company creates a new position and/or workstation, it requires a number of materials. If the warehouse does not contain them, the enterprise must generate concrete orders to purchase the materials.

As part of a movement toward paperless offices, employees now have the ability to requisition materials at a specific price directly online. They do not need to fill in a form and send it along for further processing. The R/3 System contains an application that processes purchase requisitions. The application determines if warehouse stocks already contain the article in question or if the enterprise must order it. This R/3 application requires detailed knowledge to handle the transaction.

The *Requirement Request* IAC provides all employees with an easily operated interface to requisition the materials they need for their work. They can select the articles from a catalog and enter both the quantity and delivery date desired. The IAC also displays the availability of the requested materials.

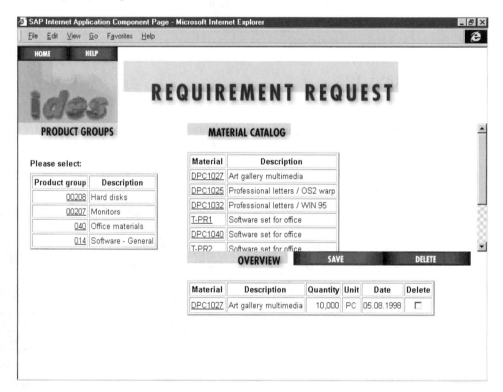

Figure 5.8   Requirement Request IAC

Preconditions

When an employee creates a requisition in the R/3 System, the notification includes the identity of the person making the request. This person must be an R/3 user.

Flow

An employee installs the latest version of a software package. This version requires significantly more memory than the previous version. To use the software, the employee needs additional main memory. The employee enters a purchase requisition as follows:

- *Login by the employee*
  Creating a purchase requisition demands authorizations that can differ from employee to employee. The user must therefore log in to the R/3 System with an R/3 login.

- *Displaying the material groups and materials*
  The first page enables the employee to select between various material groups in the catalog. The system then displays the corresponding materials in the right window. After selecting a material, the user enters the quantity and desired delivery date to initiate an availability check. If no date appears, the system uses today's date.

- *Availability check: quantity*
  Before creating the request, the user executes an availability check with the Check pushbutton. The check returns the material available on the desired date. If none, or only part, of the material is available, the system displays the next possible delivery date.

- *Recording in the supplies list*
  After the availability check, the employee records the material in a list of supplies with the Add pushbutton. The employee can add additional materials to the list in the same manner. A particular material, however, can appear in the list only once.

- *Saving the request*
  Once the list contains all the required materials, the system saves the purchase requisition. The system provides the user with a requisition number to enable later queries on the processing status. If the material is not available, it must be ordered from an external source. In this case the R/3 System automatically creates a purchase order (PO). If the warehouse contains the material, the system generates a reservation.

Technical information

Table 5.18 Technical information for the Requirement Request IAC

Service	Users	Transaction	Development class	Module pool	Function group
MEW1	Intranet	MEW1	MEW	SAPMMWE1	MEWR

Default settings

Material groups are displayed on the Web only if they are marked as web-enabled . To do so, first enter all the material groups in table T023. Next, enter the value WWMM in the field for the authorization group (BGrp). The intervals of the number ranges of reservations in inventory management also require adjustments in Customizing:

- Change the 'to' number in interval 01 to 0019999999

- Insert a new interval (number 10) from 0090000000 to 0099999999

This application takes the mandatory values needed to create a purchase requisition in the R/3 System from the user parameters of the R/3 login. The parameters in Table 5.19 must have valid entries.

Table 5.19   User default values for the Requirement Request IAC

Parameter	Description
WRK	Plant for which the material is maintained
LAG	Storage location
BSA	Document type used to create the purchase requisition
BWA	Transaction type for the reservation
EKG	Purchasing group
CNT	Cost center that will post the purchase order or reservation

Authorizations

Execution of this application requires the authorizations in Table 5.20 for R/3 identification:

Table 5.20   R/3 authorizations required for the Requirement Request IAC

Authorization object	Description
M_BANF_BSA	Document type in the purchase requisition
M_BANF_EKG	Purchasing group in the purchase requisition
M_BANF_EKO	Purchasing organization in the purchase requisition
M_BANF_WRK	Plant in the purchase requisition
M_MRES_BWA	Reservations: transaction type
M_ MRES_ WWA	Reservations: plant

Differences between the IAC and R/3 transactions ME51 and MB21

This Internet application rests upon transactions ME51 (create purchase order) and MB21 (create reservation). However, unlike transaction ME51, the IAC does not permit source determination. It does not permit account assignment data or entry of texts. Unlike transaction MB21, the IAC does not permit setting transaction types.

Interfaces

Table 5.21   Interfaces used in the Requirement Request IAC

Interface	Description
BAPI_MATERIAL_AVAILABILITY	Checks material availability
BAPI_REQUIREMENT_CREATE	Creates a requirements request
MM_MATERIALS_FOR_GROUP	Selects materials for a specific materials group
MM_SELECT_MATERIAL_GROUPS	Selects all the materials groups with authorization group WWMM

5.4.2 Requirement request status

After creation of a purchase requisition with the appropriate IAC, the employee wishes to inquire on the status of the request. Telephone calls are no longer necessary to do so.

The employee can use *Requirement Request Status* at any time to learn the current processing status (if an order has already been placed, for example).

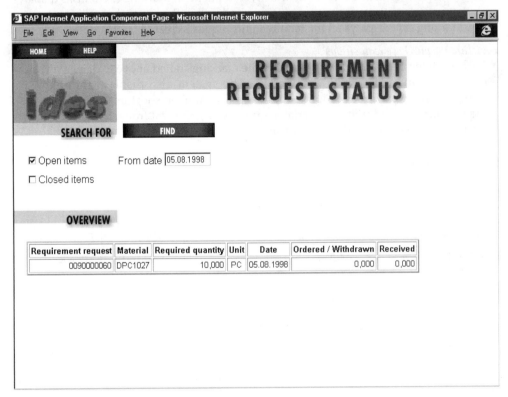

Figure 5.9   Requirement Request Status IAC

Preconditions

The user needs an identification to log in to the R/3 System. To display the status, the employee must have already created a purchase requisition.

Flow

The employee in the previous scenario has already entered a request for additional main memory. However, the employee has not received any reaction to the request. The employee now wishes information on the status of the request:

- *Login by the employee*
  A status query on the purchase requisition rests upon a logged-in R/3 user. Therefore, the employee must log on with an R/3 identification.

- *Selection criteria*
  The user can mark specific criteria to target certain requirements requests for inclusion in the display. One criterion might be *open items*. This criterion lists all the requests with a quantity greater than the ordered or delivered quantity. Marking *closed items* displays all the requests with a quantity equal to or smaller than the ordered or delivered quantity. Marking *date* displays all the requirements requests created on that date.

- *Listing the purchase requisitions*
  The search for matching requisitions uses the markings noted above to display the purchase requisitions in the lower window. The system also displays the following information for each requisition request: activity number, short text for the material, request quantity and unit of material, required date, removal from storage, orders created, and goods receipts that have already occurred.

Technical information

Table 5.22   Technical information for the Requirement Request Status IAC

Service	Users	Transaction	Development class	Module pool	Function group
MEW2	Intranet	MEW2	MEW	SAPMMWE1	MEWR

Default settings

This application requires no additional settings.

Authorizations

Only authorized users may have access to status information on purchase requisitions. The application requires the following authorizations:

Table 5.23   R/3 authorizations required for the Requirement Request Status IAC

Authorization object	Description
M_BANF_BSA	Document type in the purchase requisition
M_BANF_EKG	Purchasing group in the purchase requisition
M_BANF_EKO	Purchasing organization in the purchase requisition
M_BANF_WRK	Plant in the purchase requisition
M_MRES_BWA	Reservations: Transaction type
M_MRES_WWA	Reservations: Plant

Interfaces

Table 5.24   Interfaces used in the Requirement Request Status IAC

Interface	Description
BAPI_REQUIREMENT_GET_LIST	Determines a list of detailed information on the status of the purchase requisitions

5.4.3   Collective release of purchase requisitions

Purchase Requisitions are internal documents that define requirements and trigger purchasing to generate an order. For example, the purchase requisition of a given employee illustrates a requirement. However, purchase requisitions do not automatically lead to an order. If the purchase requisition fulfills certain conditions (a value above $5000, for example), a higher instance must approve the request. The R/3 System uses a release procedure with various release strategies to apply to the approval process. Each person involved in the approval must enter a release code before the purchasing department can order the material.

The *Release of Purchase Requisitions* IAC enables simple release of these requests. This feature provides a distinct advantage to the untrained R/3 user, especially when the user's primary responsibilities do not involve such releases.

The IAC automatically creates a list of all purchase requisitions that require release by the user. The user can select an entry and release it – without entering a specific release code. The IAC however, does not support simultaneous release of all items. Once entered, the user can reset (rollback) the release.

Preconditions

This IAC creates an individual list for the R/3 user logged into the system. The user must have an R/3 login with the appropriate authorizations and user default values.

Flow

A department will have five new employees next month. A current employee submits a requirements request for each new employee, requesting a work station computer for each one. Since the total value of the order exceeds a predefined limit, the department head must approve the order:

- *Login*
  Not every employee can release purchase requisitions. The user must log in with an R/3 identification.

- *Releasing a purchase requisition*
  The application lists all the purchase requisitions that the user may release in the left window. Appropriate selection displays detailed information in the right window. The user can now release a purchase requisition, which then receives the status of *released*.

The lower window displays a list of released elements. The application does not support the simultaneous release of all purchase requisitions assigned to the user.

- *Resetting (rolling back) a release*
  The user can rescind the release of a purchase requisition. If the user does so, the purchase requisition again receives the status *to be released*.

Technical information

Table 5.25   Technical information for the Collective Release of Purchase Requisitions IAC

Service	Users	Transaction	Development class	Module pool	Function group
MEW3	Intranet	MEW3	MEW	SAPMMWE2	

Default settings

So that the user does not need to enter a release code explicitly, the user default values must be set as in Table 5.26.

Table 5.26   User default values for the Collective Release of Purchase Requisitions IAC

Parameter	Description
FAB	Release code with which the user works
FGR	Release groups to which the release code is allocated

Authorizations

Release of purchase requisitions requires the authorizations in R/3 identification given in Table 5.27.

Table 5.27   Authorizations required in the Collective Release of Purchase Requisitions IAC

Authorization object	Description
M_BANF_BSA	Document type in the purchase requisition
M_BANF_EKG	Purchasing group in the purchase requisition
M_BANF_EKO	Purchasing group in the purchase requisition
M_BANF_WRK	Plant in the purchase requisition
M_EINK_FRG	Release code and release group in purchasing

Difference between the IAC and transaction ME55

Compared to the standard transaction ME55, the IAC supports fewer entry fields. The IAC does not support changes to the data or the display of additional detailed information. It does not support a general release of all purchase requisitions.

Interfaces

Table 5.28   Interfaces used in the Collective Release of Purchase Requisitions IAC

Interface	Description
BAPI_REQUIREMENT_GET_LIST	Determines all the purchase requisitions to be released
BAPI_REQUISITION_RELEASE	Release the purchase requisition
BAPI_REQUISITION_RESET_RELEASE	Resets a released purchase requisition

5.4.4   Collective release of orders

The section on the *Collective Release of Purchase Requisitions* IAC described a release procedure. A similar procedure applies for the release of orders. If an order fulfills certain conditions, such as a value over $10,000, a duly authorized person must first release the order before the purchasing department can send it to a vendor. To release the order, each person involved in the process must use a release code in a release transaction.

The Internet application for *Collective Release of Orders* meets the same requirements as the IAC described previously. It provides a simple and comfortable user interface that permits even the untrained R/3 user to perform releases without concrete entry of a release code.

Preconditions

Only authorized persons may perform releases. Accordingly, the IAC requires an R/3 user.

Flow

The purchasing agent responsible for all orders must decide if a vendor should receive a particular order. The agent lists all the orders that require release as follows:

- *Login*
  To determine all the orders that require release, the system must operate with an R/3 user. The user must log in to the system with an R/3 login. In addition, only duly authorized persons may release orders.

- *Releasing an order*
  The application lists all the orders that require release on the left side. After selection of a particular order, it lists the corresponding detailed information in the right window.

If the user releases an order, the application records the status *released* in the overview list that appears the lower window. The vendor can now receive the order.

- *Canceling a release*
  To cancel the release of an order, the user selects the order in the overview list and sets the status to be released. The order then returns to the list of orders that still require release.

Technical information

Table 5.29   Technical information for the Collective Release of Orders IAC

Service	Users	Transaction	Development class	Module pool	Function group
MEW5	Intranet	MEW5	MEW	SAPMMWE3	

Default settings

The user default values given in Table 5.30 allow the user to perform a release without entering a release code explicitly.

Table 5.30   User default values for the Collective Release of Orders IAC

Parameter	Description
FAB	Release code for the user
FGR	Release group allocated to the release code

Authorizations

Release of an order requires the authorization given in Table 5.31.

Table 5.31   Required authorization in the Collective Release of Orders IAC

Authorization object	Description
M_EINK_FRG	Release code and release group in purchasing

Differences Between the IAC and the R/3 Transaction

The application does not permit changes to the data for an item or a release of all items simultaneously. The IAC does not support a complete, detailed display of a release strategy or a material, for example.

Interfaces

Table 5.32   Interfaces used in the Collective Release of Orders IAC

Interface	Description
BAPI_PO_GET_LIST	Displays orders that require release
BAPI_PO_RELEASE	Releases an order
BAPI_PO_RESET_RELEASE	Rests (rolls back) a release

5.4.5   Collective release of service entry sheets

If a service entry sheet meets a certain threshold, such as a value above $10,000, a higher instance must approve the release. A release procedure handles the approval process. As in the case of similar collective releases, the system requires entry of a release code by a duly authorized person.

The Internet application for *Collective Release of Service Entry Sheets* simplifies the release *service entry sheets*. The system displays a list of the service entry sheets that the user must process. The user can release a list element by selecting it, even without knowing the proper release code. A default user value in the R/3 identification stores the release code. The IAC also permits cancellation of the release.

Preconditions

To release service entry sheets, the user requires an R/3 identification with the appropriate authorizations.

Flow

The person responsible for the release of service entry sheets wants to display an overview of the service entry sheets that require release and to release individual sheets. The user must perform the following tasks:

- *Login*
  Only duly authorized persons can perform a release. The user must log in to the system with the appropriate R/3 login.

- *Releasing a service entry sheet*
  A list displays all the service entry sheets that require release. Selection of one sheet lists the corresponding information. If the user releases the selected sheet, it receives the status *released*.

- *Canceling a release*
  If users release a service entry sheet in error, they can cancel (reset) the release. The cancellation resets the status to *to be released*.

Technical information

Table 5.33   Technical information for the Collective Release of Service Entry Sheets IAC

Service	Users	Transaction	Development class	Module pool	Function group
MEW7	Intranet	MEW7	MEW		MEW4

Default settings

The R/3 System must have an active release procedure and one or more service entry sheets that require release. Release also requires the user default values shown in Table 5.34.

Table 5.34   User default values for the Collective Release of Service Entry Sheets IAC

Parameter	Description
FAB	Release code with which the user works
FGR	Release group allocated to the release code

Authorizations

The user must have the authorization given in Table 5.35 to perform a release.

Table 5.35   Required authorizations for the Collective Release of Service Entry Sheets IAC

Authorization object	Description
M_EINK_FRG	Release code and release group in purchasing

Differences between the IAC and the R/3 transaction

The R/3 transaction covers a much wider range and offers more entry fields and functions. The IAC does not support changes to data in service entry sheets (blocking indicators, 'delivery completed' indicators). The application does not support the simultaneous release of all service entry sheets.

Interfaces

Table 5.36   Interfaces used in the Collective Release of Service Entry Sheets IAC

Interface	Description
BAPI_ENTRYSHEET_GETDETAIL	Displays details of the service entry sheet
BAPI_ENTRYSHEET_GETLIST	Determines a list of the service entry sheets
BAPI_ENTRYSHEET_RELEASE	Releases a service entry sheet
BAPI_ENTRYSHEET_RESET_RELEASE	Resets (rolls back) the release of a service entry sheet

5.5   Customer service

Close customer service is a significant precondition for the success of an enterprise and gives the services provided to customers an important role. Good customer service means close contact with the customer and good communications.

SAP has fulfilled these requirements with the Internet applications given in Table 5.37.

Table 5.37   R/3 Internet applications for customer service

Scenario	Description
Quality certificate	Outputs certification of product quality
Quality notification	Creates stocks of defective products
Service notification	Notification of a breakdown
Measurement and counter readings	Enters measurements and counter values for rented or leased equipment
KANBAN	Checks the containers in a material flow control according to the KANBAN method
Consignment stocks	Checks the consignment stocks of the supplier at the customer location

5.5.1   Quality certificates

If a customer, rather than a product, returns, an enterprise has made a product of quality. The R/3 System can certify the quality of individual products with quality certificates that can accompany deliveries. The vendor can determine the contents of the certificates in consultation with the customer. Examples include specifications or data from inspections. The enterprise can also consider individual customer inquiries when creating certificates. The enterprise can print the certificates and send them to the customer.

The Internet application *Quality Certificates* allows the customer to call certificates in a batch from the vendor at any time over the Internet. The certificates contain information agreed to by the vendor and the customer. If the customer's expectations differ from the results of an internal inspection, the customer can compare those results with the results reported by the vendor. Direct access to certificates saves the vendor from sending documents along with a delivery. An actual request for information from the R/3 System triggers creation of the certificates. This process makes use of templates that specify the contents.

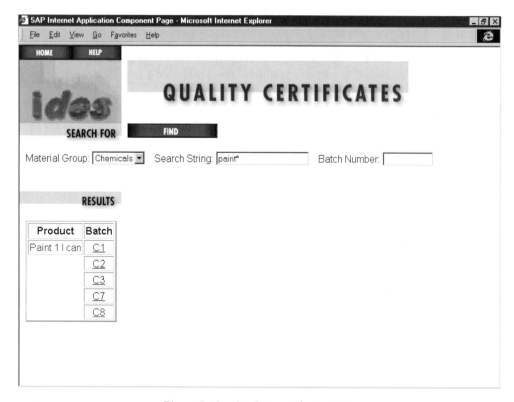

Figure 5.10   Quality certificates IAC

Preconditions

To access quality certificates, the customer must have a customer number and a password (type: KNA1 (customer)). To create a certificate, the system must contain a quality certificate determination for the customer.

Flow

A customer has received a delivery and has already used the products. If a quality problem appears, the customer must examine the quality certificate to determine the cause of the problem. To do so, the customer must perform the following actions:

- *Login by the customer*
  Only specific customers may examine certificates. The system requires identification of the customer by customer number and password.

- *Selecting the batch*
  Certificates are selected according to batch. The user must therefore select the correct batch. The application offers the following search criteria: *product group*, *search text* or *batch number*.

After the user selects a product group, the application displays all the batches for the group in the right window. The R/3 System preselects the list of product groups that appear in the display. If the user enters a search text, the system examines materials with the material short text. Entry of an asterisk (* = any character string) or a plus sign (+ = any character) allows a generic search. The system again displays the hits for the batch on the right side. If customers have the correct batch number, they can enter it directly. They can also enter individual or combined criteria. A logical AND links combinations.

The list of results contains the appropriate batches, including plant and expiration date.

- *Generating a certificate*
  The customer selects the desired batch from the list of results and receives the certificate generated by the system in Portable Document Format (PDF). The browser must contain an entry for a viewer that supports this format. The certificate template determines the contents of certificates. The template selects the information directly from the R/3 System. The template also defines the form used, data, texts, characteristics and the amount of information that appears for each characteristic. The customer master determines the language used in the certificate.

Technical information

Table 5.38   Technical information for the Quality Certificates IAC

Service	Users	Transaction	Development class	Module pool	Function group
QC42	Extranet	QC42	QC	SAPMQCWA	

Default settings

The system can generate a certificate only if it already contains all the properly maintained data necessary for the certificate. The customer must also successfully locate a certificate template. Customizing for the Quality Management module must also contain the following settings:

- View V_T001G_QM requires entries for program SAPLQC07. All company codes whose plants will generate certificates must be maintained.
- Sender texts must exist in the working client. Use transaction SO10 to generate them. Texts and forms must exist for all languages in which the system will generate certificates.

Authorizations

The R/3 identification used to view and generate certificates requires the following authorizations in Table 5.39.

Table 5.39   Required authorizations for the Quality Certificates IAC

Authorization object	Description
F_KNA1_APP	Customer: application authorization (activity: 03, application authorization: F)
Q_TCODE	Transaction authorization for QC42

Differences between the IAC and R/3 transaction QC22

The Internet application differs from standard transaction QC22. The system takes the language used in the certificate from the customer master. It finds the certificate templates automatically, and does not support the use of alternative templates. Sender texts at the company code level belong to program SAPLQC07, rather than to program RQCAAP02.

Interfaces

Table 5.40   Interfaces used in the Quality Certificates IAC

Interface	Description
BAPI_DEBITOR_CHECKEXISTENCE	Checks the existence of a customer in the R/3 System
BAPI_CUSTOMER_CHECKPASSWORD	Checks the customer password
BAPI_CUST_SAREAS_MATERIALS_GET	Generates a list of materials for a customer's sales area
BAPI_MATERIAL_BATCHES_GET	Determines the batch list for a material
BAPI_MATERIAL_BATCH_CERTIF_PDF	Generates a Quality Certificate for the batch in PDF format
SD_SELECT_MATERIAL_GROUPS_WWW	Determines the list of material groups for the WWW

5.5.2   Quality notification

If a delivery contains a product of substandard quality, the R/3 System supports the generation of complaints, or quality notifications. To avoid angering the customer with long processing times, customer service must operate efficiently. Contact between the customer and the supplier should take place as quickly as possible.

Use of the Internet application for *Quality Notification* enables the customer to submit notifications with a minimum of effort and at any time. The Quality Management module of the R/3 System then processes the notifications. The supplier or service center can react to the notification immediately. This application permits the customer to limit and describe the problem by using predefined defect codes. Customers can also query the processing status of the notification at any time.

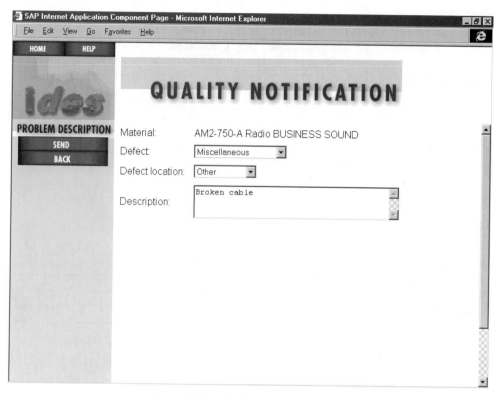

Figure 5.11   Quality Notification IAC

Preconditions

The customer's contact person generates quality notifications. The customer master record must contain an entry that identifies this person. To enter a notification this customer employee needs the number stored in the customer master record and the Internet user from transaction SU05. The correct type is BUS1006001 (employee of a business partner).

Flow

A retail concern sells PCs that it procures from an enterprise. The enterprise offers the required IACs. If the retailer discovers defects in a delivery, an employee can inform the enterprise of the defect with a quality notification. The employee must perform the following actions:

- *Login by the contact person*
  Only a customer who has received a material can issue a quality notification on the material. The customer master record must identify the contact person by number and password. The system uses the identification to display a list of materials about which the customer can generate a notification. The customer material master record must contain this list of each customer. At login, the customer decides if the system should enter a new notification or display an older one.

- *Creating the notification*
  The customer first selects a material from the customer-specific list of materials and then moves to the problem description. The customer selects a defect code and defect location as well as a description of the defect on the next Web page. The default values refer to the material selected. This reference guarantees that the customer can select only defect codes that apply to the material. After saving the notification, the customer receives a quality notification number.

- *Displaying the notification list*
  The customer can determine the status of a quality notification by listing all the notifications. The notification list contains the notification number, description, material, date and status of each notification.

Technical information

Table 5.41   Technical information for the Quality Notification IAC

Service	Users	Transaction	Development class	Module pool	Function group
QMW1	Internet, Extranet	QMW1	QQM		SAPQMWWW

Default settings

For this application to send a complete notification, the starting notification type for transaction QM01 (Create Quality Notification) must be set. During creation of a notification, the system first checks if all the mandatory roles for the notification type contain data. The Internet application uses only the notification type Q1, which uses only the roles of AG (ordering party) and AP (contact person). The partner scheme in Customizing should not contain any additional mandatory roles.

Authorizations

To create a quality notification, the R/3 identification requires the authorizations given in Table 5.42.

Table 5.42   Required authorizations for the Quality Notification IAC

Authorization object	Description
Q_QMEL	Type of login
Q_TCODE	Transaction authorization for QMW1
Q_MATERIAL	Material authorization
Q_GP_CODE	Use of group codes

Differences between the IAC and R/3 transaction QM01

Unlike the R/3 application (transaction QM01), the IAC does not support the entry of multiple items, such as cause, measures and action. It does not support functions for priorities, dates and internal processing.

Interfaces

Table 5.43   Interfaces used in the Quality Notification IAC

Interface	Description
BAPI_PAR_EMPLOYEE_CHECKEXISTEN	Checks the contact person's number
BAPI_PAR_EMPLOYEE_CHECKPASSWOR	Checks the contact person's password
BAPI_MATERIAL_GETCATALOGPROFIL	Determines the report scheme from the material master
BAPI_QNOTIFICAT_CREATE	Creates a quality notification
BAPI_CUSTOMER_QNOTIF_GET_LIST	Determines a list of quality notification for a customer
BAPI_CUSTOMER_QNOTIF_GET_MAT	Determines the material list for which a customer material information record exists

5.5.3   Service notification

When purchasing equipment, such as a copier, the customer often signs a service contract that guarantees quick service to limit the down time. To fulfill these requirements, the vendor or service provider must enter service notifications with little effort and establish contact with the customer rapidly.

The Internet application for *Service Notification* provides a first and important step on the road to rapid responses to service requests. This application allows the customer to enter service notifications directly into the R/3 System of the vendor or service provider. The notification serves as the basis for service requests that plan and execute individual services in detail.

The advantage of this application lies in its complete availability. Equipment needs service beyond the business hours of those who supply it. In the past, service requests had to wait until the start of the next business day. The application also provides the vendor or service provider with a pool of new notifications immediately after customers have entered them. The vendor can thus respond to the customer very quickly. The application permits the customer to query the processing status of the notification at any time.

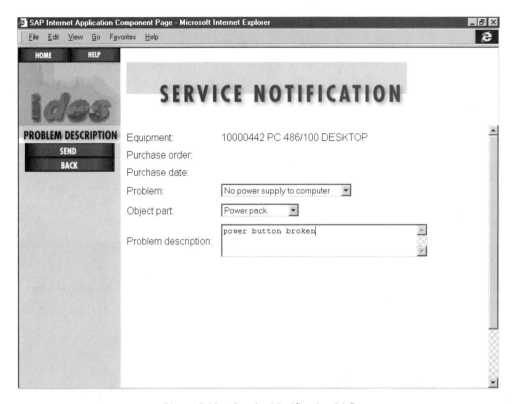

Figure 5.12   Service Notification IAC

Preconditions

A contact person at the customer site generates the notification. The customer master record of the R/3 System at the service provider must contain data for this person. To create a notification, the system requires the contact person's number and password for identification (type: `BUS1006001` (employee of a business partner)).

Flow

A customer has purchased a copier from an enterprise that offers on-site service. After a time, the copier fails. The customer can use the Internet application *Service Notification* to request service. The customer must perform the following steps:

- *Login by the customer*
  Only the contact persons designated as such by the customer can enter a service notification. The user must log in with a (contact person) number and appropriate password. At login, the system asks the user to decide between creation of a new notification and display of a list of existing notifications.

- *Creating a service notification*
  Customers can create service notifications only for products allocated to that customer in the R/3 System. The system displays an individual list to all customers so that they can select a product. To specify the product more exactly, customer can also enter the order and order date. At first, the problem description lists predefined problem codes from which the customer may select. This selection process guarantees that the service provider receives a well-articulated report on the defect. The customer must also enter a description of the problem. After a user has sent the notification, the system returns an overview of the message that contains a notification number. Users can later check on the processing status of the notification with this number.

- *Outputting the list of service notifications*
  Customer can check the status of one or more service notifications by outputting a notification list. Each notification contains the notification number, notification text, date and status.

Technical information

Table 5.44   Technical information for the Service Notification IAC

Service	Users	Transaction	Development class	Module pool	Function group
IWWW	Internet, Extranet	IWWW	IWWW	SAPMIWOW	

Default settings

The starting notification type for transaction IW51 (create service notification) must exist for successful processing a notification in the R/3 System.

Authorizations

To create a service notification successfully, the R/3 user must have the authorizations given in Table 5.45:

Table 5.45   Required authorizations for the Service Notification IAC

Authorization object	Description
I_BEGRP	Authorization group
I_IWERK	Plant maintenance planning plant
I_SWERK	Maintenance plant
I_QMEL	Notification type
I_TCODE	Transaction authorization for IWWW

Differences between the IAC and the R/3-transaction

Unlike the standard transaction, this IAC does not support the creation of multiple items, or causes, measures and actions. It does not support entry of priorities, dates and internal processing.

Interfaces

Table 5.46   Interfaces used in the Service Notification IAC

Interface	Description
BAPI_PAR_EMPLOYEE_CHECKEXISTEN	Checks the contact person's number
BAPI_PAR_EMPLOYEE_CHECKPASSWOR	Checks the contact person's password
BAPI_CUSTOMER_EQUIPMENT_LIST	Determines all the service equipment of a customer
BAPI_EQMT_GETCATALOGPROFIL	Determines the parts of a machine
BAPI_SERVICENOTIFICAT_CREATE	Creates a service notification
BAPI_CUSTOMER_NOTIFIC_LIST	Determines all completed service notifications

5.5.4   Measurement and counter readings

Many enterprises rent equipment that contains counters. Examples include copiers and automobiles (odometer readings). This equipment often requires (preventative) maintenance at intervals determined by the counter reading. To determine the counter reading, service technicians from the renting company must read the meters on site, or the renter must charge a given employee with the task. The employee would then register the counter reading periodically with a fax or telephone call.

This category also includes measurement readings . An apartment complex must measure the supply of heating oil periodically, even if the complex does not employ a full-time maintenance employee. A rental management company must often estimate the supply of heating oil in its buildings so that it can order additional supplies when necessary.

With the Internet component *Measurement and Counter Readings*, an enterprise or a particular employee can take the measurements and readings and then enter them into the service provider's R/3 System over the Internet. The service provider thus has an overview of current use and conditions. Since taking the readings and measurements requires less effort, the service can operate a lower cost.

Preconditions

To enter measurement and counter readings in the R/3 System, the user must have an R/3 login and the authorizations listed below.

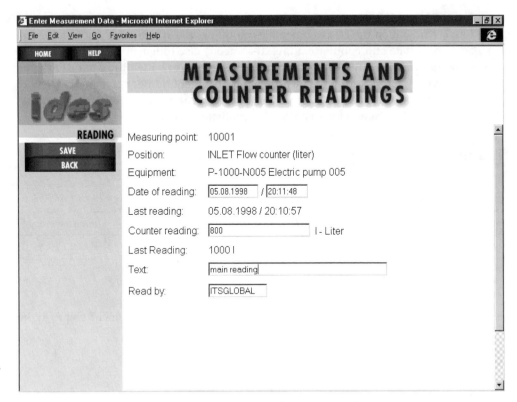

Figure 5.13   Measurement and Counter Readings IAC

Flow

The company renting a copier periodically reads the unit's counter and reports the measurement to the renting company. The customer takes the readings and enters them in the application as follows:

- *Login by the customer*
  The application does not require special identification. Nonetheless, we recommend that only duly authorized persons enter measurement values. To do so, the user needs an R/3 login and appropriate password.

- *Entering the measurement point*
  The system identifies every measurement station as a measurement point. The user enters the description of the measurement point and then inserts the new measurement.

- *Inserting a measurement*
  To permit inspection, the next page displayed by the application shows an exact description (measurement position and equipment) of the measurement point. If the readings have already been taken, the user should also change the measurement date,

as the system would otherwise use today's date by default. The user can also enter an optional comment on the measurement. For auditing, the system also displays the last measurement date and counter reading. If someone else (other than the current user) took the reading, the entry should indicate that employee's identity. After saving the measurement, the user receives a measurement document number and an overview of successfully entered readings. The service provider can now use the document that exists in the R/3 System to forecast needs or evaluate trends.

Technical information

Table 5.47   Technical information for the Measurement and Counter Readings IAC

Service	Users	Transaction	Development class	Module pool	Function group
IK71	Extranet, Intranet	IK71	IMRI		IMRI

Default settings

To enter measurement and counter readings, the appropriate measurement points in the R/3 System must be maintained.

Authorizations

Table 5.48   Authorizations required for the Measurement and Counter Readings IAC

Authorization Object	Description
I_BEGRP	Plant maintenance authorization in general
I_TCODE	Transaction code

Differences between the IAC and R/3 transaction IK11

The Internet application does not support resetting the counter externally or changing the counter apparatus. The application does not display certain information, such as the object structure or the list of measurement documents.

Interfaces

Table 5.49   Interfaces used in the Measurement and Counter Readings IAC

Interface	Description
MEASUREM_DOCUM_DIALOG_LIST_1	Dialog measurement document: List processing for changing measurement point objects
MEASUREM_BUFFER_INITIALIZE	Initializes the update-relevant dialog buffer for measurement points and measurement documents
MEASUREM_POINT_READ_DIALOG_BUF	Determines the measurement point from the dialog buffer or from the database
MEASUREM_DOCUM_READ_LAST	Determines the last (non-cancelled) measurement document for a measurement point

5.5.5   KANBAN

The *KANBAN* system provides a special procedure for controlling production and material flow. The system rests upon retrograde links of processing in assembly. The system triggers a material flow only when an assembly level actually requires the material.

The request for materials follows in the form of a card that contains all the information on the material (the amount of material, the quantities and the delivery location). The manufacturer sends the card (KANBAN in Japanese) to the vendor who supplies the material. The advantages of this system include low warehouse levels and automated transmission of data for re-supply. To procure the material or to receive the goods, the system must only read the barcode.

The vendor can now request information on empty containers with the *KANBAN* Internet application and react to the information appropriately by creating a delivery due list. The vendor can also confirm planned deliveries directly over the Internet. The application offers the supplier a quick overview of product levels. The vendor can use this information to decide what quantities of a given product to deliver.

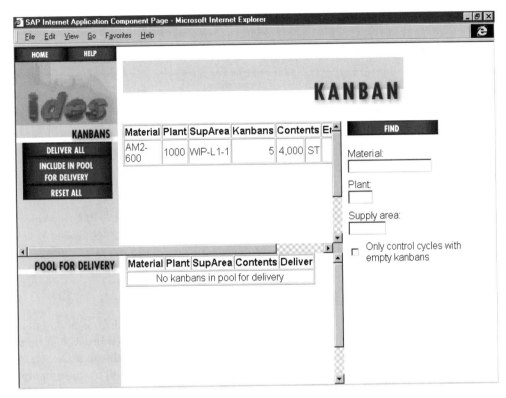

Figure 5.14   KANBAN IAC

Preconditions

A vendor master record for the vendor must exist in the R/3 System. The user also requires a supplier number and a password (type: BUS1008 (vendor)).

Flow

A vendor handles material flow control with a customer with the KANBAN process. The customer has already used the materials needed for production and sets the KANBANS to 'empty.' The vendor now looks through the various control cycles with the IAC and creates a delivery due list. A control cycle describes the flow of materials and the demand for them:

- *Login by the vendor*
  Each vendor should have access only to the control cycles for which it supplies deliveries. Vendors must therefore identify themselves by vendor number and password.

- *Overview of all control cycles*
  After login, the system displays all the control cycles for the vendor number. The overview contains the following information for each control cycle:

  Material number: The vendor and customer often use different material numbers for the same material. The system displays either the vendor's material number (if maintained in the contract or the delivery plan) or the customer's.
  Plant: Plant defined in the control cycle.
  Production provisioning area: The workstation that requires the material.
  Number of KANBANS per control cycle: The R/3 System sets number of circulating containers for each control cycle.
  Contents (quantity) of a KANBAN: The R/3 System also sets the quantity (and the unit for the quantity) of a container for each control cycle.
  Number of empty containers per control cycle: This number tells the vendor the number of containers that the customer has set to 'empty.'
  Number of KANBANS for delivery: The vendor enters the number of containers delivered per control cycle.

- *Limiting the display of control cycles*
  After login, if users find the list of all control cycles too long, they can limit the number of control cycles displayed. They can select the following criteria in the right window: *material number, plant, production provisioning area*, and *ID for 'only empty containers.'* Customer entries for these criteria selected the appropriate control cycles.

- *Creating the delivery due list*
  Based on the listing of the control cycles, the vendor creates the delivery due list. The vendor enters the number of containers to be delivered for each control cycle selected and records them in the delivery due list. The system displays the delivery due list in the lower window.

- *Confirming the KANBANS for delivery*
  The vendor confirms the delivery due list with the customer. The application automatically sets all KANBANS in the delivery due list to 'in process' in the customer system. After successful confirmation has taken place, the application again lists all posted KANBANS for inspection by the vendor.

Technical information

Table 5.50   Technical information for the KANBAN IAC

Service	Users	Transaction	Development class	Module pool	Function group
PKW1	Extranet	PKW1	MDW2	SAPMMPKW	MPKW

Default settings

This application requires maintenance of data for KANBAN with the 'external procurement' replenishment strategy. This type of maintenance applies to control cycles, the corresponding replenishment strategies, information records, contracts and scheduling agreements. It does not apply to control cycles with a replenishment strategy of control type 5 (processing from a source list).

Authorizations

Inspection and refilling of product levels requires the following authorization for the R/3 identification used by the user:

Table 5.51   Authorization required for the KANBAN IAC

Authorization object	Description
F_LFA1_APP	Vendor: application authorization

Differences between the IAC and the R/3 transaction

Unlike the standard transaction, this IAC handles execution by the vendor. It represents a specially tailored cross-section of the KANBAN and therefore has a different range of functions. The IAC supports creation of various control cycles online, according to specific criteria. The vendor can also create a delivery due list and confirm it immediately. The IAC, however, can only set the KANBAN status to 'in process.'

Interfaces

Table 5.52   Interfaces used in the KANBAN IAC

Interface	Description
BAPI_CREDITOR_CHECKPASSWORD	Checks the vendor password
BAPI_KANBAN_GETLISTFORSUPPLIER	Supplies KANBAN data for the vendor
BAPI_KANBAN_SETINPROCESS	Sets the KANBAN status to 'in process'

5.5.6   Consignment stocks

A consignment defines the placement of materials owned by a vendor into the warehouse of a customer. The materials become the property of the customer only when the customer removes materials from storage in the consignment warehouse at the current daily price. Notification of removal takes place periodically, often monthly. The vendor's system carries the materials as customer consignment stocks, while the customer's system carries them as vendor consignment stocks.

The Internet application *Consignment Stocks* permits regular and comfortable queries on stocks directly from the R/3 System. The application can be used in one of two ways: at the customer site or at the vendor site. The customer can inspect the stock level in the vendor's system and compare those levels to the stocks physically present at the customer site. The vendor can also inspect stock levels to estimate expected revenue and create plans for later replenishment. Neither customer nor vendor can use the Internet for consignment orders, schedule lines or contract release orders.

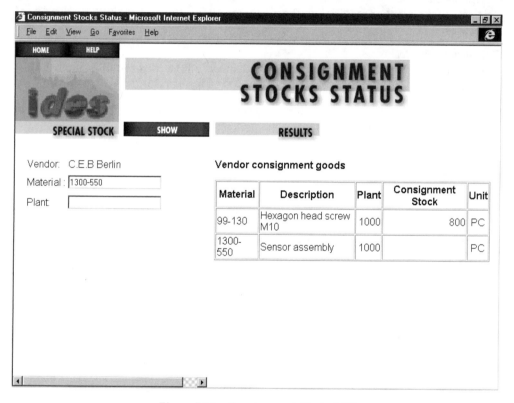

Figure 5.15   Consignment Stocks IAC

Preconditions

Only customers and vendors known to the R/3 System may query stock levels. In addition to a customer or vendor number, the user must also possess a password: user type BUS1008 (for the vendor) and user type KNA1 (for the customer).

Flow

The warehouse of a distributor of data processing products contains a consignment stock of printers made by Print, Inc. The vendor wishes to inspect the consignment stock level of the distributor for the current quarter to estimate expected revenue and to plan to for later replenishment. The vendor must perform the following steps:

- *Login by the vendor*
  In the first step, users identify themselves with a vendor number and password for authorized access to the stocks.

- *Selecting the stocks*
  Selection of a plant or material on the next page allows the user to limit the display of stocks.

- *Displaying the stocks*
  Based on the selection of stocks, the system displays all the corresponding stock levels. The vendor can then evaluate the data.

A customer who wishes to compare the physical stock levels with the consignment stock levels would perform analogous steps.

Technical information

Table 5.53   Technical information for the Consignment Stocks IAC

Service	Users	Transaction	Development class	Module pool	Function group
MBW1	Extranet	MBW1	ECMM	SAPMMBW1	

Default settings

This application requires no additional default settings.

Authorizations

The R/3 identification requires no additional authorizations.

Differences between the IAC and the R/3 transactions MB54 and MB58

Compared with transactions MB54 (display vendor consignment stocks) and MB58 (display customer consignment stocks), the Internet application has a more narrow focus and offers fewer selection screens and functions. The Internet application, however, presents a better overview of lists.

Interfaces

Table 5.54   Interfaces used in the Consignment Stocks IAC

Interface	Description
BAPI_CUSTOMER_CHECKPASSWORD	Checks the customer password

5.6   Employee self-service

In addition to processing business processes, the R/3 System also administers personnel data. Individual employees may well find some of this information, such as a colleague's telephone number, of particular interest. With the following scenarios, SAP delivers the foundation for employee self-service that permits easy access to personnel data in the R/3 System.

Table 5.55   R/3 System Internet applications in the employee self-service area

Scenario	Description
Employee directory	Displays employee information, such as telephone number and so on
Calendar of events	Lists information on events sponsored by the enterprise
Booking attendance	Books a selected event
Booked events	Lists the events booked by an individual
Cancel attendance	Cancels an already booked attendance
Employment opportunities	Announcement of vacant positions and entry of an application
Application status	Checks the processing status of an application
Time reporting	Lists the hours actually worked

5.6.1   Employee directory

The larger an enterprise is, and the more quickly it grows, the more difficult it becomes to find information on employees: telephone numbers or office numbers, for example. Employees can, of course, use a telephone list, but these readily become obsolete during rapid growth or a reorganization. Many enterprises make such information available with an electronic mail system. An international enterprise, however, can operate several different mail systems, each with a differently structured address book. Since a productive business system usually administers the information, personnel data requires frequent maintenance.

The Internet application *Employee Directory* offers a more sensible alternative. The application calculates the information directly from the personnel data in the R/3 System.

Use of the application eliminates the need to store data twice and permits central administration of personnel data at headquarters. The application supports uniform access for all subsidiaries, regardless of the mail system in use. The Intranet also offers an additional advantage: the information on a given employee can also contain other data, such as a photograph or signature.

Note: The application permits users to search for limited personnel data not protected by privacy laws.

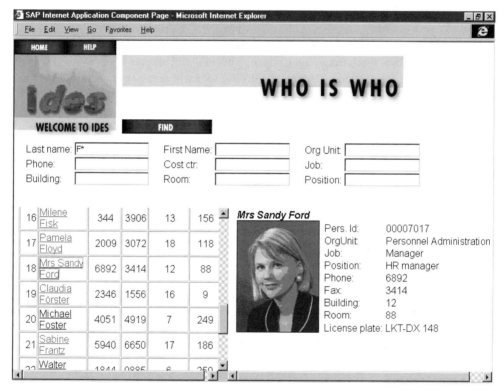

Figure 5.16   Employee Directory IAC

Preconditions

Because the application normally runs only on the Intranet and provides information to all employees, it does not require an authorization check.

Flow

An employee needs the telephone number of a colleague whom he or she has not yet met in person. The employee also wishes to see what the colleague looks like and where the colleague works. The employee must perform the following steps:

- *Entering selection criteria*
  During a search for a specific person, the application should return as short a list of results as possible. The user can limit the search by using the following criteria: *given name, family name, telephone number, building, room number, organizational unit, position, function* and *cost center*. The user can enter these criteria individually or in combination. A logical AND joins multiple entries. The application supports use on an asterisk (*), even when combined with a text.

- *Selecting the person desired*
  If several persons meeting the search criteria exist, the application lists them in the left window. Selection of a particular person displays additional information in the right window. If available, the detailed information includes a picture of the person.

Technical information

Table 5.56   Technical information for the Employee Directory IAC

Service	Users	Transaction	Development class	Module pool	Function group
PAW1	Intranet	PAW1	PBAS	SAPMPW01	

Default settings

To depict personnel information, the following information types (various categories or characteristics that can exist for a person) shown in Table 5.57 must be maintained:

Table 5.57   Information types used in the Employee Directory IAC

Info type	Description
0001	Organizational unit
0002	Data on the person
0032	Internal company data
0105	Communication

One location, which the Web server can access, should store the photographs or signatures. The location may be an optical archive or the file system of the Web server.

Authorizations

To make the application as accessible as possible, it does not require any additional authorization. If, however, administrators wish to limit display to specific persons, they must maintain the corresponding authorizations. In this case all users require an R/3 login.

Interfaces

Table 5.58　Interfaces used in the Employee Directory IAC

Interface	Description
BAPI_EMPLOYEE_GETDATA	Calculates employee data (information types 1, 2, 32)

5.6.2　Employment opportunities

An enterprise expends great effort in filling vacant positions. Advertisement, preselection, administration and processing require a great deal of time and accumulate tremendous costs.

The Internet application *Employment Opportunities* supports the human resources department in performing these tasks. Since no time zone limits operation of the Internet, it offers an ideal medium for the announcement of current employment opportunities. An Internet user can take advantage of the application to display the vacant positions at an enterprise. Each position includes a description of and requirements for the position. The application takes this information from records in the Recruitment component. This IAC also permits direct application for a given position. It also supports unsolicited applications.

Exclusive use of this medium to publicize vacant positions is hardly realistic, as too few candidates (can) use it. As a supplement to traditional methods, however, it offers several advantages. It provides a low cost alternative to newspaper advertisements; it addresses and reaches a much wider group of potential candidates. Preselection of candidates lightens the burden on the human resources department and the candidates. When candidates use this medium to submit their applications, the human resources department can decide if a particular candidate possesses the required qualifications and should continue the application process. The candidate can thus save the expense involved in sending application materials.

Preconditions

The public should have access to Employment Opportunities. Accordingly, the application requires no additional identification.

Flow

A recent graduate looks for an opportunity to enter the business world. A Web site listing various jobs contains a link to the Web page of an enterprise that uses the *Employment Opportunities* IAC to advertise all its vacant positions. To view information on a position or to submit an application, the candidate must perform the following steps:

- *Displaying open positions*
  After starting the application, candidates can display all open positions or only those in a specific region. In the latter case, they select an area in a graphic. Depending on the selection, the application displays a list of all open positions.

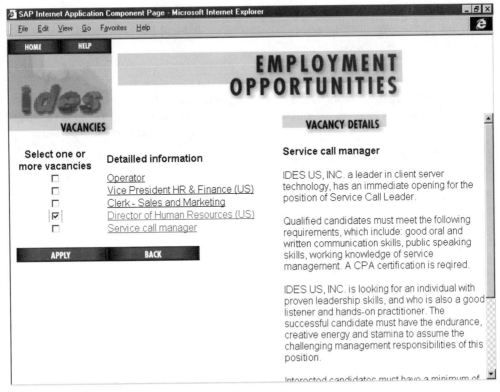

Figure 5.17   Employment Opportunities IAC

- *Selecting a position*
  The candidate selects a particular position to display additional information. The right window then displays an exact description of the position and the requirements for the candidate. In addition to text, the description can also contain multimedia elements such as images or video.

- *Completing the application form*
  If the description of a position interests the candidate, he or she can continue to use the IAC to apply for the position online. The user simply marks the position and selects the pushbutton APPLY. The left window then displays an application form that the user can complete with personal entries. The form contains several sections: users can navigate between the sections with the tab key: *personal data, education, qualifications* and *previous occupations*. The user makes the appropriate entries for each point, including information on the person. After completing the form, the candidate transmits it to the enterprise with *Send*.

- *Checking the entries*
  The R/3 System then checks the incoming application for its validity. It checks that all required fields contain an entry, for example. If the system accepts the application, it

sends the information to the human resources department. If it rejects the application, the system displays an appropriate error message that requires the candidate to change the invalid entries and resend the form.

- *Confirming the application*
  After successful transmission, the system sends the user a confirmation of the application. To permit later checks to the processing status (see the Application Status IAC), the candidate also receives a number and password. The user can change the password at will. The system creates the Internet user automatically (user type: APPLICANT).

The IAC also supports unsolicited applications. In this case, the user can enter additional information.

The human resources department evaluates the application. It can contact the candidate by letter, telephone or e-mail (if the user has entered an e-mail address).

Technical information

Table 5.59   Technical information for the Employment Opportunities IAC

Service	Users	Transaction	Development class	Module pool	Function group
PBW1	Internet	PBW1	PAPL	SAPMPW02	APPL, VAP1

Default settings

In addition to normal customizing activities for the human resources component, the Internet application requires further settings. The settings apply to the display of vacant position and the creation of applications.

Display of vacant positions

The output of a list of vacant positions implies that the R/3 System can calculate the positions. To do so, the settings given in Table 5.60 are necessary.

Table 5.60   Tables for the display of advertisements

Table	Actions
T750B	Create several advertisements for each recruitment instrument.
	Allocate a vacancy to each advertisement.
	Maintain texts for the advertisements. The system uses the text to describe the vacancy (responsibilities, required abilities, additional qualifications, and so on).
T750C	Create recruitment instrument for each region and allocate a medium type, defined with an ITNET characteristic, for each region.
T750D	Create Internet medium.
T750X/P1007	Maintain vacancies with one of the tables.

The ITNET characteristic defines the medium, applicant group, applicant range, personnel area, personnel subarea, unsolicited applicant group, references and the Internet address for e-mail.

Entry of applications

An application entered on the Internet requires data on the candidate such as name, address or qualifications. To accept this information, the application contains several forms that correspond to the info type records of the R/3 System. The following tables must be maintained to check for acceptable entries.

Table 5.61   Tables for the entry of applications

Table	Description
T522T	Salutation
T002	Language key for correspondence with the applicant
T005	Countries
T005U	Taxes: state/province key: texts
T517T	Descriptor for school type
T519T	Degrees/certifications
T518A	Check table for education
T518B	Descriptor for education
T538C	Acceptability of time/measurement units for the info types
T517X	Major area of study
T517Y	Check table for the majorr area of study
T517Z	Permissible combinations of tables T517T and T517Y
T517A	Permissible combinations of tables T517T and T519T
T574B	Descriptor for qualifications
T016T	Descriptor for sectors
T513C	Responsibilities at other/earlier employers

Authorizations

Because of its wide availability, the IAC requires no authorizations for the R/3 identification.

Interfaces

Table 5.62   Interfaces used in the Employment Opportunities IAC

Interface	Description
BAPI_APPLICANT_CREATE	Creates applicant
BAPI_APPLICANT_INITPASSWORD	Initializes the password
BAPI_APPLICANT_CREATE_PW_REG	Creates an entry for the applicant password
BAPI_APPLICANT_CHANGEPASSWORD	Changes the applicant password
P_APP_GET_LIST_OF_VACANCIES	Lists vacancies according to preselection by region
P_APP_GET_DETAIL_OF_VACANCY	Calculates the position description of a vacancy for the advertisement
P_APP_GET_INTERNET_DEFAULTS	Calculates the default values for Internet applications
P_APP_GET_SELECTION_DATA	Entry options for application form

5.6.3   Application status

A flood of applications usually accompanies an advertisement for an open position. In addition to confirmations, rejections, invitations and so on, the human resources department must deal with the heavy burden of constant inquiries on the telephone regarding the status of an application.

An application entered with the *Employment Opportunities* scenario offers the advantage of no written communications. The Internet application *Application Status* provides the candidate with the opportunity to check the status of an application at any time. Even if the application arrived in traditional form, the enterprise can allow the candidate to check its status on the Web. A confirmation letter can contain the application number and password.

Preconditions

Access to the information in the Application Status IAC requires an application number and password. The *Employment Opportunities* IAC assigns the number and password when it accepts an application. Accordingly, only the candidate can query the status of their application.

Flow

Some two weeks after submitting an application, the graduate in the *Employment Opportunities* scenario has not yet received any reaction from the enterprise. The graduate proceeds as follows:

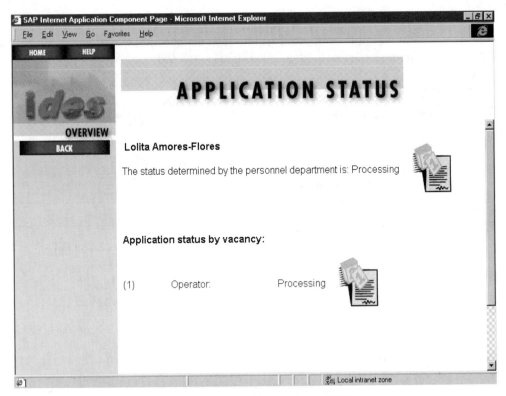

Figure 5.18   Application Status IAC

- *Login by the applicant*
  Applicants can query the status of their own application only. Each applicant must first enter the application number and password generated by the *Employment Opportunities* IAC.

- *Displaying the status*
  Using the application number, the application selects the status in the R/3 System and displays it on the following page. The status can indicate the following values: *in process, invite for interview, no suitable position currently available, offer made, applicant rejected the offer, hired.*

Technical information

Table 5.63   Technical information for the Application Status IAC

Service	Users	Transaction	Development class	Module pool	Function group
PBW2	Internet	PBW2	PAPL	SAPMPW03	APPL, VAP1

Default settings

The description of the application status requires text maintenance with transaction SO10. Entry of PAWW in the Text ID field links the status to the text.

Authorizations

Other than identification of the applicant, the IAC requires no additional authorizations.

Interfaces

Table 5.64   Interfaces used in the Application Status IAC

Interface	Description
BAPI_APPLICANT_CHANGEPASSWORD	Changes the password
BAPI_APPLICANT_CHECKEXISTENCE	Checks the existence of the applicant
BAPI_APPLICANT_CHECKPASSWORD	Checks the applicant password
BAPI_APPLICANT_GET_STATUS	Calculates the status of the application

5.6.4   Calendar of Events

An enterprise that offers training, seminars or events in general to its own employees or a wider group should publicize the events in a manner that reaches a broad range of interested parties. If the enterprise already uses the Event Management component in its R/3 System, it can administer and process these events with its R/3 System.

The *Calendar of Events* Internet application can publicize such information and make it available to the entire Intranet and Internet communities. The application uses a Calendar of Events, subdivided into topic areas, that makes current information on dates, contents, facilitators, available slots and price available around the clock. This type of publication saves the costs of printing and advertising.

Preconditions

All interested parties should have access to this service. Accordingly, the IAC requires no identification.

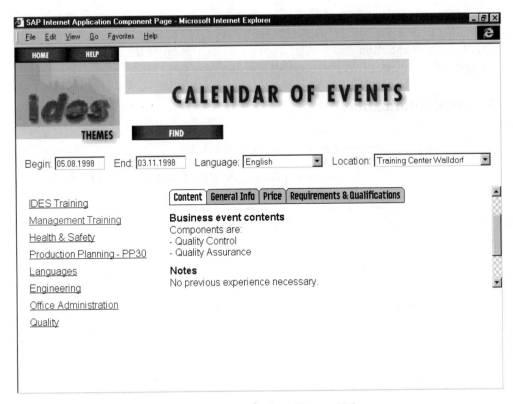

Figure 5.19   Calendar of Events IAC

Flow

A user with interest in an Internet course wishes to view the current offerings of a training company. The user wants information on the courses available, dates, contents and prices. The user would proceed as follows with the *Calendar of Events* IAC:

- *Listing the event offerings*
  Entry of a location, language and date (interval) can limit the listing of available events. The application already contains the values for the date interval: today's date as the start date and an end date suggested by the R/3 System. The user can change both dates. The lower left window displays the results of the search as a list of all applicable topic areas.

- *Selecting a topic area*
  Selection of a topic area displays the individual event offering for a given area in the right window.

- *Displaying an event*
  Detailed information on an offering becomes available by selecting a particular event with the I pushbutton. The screen displays a description of the contents along with organizational data, price, prerequisites and qualifications.

Technical information

Table 5.65   Technical information for the Calendar of Events IAC

Service	Users	Transaction	Development class	Module pool	Function group
PV0I	Internet, Intranet	PV0I	PP09		RHVI

Default settings

The use of this application requires the *Event Management* R/3 component. In addition, the R/3 System must contain a Calendar of Events with event offerings. See the online help for Calendar of Events for additional information.

Authorizations

A new activity group that contains transaction PSV2 must be created for authorization in the R/3 identification. The group can generate the required authorization profile.

Interfaces

Table 5.66   Interfaces in the Calendar of Events IAC

Interface	Description
BAPI_BUS_EVENTGROUP_LIST	Calculates the event group hierarchy
BAPI_BUS_EVENTTYPE_LIST	Lists the event types for an event group
BAPI_BUS_EVENT_LIST	Calculates event dates for an event type
BAPI_BUS_EVENTTYPE_INFO	Calculates the event types for an event group
BAPI_BUS_EVENT_INFO	Calculates data for an event type
BAPI_BUS_EVENT_LANGUAGE	Calculates the language for the event
BAPI_BUS_EVENT_LOCATION	Calculates the location for the event
BAPI_BUS_EVENT_SCHEDULE	Calculates the schedule for an event
BAPI_BUS_EVENT_INIT	Calculates default values for creation of an event offering

5.6.5   Booking attendance

If the *Calendar of Events* IAC awakes interest in an event, the user can register for it directly with the *Booking Attendance* Internet application.

To book an event, the user begins at the Calendar of Events, divided into topic areas. The Calendar of Events provides the user with information on dates, contents, facilitators, available slots and costs. The user can select an event from the list of offerings and book it. The *Booked Events* IAC provides a list of events previously booked for the user.

Preconditions

Users can execute this application with an internal R/3 identification (service PV3I) or an Internet user (service PV4I; type: PDOTYPE_PT (participant)). The user must have the identification that corresponds to the service employed.

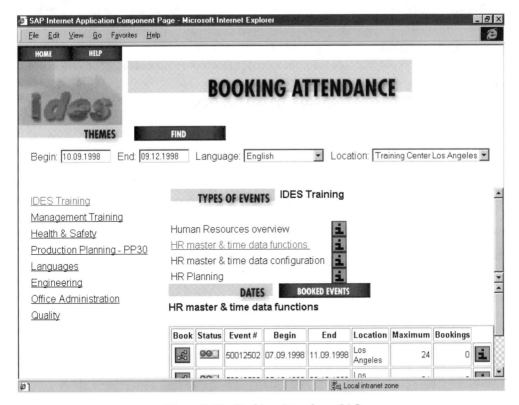

Figure 5.20   Booking Attendance IAC

Flow

The user interested in Internet courses from the last IAC now wishes to book a course concretely. To do so, the user proceeds as follows. The *Calendar of Events* IAC depicts the flow required to display the desired event. The following treats only the additional steps.

- *Login*

- *Listing the event offerings*

- *Selecting an event*
  After the user has selected a specific event, the right window displays all the dates for the event. The display also shows the status, location, maximum number of participants and completed bookings for each date.

- *Booking an event*
  After selecting the booking icon for one of the dates listed, the user sees another display of the desired event. The user can now book the event with the Confirmation pushbutton. The next overview display will show one more booking for the event.

- *Displaying detailed information*
  The I pushbutton displays detailed information for a particular date, if the user has not already seen it.

Technical information

Table 5.67   Technical information f or the Booking Attendance IAC

Service	Users	Transaction	Development class	Module pool	Function group
PV3I	Intranet	PV3I	PP09		RHVI
PV4I	Internet	PV4I	PP09		RHVI

Default settings

This application requires no default settings other than those in the *Calendar of Events* IAC.

Authorizations

This application requires no addition authorizations.

Interfaces

Table 5.68   Interfaces used in the Booking Attendance IAC

Interface	Description
BAPI_BUS_EVENTGROUP_LIST	Calculates the event group hierarchy
BAPI_BUS_EVENTTYPE_LIST	Calculates the event type for an event group
BAPI_BUS_EVENT_LIST	Calculates the event dates for an event type
BAPI_BUS_EVENTTYPE_INFO	Calculates an event type from data
BAPI_BUS_EVENT_INFO	Calculates an event from data
BAPI_BUS_EVENT_LANGUAGE	Calculates the event language
BAPI_BUS_EVENT_LOCATION	Calculates the event location
BAPI_BUS_EVENT_SCHEDULE	Calculates the schedule for an event
BAPI_BOOK_ATTENDANCE	Event management: book attendance
BAPI_ATTENDEE_BOOK_LIST	Calculates the bookings of a given attendee

5.6.6   Booked events

Interested parties receive information on events from advertisements in the media and from the *Calendar of Events* IAC. Bookings can take place in traditional ways (fax or telephone) or with the *Booking Attendance* IAC. The R/3 System administers every incoming booking, regardless of how it was entered, and can display every booking.

The *Booked Events* IAC provides event participants with constant access to all the important information on the events that they have booked (both before and after the event takes place). The information includes dates, contents, qualifications attained by attendance, facilitators and costs. The application also allows the display and administration of prebookings for courses, seminars and so on.

Two different user groups, with different authorizations, can execute this application:

- *Intranet: R/3 User (service: PV1I)*
  Within a firm, an R/3 login can provide additional authorization to certain persons, who can then view more information. For example, with proper authorizations, a department supervisor could see the events booked by department members and the qualifications the members earn. Such a user must log in to the application with an R/3 login.

- *Intranet/Internet: Web User (service: PV2I)*
  All other users (Intranet and Internet) can access all information on their individual bookings and reservations with general R/3 identification, without additional authorizations. Login takes place with an Internet user.

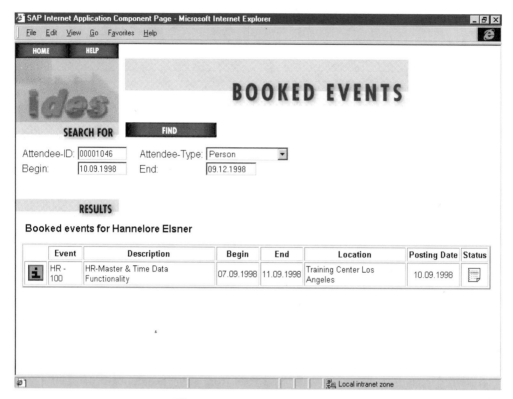

Figure 5.21   Booked Events IAC

The applications differ only in the service they use. The service for the R/3 user leaves the login parameter blank; the service for a Web user contains a general R/3 identification.

Preconditions

This IAC supports two types of authorization checks. R/3 users require an R/3 login (with the appropriate authorizations) to log into the R/3 System. To list booked events, the user also needs a participant ID. Web users requires an Internet ID (type: PDOTYPE_PT (participant)), that consists of the participant ID and the corresponding password.

Flow

A user who has already booked specific events now wishes to check if an additional date conflicts with an event already booked. To prepare for the next planned event, the user also wishes to list the contents for that event. The user starts the applications and can proceed as follows:

- *Login by the user*
  Users can log in to this IAC either with an R/3 identification or with an Internet ID (depending on the authorization assigned to the user). Identification is absolutely required, since the system uses it to calculate the appropriate list of bookings.

- *Listing booked events*
  If users logged in with service PV1I and an R/3 login, they must then enter a participant ID and participant type (containing the appropriate authorization) to list the booked events. The IAC does not require this step if login took place with an Internet user (service PV2I), since the participant ID is already present after login.
     Users can limit the list of bookings for a participant by entering a time period. Selection of the SEARCH pushbutton then finds all the reserved and booked events in that period and displays them in a table in the lower window.

- *Displaying detailed information*
  The I pushbutton and tab key display additional information on an event, such as *contents, qualifications, fees/costs, starting time, language, room* or *facilitator*.

Technical information

Table 5.69   Technical information for the Booked Events IAC

Service	Users	Transaction	Development class	Module pool	Function group
PV1I	Intranet	PV1I	PP09		RHVI
PV2I	Internet	PV2I	PP09		RHVI

Default settings

This application builds on the Calendar of Events IAC and therefore has the same default settings. The application can display bookings only if the default settings are in place.

Authorizations

The profile generator for transaction PV1I sets up the special authorizations for this application.

Interfaces

Table 5.70   Interfaces used in the Booked Events IAC

Interface	Description
BAPI_ATTENDEE_CHECKPASSWORD	Checks the participant's password
BAPI_ATTENDEE_CHANGEPASSWORD	Changes the participant's password
BAPI_ATTENDEE_BOOK_LIST	Calculates the bookings for a participant
BAPI_ATTENDEE_PREBOOK_LIST	Calculates the prebookings (reservations) for a participant
BAPI_ATTENDEE_TYPE_LIST	Internet-relevant types of participants
BAPI_COMPANY_BOOK_LIST	Calculates all the bookings for a collective participant
BAPI_COMPANY_PREBOOK_LIST	Calculates all the prebookings (reservations) for a collective participant
BAPI_BUS_EVENTTYPE_INFO	Calculates the event group from event types
BAPI_BUS_EVENT_INFO	Calculates an event type from data

5.6.7   Cancel attendance

Other appointments or commitments often require users to cancel already-booked events. Rather than performing this task with long telephone calls, users can employ the *Cancel Attendance* IAC to cancel their participation over the Internet. Users save time and know that they have canceled the correct event.

Preconditions

As in the *Booked Events* IAC, the user here requires an R/3 login (for service PV5I) or an Internet user (service PV6I; type `PDOTYPE_PT` (participant)).

Flow

A person who has already booked an event now wishes to cancel it because of scheduling conflicts. The system requires the following steps. The *Booked Events* IAC describes the flow for listing booked events. The following describes the flow only for cancellation:

- *Login by the participant*
- *Listing booked events*

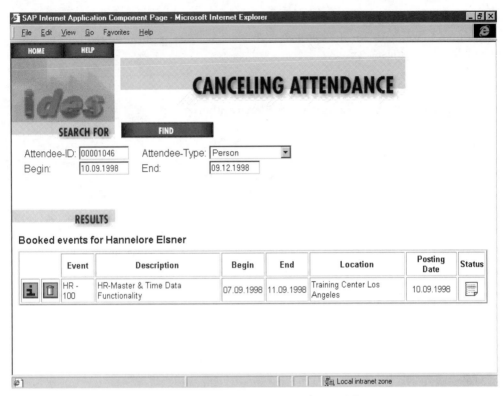

Figure 5.22 Canceling Attendance IAC

- *Canceling an event*
  The IAC displays a wastebasket icon next to every event list. Selecting the icons displays the event to be canceled and a CONFIRMATION pushbutton. Selecting the pushbutton cancels the registration.

Technical information

Table 5.71 Technical information for the Cancel Attendance IAC

Service	Users	Transaction	Development class	Module pool	Function group
PV5I	Intranet	PV5I	PP09		RHVI
PV6I	Internet	PV6I	PP09		RHVI

Default settings

Other than those made for the *Calendar of Events* IAC, this application requires no additional default settings.

Authorizations

Executing the application requires no additional authorizations.

Interfaces

Table 5.72   *Interfaces used in the Cancel Attendance IAC*

Interface	Description
BAPI_BUS_EVENTGROUP_LIST	Calculates the even group hierarchy
BAPI_BUS_EVENTTYPE_LIST	Calculates the event types for an even group
BAPI_BUS_EVENT_LIST	Calculates the event dates for an event type
BAPI_BUS_EVENTTYPE_INFO	Calculates the event type from data
BAPI_BUS_EVENT_INFO	Calculates the event from data
BAPI_BUS_EVENT_LANGUAGE	Calculates the event languages
BAPI_BUS_EVENT_LOCATION	Calculates the event locations
BAPI_BUS_EVENT_SCHEDULE	Calculates the schedule of an event
BAPI_ATTENDEE_BOOK_LIST	Calculates the bookings of a participant
BAPI_ATTENDEE_CANCEL	Cancels a booking

5.6.8   Time reporting

Employees are normally paid per hour or at a weekly rate that includes a minimum number of hours, provided that no non-pay-scale or partial payments are made. In enterprises with flexible work hours, management often asks how many hours have actually been worked in the current or previous pay period.

The *Time Reporting* Internet application permits employees (and their superiors) to call up their own time reports over the Intranet or Internet. The application supports flexible work hours and the entry of hours with 'come and go' postings.

This application rests upon the results of personnel time evaluation in the R/3 System, part of the Human Resources module.

Preconditions

R/3 identification is required for users to check their own statement of hours worked.

Flow

An employee wishes to check the hours he worked in the previous week:

- *Login by the employee*
  Only employees themselves have access to the time report . They must therefore log in with their R/3 login.

- *Listing the hours worked*
  Employees enter a time period, and the application lists the hours worked in that period.

Technical information

This application rests upon a function module, HR_TIME_SHEET_TO_HTML, rather than a transaction. The system calls the function module directly, with service XGWFCT (development class: PTIM; function group: RPTI).

Default settings

The communication info type (0105) enables linking an R/3 user with an employee number. The system assigns an employee number to every employee created in the Human Resources component. Linking a user to an employee numbers enables the system to locate time statements.

The subtype system user name SAP System (SY-UNAME) (subtype 0001) of the communication info type (0105) must be maintained. Maintenance of the info types takes place in the Human Resources component.

Authorizations

This application requires no additional authorizations.

5.7   Internal Services

Internal Services describe a collection of services that users can execute only locally on the Intranet. These service include the scenarios shown in Table 5.73.

Table 5.73   R/3 Internet applications in the Internal Services Area

Scenario	Description
Integrated Inbox and Workflow Management	Views the personal messages, general folders and list of work items of an R/3 user
Workflow Status Report	Status information on the user's workflows and work items
Internal Activity Allocation	Creates a document for allocating internal services (and/or costs)
Internal Price List	Lists prices used within a company
Project Data Confirmation	Reporting by project employees
Project Documents	Lists all the documents in a project
Asset Information	Information on an enterprise's assets
Web Reporting Browser	Collection of executable reports, arranged in a tree

Execution of all applications requires an R/3 login with the appropriate authorizations.

5.7.1   Integrated inbox and workflow management

Good communications among employees make an essential contribution to the success of an enterprise today. Frequently, however, the issues raised by frequent travel and employees working outside traditional office space hamper good communications. These difficulties separate communications from specific decision-making processes in the enterprise.

The R/3 System offers a means of distributing information to all employees with the SAP*office* component. The component permits viewing messages or general documents in public folders in addition to receiving and sending messages. Travelers may not always have the ability to access SAPoffice, however, since not every computer has a SAPGUI installed.

The Internet application *Integrated Inbox* and *Workflow Management* offers broad-based availability of office information. The IAC permits access to incoming messages and work items for the logged-in user, as well as folders and documents in general storage. The employee can also process user decisions over the Internet. The IAC can also display work items that the employee has set for resubmission.

Note: User decisions are decisions defined as a step within a workflow. User decisions constitute part of the employee's personal worklist, stored in the Workflow folder of the Inbox. A worklist constitutes a list of all work items allocated to the employee that require processing.

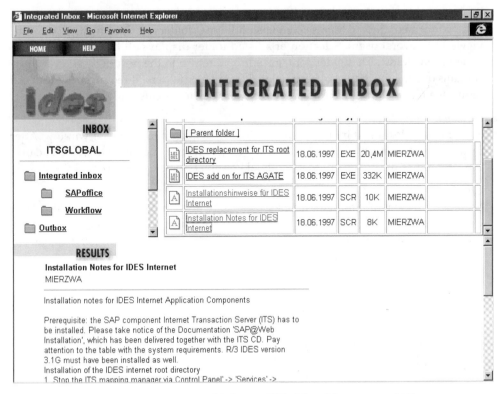

Figure 5.23   Integrated Inbox and Workflow Management IAC

Preconditions

The user requires R/3 identification to access work items and personal messages.

Flow

At the start of the working day, an employee wishes to display all the work items assigned to him and all his messages:

- *Login by the employee*
  The employee logs in to the system with his R/3 login, since the system will display only documents and work items intended that employee.

- *Listing documents or work items*
  The left window contains three main folders: Inbox, General Storage and Trash. The folders enable the user to select lists of various elements. The *Inbox* contains two additional folders: SAPoffice and Workflow. Selection of SAP*office* displays all incoming personal messages in the right window, listed with entries for the date received, the

document type and the author. Selection of the *Workflow* folder lists all the work items to be performed. *General Storage* contains additional folders or documents that can be viewed by several users. Selection of a listed folder displays all the documents contained in the folder. The folder contains a link to return to the next highest level. *Trash* contains documents that have been deleted from other folders. If required, the user can return them to their original folders, if they were deleted accidentally.

- *Displaying documents*
  Selection of a document in the document list will display it in the lower window. After reading it, the user can use the DELETE key to transfer the document to trash. The user can later return the document to its original location or delete it entirely.

- *Creating a message*
  From within General Storage, the user can create documents directly with this IAC. Users select the CREATE MESSAGE pushbutton. They then enter a title and text in the form that appears in the lower window. After the user saves the message, it appears as a new message in the appropriate folder, displayed in the upper right window.

- *Processing a user decision*
  Selection of a user decision from the *Workflow* folder displays the long texts defined as part of that decision. The Workflow System has already replaced the text variables with information from the current workflow containers. The pushbuttons displayed permit the employee to select an alternative decision. The new decision will influence further steps in the R/3 System, depending on the workflow definition in use.
  Note: The user decisions displayed by the system are always part of the employee's personal work list.

Technical information

Table 5.74   Technical information for the Integrated Inbox and Workflow Management IAC

Service	Users	Transaction	Development class	Module pool	Function group
BWSP	Intranet	BWSP	BWWF		LBW02

Default settings

The system can display SAPoffice documents only when table bwwf_mime has been maintained for the appropriate document type. The table contains all common types. The table must be expanded to include any new types.

Authorizations

For the IAC, the user requires an R/3 login with the authorizations of an office end user. The profile S_A.USER (administrator (basis rights)) contains the required authorizations. Display of user decisions is limited to users who belong to the *selected agents* of the user decision.

Differences between the IAC and the R/3 transaction

The IAC does not offer all the full range of functions of SAPoffice. The IAC does not support creating attachments, transmitting documents, displaying documents from personal folders or defining a resubmission.

Workflow Management in the IAC does not support secondary methods for a user decision and the creation of attachments. The IAC does not offer an explicit function to confirm the end of processing for a user decision.

Interfaces

Table 5.75   Interfaces used in Integrated Inbox and Workflow Management IAC

Interface	Description
BWWF_GET_WORKITEM	Work item: Read a work item (decision)
BWWF_WORKITEM_COMPLETE	Work item: Complete a work item (decision)
BWWF_GET_MIME_TYPE	Allocation of a MIME type according to the conversion key
SO_AUTHORITY_CHECK	SAPoffice: Calculates the authorization for an object
SO_FOLDER_READ_API1	SAPoffice: Reads the contents of a folder externally
SO_DOCUMENT_INSERT_API1	SAPoffice: Creates a new document in Office externally
SO_DOCUMENT_READ_API1	SAPoffice: Reads an object from a folder externally
SO_DOCUMENT_SET_STATUS_API1	SAPoffice: Sets various statuses externally
SO_DOCUMENT_DELETE_API1	SAPoffice: Deletes a document externally
SO_ATTACHMENT_INSERT_API1	SAPoffice: Creates an attachment (external)
SO_ATTACHMENT_READ_API1	SAPoffice: Reads an attachment (external)
SO_ATTACHMENT_DELETE_API1	SAPoffice: Deletes an attachment (external)
SO_OBJECT_REMOVE	SAPoffice: Removes a document (from the trash, for example)
SO_USER_READ_API1	SAPoffice: Reads SAPoffice user data for external access

5.7.2   Workflow status report

In addition to its transaction-oriented Internet applications, SAP also delivers portions of Workflow Reporting for use on the Internet. The *Workflow Status Report* IAC comprises the functions based on Web reporting technology (see Section 7.3.3: Standard Reports on the Web). The reports display already-completed work items or those work items linked to specific objects. The IAC also display work items linked to the *purchase order* object type.

Two types of work items exist: dialog (type W) and Workflow (type F). *Dialog work items* are those displayed in the list of work items. Within a workflow, they represent a single-step task that requires a dialog with the user. The system monitors the dialog steps according to date. Such a work item appears in the Integrated Inbox of all selected employees with the status ready. As soon as any agent processes the work item, the system removes it from the inboxes of the remaining agents. Processing length for a work items begins with the status *in process* and ends with the status *completed*.

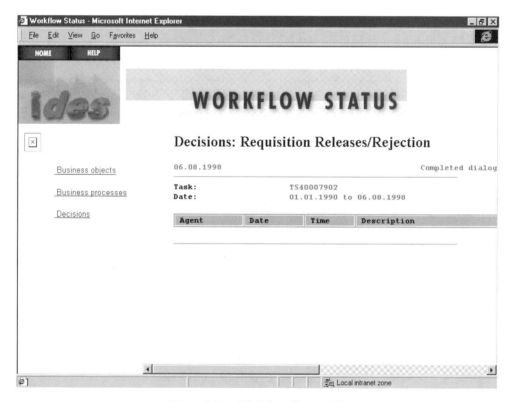

Figure 5.24   Workflow Status IAC

A *workflow* represents a multistep task (workflow task/workflow template). The start of every multistep task generates a workflow. Unlike dialog work items, these tasks do not appear in the list of work items.

Preconditions

To execute reports, the user requires an R/3 login with the appropriate authorizations.

Flow

The Internet application permits execution of specific reports, called from the start page. The reports include the following areas:

- *Completed work items*
  This report lists the work items, current agents and processing length of all work items with the status *completed*. The following selection parameters can limit the number of displayed work items during execution of the report:
  Evaluation period: Selection of all work items completed in this period.
  Agent: Person currently processing the work items.
  Task: Selection of all work items that represent a single-step task.

- *Status of a purchase order*
  This report selects all workflows and work items that represent only single steps, if the steps relate to a specific item in a purchase order. The application lists the items along with type, status, starting data and work item text. The list does not include the work items that belong to a workflow. Users can enter purchase order number and item number as selection criteria.
  Note: A relationship exists between a purchase order and a work item whenever an element in the work item container or workflow container references the purchase order.

- *Overview: purchase orders*
  As in the case of the previous report, this list includes only single-step workflows and work items related to a purchase order and entered after the date specified. The list also includes type, status, start date and work item text.

Technical information

The IAC uses the reports shown in Table 5.76.

Table 5.76   Reports in the Workflow Status Report IAC

Report	Description
RSWIDONE	Completed work items according to agent and task
RMW3OINS	Status of a purchase order
RMW3OTYP	Overview of purchase orders

Default settings

Reports do not require any additional default settings.

Authorizations

The reports used in this IAC are all part of an authorization group. To execute reports, the user requires authorizations for the following authorization groups:

Table 5.77   Authorization groups of reports in the Workflow Status Report IAC

Authorization group	Description
SWI_WLA	Completed work items
SWI_OA	Status of a purchase order, overview of purchase orders

To start a report, a user also needs additional authorizations for object S_PROGRAM (Table 5.78).

Table 5.78   Required authorizations for reports in the Workflow Status Report IAC

Authorization	Description	Meaning
S_WF_INF_OA	Selects work items for a business object	"SUBMIT" authorization for reports in authorization group SWI_OA
S_WF_INF_WLA	Execute workload analysis	"SUBMIT" authorization for reports in authorization group SWI_WLA

5.7.3   Internal activity allocation

Internal Activity Allocation enters the cost of internal operating expenses, such as repairs and consulting services. The R/3 System measures, enters and calculates the cost of these services. The cost center that provided the service then posts to the account of the recipient.

The *Internal Activity Allocation* Internet application enables worldwide entry of such services. The application contributes to rapid entry and immediate calculation: verification of costs appear in the affected cost center immediately after entry. The system can debit the cost center immediately after provision of the service. The prices (tariffs) for internal services can be taken from the *Internal Price List* IAC.

Preconditions

To enter internal services, the user requires an R/3 login with the appropriate authorizations.

Flow

A piece of equipment fails in an productive enterprise. An internal shop is designated to perform the required repairs. After completion of the repairs, the associated costs are to be debited to the productive department.

- *Login by the services entry clerk*
  Only certain persons may enter services. Users must first log in to the R/3 System with an R/3 identification. Individual entries are made on the following page.

- *Completing the document header*
  In addition to information on the specific service, the user must also enter general information in the document header (left window) such as the sender's cost center and the type of service. The user can overwrite the values suggested by the system for the posting date and controlling area. The document header also indicates the object to which the services will be settled. The user can select between *cost center*, *tasks* and *Project Structure Plan (PSP) elements.*

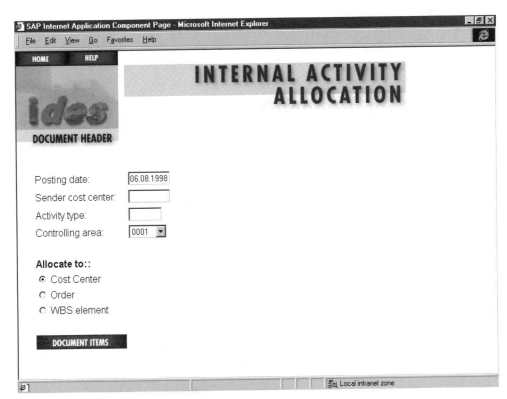

Figure 5.25   Internal Activity Allocation IAC

- *Entering document items*

  The pushbutton for document items permits entry of up to five document items in the right window. Entries here include the consumption of services and the receiving object. The application automatically takes the service unit from the service type. To check the entries, the user can display a control total before saving them. This system also displays controlling area currency, positive or negative totals and the fixed portion of settled costs. After the user saves the document, the system returns the document number used to post the service settlement.

Technical information

Table 5.79   Technical information for the Internal Activity Allocation IAC

Service	Users	Transaction	Development class	Module pool	Function group
ILV1	Intranet	KB22	KBAS	SAPMK23B	

Default settings

To enter services on the Internet, the appropriate service type must exist in the R/3 System. The cost center of the recipient is debited with the product of the plan activity price and the quantity entered. Both cost centers must recognize the plan activity price for the type of service.

Authorizations

To enter services, the R/3 login requires authorization for internal service settlement (Table 5.80).

Table 5.80   Required authorization for the Internal Activity Allocation IAC

Authorization object	Description
K_VRGNG	CO: transaction, actual postings and plan/actual settlements

Differences between the IAC and the R/3 transaction KB21

Compared with the standard R/3 transaction KB21, this application offers limited functions. Settlement, for example, can take place only in version 0 (plan/actual). In addition, the IAC does not support manual entry of document numbers (external number assignment). The system always generates document numbers automatically (internal number assignment). The application does not support entry of senders and receivers in the same list screen. Users must enter all receivers for a fixed sender before they can enter the next sender. The IAC offers entry templates for internal cost allocation only to cost centers, tasks and PSP elements. Cost objects, customer orders, run schedule headers and business processes are not considered receivers for internal cost allocation on the Internet.

Interfaces

The IAC uses the interfaces of module pools SAPMK23B, generally used for R/3 transaction in the area of *actual postings*.

5.7.4   Internal price list

The system settles internal services based upon the tariffs contained in internal price lists. Use of the *Internal Price List* lists the settlement tariffs valid on a particular date. This application has two major functions. First, users can check the accuracy of services already settled. Second, users can determine the price of services at different times and from different cost centers before taking advantage of the service.

Preconditions

Only specific persons may list internal price lists. Users therefore require an R/3 login with the appropriate authorizations.

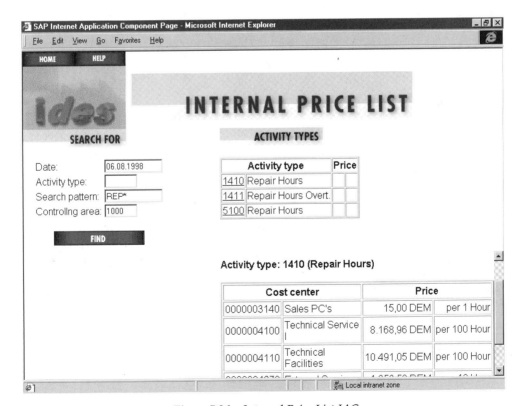

Figure 5.26   Internal Price List IAC

Flow

An internal shop repairs a defective machine. The cost center of the receiver is then debited with the cost of the internal services. The person responsible for the cost center then requires the tariffs used in posting the services:

- *Login by the user*
  The user must first log in with an R/3 identification as an authorized user.

- *Selection of the service types*
  The corresponding service type manages the display of tariffs. Accordingly, the user must first select the service types desired. The user can limit the number of service types with the following search criteria: *date, service type, search term* and *controlling area*. The user must enter a date. The application then calculates the tariffs for the appropriate period (month/year). Entry of key for one service type will select exactly that service type. Users can also perform generic searches. If the user enters a search term, the search returns all the service types that contain the search text in the key, name or description. A logical AND links user entries.

- *Displaying tariffs*
  The application displays the selected service types in the upper right window. Selection of a particular service type displays all the corresponding tariffs and cost centers in the lower window.

Technical information

Table 5.81   Technical information for the Internal Price List IAC

Service	Users	Transaction	Development class	Module pool	Function group
ILP1	Intranet	KW3P	KINT		KW3P

Default settings

The system replaces the date field with the current date whenever the application starts. It also uses 1000 as the value for the controlling area. However, the HTML template, SAPLKW3P_1010.HTML, rather than the transaction, stores the value. Users can set the display of the controlling area by using the following values in the CO_AREA_MODE field: HIDE suppresses display of the controlling area, SHOW displays it and INPUT declares the field as an entry field.

The application is similar to the tariff report available in the R/3 System. If the tariff report was generated over more than one period, however, the tariffs are calculated accordingly. The values generated by the R/3 System can therefore differ from those generated by the Internet application.

Authorizations

Display of internal prices requires display authorization for all controlling areas and for the service type master in the desired controlling area.

Table 5.82   Authorizations required for the Internal Price List IAC

Authorization object	Required authorization	Description
S_TABU_DIS	ACTVT = 03, DICBERCLS = KC	Display authorization: controlling area
K_CSLA	ACTVT = 03, KOKRS	Service type master record in the controlling area
S_TCODE	KW3P	Transaction authorization

Interfaces

Table 5.83   Interfaces used in the Internal Price List IAC

Interface	Description
BAPI_ACTIVITYTYPE_GETLIST	Calculates the list of service types according to the selection criteria
BAPI_ACTIVITYTYPE_GETPRICES	Calculates the tariffs for service types on a particular date
BAPI_CONTROLLINGAREA_GETDETAIL	Calculates detailed information for the controlling area

5.7.5   Project data confirmation

Project managers always require a quick overview of the current activities in a project. To provide an overview, employees working on the project must confirm the tasks they perform. Project managers often travel or must work at customer sites. The telephone frequently remains the only communications alternative.

The *Project Data Confirmation* Internet application offers a much more elegant solution. The application enables project participants to confirm their data over the Internet. The application also supports creation of reports. Quick confirmations offer an obvious advantage: early recognition of problems and introduction of corrective measures. Confirmations also provide the basis for actual schedules and actual costs. Processes in a project area based on a network that determines the order and dates in which tasks are performed. Confirmations, therefore, always refer to a process in the network. Confirmations that enter the R/3 System over the IAC are processed in the same manner as confirmations entered directly into the system.

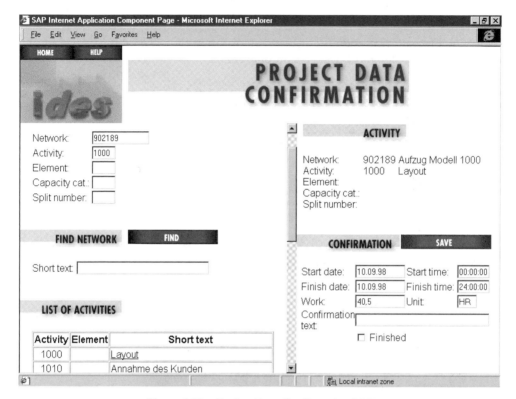

Figure 5.27   Project Data Confirmation IAC

Preconditions

Only authorized project members may enter notification. The members therefore require an R/3 login.

Flow

A firm manages a large project involving many subordinate areas of the customer's business at several different sites. To coordinate the subprojects, the project manager travels a great deal: her talents do not include bilocation. To maintain the schedule agreed upon at the start of the project, the manager needs an overview of the current situation and the progress made on the subprojects. Project members contribute to the overview by entering confirmations related to a network activity:

- *Login by the project member*
  The user logs in with R/3 identification to confirm identity and to permit an authorization check.

- *Selecting the type of confirmation*
  On the first page, the user decides to enter a confirmation for an individual activity or for a group of activities. The latter would involve a collective confirmation. The next page offers the user the opportunity to limit, according to the following search criteria, the number of networks displayed by the system: *network, activity, element, capacity type, split number.*

- *Entering the confirmation*
  Depending upon the selection made by the user, the system displays a list of all the relevant networks or pools of confirmations. Selection of a list item allows the user to enter detailed information on the activity, such as *starting date, ending date, work, short text* or *closed activities.* To update the R/3 System, the user must now save the confirmation. The project manager has access to the information immediately after the user saves it.

Technical information

Table 5.84   Technical information for the Project Data Confirmation IAC

Service	Users	Transaction	Development class	Module pool	Function group
CNW1	Intranet	CNW1	CNWW	SAPMCNW1	

Default settings

This application automatically provides default values for dates and work. It also takes the service type and plant from information supplied in the activity.

Authorizations

Only persons whose R/3 login includes the authorizations in Table 5.85 may create confirmations.

Table 5.85   Authorizations required for the Project Data Confirmation IAC

Authorization	Description
C_AFKO_AWK	CIM: Plant for the request type
C_AFKO_DIS	Network: Material requirements planning group (plant) and transaction type
C_AFRU_APL	Confirmation: Authorization for actual workstation
C_MLST_BGR	PS: Milestone (authorization group)
C_PROJ_TCD	PS: Transaction-dependent authorizations in the Project System
M_MSEG_BWA	Goods movements: Movement type
M_MSEG_WWA	Goods movements: Plant
PLOG	PD: Human Resources Planning
P_ABAP	HR: Reporting
P_ORIGIN	HR: Master data
P_ORGXX	HR: Master data additional check
P_PCLX	HR: Cluster
S_TCODE	Checks the transaction code at the start of the transaction

Differences between the IAC and the R/3 transaction

The Internet application does not support setting the user status or the entry of a long text. If an error appears in costing, the IAC cannot display the error log.

Interfaces

Table 5.86   Interfaces used in Project Data Confirmation IAC

Interface	Description
CO_RU_CONFIRMATION_ADD	Inserts a confirmation (without checking)
CO_RU_CONFIRMATION_POST	Final routine: inserts/cancels a confirmation
CO_RU_DEQUEUE_ALL	CIM Confirmation: unlocks all unposted activities
CO_RU_DATA_RESET	CIM Confirmation: resets tables
CO_RU_CONFIRMATION_CHECK	CIM Confirmation: checks confirmation data
CO_RU_CONFIRMATION_PREPARE	CIM Confirmation: checks confirmation key and prepares activity data

5.7.6 Project documents on the Internet

A host of documents usually accompany projects: logs, schedules, specifications, calculations or graphics. Every project member should have access to these documents at all times from any location.

The *Project Documents* application provides ideal access to these documents. Every project member can access project-related information administered in the document management system of the R/3 System. This ability has important implications for decentralized project planning and control. The application can display all types of documents stores in the project information system except for *Project System* (PS) texts.

Preconditions

To access project documents, the user requires an R/3 login with the appropriate authorizations.

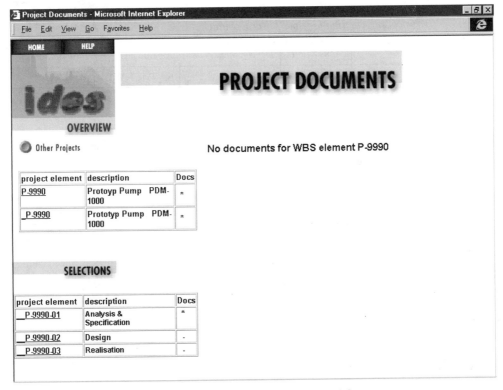

Figure 5.28   Project Documents IAC

Flow

A project member would like to have information on the last meeting with the customer. The member displays the minutes of the meeting:

- *Login by the project member*
  Only members of the project may access project documents. The user must therefore log in with an R/3 identification that contains the required authorizations.

- *Displaying a document*
  After the user selects a project, the right side of the display lists all the corresponding documents. The display includes a description of the documents and *document type*, *title* and *version*. Selection of a document transmits the corresponding file to the browser. Depending on the MIME type, the application may also start the proper viewer with the document.

Technical information

Table 5.87   Technical Information for the Project Documents IAC

Service	Users	Transaction	Development class	Module pool	Function group
CNW2	Intranet	CNW2	CNWW	SAPMCNW1	

Default settings

Presentation of project documents in the R/3 System requires generation of a hierarchy that lists the project elements and their documents.

To create the hierarchy, users select TOOLS | INTRANET | HIERARCHY   FOR DOCUMENTS in the Project Information System. They then set the selection criteria that determine which project elements should appear in the hierarchy. They must also define the level of detail for the hierarchy.

Authorizations

To access project documents, the R/3 identification requires the authorizations in Table 5.88.

Table 5.88   Authorizations required for the Project Documents IAC

Authorization object	Description
C_DRAW_BGR	CA: Authorization group
C_DRAW_DOK	CA: Original data
S_TCODE	Checks the transaction code at the start of the transaction

5.7.7   Asset information

The Asset Management (AM) component of the R/3 System administers and controls assets that exist in an enterprise. The component handles depreciation, interest, insurance and so on for individual assets.

The kernel of the *Asset Information* Internet application displays accounting information on these assets. The application permits employees without training in asset accounting or access to an R/3 System to view this information. A business traveler in an international enterprise can examine local assets over the Internet before beginning the trip.

Preconditions

Only authorized employees can access asset information. These employees require an R/3 login with the appropriate authorizations.

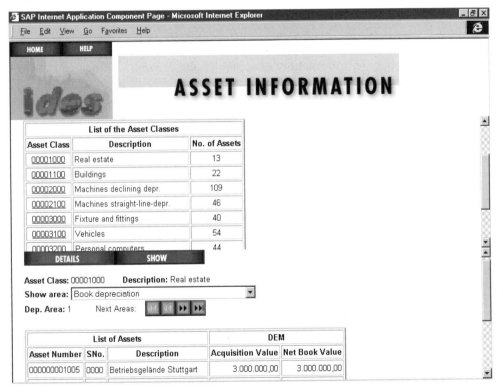

Figure 5.29   Asset Information IAC

Flow

The CFO of an European enterprise wishes to view the residual book value of specific assets in an American branch. The CFO starts the IAC on the R/3 System used at the local branch (provided that the local system maintains the assets):

- *Login*
  To retrieve information on assets, the user must log in to the R/3 System with R/3 identification.

- *Entering selection parameters*
  Selection of specific assets first requires entry of certain selection parameters. The display of assets can be limited by the mandatory company code and *business area, plant, asset class, fixed assets, manufacturer, property, cost center* and *customer-specific groupings.*

- *Displaying the asset overview*
  The selection first produces a display of asset classes and quantities in the left window of the following page. An additional selection of an asset class displays all the assets for the class in the right window with acquisition and production costs and with residual book value.

- *Displaying detailed information on assets*
  Selection of an asset displays detailed information on the next page. The application displays the following information: *asset number and description, activation date, cost center, manufacturer, customer (vendor), evaluation group (1-5), investment tax ID* and *residual book value.*

Technical information

Table 5.89   Technical information for the Asset Information IAC

Service	Users	Transaction	Development class	Module pool	Function group
AWW1	Intranet	AWW1	AA	SAPMAWW1	

Default settings

The application requires no additional default settings.

Authorizations

The IAC requires the authorizations of asset accounting to maintain master data for the assets being evaluated (authorization objects: company code/plant, company code/business area, company code/asset class).

Interfaces

Table 5.90 Interfaces used in the Asset Information IAC

Interface	Description
FI_AA_VALUES_CALCULATE	Calculates all meaningful value fields from table ANLC
GET_NEXT_ANLC	Prepares table ANLC for the next asset

5.7.8   Web reporting browser

The display of various facts or numbers does not always require a transaction as an application. Often, reports executed on a regular basis prove sufficient. SAP delivers a variety of standard reports, and customers can easily develop additional reports with far less effort than that required by transactions.

The *Web Reporting Browser* IAC enables execution of reports over the Web in much the same manner as the Workflow Status scenario. A report tree lists the reports. Users can navigate among the reports and execute them directly from the tree. Report trees are hierarchical structures that contain standard or user-specific reports arranged according to application and application area. Users can change, modify or regenerate the standard report trees delivered with the R/3 System. The primary advantage of Web reporting is speed: a newly developed report can be executed immediately on the Web, without having to add any Web-specific supplements to it.

Preconditions

Security concerns demand that users of Web reporting log in to the system with an R/3 login.

Flow

A user has already created an individual report tree in the R/3 system. The tree contains the user's most important reports. To execute the reports over the Web, the user proceeds as follows:

- *Login*
  To execute reports on the Web, the user must first log in to the R/3 System.

- *Navigating in the report tree*
  The report tree is divided into various application areas. The user selects the proper area to navigate to the required report. A click of the mouse on the report name executes the report.

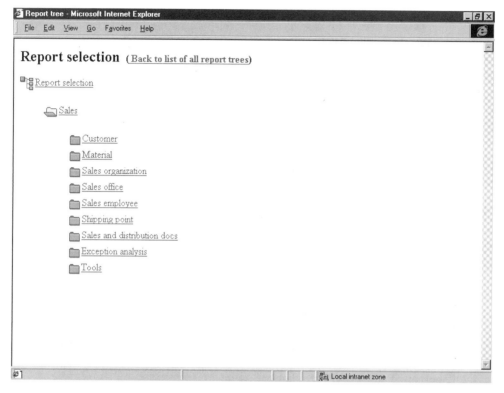

Figure 5.30　Web Reporting Browser IAC

- *Executing a report*

  Depending upon the report, the user may have to enter selection parameters before executing the report. A click of the mouse on the OK button executes the report and displays the result on the following page.

Technical information

This IAC is not based on a transaction. See Chapter 7 for a description of executing reports over the Web. The application uses the WWW_GET_TREE_LIST function module to display the report tree.

Default settings

This application rests upon the report tree in the R/3 System. Transaction SERP generates the report tree. Additional settings depend upon the individual reports.

Authorizations

Authorizations for this application depend upon the individual reports in the report tree.

Web functions

Navigation in the report tree and execution of reports takes place with the web-enabled function modules given in Table 5.91:

Table 5.91   Function modules for access to reports in a report tree

Function Module	Description
WWW_GET_TREE_LIST	Displays all report trees
WWW_GET_TREE_NODE	Displays the contents of a node
WWW_GET_NODE_LIST	Displays a list of nodes
WWW_GET_SELSCREEN	Outputs the entry screen for a report
WWW_GET_REPORT	Executes a report

5.8   Distributed business applications

The use of previously developed Internet applications stretches the operation of R/3 functions to the reach of a much wider group of users. Such applications supplement business processes internally. The applications also implement and employ the processes beyond the boundaries of the enterprise. In addition, however, the business-to-business area offers intriguing possibilities for the design of business processes. Section 1.4 presented the requirements of supply chains in the future: chains that demand an information flow that extends beyond any one enterprise. The supply chain thus takes on a new meaning. It becomes a communication system that permits the individual entities to act as independent units, but binds the entities together in an information flow that drives the supply chain with customer demand.

The applications described above limit themselves to the interaction of one user with one concrete business system. Even here, designs can stretch integration to additional applications. For example, at this time in the KANBAN IAC, a vendor can only examine containers at a customer site and confirm additional deliveries with the customer. The vendor cannot yet simultaneously create a new delivery for the customer in its own business system.

The simultaneous integration of several parties into the supply chain demands seamless interaction between different business applications, all of which operate on different or distributed systems. In recent years, industry sectors that particularly depend upon smoothly flowing information in the supply chain (such as the automobile industry) have taken measures to install such cross-system processes. Instead of traditional paper documents, enterprises can transmit business messages directly with Electronic Data

From EDI to a distributed transaction

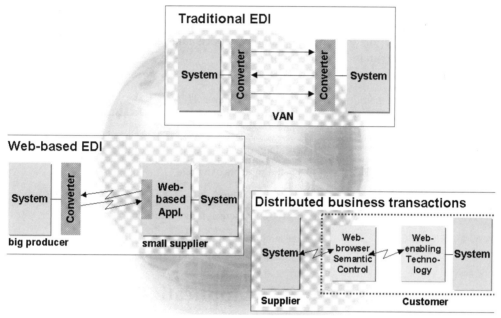

Figure 5.31   The evolution of EDI

Interchange (EDI). These transmissions can accelerate logistics processes significantly. Standard EDI messages exist for the most important processes, such as quotation and order, that can trigger a transaction in the target system. Despite the uncontested advantages, use of EDI has not spread beyond certain industries. The limitations of EDI provide the reason for its limited use. EDI systems are expensive to create and operate, are complex to maintain and currently operate in only certain sectors. The basic network infrastructure for Value Added Networks (VANs) is not public; fixed business relationships operate in the long-term.

For some sectors, the asynchronous character of EDI technology poses a decisive problem. The transmitting system generates and sends a message that reflects a specific state of information. Consider an article at a particular price as an example. When it sends a message, the transmitting system does not know if the target system has a suitable information environment. In this case, the article costs $5.00. The transmitting system knows that the recipient has a suitable environment only when it receives a confirmation from the recipient.

The use of Internet technology and the creation of business-to-business scenarios can partially solve these problems. 'Semantic integration' of the two systems that enable such distributed business transactions plays a decisive role. One transaction handles information from both systems (customer and vendor). A common information base can then trigger a business process that both system process synchronously. For example, buyers would reliably know the price and availability of a product when making and order, since information would come from the vendor's system. The two systems could then exchange the information about the resulting 'business objects,' such as order and customer request. The use of such scenarios and systems can include many more parts of the supply chain in the business processes of each enterprise than could previous scenarios and systems.

SAP took the first step in the direction of distributed business applications with the *Procurement via Catalogs* IAC, implemented in R/3 release 4.0A. Previously, when the warehouse did not contain a material requested by an employee, the purchasing department had to create a purchase order for the vendor from the requisition. This process was not only slow, but also demanded several resources on both sides to create and accept the order.

The integration of requisitions of an enterprise with the product catalog of a vendor provides a much more efficient solution. An employee can transfer the data on the required material directly from the vendor's product catalog into the requisition. At the same time, the business system of the vendor would generate a customer order. The following chapter discusses this application in detail.

5.8.1   Procurement via catalogs

Within an enterprise, many employees requisition materials. Examples include office supplies for secretaries and screws for the production department. The *Purchase Requisitions* IAC implements requests for supplies. Because the application includes the vendor's catalog, it simplifies procurement of materials and makes it more comfortable. An employee can search to procure a desk chair both in the R/3 System's catalog and in external catalogs. The system then records the selected chair in the list of materials for procurement. The user need not know the material number to complete the transaction. When the system records the selection, it automatically takes the material number from the internal or external catalog. If the user happens to know the number, the user can enter it directly. If the catalog does not contain the material, the user can enter a description along with the requisition. The user need not know if the R/3 System creates a reservation, a purchase order or an order to satisfy the requisition.

When the application uses a link to an external catalog, it closes the catalog after the user selects the material and then creates an order in the IAC. If the user made a selection from the SAP product catalog, the system reopens the catalog with the order data after the user has selected an item. It then generates a customer order and returns a customer order number to the user. Once the system has created the number, the system can update the order.

Preconditions

To procure materials with the IAC, the user requires an R/3 login with the appropriate authorizations.

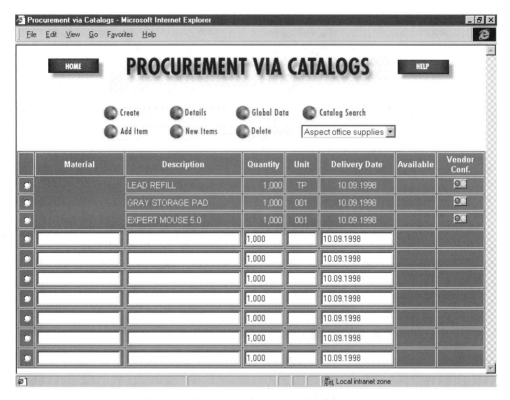

Figure 5.32   Procurement via Catalogs IAC

Flow

An employee wishes to requisition 100 transparencies for an overhead projector and a
new set of markers for the transparencies. The user enters the requisition on the Internet
as follows:

- *Login by the employee*
  The purchase requisition must contain the name of the person making the request. The
  user must therefore log in to the system with an R/3 identification. The following entry
  template permits the user to enter a description of the material directly, or to search for
  it in an external catalog.

- *Searching with a catalog*
  If users wish to search for the material through a catalog, they can select a catalog from
  the list of possible entries (above right) and then branch to the selected catalog with the
  CATALOG SEARCH pushbutton. A successful search takes the material, the source, and
  the price from the catalog and transfers the data to the IAC. In this case, the system
  uses the entries to generate a new item in the overview screen of the IAC. If possible,
  the catalog returns the SAP material number to the IAC. If the system can return only

the vendor's material number and the vendor number, it searches the info records for
the vendor with these entries. If the system can return only the manufacturer part
number, it searches the material master record with these entries. If the system can
determine the SAP material number, it executes an availability check and displays the
result graphically.

- *Displaying detailed information*
  The user can display detail data for each item with the DETAILS pushbutton. The
  details can include information on quantity, date, requester or item text. If the item
  refers to an SAP material master, the system also displays the availability data. From
  this display, the user can again branch to the catalog; the system transfers the description of the material as a search criterion. If the user has changed the quantity, the
  system can reconfirm availability of the item from the vendor.

- *Maintaining global data*
  Users can employ the GLOBAL DATA pushbutton to maintain data valid for all items
  (materials group, document type or account-assignment category).

- *Saving the items*
  Once the user has entered all the materials for a requisition, the CREATE pushbutton
  saves the items. The system then displays a confirmation screen.

Depending on the settings in Customizing, the R/3 System generates purchase orders,
reservations and/or orders from this application. If the application has taken a material
from the SAP product catalog, the R/3 System creates an order and then uses the order to
create a customer order in the Sales and Distribution component. The system writes the
customer order number into the order confirmation number for the item. The confirmation screen thus displays both the order number and the customer order number.

Data exchange between the IAC and a catalog

Communication with an external catalog takes place over an exactly specified interface. The
IAC, however, is not linked to catalogs from specific software firms. As long as a catalog can
be addressed over the defined interface, the IAC can use any external catalog application.

Communication between the applications

This IAC implements, for the first time, the interaction between two different Internet
applications that store passed values in a URL. When called, the catalog application
receives a *Return URL* (called a HOOK-URL in Customizing). This URL allows the system
to transfer the data selected in the catalog application into the input mask of the current
IAC. The catalog system expands the URL with the appropriate parameters and values in
the catalog application. The Internet application holds fields ready to accept this data; the
URL must fill the fields.

Data transfer from the IAC to the catalog application

Before running this IAC all information required to start a catalog application must be entered in Customizing for permissible catalogs (see below). For each catalog, this information must include the Return URL and address data such as the user name or a category. The data, however, depends on each catalog and is maintained with view VC_TMW03. With the R/3 System, SAP also delivers model settings for the SAP product catalog and for the catalog of the firm Aspect.

Data transfer from the catalog application to the IAC

The following fields in the R/3 transaction are intended to retrieve data on a selected material from a catalog. The catalog application must fill the fields with the Return URL (Table 5.92).

Table 5.92   Entry fields for data transfer from a catalog

Name	Description
NEW_ITEM-DESCRIPTION	Description of the material
NEW_ITEM-MATNR	Number of the material master record
NEW_ITEM-QUANTITY	Quantity ordered
NEW_ITEM-UNIT	Quantity unit
NEW_ITEM-PRICE	Price for the material in the catalog
NEW_ITEM-PRICEUNIT	Unit to which the price applies
NEW_ITEM-CURRENCY	Currency
NEW_ITEM-LEADTIME	Number of working days for the material to become available (lead time)
NEW_ITEM-VENDOR	Vendor number, if the material is procured from a broker
NEW_ITEM-VENDORMAT	Vendor material number
NEW_ITEM-MANUFACTMAT	Manufacturer material number
NEW_ITEM-MANUFACTCODE	Manufacturer number

These fields have fixed length which users cannot exceed. See the online documentation of the R/3 System for additional information.

Customizing settings

A Customizing transaction has been developed for this application that enables the following settings:

- Material groups for a purchasing group and the documents generated during a save. Table TMW01 holds these entries.

- Permissible catalogs.

The settings for permissible catalogs depend on material groups and plants. These settings determine which catalogs the system permits and includes in the list of possible entries. A new table, TMW02, was created to contain the material group, the plant, a catalog identifier and a vendor number (optional).

View VC_TMW03 stores the individual values required to address the catalog application. The view can contain field names and contents for the catalog identifier. The contents of the Name field differ for each catalog. This structure enables dynamic generation of catalog calls. Table 5.93 displays model entries for the catalog from Aspect.

Table 5.93   Sample entries for view VC_TMW03

Catalog ID	Counter	Name	Contents
Aspect1	1	USERNAME	SY-UNAME
Aspect1	2	SERVICE	3
Aspect1	3	CATEGORY	XYZ
Aspect1	4	HOOK-URL	www.sap...

Various catalog identifiers implement the different categories of catalogs. Table TMW3TEXT stores a language-dependent description of the catalog. Users can also block individual catalogs.

Additional technical information

Table 5.94   Technical information for the Procurement via Catalogs IAC

Service	Users	Transaction	Development class	Module pool	Function group
MEW0	Intranet	MEW0	MEW	SAPMMWE0	

Default settings

Users should make the following default settings or check them before using the IAC.

Under *Internet Application Components*, Customizing for Purchasing sets the documents (purchase order, reservation, order) generated during a save according to material group and purchasing group. The SAPLMEWP enhancement determines the object generated. The catalogs permitted for each material group must also be set to determine how the system calls the catalogs (see *Customizing Settings*, above).

User-specific parameters can preallocate important user information that the application requires. If no entries are present, the application asks for the data directly. The following values can be preallocated:

Table 5.95   Default parameters in the Procurement via Catalogs IAC

Parameter	Description
WRK	Plant for which the materials are maintained
LAG	Storage location
BSA	Document type used to create the purchase order
BWA	Movement type for reservations
EKG	Purchasing group
CNT	Cost center to which the purchase order or reservation is posted

Authorizations

Creation of requisitions with this application must depend on settings in Customizing and include allocation of the following authorizations with activity 01 (create):

Table 5.96   Authorizations required for the Procurement via Catalogs IAC

Authorization object	Description
M_BANF_BSA	Document type in the purchase order
M_BANF_EKG	Purchasing group in the purchase order
M_BANF_EKO	Purchasing organization in the purchase order
M_BANF_WRK	Plant in the purchase order
M_BEST_BSA	Document type in the order
M_BEST_EKG	Purchasing group in the order
M_BEST_EKO	Purchasing organization in the order
M_BEST_WRK	Plant in the order
M_MRES_BWA	Reservations: Movement type
M_MRES_WWA	Reservations: Plant

Interfaces

Table 5.97   Interfaces in the Procurement via Catalogs IAC

Interface	Description
BAPI_HELPVALUES_GETLIST	Determines valid entry values (F4) for fields in BAPI parameters
BAPI_MATERIAL_AVAILABILITY	Availability information
BAPI_MATERIAL_GETLIST	Calculates a list of materials from a transferred search criterion
BAPI_RESERVATION_CREATE	Creates a reservation
BAPI_PO_CREATE	Creates an order
BAPI_REQUISITION_CREATE	Creates a requisition
BAPI_INFORECORD_GETLIST	Displays purchasing information records
BAPI_CREDITOR_FIND	Determines the creditor
BAPI_PROCOPERATION_GETCATALOGS	Determines valid catalogs as F4 Help
BAPI_PROCOPERATION_GETINFO	Analyzes the objects to be generated in purchasing

6 Enhanced use of ITS technology

With the Internet Transaction Server (ITS), SAP permits operation of R/3 System applications over the Internet. Standard IACs seek to provide as universally valid as possible and interesting scenarios with simple and intuitive operation to a wide range of users. The firm iXOS Software AG has developed new scenarios in the form of technology studies. The new scenarios include additional flow techniques and permit more user access to the R/3 System. One such technology implements Web access to business documents stored in an electronic archive system linked to an R/3 System. Another technology uses mobile equipment as a front end.

6.1 Business documents on the Internet

Within an enterprise, business processes trigger numerous business documents or run with the same documents. The larger an enterprise, the more documents it must administer and store. Such documents include contracts, proposals, orders, invoices, delivery notes, applications and correspondence. As long as these documents are produced only once, placed in a file and never seen again, the enterprise requires no help in dealing with them. However, problems develop as soon as someone looks for an invoice from the previous fiscal year or for work on a contract within a workflow, when several employees had access to the contract. Availability of documents beyond the confines of national borders plays an important role in the internationalization of many enterprises. Without assistance, subsidiaries must administer redundant copies of the original document.

Digitalization of (paper) documents with a scanner and later administration of the electronic documents in a document management system (DMS) offers a much more efficient and elegant method of reaching a wide range of users. Documents centrally administered in such a system become available to all authorized users without the creation of redundant copies. The market already offers several document management systems that feature direct integration with a productive business system. Electronic archiving relates very closely to linking administration of a document system with a business system. AWV, the German professional organization for business administration (Arbeitsverband für wirtschaftliche Verwaltung), has done research that illuminates the potential savings provided by an electronic archiving system:

- 0–90% reduction in processing time;

- 10–35% reduction of professional staff;

- 10–75% increase in productivity;

- 20–40% reduction (per unit) in processing costs;

- 30–50% savings in office space.

Enterprises that use an R/3 System already possess a system that offers the essential foundation for integration of business processes with the corresponding business documents. The linkage of an archiving system to an R/3 System can permanently assign documents to specific business processes. For example, users can uniquely link the original invoice with the document record for the invoice. Users can then find and examine the invoice at any time. This feature enables administration of business documents to become especially efficient for the first time. An archive system stores documents separately, outside of the R/3 System. Documents that must be stored for a long time but that are examined rarely therefore do not place a burden on the R/3 System. The integrated linkage means that several persons can simultaneously retrieve documents from the archive system within seconds and display them in the appropriate R/3 applications. In addition to traditional paper documents, enterprises have also come to manage numerous types of documents, such as images, files, graphics, e-mails or videos. These documents already exist in electronic form. After electronic generation, many documents never see paper. Authors send them to recipients in electronic form. Examples include faxes created in word processing programs and transmitted directly to the recipient as well as order confirmations and invoices from the R/3 System. An archive system must also provide access to these documents.

The use of an R/3 System linked to an archiving system permits global access to all the business documents of an enterprise. Nevertheless, users must enjoy competency with the R/3 applications before they can access the documents. Such competency usually demands extensive training usually available only to professional staff members. Users must also have a computer with a SAPGUI installed. Business processes do not only require professionals trained in the use of the SAPGUI. Rather the processes require attention interaction from various groups: employees or managers, for example. Comfortable selection of archived documents over the Web would enable these persons to become involved in handling the business processes. Special, easy-to-operate Internet applications offer such access to every user. The following section describes the special mechanism required to permit all users access.

6.1.1   Access to archived documents

SAP and iXOS Software AG collaborated on development of the *Internet Transaction Server*. The server's design does not consider direct access to an archive system and its documents. As a company concerned with business documents, iXOS has expanded the architecture of its archive to permit access over the Web. Users can now display archived documents over a hyperlink in the browser. The information needed to select documents is taken from the R/3 System over the *ArchiveLink* interface. A previous version of the ITS included an additional component (sapawl.dll) to access the archived documents of an iXOS-Archive. This component no longer exists.

Expanded architecture

Section 6.1.2 describes a scenario that permits access to archived documents in the Document Management System of the R/3 System. After the user enters selection parameters correctly, the browser displays a hit list of documents. If list elements indicate an archived document, the elements appear as hyperlinks. Selection of a hyperlink finds the document in the archive system and displays it in the browser.

Selection of a document from iXOS-ARCHIVE requires an archive ID and a document number provided by the archive system. The R/3 System determines this data, and the ITS places hyperlinks in the HTML template to access a document in the archive. Figure 6.1 displays the expanded architecture.

The following individual steps display a document:

- *Starting the application and displaying a document*
  The R/3 System created the documents considered here; the ArchiveLink interface archived the originals. A *document information record* exists for each document. The record contains various attributes required to administer the documents. After starting the application and entering the selection criteria, the user selects the appropriate documents in the R/3 System. Selection includes the info records and the information needed to access the archived document, such as the identity of the archive and the document number.

- *Displaying the hit list*
  The browser lists the documents selected. If the archive contains an original, the list element for the original appears as a hyperlink to the archived document. The hyperlink has the following structure:

```
<a
href="http://server/archive.dll?get&contRep=EF&docId=123.1231231
231.123">
```

- *Selecting in the archive*
  A click on the hyperlink triggers the web-enabled archive to retrieve the selected document. The file corresponding to the document is sent from the archive directly to the browser.

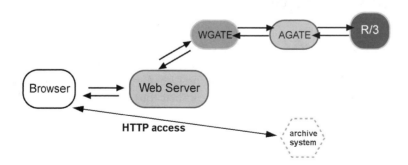

Figure 6.1   Expanded architecture

- *Displaying in the browser*
  If the Web server sends the browser a Word document (rather than an HTML file), the browser redirects it to Word, since the browser cannot display it. A *mime table*, maintained in the browser, assigns file formats to specific applications. For example, a hyperlink to a Word document would first store the file locally and then display it in Word.

  Depending on the archived file, a viewer must be entered in the table to enable display of the document. Scanned documents usually appear in tiff format; a tiff viewer suffices for display.

Users can employ this architecture without any problems as long a person's record has associations to only a single file (such as an image or a Word file). An external application, such an office application, can display the single file. Business documents, however, such as a contract, usually consist of several pages, including annotations. The archive stores such a document in several components (files). To view all pages of this document, a viewer must connect to the archive. Use of the appropriate archive viewer provides access to the full functions of the archive. The archive viewer supports reduction, enlargement, cropping and annotations. To use the viewer, the browser must call it with the required information. The viewer establishes a direct connection to the archive system and can therefore use the full functions of the archive. Users can call the archive viewer in two ways:

- *Java viewer*
  The browser can call an Applet that functions as a Java viewer for iXOS-ARCHIVE directly. The call of the Applet provides it with the information required to establish a connection to the archive system and the selected document.

- *Windows viewer*
  The Windows viewer offers another option. The http-interface of the archive must extract the information on an archived document from the archive and then transfer it to the viewer. The viewer then establishes a connection to the archive.

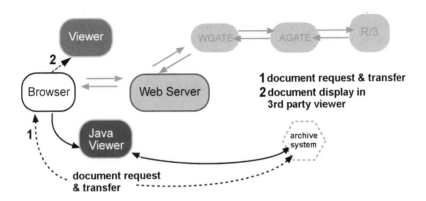

Figure 6.2   Access to the archive system over a viewer

Web access to business documents stored with iXOS-ARCHIVE efficiently and electronically can be integrated into existing applications and optimize the use of such applications. Examples include the standard IACs:

- Employee Directory;

- Electronic Product Catalog (with and without the order function).

The Web server does not store the images for the product catalog. Rather, the R/3 System maintains images consistently and iXOS-ARCHIVE stores them securely. The same holds true for the Employee Directory. Obviously, these documents require significantly administrative effort than do traditional documents.

Numerous scenarios can enable direct integration of business documents and open new doors for the design of business processes. For example:

- Customers can verify their own orders and then receive or check the invoice over the Internet.

- The external sales forces can request blueprints and construction plans online.

In addition to extended access to business documents, coordinated access to R/3 application data means a completely new way of using the R/3 System. The following section treats *document-oriented* access to the R/3 System.

6.1.2   Document-oriented access to the R/3 System

Documents, such as orders, usually trigger and accompany business processes. A great deal of R/3 application data derives from documents. Users then allocate the (paper) documents to the document data generated in the R/3 System (simultaneously, earlier or later) and then store the originals in the archive system. Because generation of documents in the R/3 System presupposes the physical presence of documents (even electronic), some application should provide documents-oriented access to the R/3 System.

Such access does not necessarily mean the display of a document that can store the document data recorded in the R/3 System. It rather involves a process that uses a document and its context as a point of departure. Such a document might be an invoice for a customer, for example. Via the SAPGUI, a user can search for an invoice and its original document in a targeted manner. However, the user may not feel naturally 'born' to the task. The possibilities of the World Wide Web and R/3 Internet applications permit the implementation of interesting procedures. The new options enable a wide range of users to have a new type of access to the business information of an R/3 System. A user, for example, can search for the original document referenced by document data in the R/3 System with knowledge of the document's context.

The following three sections present technological studies on these possibilities and clarify the potential of document-oriented access to an R/3 System.

Document flow on the Internet

A large number of documents accompany a sales process. The customer first sends a request for price information and the availability of a certain product. The enterprise replies with a proposal. If the proposal satisfies the customer who then wishes to place an order, a purchase order is then created. Once delivery takes place, delivery notes, invoices and other documents are generated. Cancellations, dunning notices and additional documents can also come into play and generate additional correspondence.

Depending on the size and scope of the order, persons involved in processing can quickly lose an overview of the entire process. Efficient access to the complete business process and the original documents associated with it demands a structured presentation. In this manner, a firm can process customer complaints more quickly; the agent can audit the entire flow of the business process immediately. An inquiry might read, 'my order requested 30 units, but the second delivery still came up five units short.' Exact verification of the inquiry requires more than checking the data in the R/3 System. Someone must still examine the original documents. An employee can also use this method to examine the previous business deal before visiting the customer.

To satisfy these requirements, iXOS has developed an Internet application that presents an overview of all the documents belonging to a given business process. The application initially shows only a portion of the documents currently required but can also display additional information on a particular document if required. The overview of the document flow does more than provide an untrained R/3 user immediate access to the data. It also simplifies processing of customer inquiries with a structured procedure and the display options of the browser.

An agent can complete work on the customer inquiry described above by taking the following steps:

- *Requesting the document number or the customer number*
  To process the inquiry, the agent must see the document flow associated with the business deal. To select a document flow, the agent uses a document number contained in the flow, such as an order number. The agent requests the number from the customer. If the customer cannot provide an order number, the system can determine it from the customer number or customer name. At entry of the customer number, the system lists all the business processes for that number. The agent can then select the process involved in the inquiry.

- *Presenting the document flow*
  Documents in a sales process belong to one of three categories: *sales, transport* and *invoices*. The system therefore places the documents in three different areas. The system first displays the sales documents (inquiry, proposal and order) as well as corresponding deliveries (symbolically, with a truck icon). The user thus has a quick overview of

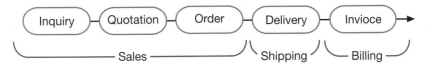

Figure 6.3   Sales process

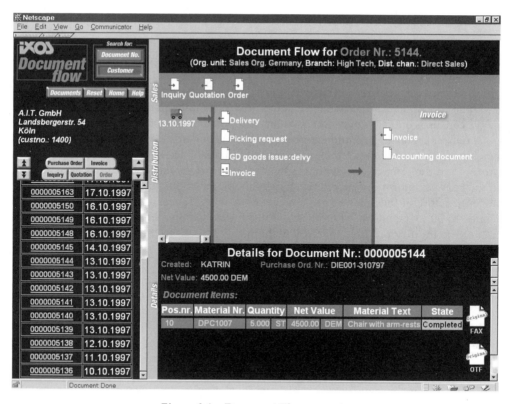

Figure 6.4   Document Flow scenario

deliveries that have already occurred. A click on the truck icon displays the documents
in the *transport* area. An additional symbolic link in this area represents the invoice. A
click on the invoice icon displays all the documents related to invoices for the order in
the *invoices* area. If the user wishes to display documents from a different delivery, a
click on the corresponding truck icon suffices.

- *Displaying details*
  Details become visible by selecting a document. The details include individual items
  and additional administrative information such as date and creator. The detail view
  also enables access to the archived original document, if available.

- *Displaying the original*
  Selection of the original document triggers the web-enabled archive to retrieve and
  transmit the selected document to the browser. A viewer, corresponding to the file type,
  displays the document. The original document will reveal the quantity originally
  ordered by the customer.

In addition to easier processing of customer inquiries, the application can also inform
users about the purchasing habits of the customer. The application can analyze the last ten
orders placed by the customer.

Web research with the Document Management System of the R/3 System

Several documents accompany many activities within an enterprise. For example, in addition to requirements specifications, a software project includes documents for varied specifications and other external documents, many of which can serve as the basis for development. These documents require orderly and clear administration: users must be able to find them. Version creation for the document being created or classification of individual items plays an important role in a quick and specific search. A system should also administer press coverage, making this material available to all employees.

With the R/3 *Document Management System* (DMS), SAP provides an application that meets these requirements. The application can administer documents, classify them, place them in a hierarchy and provide version creation for them. Originals can be stored in the R/3 database, in the file system or in the archive system. The DMS provides its most important function in offering access to and researching documents. At creation, documents can receive a particular characteristic that allows users to find the documents efficiently.

Such research remains the province of trained R/3 users. On some projects, however, it may prove useful for all project staff to have access to central documents. An Internet application that permits research over the Web can prove helpful here. The application aims at providing the user with as simple a means as possible to select a document from within a given class, to call the document from a hit lit and to display the document.

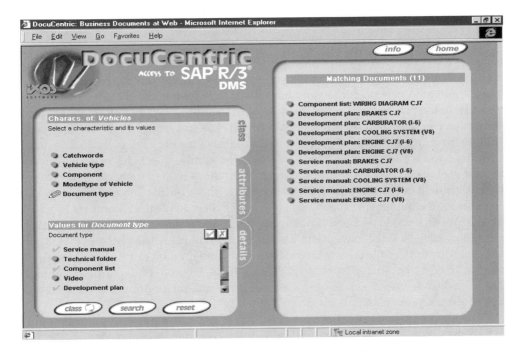

Figure 6.5   DMS: research over the Web

To enable efficient searching, the user assigns all documents a class with valuation characteristics at the time of creation. Selection over the browser takes places as follows:

- *Selecting a category*
  The user selects the class for the searchable documents at the beginning of the application. The R/3 System then selects all the corresponding characteristics and displays them in the browser. The user makes selections by evaluating the characteristics.

- *Assigning values to characteristics*
  After selecting a characteristic, the user must enter valuations for it. The user can enter the evaluations as freely defined text or the system can propose a list of values for a characteristic. The user must then select from the list. A logical OR can link valuations within a characteristic. Linkage between the characteristics takes place with a logical AND.

- *Selection in the R/3 System*
  After entry of the selection criteria, the application selects the corresponding documents in the R/3 System and displays the results list in the browser. If the archive contains the original of a document, the browser indicates the presence of the original.

- *Displaying the original*
  Selection of a document transmits the original to the browser. Depending on the type of document, the application starts the appropriate viewer (or program) and displays the document.

The application consists of an input mask and a results list. The user can enter a new search or limit the current search at any time – without additional navigation.

Creating documents on the Web

Traditional business practice sees employees create documents and then enter them into the R/3 System. A new practice would have the system itself create the documents automatically. In the past, when a potential customer requested a proposal or quotation for a product, an employee had several tasks to perform. The employee created the document, sent it to the customer, archived it, and stored a record of the proposal in the R/3 System.

Internet applications enable processing of orders and requests for products on the Internet itself. Such process would not include products with extremely high prices or those with delivery conditions that make selling them on the Internet problematic. Nonetheless, the multimedia capabilities of the Web offer an ideal environment in which to configure such products. For example, an Internet application could configure an automobile according to a customer's taste. The application could also display the color, wheel rims and other options the customer requested. The configuration can also produce a quotation immediately. So far, such applications have labored under a disadvantage. Customers had to write down the particulars of the quotation (or print it) and then repeat the entire configuration and pricing process at the dealer.

A much more elegant process would dynamically generate a proposal (including pricing), display it in the browser, automatically link it to a quotation document in the R/3 System and archive it. The customer can print the document and then hand it to the dealer. The customer would ask the dealer to order the exact product (automobile), in the exact configuration at the same price. To check the accuracy of the document, the deal would select the original document from the archive system and use it to create an order in the R/3 System. This process saves the dealer a great deal of work.

An additional application has implemented this strategy. A leasing company lets a customer configure a vehicle and a lease directly over the Web (see Figure 6.6):

- *Configuration of the automobile*
  In the first step, the customer configures interior and exterior colors, motor, wheels and additional options. The browser displays the color combination, giving the customer an image of the automobile. Because some combinations are impossible (color, for example), the system checks the configuration before generating a quotation.

- *Entering the leasing details*
  After configuration, the customer receives a price quotation for the selected automobile. The customer can now configure a personal lease, including initial payment, monthly lease payments, duration and so on. Confirmation of the quotation creates an offer in the R/3 System. It also produces a document (in RTF format) that includes all the configuration data. The system links the document to the quotation and stores it in the archive system.

Using the Web browser, the customer can now use another application to display the price quotation. The customer can print the document and take it to the dealer. The dealer selects the document in the R/3 System and can immediately generate a request from it.

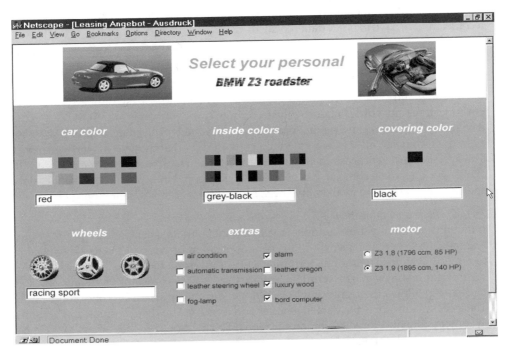

Figure 6.6   Configuration on the Web

6.2   Mobile access to the R/3 System

Much like the Internet, mobile communications have revolutionized the world of information and communications. Work processes in many industry sectors presume that the enterprise can be reached from anywhere. For example, service and sales personnel often need to communicate with the home office and request information while they work at a customer site.

The combination of Internet technology and mobile communications offers new opportunities for applications and, joined with an R/3 System, opens a new dimension. ITS technology enables comfortable access to an R/3 System over the Internet. Mobile telephones now offer integrated browsers, as do small notebooks or handheld PCs. These units use a special PC card to connect to a mobile network, such as the Global System for Mobile Telecommunications (GSM). This is a uniform, mobile system that satisfies certain requirements such as quality of speech, low equipment and service costs, support for handheld units, and ISDN compatability. GSM defines the standard for all of Europe and supports SMS. These connections to this network can make contact with the Internet. The Internet applications of the R/3 System, based on the ITS, will soon support the design of mobile terminals.

During a service call at a customer site, communications between a service technician and the R/3 System over a mobile terminal can occur in one of three ways:

1. *Online connection*
   Mobile terminals can connect to the telephone network. That connection provides the terminals with an online connection to the R/3 System or the Internet. The communications costs for such connections remain quite high, however. A sudden outage or the inability to establish a connection can hinder the technician's work. In some cases, the technician may have to enter data repeatedly.

2. *Offline connection*
   Offline solutions do not require a connection to the R/3 System. These solutions can offer an advantage: the technician can query service requests from the R/3 System in the morning and then record them in the offline system. The local, offline system temporarily stores any entries made by the technician during repair work. At the end of the day, the technician reconciles the local system and the R/3 System. In this case, however, the technician always works with a copy of data that may no longer be current. The system must reprocess the data when the technician returns from a service call. While working, the technician has no access to additional information that applies only sporadically, such as an availability check for additional replacement parts.

3. *Asynchronous communication*
   If mobile applications transfer only small amounts of data, such as the entry of values read at a customer site, asynchronous communication provides a low-cost connection to an R/3 System. The mobile terminal sends a message to the R/3 System without waiting for an answer. The terminal automatically signals receipt of an answer. This mechanism allows the technician to send a message even when no connection exists. The local system stores the data in a buffer and transmits it when a connection becomes available: store-and-forward communications. The method provides access to the most current data at all times.

The Innovation Department at iXOS Software AG studied the technology of the asynchronous solution. The study sought a standard solution that would connect mobile terminals to various applications of the R/3 System. The study determined that the communication architecture between the browser and the R/3 System could remain in force, although it also required additional components to handle the special requirements of mobile terminals. The following section describes this expanded architecture.

All situations that previously used a telephone can now enjoy direct access to an R/3 System. This access provides simple operation, attractive communications costs and secure data transfer. In addition to the Service Management application described below, this technology is ideally suited for all mobile applications that involve small amounts of data and uncomplicated dialogs. Depending on the type of terminal, the applications must consider the size of the browser. The browser integrated into a mobile telephone, for example, can display only a couple lines. It cannot accept or display images or HTML frames.

6.2.1 Architecture

In this solution as well, the browser communicates with a Web server that has access to an R/3 System over the Internet Transaction Server. The solution implements only the connection and the data exchange between the browser and the Web server differently. The original communications architecture of the ITS included a permanent connection between the Web server and the browser. Data exchange during asynchronous communications, however, takes place with messages transmitted by radio. After transmitting a message, the user does not wait for an answer, but continues with other work. The system signals the user when it receives an answer and automatically inserts the contents of the answer in the corresponding request. Quick response times permit the messages to remain within the context of the process or activity. The system organizes local data storage as a cache, rather than a replication. This method avoids consistency conflicts.

Figure 6.7 illustrates the architecture for mobile access to an R/3 System. Data exchange occurs asynchronously in *short messages* with the Short Message Service. This is a bidirectional service to send brief alphanumeric messages (up to 160 bytes) with the *store-and-forward* procedure. The mobile terminal transmits messages by radio to an SMS Center. The center than redirects the data either over an ISDN connection or over radio to an SMS gateway, developed especially for this application. The gateway prepares the information for further redirection to the Web server for interpretation by the ITS. In the opposite direction, the gateway determines the required information from HTML pages transmitted by the Web server and converts it into a message in SMS format. The SMS center then redirects the message to the mobile terminal. SMS uses a *store-and-forward-*process to transmit messages. If no connection exists at a particular point, the system temporarily stores the message. When a connection again exists, the system automatically retransmits the message.

6.2.2 Service management 'on the road'

Service has become an increasingly important factor in the success of an enterprise. It also offers a pivotal way for a company to differentiate itself from its competitors. R/3 Service Management can handle service issues and contribute to the improved quality of service in general. The first use of mobile access to an R/3 System involved the development of an application to process service requests. The application included several smaller appli-

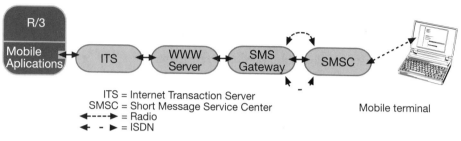

ITS = Internet Transaction Server
SMSC = Short Message Service Center   Mobile terminal
◄----► = Radio
◄ - ► = ISDN

Figure 6.7   Architecture for mobile access to an R/3 System

cations for time recording, availability checks, withdrawals, entries of services performed, displays of service notifications, and so on. These smaller applications covered various aspects of a service contract. A model scenario could appear as follows:

A service technician from a firm that manufactures copiers has received a service request to repair a copier. Completion of the request occurs with the help of a mobile terminal that supports direct access to the firm's R/3 System:

- *Creating the work list*
  The service technician transfers current data on service requests from the R/3 System on a regular basis (daily or weekly, for example). The technician's local system thus has a work list of service contracts that contains all the relevant data from R/3 service notifications and R/3 service contracts. The technician can navigate in the data and create a work plan (schedule).

- *Preparing and performing the repair*
  Once on site, the technician checks the defect notification that the customer entered in the R/3 System and that now appears on the terminal. While examining the copier, the technician discovers a defective part that requires replacement. If the technician's truck has the part in stock, the technician can debit the part directly in his R/3 stock and settle it immediately. If the material is not in the truck, however, the technician can perform an availability check in the R/3 System. If the manufacturer has the part in stock, the technician can reserve it for the repair request. If it is not in stock, the technician can order it.

- *Completing the repair*
  After a successful repair, the technician uses the R/3 System to assign the status *closed* to the request. The technician also posts the hours worked and adds the costs to the service request. If the warehouse does not have some replacement parts that must be ordered, the technician can use the availability check to set another appointment for repair.

The mobile terminal updates all activities directly in the R/3 System. In addition, the technician can request other information, such as availability or technical documents, from the front end on the mobile terminal. After completion of the service request, the R/3 System stores all the activities related to the repair. The system can now calculate the costs and issue an invoice, and thus close processing on the request. The R/3 System can also administer the stock in the technician's truck. Later manual entry or processing of data is no longer necessary.

7 Programming guidelines for Internet applications

SAP supports various methods of implementing Internet applications for the R/3 System (see Chapter 3, The SAP R/3 System and the Internet). Portability, performance and type of connection to the R/3 System distinguish the methods from each other. SAP uses the term *Web-Basis* to refer to all three methods. These guidelines treat only the creation of Internet applications that use the Internet Transaction Server (ITS). This product represents a cooperative development by SAP and iXOS Software. The Internet Transaction Server (ITS) enables development of dialog-capable Internet applications with the ABAP/4 programming language in the R/3 System and running the applications in the system. The applications do not differ from normal ABAP/4 dialog applications in any significant manner. Enhancements to the Internet Transaction Server enable uses to call any desired reports and special function modules in the R/3 System and to display the result on the Web.

The present description of the ITS refers to ITS version 2.0, delivered with version 4.x of the R/3 System software. This ITS version also works with earlier releases (as of 3.0D). With earlier versions, however, users cannot take advantage of all the features of the ITS. The following text will indicate if and where differences in the programming model apply to older versions of the ITS and the R/3 System software.

7.1 The SAP product

The specific characteristics of the SAP System and the Internet require a special coupling program between the two systems. The type of coupling also demands a special programming model for ABAP/4 development. This section first describes the technical principles of coupling and various components. It then treats contextual issues that developers must consider when programming Internet applications.

7.1.1 Technical principles

Users cannot call the SAP System directly from the Web server. The type and method of data exchange between the Web server and external programs represent one reason for this inability. Instead of a direct call, the Web server starts a program that connects it to the R/3 System. This method uses the *screen interface* of the SAP System as the technical transmission channel. The R/3 System and the front end designated as the SAPGUI communicate with each other over this interface. To the R/3 System, the coupling program behaves similarly to a normal SAPGUI. It converts screen data from the SAP System into HTML documents and vice versa. In the process, HTML templates server serve as models the following advantages for the Web pages created by the system. This approach provides a simple way to make ABAP/4 applications capable of use on the Internet. The approach offers the following advantages:

- Development and testing of the Internet application can take place almost completely in the R/3 System.

- Connections use only proven interfaces of the R/3 System.

- The various components of the Internet applications can operate with the Correction and Transport System of the R/3 System without any difficulties. This feature enables a simple way to upgrade the standard Internet Application Components (IACs) delivered by SAP. Just as they do with other applications, customers can develop Internet applications in a test system and then transport them into the production system.

- The R/3 System can store all the components of an application, even when the applications must operate externally at runtime.

- To generate language-independent HTML documents, the Internet applications can use the automatic language features of the SAP System.

We must strongly emphasize, however, that developers must optimize the application running in the R/3 System to meet the demands of the Web. Although web-capable R/3 applications can run in the R/3 System and, independently of the Web, undergo testing there, they do not meet the demands made on pure R/3 applications. The procedures chosen by SAP enable development of Internet-capable R/3 applications. It remains impossible, however, for any existing R/3 application to run on the Web without any modifications. Web applications aim at a different group of users than do applications that operate over the normal SAPGUI. Accordingly, new development must occur in any case, and thus represents no real handicap.

Although the coupling program is complex, it remains a completely transparent application to developers and to users. In addition to its obvious tasks, exchanging data between the Web and the R/3 System and converting screen and HTML documents into each other (in both directions), the program must perform additional, system-oriented tasks. These tasks include the administration of various Web users, system resources and various Internet applications in addition to the maintenance of security standards. The *Internet Transaction Server* (ITS) performs all these tasks. Although the ITS consists of several components, the individual components have no significance in this discussion. Accordingly, the following will speak of the ITS even when treating one component of the coupling program.

7.1.2   Component parts of Internet applications

While creating an Internet application, a developer encounters various tools and other diverse objects. The tools include executable programs and control files. The objects include various logical objects. Each developer must operate or generate some of these tools and elements.

ITS

ITS is the abbreviation for the *Internet Transaction Server*, the actual coupling program between the Web sever and the Internet on one side and the R/3 System on the other side. Developers have no direct access to this program.

The ITS performs all the tasks required at runtime:

- communication with the Web server;

- evaluation of user requirements;

- communication with the R/3 System;

- generation of HTML pages.

Virtual ITS

Several instances of the ITS can run on one server. Each instance has subdirectories for IAC files. The feature enables various R/3 Systems to work with an ITS. Such a situation exists in large development environments that operate separate development, test and production systems. A virtual ITS is simply one of the instances of the program.

ITS Debugger

The ITS Debugger is a special function of the ITS, not an independent product. It permits the Web application to switch to a normal SAPGUI in parallel so that the application becomes visible on the Web and the SAPGUI simultaneously. Within the SAPGUI, the expected functions of the R/3 System remain available. This feature also enables use of the R/3 Debugger and debugging of a running Web application.

SAP@Web-Studio

SAP@Web-Studio, abbreviated as Studio in the following, helps generate and process files stored in the file system of an NT computer (that is, outside the R/3 System) that runs the ITS. That computer may also run the Web server, so simply have a network connection to the Web server. The following describes the files used by the ITS. The Studio also places any modified files back into storage in the R/3 System after processing. Every developer must have access to the Studio tool to create Internet applications. The Studio runs outside of the R/3 System.

Service

The term *service* identifies an Internet application. A service name, rather than an R/3 transaction code, describes applications outside of the R/3 System. The service name can consist of up to 14 characters. Within the R/3 System, the service name identifies the diverse objects of an Internet application. Accordingly, developers must adhere to SAP guidelines for the naming environment. Service names in customer systems must therefore begin with the letter Y or Z.

Theme

Specification of a *theme* can reference one of several design versions of a *service*. The differences remain purely visual, as the service sets the functions. The theme is a two-place descriptor.

Global service description

To log in to the R/3 System, the ITS requires a great deal of information, including the name of the SAP System, login data and so on. The global service description stores these types of data that do not otherwise belong to a special service. Installation of the Web server generates the global services file. A user – normally only the system administrator – can later change the file manually.

Individual service description

You must create a service description for each R/3 application that will run over the Web. This file contains parameters required by the ITS to call an R/3 transaction. Service files are essential: they contain the name of the SAP transaction that will be called. Parameters in this file overwrite settings in the global service file.

The Web-Studio always creates a service file when the Studio generates a new service. The Studio queries the required entries from the user or determines them automatically. Developers can also edit a service file manually.

Application templates

Templates define HTML pages that contain supplemental information on the R/3 data that you wish to merge into a document. They also specify where the merge occurs. Every template corresponds to a screen of an R/3 application. A template belongs to exactly one service and to exactly one theme within the service, if the service contains more than one theme.

Application templates can exist in language-dependent and in language-independent variants.

Application templates undergo frequent changes during development. At first, developers initiate the changes, but later Web designer also make changes that affect the visual design of the page.

System templates

If the application in the R/3 System cannot capture an error that occurs while processing, the ITS must generate an error message. In other cases, the ITS must query supplemental entries from users (login name, password, login language) independently, without communicating with the R/3 System. For such cases, default HTML templates exist that the ITS can use to generate the final HTML pages if necessary.

System templates can be generated and addressed as language-dependent templates, but cannot be subdivided into themes.

Customers may not change system templates. Nonetheless, a second set of templates exists: customers take full responsibility for any modifications made to the second set. A parameter in one of the service files determines which of the two template versions the ITS should use.

HTML^{Business}

HTML templates contain supplemental metastatements. The commands do not follow the HTML standard, and the Web browser does not evaluate them. They exist only to support the work of the ITS. Pages sent from the server to the browser do not contain any metastatements.

SAP terminology uses *HTML^{Business}* to refer to metastatements. For the sake of simplicity, this chapter will use these metastatements.

Language resources

An HTML template can contain placeholders for text elements. Depending on the login language, the ITS replaces the placeholders with texts from a language resource file. A language resource file exists for every theme. If no theme exists, the file exists within a service.

You can process language resources in a file system outside of the R/3 System, preferably with SAP@Web-Studio. This method becomes mandatory during development. Language resources can also be processed, or translated, in the R/3 System with the tools available there.

Binary objects

Web applications also include graphics, sound files and additional objects. The Web server, rather than the ITS, inserts these objects into the HTML pages. Unlike the elements described above, such as templates or language resources, these objects do not influence the work of the ITS directly. The objects are not stored in the ITS directory, but in a subdirectory on the Web server. The objects do, however, belong to an Internet application and must meet some ITS requirements for dependence on a language or for a theme. Storage in a special directory branch allocates these elements to an Internet application. Within temples, a special HTML^{Business} function can hold the correct URL for a binary file.

RFC channel

Various transmission channels exist within the screen interface. R/3 applications can use an RFC channel, much as the R/3 System uses the DIAG channel to transmit screen data. The application server and the front end use the RFC channel to exchange data bidirectionally. Internet applications can use this channel to exchange mass data with the ITS. Therefore, the channel is also called the mass data channel.

Web RFC

A second RFC option also exists in addition to the mass data connection between the R/3 System and the SAPGUI interface. This option rests on a different technical solution and permits external applications to call special function modules of the R/3 System.

7.1.3   Workflow for generating an IAC

Generation of a Web application is an iterative process that passes through the development cycle described below. Practice has proved it almost impossible to generate Web objects for an R/3 application without changing the R/3 portion of the application.

Generating the R/3 transaction

An executable R/3 application serves as the starting point for a Web application. Because considerable differences exist between the Web and the SAP System, developers must adjust the R/3 application to the characteristics of the Web. Details on this point are provided later. Executable does not mean that the application must fulfill the same ergonomic and visual requirements of a functional transaction that users would encounter when working with the SAPGUI. In this context, an executable R/3 application must simply function correctly and be operable considering some compromises in the R/3 System.

Developers can employ the normal development tools of the R/3 System without any restrictions to create and test the application.

Creating or changing the service description

A service description must exist on the file system on the ITS computer for each Web application. This file contains all the information that the ITS needs to call an SAP transaction. If you must create a service description, you must always create it with the Web-Studio. A normal text editor can handle any later changes to the description.

Creating or changing language resources

HTML templates should not contain any hard-coded language-dependent texts. When working with language-dependent graphics or texts not delivered directly from the R/3 System, developers must use language resources. Language resources maintain language-dependent texts or language-dependent file names: the templates contain only placeholders. For language-independent templates, a language resource must exist for every login language so that the ITS can find the template. If the template doesn't contain any text elements, the resource file can remain empty.

If development does not involve any language-dependent templates, create at least one language resource for the language used in developing and testing the application.

Creating or changing templates

An HTML template must exist for every screen of the R/3 transaction. The template must contain various HTML[Business] statements that create references to the corresponding screen fields. The Web-Studio can generate such a template from a screen description. The Studio automatically generates the required placeholders and control statements. In almost every case, an automatically generated page requires manual editing. Any screen changes will also require reworking of the templates. If the screen has changed, developers can enter the changes into the template manually or generate a new page automatically from the new screen description. In the latter case, the new template would not contain any edits made previously. We recommend making backup copies of previously generated templates before creating any new ones.

Editing a template does more than improve the visual appearance of Web pages. Special programming techniques or frame applications require HTML[Business] statements to guarantee the interplay of HTML pages and SAP screen. Developers must insert such instructions manually.

Testing the application

After creating or changing objects, you must test the application. The test must run with the Web application to check the interplay of all components. A range of possible errors exists outside of the R/3 System. Any of these errors may well cause an application that works correctly within the R/3 System to malfunction on the Web. Tools, among them the ITS debugger, can help locate the error.

7.1.4   Programming model

All R/3 applications that run on the Web must meet special requirements. Developers must consider this context when programming their own applications. This section describes the reasons for the limitations and the effects of the limitations on the programming model. The presentation covers the function range of the HTML standard, but does not consider proprietary enhancements of various supplier or script languages. Not using these enhancements guarantees that the Internet application remains compatible with the majority of browsers.

Problems

Significant differences exist between HTML documents and SAP screens. In an HTML document, programmers cannot use all the objects available in a screen or ABAP/4 application. In addition, some objects in screens rest on special programming techniques and thus require the use of special ABAP/4 commands. HTML does not contain these types of elements in the same form. Programmers must create suitable substitutes for the HTML documents. This section describes the problems related to the differences between HTML documents and SAP screens. Another section provides numerous examples that demonstrate concrete effects on R/3 applications.

Menus

An HTML browser has a menu that operates it. The HTML standard does not support any commands to generate additional menus in Web pages or to add items to existing menus. R/3 applications that run on the Web must therefore operate without their own menus. Only pushbuttons can operate such applications. This same holds true for the actual R/3 applications. Contrary to the usual expectations, it is neither necessary nor reasonable to set a status for an R/3 application, except in the scroll interface for step loops.

Popups

The HTML standard currently recognizes only one form of presenting HTML documents. The browser always displays the documents completely in a window. No popups exist. R/3 applications, however, frequently use popups for possible entries, error messages (type I), security queries or confirmations. Internet applications do not permit use of such elements. The ITS suppresses them or a simulation of the enter key ends them. Problems can occur if the enter key triggers a different function that ends the popup. For example, the enter key may branch to another application.

Possible entries

An HTML browser cannot evaluate the F1 and F4 keys in relation to documents and cannot display any popups. Accordingly, it cannot offer a function similar to that offered in the R/3 list of possible entries. Two programming techniques can provide a substitute, but both require special coding in the R/3 application. The first technique uses a special entry element in HTML documents. The elements permit the user to select from default values. The R/3 System can fill the value sets at runtime. The second technique programs individual lists for possible entries. These lists are derived from the possible entries on a normal screen.

Checkboxes and radio buttons

Both field types exist in both screens and HTML documents, but are implemented differently. R/3 screens have a unique input field of length 1 for each radio button. HTML uses only a single field for all radio buttons that form a logical unit. This field length may be greater than 1. Various values in this field symbolize different conditions. The R/3 System does not support direct depiction of the field contents in radio buttons.

To permit easy searches for errors in an R/3 application, screens should not contain any radio buttons. The application should use the HTML model and use a single input field with fixed set of values (domains with fixed values).

Although the Web's use of checkboxes is similar to that of the R/3 System, problems still exist when representing Web fields in screen fields. Transfer of field values currently functions correctly only when the screen uses simple, one-place input fields rather than true checkboxes. The ABAP/4 program does not evaluate these fields any differently than normal. It treats also treats true ABAP/4 checkboxes as type C fields of length 1. Correct transmission of all checkbox information requires some additional statements in the HTML template.

Multi-line input fields

In addition to the usual single-line input fields, HTML documents also contain multi-line fields, or *text areas*). These fields enable the user to create long texts. Analogous screen fields do not exist. The ABAP/4 application must therefore convert the text areas in step loops. The application must also support a break from the text area into the step loop. The break requires special statements in the HTML template. A mass data channel can substitute for the special statements to handle data exchange with text areas.

Step loops

The step loops used in the R/3 System require special statements in the flow logic. In addition, the fields in a column all possess identical names, which makes converting them into an HTML document more difficult. Limitations on the number of table lines delivered by the R/3 System pose an additional problem. The system prepares only the number of lines defined in the screen, even when a variable loop is involved. Accordingly, the application design must permit scrolling in the dataset with pushbuttons in the HTML document. As an alternative, the use of special ITS properties with a scrollbar in the HTML document can scroll through the entire dataset.

   The context of step loops also permits the use of a mass data channel. Such use, however, also limits the programming model.

   See the following examples for more details on handling step loops.

Synchronization

Internet applications place a new problem before the programmer. R/3 applications always find themselves in a clearly defined status (state). Movements from one status to another occur at defined times controlled by the application. The R/3 System steadily restructures every screen and resupplies it with current data.

   The HTML browser operates differently. To limit the load on the network, the browser places HTML documents in intermediate storage, in a local cache. In addition to navigation with hyperlinks, the user can employ menu functions in the browser to scroll through the list of cached pages. The status visible in the browser can thus differ from the status of the application in the R/3 System. The coupling procedure between the Internet and the R/3 System, however, demands that the data delivered over the Web can be merged with that of the current screen. The status on the Web must agree with the status in the R/3 application. If this were not the case, the Web would deliver data that the ITS could not transfer to the R/3. This condition would cause a runtime error.

   The ITS can rather easily determine that the page sent by the browser does not correspond to the current status of the R/3 application. The ITS can then inform the application of this condition, and the application must then react accordingly. The application's reaction should correspond to the user's expectations and return a meaningful response to the user's request. Accordingly, the application must be able to create a program status corresponding to that on the Web. This ability requires a comprehensive status model for the application and a new, perhaps unfamiliar, programming style.

7.2   Practical introduction to Web programming

This section uses examples to demonstrate a programming method for the creation of Internet-capable R/3 applications. It assumes fundamental knowledge of R/3 programming and basic familiarity with the design of HTML pages.

The following ABAP/4 examples make no claim on perfection: they represent a means to an end. To assist readability, the program examples expressly avoid the use of numbered text elements and messages. Instead, they use hard-coded character strings and one universal message. The character strings consist of four placeholders for parameters that are transferred as field contents or as a constant character string when the message is triggered. You should, of course, use the correct programming method in productive applications.

The first example describes the entire development process as well as all the tools employed in the process. The remaining examples demonstrate only the special problems of IAC programming.

The largest portion of the applications consists of a *module pool*. The names of applications in the R/3 System were chosen to permit replication in all systems above 3.0D. In particular, we avoided using the expanded name range available as of release 4.0. The names of the module pools correspond to the pattern *SAPMavnn*. Here the letter *a* stands for a unique letter, such as *I* as an IAC identifier. A customer system must use a *Y* or *Z* instead of the *I* to satisfy the requirements of the naming convention. A number identifying the release level (3 or 4) replaces the *v*. The characters *nn* represent sequential numbering of the programs.

7.2.1   Example 1: A calculator

This example is quite simple. It requires only a few activities that must execute outside of the R/3 System. Except for avoiding menus, none of the limitations noted above offer concerns in the example. The application offers a simple calculator that can link two whole numbers with the four basic arithmetical functions.

This example demonstrates the workflow involved in creating Internet applications and operation of the various tools in the process.

The R/3 application

The first application goes by the name SAPMI401. Figure 7.1 illustrates the first screen of the application. Two input fields serve to enter the two numbers; four pushbuttons determine the operation to be executed; an additional button ends the application. All fields or pushbuttons have unique identification, such as BUTTON_MUL for the multiplication button. Two additional key fields (text fields) have the same names as the two input fields. To provide a clearer understanding, Table 7.1 displays the field list of the first screen.

Table 7.1 Field list of the first screen

Field name	Field type	Field text/Template
VALUE1	Text	Value_1
VALUE1	I/O	
BUTTON_PLUS	Push	+
BUTTON_MINUS	Push	−
BUTTON_MUL	Push	*
BUTTON_DIV	Push	/
VALUE2	Text	Value_2
VALUE2	I/O	
BUTTON_QUIT	Push	Quit
OKCODE	OK	

The application displays the result in the second screen (see Figure 7.2). For the sake of simplicity, the screen display supports true input and output fields because resetting the input attributes requires additional effort when programming the screen. In principle, both the R/3 application and the IAC being created would function if both fields were converted into purely display fields. The second screen has two pushbuttons. One triggers a jump to the previous (function code FNEW); the other ends the application (function code/NEX). The program starts with transaction IAC1.

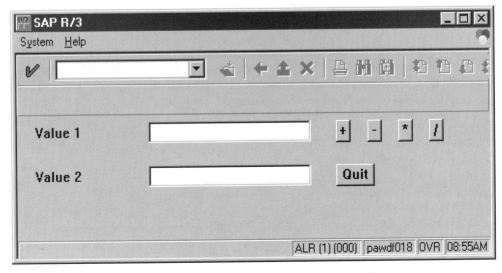

Figure 7.1 First screen of the calculator example

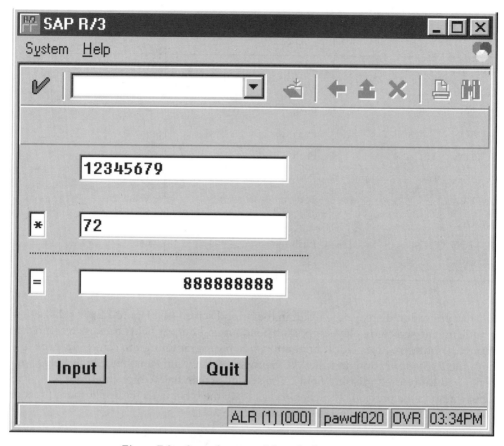

Figure 7.2   Second screen of the calculator example

The source code for the application offers no special concerns. The flow logic of the first screen shows the following. In addition to the initialization of both input fields (of no interest here) of the screen in the PBO module, the PAI module handles only simple field checks and the evaluation of the function code.

```
PROCESS BEFORE OUTPUT.
  MODULE init_0100.
*
PROCESS AFTER INPUT.
  CHAIN.
  FIELD: value1, value2.
  MODULE check_0100.
ENDCHAIN.
MODULE user_command_0100.
```

Module CHECK_0100 checks both entered numbers for the correct format. If a user entered invalid numbers, the module triggers an error message. It also triggers an error message in case of division by zero.

```
MODULE check_0100 INPUT.
  IF value1 CN '-1234567890 '.
    MESSAGE e000 WITH value1 ' is not valid!'.
  ENDIF.
  IF value2 CN '-1234567890 '.
    MESSAGE e000 WITH value2 ' is not valid!'.
  ENDIF.
  IF okcode = 'OPC/' AND value2 = 0.
    MESSAGE e000 WITH 'Division by Zero!'.
  ENDIF.
ENDMODULE.                    " CHECK_0100 INPUT
```

Module USER_COMMAND_0100 is also easy to comprehend: it must evaluate only five function codes.

```
MODULE user_command_0100 INPUT.
  CASE okcode.
    WHEN 'OPC+'.
      result = value1 + value2.
      op = '+'.
      LEAVE TO SCREEN 200.
    WHEN 'OPC-'.
      result = value1 - value2.
      op = '-'.
      LEAVE TO SCREEN 200.
    WHEN 'OPC*'.
      result = value1 * value2.
      op = '*'.
      LEAVE TO SCREEN 200.
    WHEN 'OPC/'.
      result = value1 / value2.
      op = '/'.
      LEAVE TO SCREEN 200.
    WHEN '/NEX'.
      LEAVE PROGRAM.
  ENDCASE.
  CLEAR okcode.
ENDMODULE.                    " USER_COMMAND_0100 INPUT
```

Since the call of the module consists only of an evaluation of the function code, the flow logic of screen 200 requires no repetition.

```
MODULE user_command_0200 INPUT.
  CASE okcode.
    WHEN '/NEX'.
      LEAVE PROGRAM.
    WHEN 'FNEW'.
      LEAVE TO SCREEN 100.
  ENDCASE.
ENDMODULE.                    " USER_COMMAND_0200 INPUT
```

The illustrations of both screen and the source code should explain the functions of the R/3 application sufficiently. To the sake of completeness, note the following declaration portion:

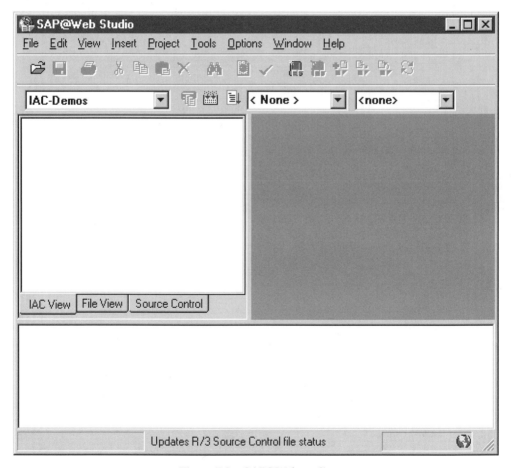

Figure 7.3   SAP@Web studio

```
PROGRAM sapmi401 MESSAGE-ID i!.
DATA:
  okcode LIKE sy-ucomm,
  value1(20) TYPE c,
  value2(20) TYPE c,
  result(20) TYPE c,
  op,
  is VALUE '='.
```

Working outside the R/3 System

The following tasks require SAP@Web-Studio. The Studio runs as an external application on a Windows NT computer. This tool can perform almost all the tasks involved in creating external IAC elements, those elements not stored in the R/3 System. Figure 7.3 shows SAP@Web-Studio in its initial condition.

The Studio requires a working directory that stores the current project and its files. You should create the directory before entering the first project in the Studio. Select the menu functions OPTIONS | STUDIO PROPERTIES and then DIRECTORIES in the following popup (Figure 7.4). Now enter the path for the project directory. If the directory does not already exist, the Studio will create it. You can create both the path and its name as desired.

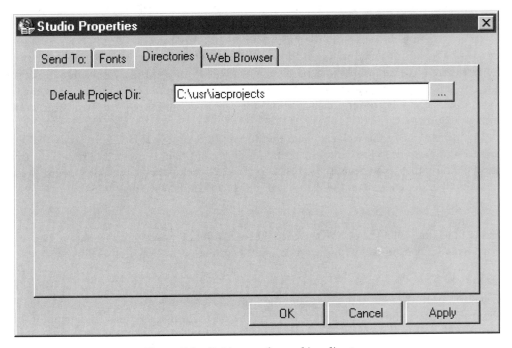

Figure 7.4   Setting up the working directory

Generating a site definition and a project

After defining the working directory, you must generate a site definition and create a project. The Studio stores the IAC files in a local working directory during processing. After processing, you move the files from that local working directory to their final position so that the ITS and the Web server can find them. To do so, you can use a special function in the Studio (PUBLISH). To ensure that this function works properly, you must first define a *site*, in which you set the target directories for the transfer and some additional technical details. You can use such a site for multiple projects. If required, you can also create several sites, particularly if you work with different R/3 Systems or Web servers. A single site usually suffices for normal development work.

A project collects all the files of an IAC. You will later generate a service description as the first step in the project. The service description contains important information for access to the R/3 System and the transaction being started.

To generate a new site, call the menu functions PROJECT | SITE DEFINITION in the Studio. A popup appears that permits you to select among three pages. The area on the left side of the popup displays a tree that shows all the existing sites. The right side contains input fields (see Figure 4.5).

You use the NEW pushbutton to generate a new site. The Studio creates a new site definition with a standard name that you should now change.

The site definition is stored as a file in the root directory of the Studio. Since a site can exist only externally, you need not observe the naming conventions of the R/3 System. You must, however, observe the naming conventions of the NT file system.

After changing the name, fill the input fields in the right portion of the popup. These entries have significant impact on the ability of the application to function correctly. Unfortunately, we cannot make general suggestions for the required values here because the concrete value depends upon the configuration of your computer and upon the system landscape. If you are unclear about the required values, request them from your system administrator.

Enter the name of the web server in the first input field (see Figure 7.5). You will later use this Web server to test your application. The second field contains the root directory for the binary files referenced in the IACs. In standard installations, this entry begins with a section that depends upon the Web server in use and ends with the following:

```
.../sap/its/mimes
```

In the third line, enter the part of the URL that is required for access to the WGATE. For standard installations, the following default value is correct:

```
/scripts/wgate.dll
```

Selection of the second page displays the input fields for the data relating to the ITS. Figure 7.6 shows the corresponding popup. The first two fields request the name of the virtual ITS and its root directory.

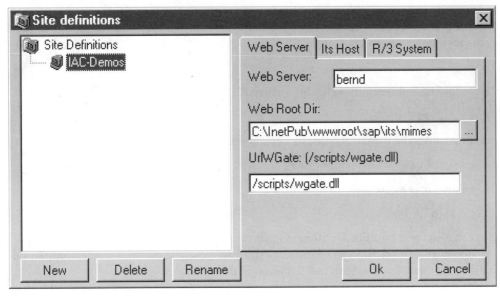

Figure 7.5   Generating a new site

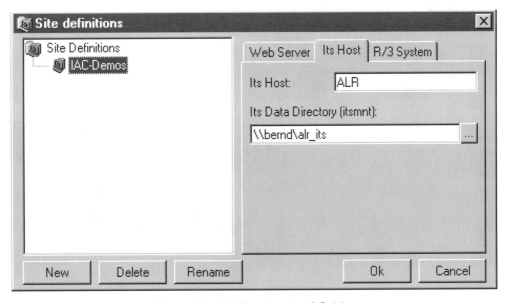

Figure 7.6   ITS data in a site definition

If you do not work with a virtual ITS, you can leave the first field empty. You must, however, enter a root directory. In a standard installation the following is the default value for a non-virtual ITS:

`itsmnt`

The following is the default value for a virtual ITS:

`<Virtual ITS>_ITS`

You must enter the directory name in UNC notation, in the following form:

`\\its-computer_name\directory`

The following is a concrete example:

`\\bernd\alr_its`

You can also use a traditional pathname that consists of a drive letter and the path.

This entry ends definition of the site. You can close the popup by selecting the OK button and then continue with the definition of the actual project.

Use the menu functions FILE | NEW to call a tool that can create a new project. Figure 7.7 shows the tool's interface. This tool appears as a popup with several sections. To generate a new project, select PROJECTS. Now you must simply enter the name of your project. This TUTORIAL uses the project name Tutorial. You can use the pathname given in the lower section of the popup without any changes.

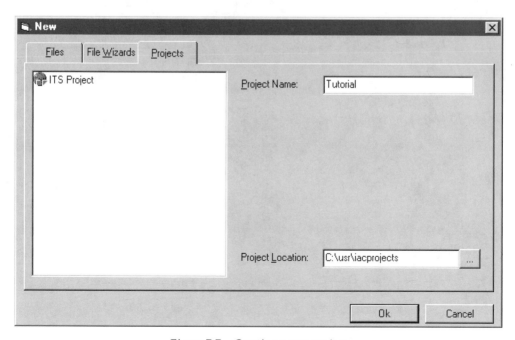

Figure 7.7   Creating a new project

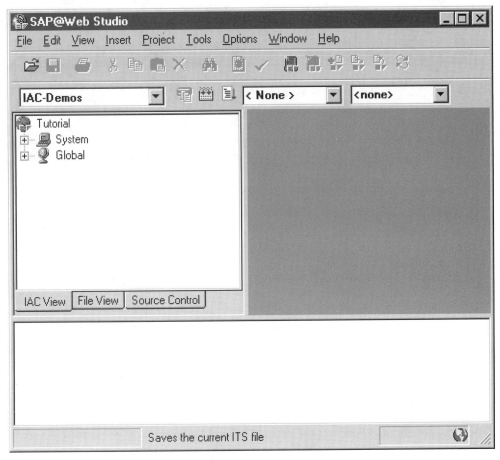

Figure 7.8   SAP@Web-Studio with an open project

After you confirm your entry with the OK button, the Studio creates the project and displays it in the left window of the Studio (see Figure 7.8).

Generating the service file

Up to now, you have only created a project. Although the project helps organize IAC files, it is not itself an IAC file. A project simply provides a utility within the Studio.

The first true IAC file that you create must be a service description. The first step involves marking the current project with a mouse click. You then use the menu function FILE | NEW (the same function used earlier to create the project) and the system displays a popup. This time, however, select FILE WIZARDS. The left part of the popup now lists the available file generators (Figure 7.9).

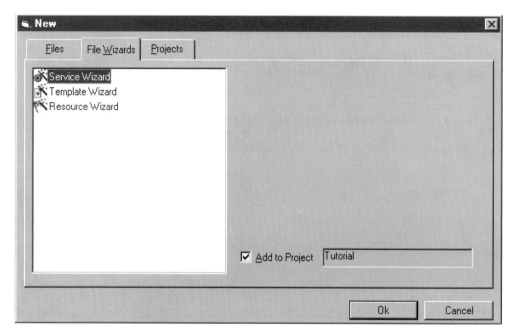

Figure 7.9   Generating a service description

Mark the entries for Service Wizard and the flag Add to Project that appear in the list. The Studio suggests the name of the project, so you should mark it before calling the file generator. Doing so saves additional writing.

Click on the OK button to begin creation of the service description. In several sequential dialogs, the Studio asks you for various values. Again, most of these values refer to the system itself. Consider the values given in the following figures only as examples.

A service description always refers to exactly one service. The service description therefore takes the name of the service as its file name. The first step in the dialog requires you to enter the name of the service (see Figure 7.10).

The service name functions within the R/3 System as an object name and in the file system of the local development computer as a file name. Accordingly, the name must have no more than 14 characters and satisfy the naming conventions of both the R/3 System and the Windows NT system. Services created in customer systems must begin with a Y or Z if the R/3 System will later store them. The NT system forbids the use of some characters, such as a backslash ('\').

This tutorial uses the service name CALC_SIMPLE, since because the sample programs were created in a SAP development system at SAP headquarters. If you wish to replicate the examples in a customer system, you must place a Y or Z before the service name.

After entering the name, use the Next pushbutton to go to the next dialog step.

An IAC always runs on an exactly specified R/3 System. The ITS must log in to that system. In all likelihood, installation of the ITS already linked it to a particular R/3 System. The global service description contains the login data. You do not need to transfer

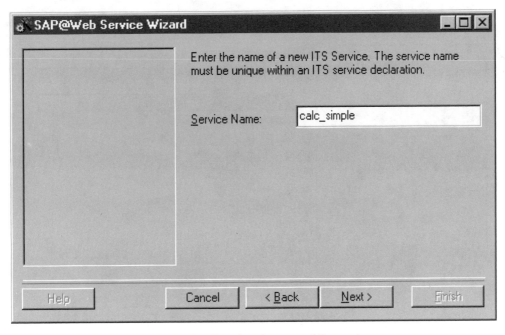

Figure 7.10   Entering the name of the service

the login data to the individual service file. In this case, you can select the uppermost entry in the selection list (NO SPECIFIC R/3 SYSTEM). Figure 7.11 shows the popup that appears in the Studio.

All other entries in the selection list come from data available in the SAPLOGON program. You can use an R/3 System listed there most easily by simply selecting the appropriate entries.

To execute an IAC, the ITS must be able to log in to the R/3 System. It can do so according to various methods. As one option, you can use a predefined user already entered in the global service description. The other option involves establishing a specific user. The Studio transfers the user's login data into the service description. Figure 7.12 displays the selection popup.

After selecting the IAC user, the Studio asks for a *timeout* period. The ITS automatically ends an Internet session if users fail to perform any activities within the time specified in the *timeout* period. Figure 7.13 shows the popup used to set the timeout.

The ITS can use two completely different channels for communication with the R/3 System. The currently operating dialog application use the *Diag-Channel*, with which the traditional SAPGUI also works. Note that the ITS cannot start dialog-enabled applications (reports or function modules) over the other communications channel, the *RFC-Channel*. A special section treats this option in more detail.

After you enter the timeout period, you complete the next dialog step by specifying the communications channel and the application to be executed in the R/3 System (see Figure 7.14). You set the application by entering the transaction code in the dialog.

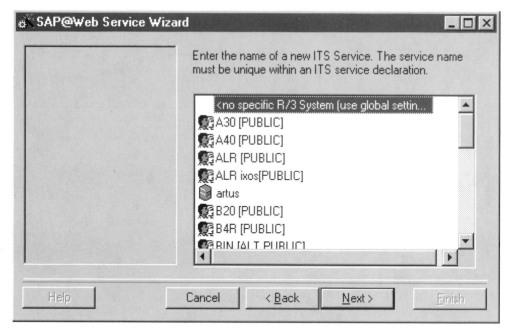

Figure 7.11   Choosing the R/3 System

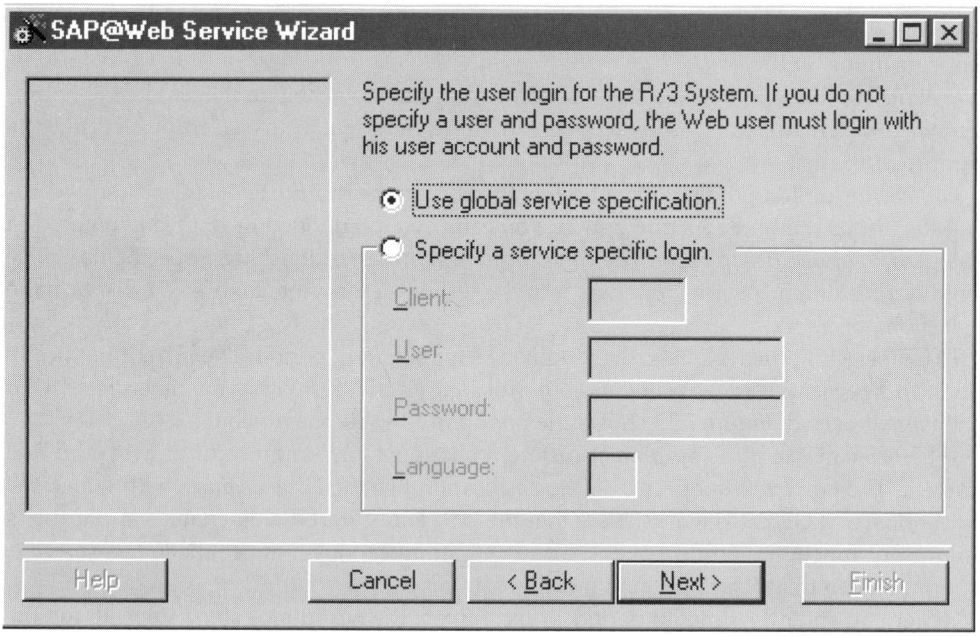

Figure 7.12   Setting users for the IAC

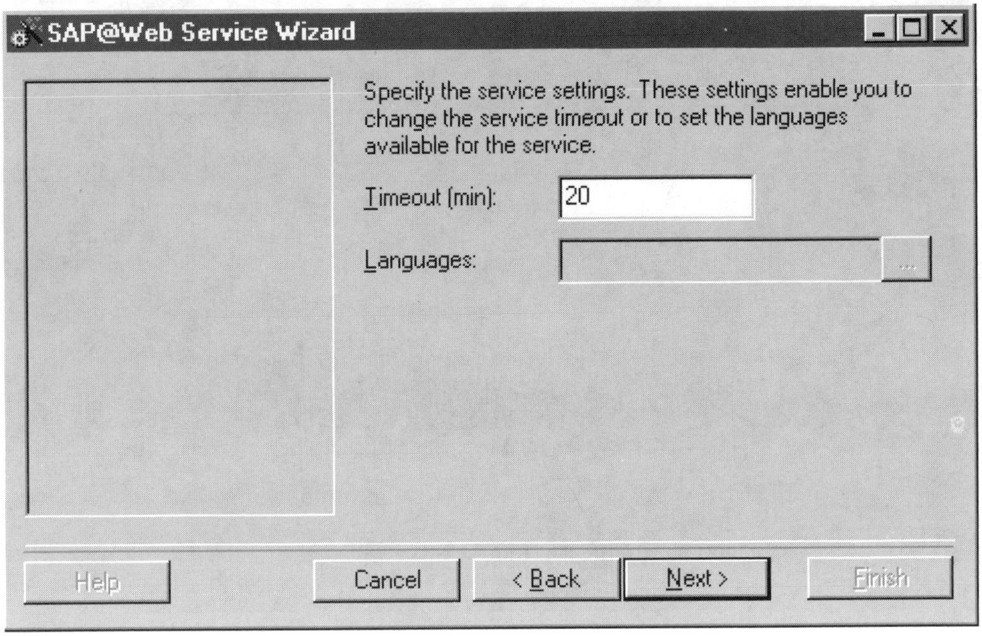

Figure 7.13   Setting the timeout for the service

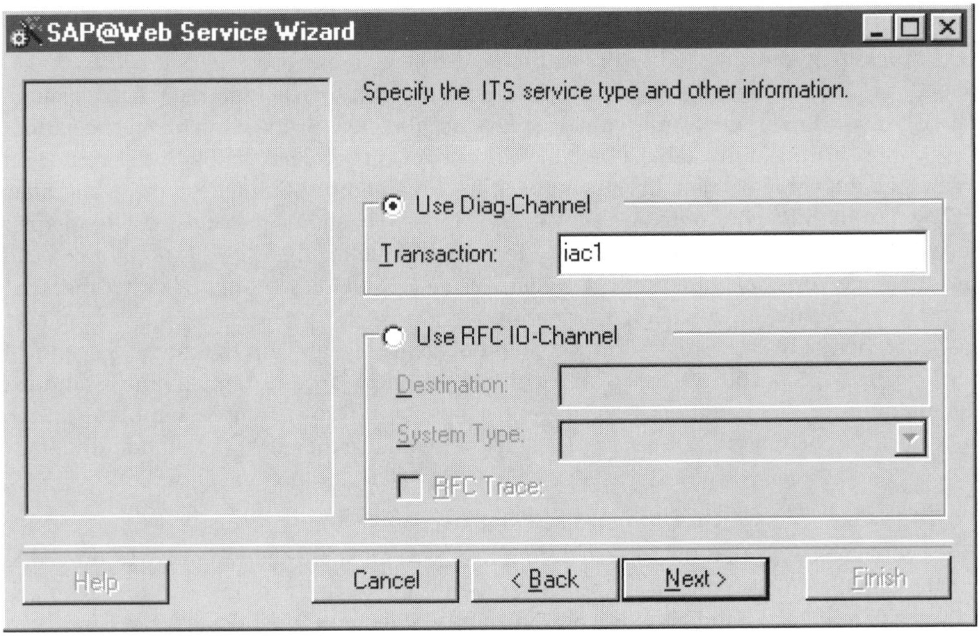

Figure 7.14   Setting the communications channel and the R/3 transaction

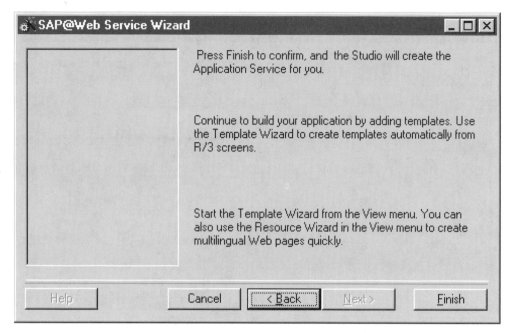

Figure 7.15   Closing confirmation

The definition of the service is now closed. To have the Studio generate the service description, confirm the previously entered settings with the FINISH button in the last popup.

If necessary, you can modify or supplement the file created by the Studio. To do so, select FILE VIEW in the left window of the Studio and double-click on the CALC symbol. The right window of the Studio now displays an overview of the contents in the service description, arranged in a table. A double-click on an entry calls a dialog that permits you to change the value of the entry. A double-click on an empty line takes you to a similar dialog that permits you to make a new entry. Figure 7.16 shows the Studio with an open service description. Use this opportunity to set the value for the LANGUAGE parameter to the language you use. Note that 3.x systems use a one-character language identifier and that 4.x systems use a two-character identifier.

Generation of the service description does not create an entry for the theme. The global service file, GLOBAL.SRVC, may well contain an entry for a default theme. Standard installations always use theme 99. The entry sets the ITS to search for templates in the subdirectories of a theme. The examples here therefore use theme 99 as a standard theme.

Creating a language resource

After you have generated the service description, you must create a language resource file for the login language entered in the service definition or in the global service file. Mark the service in the left window of the Studio and call the menu functions FILE | NEW. Then select FILE WIZARDS. Mark the generator for resource files and start it with the OK button.

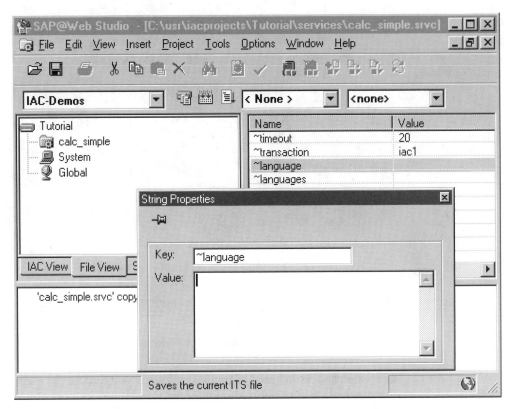

Figure 7.16   The studio with an open service description and a popup for maintaining parameters

The generator for language resources consists of a single popup (Figure 7.17) in which you enter two values: a language and a theme. The Studio creates only a empty file without any entries. Selection of the two entries completes work in this area.

The first example uses 99 as the theme. You can enter the language identifier directly or use the pushbutton next to the input field to see a list of possible entries. Versions 3.x and 4.x use different language identifiers. Because the names of external files reflect language identifiers, you must set the flag R/3 4.0 System in the popup to follow the conventions of 4.x systems. If you use an older version of the R/3 software, you can leave the flag at its default setting (unmarked).

The list of possible entries displays the languages supported by the Studio. Select one language and confirm your choice with the OK button. If you used the standard installation of the ITS and have not changed the login language in the service description, use English as the login language. After selecting the language, you return to the main window of the resource generator. Use the NEXT pushbutton to move to the next popup (Figure 7.19).

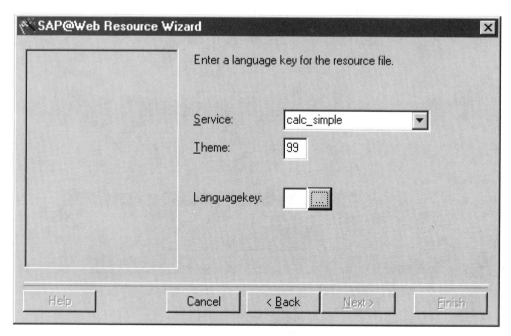

Figure 7.17   Creating a language resource

If you have already created and maintained a language resource, you can use the existing parameters when you create additional resources. Make the settings in this popup. The NEXT pushbutton takes you to the last popup that confirms your entries.

Generating and modifying HTML templates

After you have generated the service description and the language resource, you must still create both HTML templates. Again, mark the service in the Studio and call the file generator just as you did when generating the service description and the language resource. Then start the TEMPLATE WIZARD, which reads a screen description from the R/3 System and generates an HTML template from it.

The first popup to appear selects the R/3 System. You also used this popup when generating the service description. You must select an existing R/3 System in the popup; you cannot refer to the entries in the global service description. The following popup creates the log in data for the R/3 System selected. The Studio uses this data to log in to the R/3 System immediately and then to read the screen information there.

In the third popup (Figure 7.20), enter the screen to be generated. Enter the name of the program in the PROGRAM field and the screen numbers (separated by semicolons) in the SCREEN NUMBER field. To create names and store files correctly, the Studio also needs an entry for the service (obligatory), theme and language. The last two specifications are optional. You must specify a theme only when you actually work with various themes. You must specify a language only when you wish to generate language-dependent templates. In normal cases, you can leave the field blank (language-independent templates).

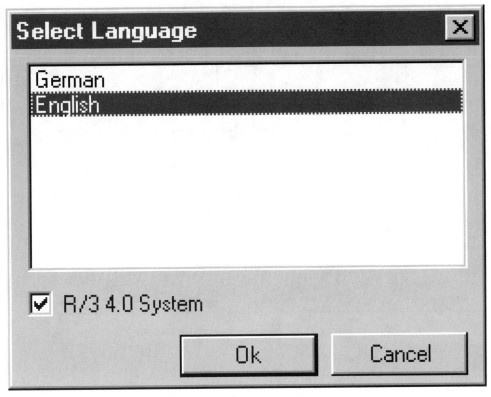

Figure 7.18   Possible entries for languages

In the following popup, you confirm previous entries. After generation is complete, the name of the template appears in the object list of the service. A double-click on the name opens the file for editing (Figure 7.21). Editing takes place in the right window of the Studio.

The generated template offers some novelties even to users with HTML experience. The following lines are number to permit easy reference in the following.

```
 1 <html>
 2 <HEAD>
 3 </HEAD>
 4 <BODY>
 5 <FORM ACTION="`wgateURL()`" METHOD="post">
 6 <p>
 7 `VALUE1.label`
 8 <INPUT TYPE="text"  name="VALUE1" VALUE="`VALUE1`"
                       maxlength='20' size="20" >
 9 <INPUT TYPE="submit" name="~OkCode=OPC+" value=`BUTTON_PLUS.label`>
10 <INPUT TYPE="submit" name="~OkCode=OPC-" value=`BUTTON_MINUS.label`>
```

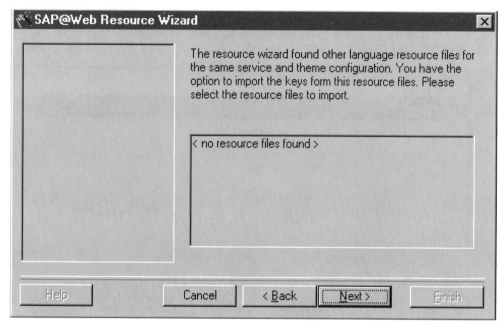

Figure 7.19   Merging language resources

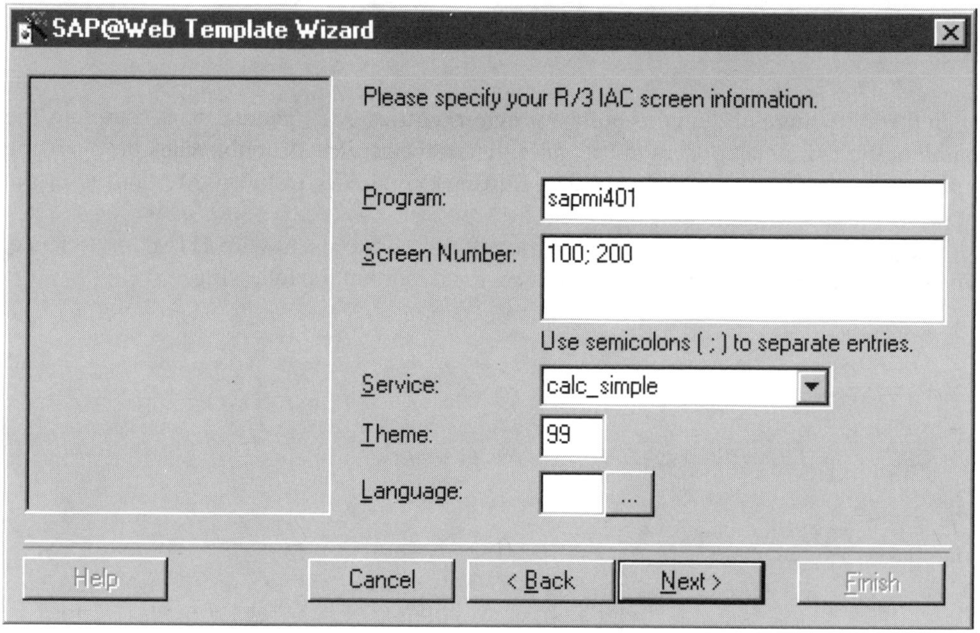

Figure 7.20   Specifications for generating templates

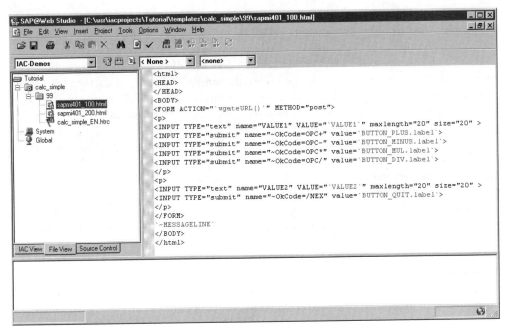

Figure 7.21   Editing a template with SAP@Web-Studio

```
11 <INPUT TYPE="submit" name="~OkCode=OPC*" value=`BUTTON_MUL.label`>
12 <INPUT TYPE="submit" name="~OkCode=OPC/"" value=`BUTTON_DIV.label`>
13 </p>
14 <p>
15 `VALUE2.label`
16 <INPUT TYPE="text"  name="VALUE2" VALUE="`VALUE2`"
                       maxlength="20" size="20" >
17 <INPUT TYPE="submit"  name="~OkCode=/NEX"
value=`BUTTON_QUIT.label`>
18 </p>
19 </FORM>
20 `~MESSAGELINE`
21 </BODY>
22 </html>
```

Lines 1–4 contain the usual HTML header and introduce the actual page description.

The first special item appears in line 5. The HTML element FORM defines an interactive element: a form. A form is not equivalent to the entire HTML document. A form consists of all the input elements between the tags FORM and /FORM. Several forms can exist within one HTML template. The FORM tag indicates the program and server that should evaluate the values from the form. A URL performs this task. The tag notes the URL as a value of the ACTION parameter. To avoid having to hard code the URL into the template, the WGATEURL() metafunction returns a URL taken from the global service description.

Backticks (`) enclose HTML enhancements. At runtime, the ITS replaces the statement with a value delivered by the function. HTML templates that use such enhancements and avoid hard coding are portable beyond the boundaries of the R/3 System.

Line 7 also contains an HTML[Business] statement. This statement inserts the description (key field) of the screen field VALUE1 into the HTML document. The name of a screen field references a screen field. Additions (here .LABEL) permit access to selected field attributes.

The statement in line 8 provides a relatively simple explanation of the data transfer principles between an HTML template and the R/3 System. The INPUT tag generates an input field. In addition to other attributes, this field receives a unique name (NAME="VALUE1") and an initial value (VALUE="`VALUE1`"). The field name must agree with the corresponding screen field. The ITS uses this name internally to allocate the HTML field and the screen field. As a result, the ITS also handles data exchange with the name. HTML syntax requires that you enclose the name in double quotation marks. The initial value is the value delivered by the R/3 System. HTML syntax requires the double quotation marks; the backticks ensure that the character string will be interpreted as a metastatement. In this special case, the statement is replaced with the contents of the specified screen field.

In addition to input fields, other interactive elements exist in an HTML template. Pushbuttons in an HTML template can also trigger actions, if an INPUT tag is generated by the pushbuttons.

The parameters of the tag are quite similar to those of input fields. However, they generally receive different values. Without knowledge of how programming interactive Web applications functions, these values can lead to misunderstandings. The TYPE parameter sets the concrete object type (input field, pushbutton and so on). The HTML standard supports two types of pushbuttons: SUBMIT and REFRESH. One pushbutton of the SUBMIT type transmits data to the Web server. The REFRESH type is used for buttons evaluated by the Web browser locally. This type merely initializes the form.

The VALUE parameter of the INPUT tag contains the text displayed in the pushbutton. The value has a completely static character and it should describe the function of the pushbutton clearly. The HTML generator takes the field text of the pushbutton for this parameter. Since the parameter has no identifying character on the Web, you can modify it as desired. You can therefore replace the value of the VALUE parameter with any character string. Use of the R/3 field text provides you with all the advantages of language-dependent design of the R/3 screen.

The NAME parameter for the pushbutton requires special handling. The ITS must transfer a function code to the R/3 application for every pushbutton. Unlike simple input fields, however, this value cannot be stored as a value for the object (VALUE parameter). The value should describe the pushbutton and must record clear text. Only the NAME parameter is available. So that the ITS can distinguish pushbuttons from normal input fields, the name must contain a unique ID for pushbutton. Accordingly, the name of the pushbutton consists of ~OKCODE= character string and the R/3 function code that the pushbutton is to trigger.

Now a special aspect of 4.0 Systems in this context is discussed. As of release 4.0, the R/3 System stores screen descriptions somewhat differently than it did in version 3.x. In addition, the HTML template generator creates entries for the NAME parameter in the following form:

```
name="~OkCode(/NEX)"
```

In this case, you may have to edit the template generated by the Studio. The parenthesis may enclose only the four-character function code: the system does not permit blanks or additions (for example E/).

In line 20, the template generator creates a metastatement to insert the ~MESSAGELINE FIELD. This field contains the text of an error message generated by the R/3 System under certain circumstance. See Section 7.2.2 for more information on handling error messages.

After generating the first template, you must generate the second. The workflow involved is identical.

```
 1 <html>
 2 <HEAD>
 3 </HEAD>
 4 <BODY>
 5 <FORM ACTION="`wgateURL()`" METHOD="post">
 6 <p>
 7 <INPUT TYPE="text"  name="VALUE1" VALUE="`VALUE1`"
                       maxlength="20" size="20" >
 8 </p>
 9 <p>
10 <INPUT TYPE="text"  name="OP" VALUE="`OP`"
                       maxlength=" 1" size=" 1" >
11 <INPUT TYPE="text"  name="VALUE2" VALUE="`VALUE2`"
                       maxlength="20" size="20" >
12 </p>
13 <p>
14 <INPUT TYPE="text"  name="IS" VALUE="`IS`"
                       maxlength=" 1" size=" 1" >
15 <INPUT TYPE="text"  name="RESULT" VALUE="`RESULT`"
                       maxlength="20" size="20" >
16 </p>
17 <p>
18 <INPUT TYPE="submit"   name="~OkCode=FNEW"
value=`BUTTON_NEW.label`>
19 <INPUT TYPE="submit"   name="~OkCode=/NEX"
value=`BUTTON_EXIT.label`>
20 </p>
21 </FORM>
22 `~MESSAGELINE`
23 </BODY>
24 </html>
```

Since all the fields of the second screen in the R/3 System are created as input/output fields, the Studio generates a true input field in the HTML template. This HTML page, however, displays only the result of the calculation. You must therefore modify the template manually. You must replace the INPUT tags with metastatements that output the five fields. To do so, delete lines 7–11 and insert the following statement:

```
`VALUE1` `OP` `VALUE2` `IS` `RESULT`
```

Testing the application

After you have completed editing the template, you can test the application. You must first transfer the newly created IAC files from the current working directory of the project to the ITS directories. To transfer the files, first mark FILE VIEW in the Studio. Then mark the service with a right click and select the PUBLISH function from the menu. You can include or exclude the files to copy in the next popup (Figure 7.22).

After you transfer the files, start a Web browser. Enter a character string in the following form for the URL and confirm it with the enter key.

```
http://<Web-Server>/scripts/wgate.dll/<Service-Name>/!
```

If the Web server and the ITS are installed locally on the same computer, a concrete URL would appear as follows:

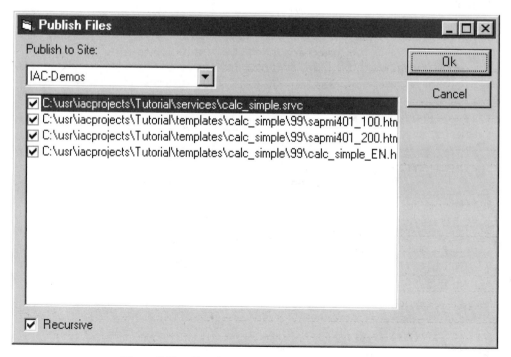

Figure 7.22   Copying IAC files to the ITS directories

```
http://bernd/scripts/wgate.dll/calc_simple/!
```

If the templates were changed correctly, the service description fits the installation and the application functions correctly in the R/3 System, the application should start and display the HTML document in Figure 7.23.

The Web browser in use may change the appearance of the displayed page slightly from the one in Figure 7.23. To arrive at a pleasing appearance, you may have to edit the temples again.

Creating and activating a new theme

The following three examples require only modifications to templates, rather than any changes to the R/3 application. We therefore recommend that you do not create a new project. Instead, perform the modifications with the current service in a new theme. You must create a new theme within the current service and copy the templates and language resources already generated into the new theme. You can then enter the current theme in the application-specific service description. After making the modifications, transfer the new files in the ITS or Web server directory and retest the application.

To create a new theme, first select FILE VIEW in the Studio. Mark the name of the service and then call the context menu for the service entry with a right click. Then select the INSERT | THEME function.

The Studio then creates a new directory for the theme. You must then set the number to the desired value. The Studio makes the input field for the number immediately available (see Figure 7.24). The following example uses theme 90.

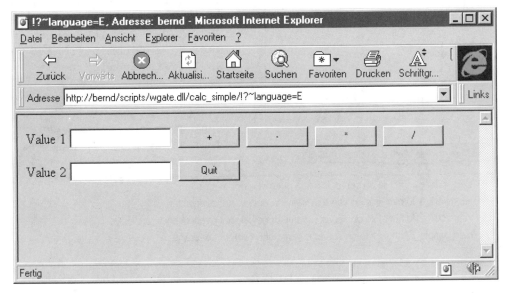

Figure 7.23   The first Web application

You can generate the IAC files from scratch or copy them with drag and drop from the files already available.

Summary

- The field values of screen fields are transferred into an HTML document by enclosing the field name in backticks. The input value provided by the browser is then transferred into the field.

  Example:
  `` `FIELD_IS` ``

- Attributes are available for some types of fields. A later fix identifies the attributes for the field names.

  Example:
  `` `NEW.label` ``

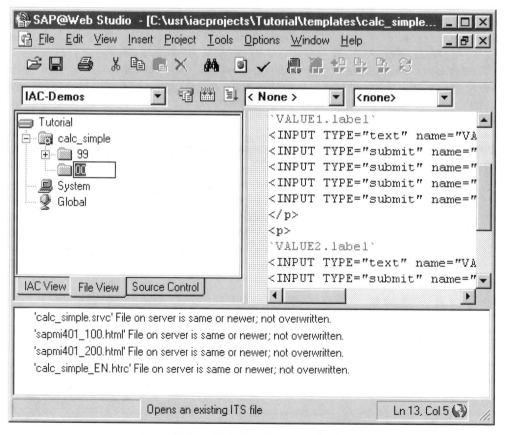

Figure 7.24   Changing the name of a theme

- The URL of the current server is available with the metafunction `wgateURL()`.

- Pushbuttons must anchor the function code to be triggered in the R/3 System in the name of the HTML object.

- Always use the function code `/NEX` to end the application explicitly.

7.2.2   Example 2: Error messages

The SAP system can signal an error condition with a message in the status line of the SAPGUI. The system generates most of these messages automatically; users cannot suppress them. A simply method allows you to insert the contents of the status line in an HTML page with an HTML[Business] statement. It is also possible to mark the field to which the error message refers. The following example demonstrates the required HTML[Business] statements. You do not need to change the R/3 application: simply enhance the templates. To do so, create a new theme (90).

Modifying the templates

The ITS automatically fills the `~MessageLine` field with the contents of the status line from the R/3 application. You can insert the field into the template at any location, as long as backticks enclose it. Otherwise, the ITS would place the field description rather than the contents of the field into the page it produces. The HTML generator assists SAP@Web-Studio to create the temple, and automatically inserts the template at the end of every template it generates.

The error messages generated with `` `~MessageLine` `` provides adequate information only in very simple cases. The system cannot transfer the long text of an error message to the Web. If you require more information on an error, you should program special help pages.

Another disadvantage: in many cases, the user cannot determine which field caused the error by examining the error message. If the R/3 application provides such information because of its programming, the HTML[Business] `~assert()` function can provide assistance.

You can insert the `~assert()` function into the HTML template with a field name as its parameter. If the R/3 application generates an error message, it sends the ITS the field name of the first field that triggered an error. The ITS then compares the field name with the parameter of the `~assert()` function. If they are equal, the ITS inserts a standard text in place of the function or, if available, the content of the `ErrorMarker` parameter. Either the global or the application-specific service description usually sets this parameter. The `ErrorMarker` parameter can contain any HTML statement. It need not be a text; you may also insert a graphic. In any case, do not allocate `ErrorMarker` to the contents of `~MessageLine`. Doing so would require recursive replacement, and the ITS does not implement this function.

Note the following quirk when using this function. In the event of an error, an R/3 application sets only the screen fields linked to the error message as ready for input. None of the other fields can accept input. In a Web application, however, switching off the ability of a field to accept input is rather involved. Users can therefore change the contents of fields on the Web even when the fields in the R/3 application cannot accept input. This would lead to an error in the application. Accordingly, you should always link all the screen fields of a screen or subscreen with an error message. Doing so ensures that all the values in the HTML page can be transferred correctly to the R/3 System. The *assert* function therefore has limited benefits in *single frame* applications. The function is more important in connection with frame applications.

If you wish to place the error message directly in the field that triggers it, you must insert the ~MessageLine parameter directly behind that field.

The following modified listing of screen 100 shows the use of both statements. The original variant of theme 99 provides the starting point. The service description uses the character string ("<<<---") to fill the ERRORMARKER parameter.

```
<html>
<HEAD>
</HEAD>
<BODY>
<FORM ACTION="`wgateURL()`" METHOD="post">
<p>
`VALUE1.label`
<INPUT TYPE="text" name="VALUE1" VALUE="`VALUE1`"
       maxlength="20" size="20" >
`assert(value1)`
`~MESSAGELINE`
<INPUT TYPE="submit" name="~OkCode=OPC+"
value=`BUTTON_PLUS.label`>
<INPUT TYPE="submit" name="~OkCode=OPC-"
value=`BUTTON_MINUS.label`>
<INPUT TYPE="submit" name="~OkCode=OPC*"
value=`BUTTON_MUL.label`>
<INPUT TYPE="submit" name="~OkCode=OPC/"
value=`BUTTON_DIV.label`>
</p>
<p>
`VALUE2.label`
<INPUT TYPE="text" name="VALUE2" VALUE="`VALUE2`"
       maxlength="20" size="20" >
`assert(value1)`
`~MESSAGELINE`
<INPUT TYPE="submit" name="~OkCode=/NEX" value=`BUTTON_QUIT.label`>
</p>
</FORM>
</BODY>
</html>
```

7.2.3   Example 3: Language-dependent text elements

The R/3 System administers field descriptions, headers and similar texts in language-dependent tables. The system merges the tables into the screens according to the login language. IACs can also use this mechanism. For example, the R/3 System can supply the descriptors for input fields of pushbuttons in the correct language. As demonstrated, the descriptors are available in the HTML templates with the supplemental `.label` options for the field name.

If you must insert texts that the R/3 System does not support, you must access external language resources. Language resources contain parameters that then receive a value. A placeholder within templates refers to such parameters:

```
#parametername
```

To create a parameter in the language resource, use the Studio. Change to FILE VIEW in the Studio and open the language resource for editing. You edit the language resources in the same manner as the serve descriptions.

You can use these types of placeholders anywhere; the placeholders do not need to contain static text. You can also use this method to store language-dependent links in language-independent templates. The method is useful when linking pages that contain static help texts. See Section 7.5 for further information.

The following listing of the template for screen 100 shows the use of language resources as headers. For this example, you can copy the files created in Example 2 for theme 90 into a new theme 80.

```
<html>
<HEAD>
</HEAD>
<BODY>
`#header`
<FORM ACTION="`wgateURL()`" METHOD="post">
<p>
`VALUE1.label`
<INPUT TYPE="text" name="VALUE1" VALUE="`VALUE1`"
                        maxlength="20" size="20" >
`assert(value1)`
`~MESSAGELINE`
<INPUT TYPE="submit" name="~OkCode=OPC+"
value=`BUTTON_PLUS.label`>
<INPUT TYPE="submit" name="~OkCode=OPC-"
value=`BUTTON_MINUS.label`>
<INPUT TYPE="submit" name="~OkCode=OPC*"
value=`BUTTON_MUL.label`>
<INPUT TYPE="submit" name="~OkCode=OPC/"
value=`BUTTON_DIV.label`>
</p>
```

```
<p>
`VALUE2.label`
<INPUT TYPE="text" name="VALUE2" VALUE="`VALUE2`"
maxlength="20" size="20" >
`assert(value1)` `~MESSAGELINE`
<INPUT TYPE=""submit" name="~OkCode=/NEX"
value=`BUTTON_QUIT.label`>
</p>
</FORM>
</BODY>
</html>
```

You can translate language resources internally in the R/3 System and externally with SAP@Web-Studio. Customer development systems will find the second option interesting because it involves less effort.

7.2.4   Example 4: Binary objects

None of the previous examples has used any visual design of the generated HTML pages. The World Wide Web greatly enjoys the ability to design the appearance of applications in any way. The following example describes how to link graphics in HTML templates. The example does not requires some any modifications of the existing R/3 application, but you must modify the templates slightly. Generate a new theme (70), and copy the files from the previous example to the new theme.

Static links

The Web server makes graphics and other binary objects (such as sound files) available for ITS applications. The pages generated by the ITS therefore contain links that refer to subdirectories beneath the root directory of the Web server. An HTML tag to insert a GIF file as a background could appear as follows:

```
<BODY background="/graphics/back.gif">
```

Of course, you can also note the links as a purely static URL in the templates. Several reasons argue against this approach:

- Hard-coded links complicate the transfer of completed applications to other systems or Web servers.

- The concept of themes was developed to give existing applications a new appearance. You can easily switch to another appearance by changing the theme entry in the global service description. The ITS uses the theme entry to generate URLs for binary files stored in other subdirectories. All applications appear with new layouts at one time. You do not need to change the templates themselves unless they contain static links.

- In some circumstances, you must make graphics or sound files available in different languages. The HTML standard does not support this function.

These disadvantages are hardly noticeable for a simple background graphic. Problems develop when working with graphics that depend on a language or theme, when dealing with a large number of binary files or when handling frequent layout changes. The HTML[Business] commands therefore contain a function that enables the ITS to generate links to binary objects. The following section demonstrates the use of this statement.

The mimeURL() HTML[Business] function

Various attributes influence the appearance of an IAC at runtime: the service, the language and the theme. The organization of binary objects must also be able to follow these criteria. Installation of the ITS creates a subdirectory tree with a structure similar to that of the templates. The subdirectory has subdirectories for each service, each of which has additional subdirectories for theme and language. An additional subdirectory is available for binary objects that apply to all applications.

When you wish to reference objects in this directory tree, use the `mimeURL()` HTML[Business] function. The function uses a maximum of four parameters: `~service`, `~theme`, `~language` and `~name`. The names of the parameters indicate their tasks. Except for `~name`, all the parameters are optional. The ITS automatically fills missing parameters with the current service, theme and language.

Unlike other HTML[Business] functions, shorthand exists for the parameters. If you maintain the sequence of parameters given above, you can omit the parameter descriptions.

SAP@Web-Studio: Inserting graphics in projects

Before you can reference graphics or other binary files in templates, you must record them in the appropriate project. You must use the Studio to record the files. First create some graphics; you can use Figure 7.25 for inspiration. The following example uses the files PLUS.GIF, MINUS.GIF, MUL.GIF, DIV.GIF, QUIT.GIF and NEW.GIF. For the moment, these files can exist in any directory.

In the Studio, use FILE VIEW to mark (right click) the target for the files you wish to insert. The target is most often a theme or a subdirectory for a language. A mouse click calls a context menu, in which you select the INSERT | FILE function. The Studio offers you a standard Windows dialog to select the files for insertion. Enter in the FILENAME field a generic name for the files you wish to find (such as `*.GIF`). A double click on a file places it in the project: the Studio copies it into a subdirectory of the project directory. If you edit the file later, you must edit the version in the project directory.

The new templates

The following template for screen 100 demonstrates the use of the `mimeURL` function. It sets a background and inserts graphics in place of the basic HTML pushbuttons. A table positions the various elements.

Since the graphics were stored as language-independent files in the directory, the `~language` parameter in the `mimeURL` function must contain an empty character string. The empty string tells the ITS that it should look for an language-independent file.

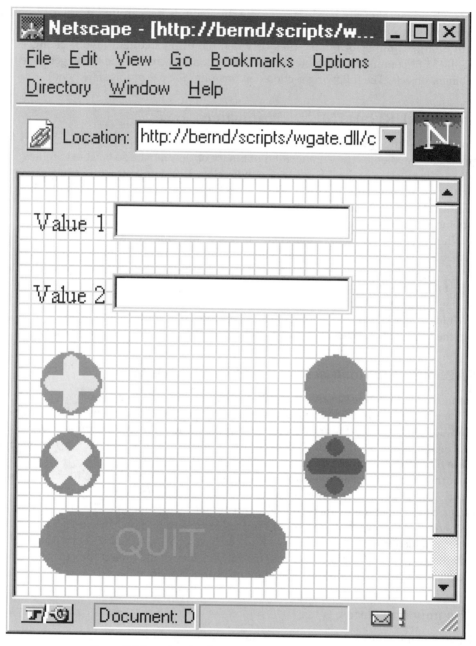

Figure 7.25   calc_simple service with designed interface

Without the parameter, the ITS would fill the parameter with the value for the current language. It would then look for the graphic in the directories for language-dependent files.

When analyzing templates, please note that you must enter the function code for graphic pushbuttons in the following form:

```
name="~OkCode(<Functioncode>)"
```

The most up-to-date variants of the template generator already conform to this requirement.

```
<html>
<HEAD>
</HEAD>
<BODY background = `mimeURL("BACK.GIF", ~language = "" )` >
`#header`
<FORM ACTION="`wgateURL()`" METHOD="post">
<p>
`VALUE1.label`
<INPUT TYPE="text"
                      name="VALUE1" VALUE="`VALUE1`"
            maxlength="20" size="20" >
`assert(value1)` `~MESSAGELINE`
</p>
<p>
`VALUE2.label`
<INPUT TYPE="text"
            name="VALUE2" VALUE="`VALUE2`"
            maxlength="20" size="20" >
`assert(value1)` `~MESSAGELINE`
</p>
<table>
  <tr> <td>
    <INPUT TYPE=image
            name="~OkCode(OPC+)"
            src="`mimeURL("PLUS.GIF", ~language = "")`"
            border = 0>
  </td> <td>
    <INPUT TYPE=image
            name="~OkCode(OPC-)"
            src="`mimeURL("MINUS.GIF", ~language = "")`"
            border = 0>
  </td> </tr>
  <tr> <td>
    <INPUT TYPE=image
            name="~OkCode(OPC*)"
            src="`mimeURL("MUL.GIF", ~language = "")`"
            border = 0>
```

```
</td> <td>
  <INPUT TYPE=image
          name="~OkCode(OPC/)"
          src="`mimeURL("DIV.GIF", ~language = "")`"
          border = 0>
</td> </tr>
<tr> <td>
    <INPUT TYPE=image
          name="~OkCode(/NEX)"
          src="`mimeURL("QUIT.GIF", ~language = "")`"
          border = 0>
  </td> </tr>
</table>
</FORM>
`~MESSAGELINE`
</BODY>
</html>
```

For the sake of completeness, the reworked source code of the second template.

```
<html>
<HEAD>
</HEAD>
<BODY background = `mimeURL("BACK.GIF", ~language = "" )` >
<FORM ACTION="`wgateURL()`" METHOD="post">
<p>
`VALUE1` `OP` `VALUE2` `IS` `RESULT`
</p>
<table>
  <tr> <td>
    <INPUT TYPE=image
          name="~OkCode(FNEW)"
          src="`mimeURL("NEW.GIF", ~language = "")`"
          border = 0>
  </td> <tr> <td>
    <INPUT TYPE=image
          name="~OkCode(/NEX)"
          src="`mimeURL("QUIT.GIF", ~language = "")`"
          border = 0>
  </td> </tr>
</table>
</FORM>
`~MESSAGELINE`
</BODY>
</html>
```

7.2.5   Example 5: Radio buttons

The previous examples have used only simple input fields and pushbuttons. The following example demonstrates how to create and evaluate radio buttons. Please create a new project for this example and another new project for the following example. The examples also require changes to the R/3 program: copy program SAPMI401 and then modify it. The examples omit graphic design.

The R/3 application

The new program is named SAPMI402 and is called with transaction ITS2. The service is named calc_radio; the project is named CALC2. This example replaces the four operations pushbuttons in the HTML template with radio buttons and a new pushbutton to start the calculation. The Web and the R/3 System display radio buttons in different ways. HTML displays related radio buttons as a single field with variable contents. For the sake of simplicity, the ABAP/4 application uses the same mechanism. This method ensures that execution on the Web processes a different program code than direct execution in the R/3 System. This type of branching significantly complicates searching for errors.

The new example is very similar to the previous example. You must adjust only screen 100. The example removes or changes some pushbuttons and adds a single-character field for the operations sign. Function code COMP triggers the pushbutton for calculation. Since the screen now has an input field, the screen must consider the field in the FIELD statement of its flow logic. This consideration ensures that the R/3 application can correctly accept this field after an error message.

```
PROCESS BEFORE OUTPUT.
  MODULE init_0100.
*
PROCESS AFTER INPUT.
  CHAIN.
    FIELD: value1, value2, op.
    MODULE check_0100.
  ENDCHAIN.
  MODULE user_command_0100.
```

Figure 7.26 shows the first screen of this application.

The flow logic of the user command module also changes. The following source code illustrates the change:

```
module user_command_0100 input.
  case fcode.
    when 'COMP'.
      case field_op.
        when '+'.
          field3 = field1 + field2.
          leave to screen 200.
```

```
        when '-'.
          field3 = field1 - field2.
          leave to screen 200.
        when '*'.
          field3 = field1 * field2.
          leave to screen 200.
        when '/'.
          if field2 = 0.
            message e002.
          else.
            field3 = field1 / field2.
            leave to screen 200.
          endif.
    endcase.
  when '/NEX'.
```

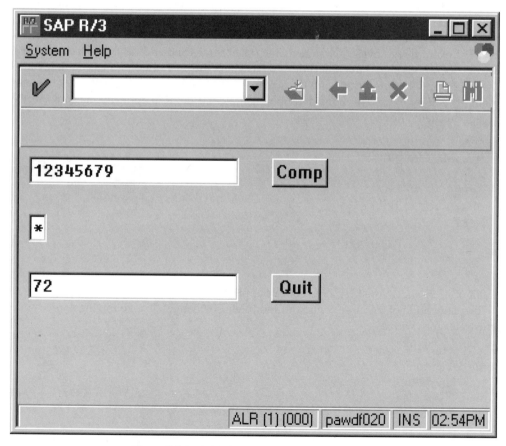

Figure 7.26   Initial screen of the second example

```
      leave to screen 0.
  endcase.
endmodule.                       " USER_COMMAND_0100 INPUT
```

Generating the template

Create the service description, language resource and template for screen 200 as you did
in the previous example. The template of screen 100 contains the only change. The following source code shows the template produced by the generator:

```
 1 <html>
 2 <HEAD>
 3 </HEAD>
 4 <BODY>
 5 <FORM ACTION="`wgateURL()`" METHOD="post">
 6 <p>
 7 <INPUT TYPE="text" name="VALUE1" VALUE="`VALUE1`"
         maxlength="20" size="20" >
 8 <INPUT TYPE="submit"  name="~OkCode=COMP"
value=`BUTTON_COMP.label`>
 9 </p>
10 <p>
11 <INPUT TYPE="text" name="OP" VALUE="`OP`" maxlength=" 1"
size=" 1" >
12 </p>
13 <p>
14 <INPUT TYPE="text" name="VALUE2" VALUE="`VALUE2`"
                      maxlength="20" size="20" >
15 <INPUT TYPE="submit" name="~OkCode=/NEX"
value=`BUTTON_QUIT.label`>
16 </p>
17 </FORM>
18 `~MESSAGELINE`
19 </BODY>
20 </html>
```

The declaration of an input field for field OP appears in line 11 of the template. Replace
this declaration with the declaration of the four radio buttons. You use the INPUT tag with
the corresponding parameters:

```
<input type=radio name="OP" value="+">addition
<input type=radio name="OP" value="-">subtraction
<input type=radio name="OP" value="*">multiplication
<input type=radio name="OP" value="/">division
```

Figure 7.27 shows the application during a test. Although the templates produced by the
generator are not particularly attractive, they can test the application.

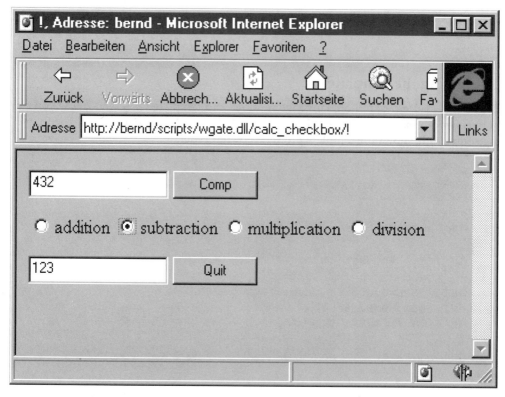

Figure 7.27   Initial screen of the radio button example on the Web

Summary

- R/3 radio buttons cannot work directly with a Web application.

- Logically related radio buttons refer to a single screen field and place various values into the field.

7.2.6   Example 6: Possible entries

The SAP System can display a list of possible entries (F4 Help) for the fields of a screen. The R/3 System determines the list of possible entries dynamically; HTML documents cannot implement an equivalent. However, you can generate and display input elements that permit selection from predefined value sets with the SELECT tag.

You can generate the value set in different ways: hard coded values in an HTML document and dynamic provision from within the R/3 application. The mechanism used to generate the value sets also enables you to transport additional data from the R/3 System to the HTML document: a mass data channel. The mechanism not only supports implementation of the list of possible entries, but also works bidirectionally with the ITS (as of version 2.0).

This example replaces the input field for the operations sign with a radio button that has a predefined value set. At runtime, the R/3 System readies permissible values for the application.

The R/3 application

You can create the sixth example (program `SAPMI403`, transaction `IAC3`, service `CALC_F4`) with a few modifications to the fifth. The operation will now no longer execute on the Web with one of the four radio buttons, but by entry of an operation sign in an field. The system should permit selection of signs from a predefined value set. Application SAPMI402 already works according to this procedure. If hard coding the possible entries in the HTML page suffices, you do not have to change the RT/3 application. You replace the declarations of the four radio buttons with the following statement:

```
<select name="OP" size=0>
  <option value="+"> Addition
  <option value="-"> Subtraction
  <option value="*"> Multiplication
  <option value="/"> Division
</select>
```

If the valid value sets are delivered from the R/3 System with the mass data channel, you must write some additional statements in the PBO portion of the first screen.

The macros `FIELD-SET` and `FIELD-TRANSPORT` handle transfer of values. The macros are in program `AVWRTCXM`; join the macros with an *Include* statement in the main program or in the *TOP-Include*.

Data must be transferred to the HTML document at the point of PBO. You should create a specific module for this task and call it in the flow logic.

```
process before output.
  module status_0100.
  module input_help_0100.

  . . .
```

Although the source code of the new module is relatively short, it requires some explanation.

```
module input_help_0100 output.
  field-set 'FIELD_OP' 1 '+'.
  field-set 'FIELD_BZ' 1 'Addition'.
  field-set 'FIELD_OP' 2 '-'.
  field-set 'FIELD_BZ' 2 'Subtraction'.
  field-set 'FIELD_OP' 3 '*'.
  field-set 'FIELD_BZ' 3 'Multiplication'.
  field-set 'FIELD_OP' 4 '/'.
  field-set 'FIELD_BZ' 4 'Division'.
  field-transport.
endmodule. " INPUT_HELP_0100 OUTPUT
```

The macros build a data structure, similar to a table, in which you can create several columns. The HTML template reads this table in a loop statement. You must fill the table in the PBO module with the FIELD-SET macro and transmit it to the HTML document with the FIELD-TRANSPORT module.

Transfer three parameters to the FIELD-SET macro: the name used to address the field in HTML document later, the sequential number (table line), and the value. The names serve only for identification in the template. No reference to existing fields is made in the R/3 application. Names must be unique in the HTML document: the screen should not contain a field with the same name. The only possible exception is in using a screen field with the same name to return one of the field contents (the selected entry) to the R/3 System. This is the case in the example.

You can note the values transmitted to the HTML document with the macros directly in the source code. Doing so, however, would require you to edit the source code for every change in the value set. Therefore, the data for a true list of possible entries should be determined dynamically by selections in tables or by reading the fixed values of a domain.

Working in SAP@Web-Studio

After creating the R/3 application, you can create the external files. The changes to the template for screen 100 reflect the only significant differences from Example 2.

Edit the declaration for field OP. According to the task, this field should have several options for selection rather than function as a simple input field. Define selection fields with the HTML SELECT tag. The OPTION tag generates one entry for a selection field. The VALUE parameter within the tag sets the returning value. You can enter an explanatory text outside of the OPTION tag. The text will then appear in the input field.

If, as in this example, you do not wish to hard code the values, but take them dynamically from the R/3 System, you must use some metastatements. Use .dim to determine the number of values in fields with several values. You can access the values by specifying an index enclosed in square brackets. With a loop statement, you can now read the individual values and create the corresponding OPTION tags.

```
<select name="OP" size=0>
  `repeat with i from 1 to FIELD_OP.dim`
    <option value="`FIELD_OP[i]`"> `FIELD_BZ[i]`
  `end`
</select>
```

The REPEAT statement sequentially assigns the variable i the values 1 to the number of elements in the FIELD_OP field. Only one OPTION tag exists within the REPEAT loop. The OPTION tag generates an entry for the each SELECT field. While evaluating the template, the ITS generates a normal SELECT tag from the metastatement and the data delivered by the SAP System.

Summary

- An alternative, bidirectional data channel exists between the R/3 application and the HTML document. You can use this channel to transfer mass data such as values for possible entries.

- Transfer takes place within the R/3 System by calling the macros FIELD_SET and FIELD_TRANSPORT.

- You must link the *Include* AVWRTCXM to declare the macros.

- You may call FIELD_TRANSPORT only once for each PBO run in version 1.x of the ITS. Multiple runs are permitted only as of version 2.0.

- An HTML[Business] field can contain several values. Access to these values takes place by specifying an index.

  Example:
  `` `FIELD_OP[i]` ``

- You can use the REPEAT HTML[Business] statement to build a loop to query the contents of fields with multiple values (vectors).

7.2.7   Example 7: Step loops

ABAP/4 applications frequently use step loops to process several data records at once. Since the fields of the individual lines of the step loop have identical names, depicting them in an HTML document requires additional effort. The following example shows the structure of a simple step loop. The example is later expanded into a frame application.

The first version of the application does not support scrolling through the data on the Web. Later examples introduce the techniques required to enable scrolling.

The R/3 application

The new application is named SAPMI404. The corresponding transaction is IAC4, the service and the project are named STEPLOOP1. The starting screen of the application (Figure 7.28) queries the name of a development class. The second screen lists some TADIR entries with objects from the development class. The list is produced in true input fields that you can edit. Editing affects the internal table and not the database table TADIR. The third screen again lists the contents of the second screen to ensure that the entries edited on the Web read the internal table maintained with the step loop. The third screen is necessary only to demonstrate the transfer of data from an HTML table on the Web into the R/3 application.

The screen (number 100) offers an input field and two pushbuttons. The input field (TADIR-DEVCLASS) takes the name of the development class to be listed. One pushbutton ends the application; the other pushbutton jumps to the second screen.

The flow logic is also simple; repetition can be omitted here. The flow logic consists only of the *user command module*.

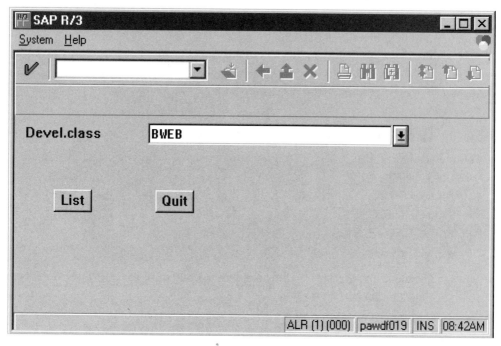

Figure 7.28   Initial screen of the step loop example

```
MODULE user_command_0100 INPUT.
  CASE okcode.
    WHEN '/NEX'.
      LEAVE TO SCREEN 0.
    WHEN 'LIST'.
      SELECT * FROM tadir INTO TABLE itadir
        WHERE devclass = tadir-devclass.
      itadir_size = sy-dbcnt.
      IF itadir_size > 0.
        LEAVE TO SCREEN 200.
      ENDIF.
  ENDCASE.
ENDMODULE.                       " USER_COMMAND_0100 INPUT
```

After you enter a development class, the system fills an internal table, ITADIR with the objects of the development class and calls the second screen (number 200, Figure 7.29). The structure of the table corresponds to the dictionary table TADIR. The second screen consists of a step loop over the fields PGMID, OBJECT and OBJ_NAME of the internal table. The screen also has three pushbuttons that permit a jump to the previous (or next) screen or end the application.

Because it must handle an internal table, the flow logic of this screen is more complex.

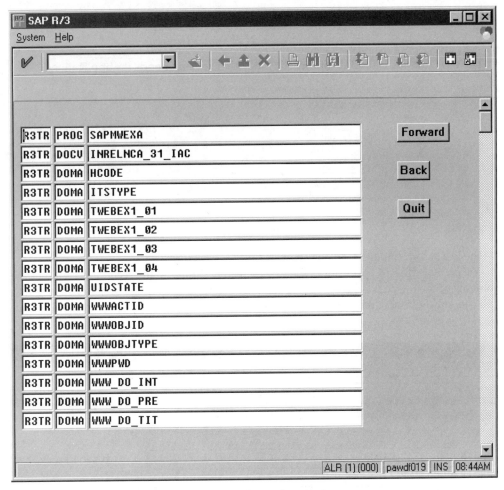

Figure 7.29   Editable step loop in the screen

```
PROCESS BEFORE OUTPUT.
  LOOP AT itadir CURSOR itadir_cursor.
  ENDLOOP.
*
PROCESS AFTER INPUT.
  LOOP AT itadir.
    MODULE aktual_itadir.
  ENDLOOP.
  MODULE user_command_0200.
```

The module that transfers the values from the step loop into the internal table consists of a single line.

```
MODULE aktual_itadir INPUT.
  MODIFY itadir FROM itadir INDEX itadir_cursor.
ENDMODULE.                         " AKTUAL_ITADIR INPUT
```

The user command module branches to the other screen or ends the application.

```
MODULE user_command_0200 INPUT.
  CASE okcode.
    WHEN '/NEX'.
      LEAVE TO SCREEN 0.
    WHEN 'BACK'.
      LEAVE TO SCREEN 100.
    WHEN 'FORW'.
      LEAVE TO SCREEN 300.
  ENDCASE.
ENDMODULE.                         " USER_COMMAND_0200 INPUT
```

The last screen (Figure 7.30) has an even simpler structure.

Within the ABAP/4 application, the third screen is similar to the second, except that the contents of the internal table are not updated and that it does not contain a pushbutton to call the subsequent screen. You can create the third screen by copying screen 200 and

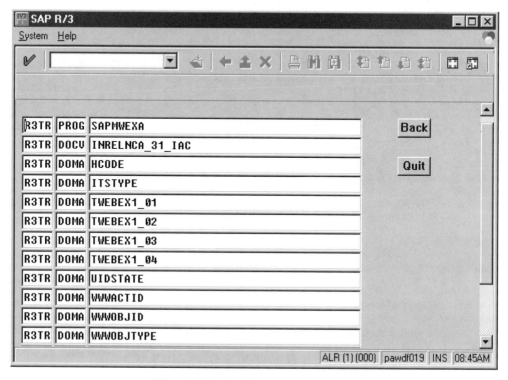

Figure 7.30   Step loop with edited lines

deleting the superfluous elements. The flow logic does not include the module for updating the internal table.

```
PROCESS BEFORE OUTPUT.
  LOOP AT itadir CURSOR itadir_cursor.
  ENDLOOP.
*
PROCESS AFTER INPUT.
  LOOP AT itadir.
  ENDLOOP.
  MODULE user_command_0300.
```

The user command module evaluates only two function codes.

```
MODULE user_command_0300 INPUT.
  CASE okcode.
    WHEN '/NEX'.
      LEAVE TO SCREEN 0.
    WHEN 'BACK'.
      LEAVE TO SCREEN 200.
  ENDCASE.
ENDMODULE.                    " USER_COMMAND_0300 INPUT
```

For the sake of completeness, the declaration portion of the program follows.

```
PROGRAM sapmi404 MESSAGE-ID i!.
TABLES: tadir.
DATA:
  okcode LIKE sy-ucomm,
  itadir LIKE tadir OCCURS 100 WITH HEADER LINE,
  itadir_size TYPE i,
  itadir_cursor TYPE i.
```

Generating the templates

Once you have created the service file and the language resource as described above, you must generate and edit the templates. The templates themselves have a relatively simple structure. The HTML[Business] statements are the most important. The first template contains the query of the development class to be listed.

```
<html>
<HEAD>
</HEAD>
<BODY>
<FORM ACTION="`wgateURL()`" METHOD="post">
<p>
`TADIR-DEVCLASS.label`
<INPUT TYPE="text" name="TADIR-DEVCLASS" VALUE="`TADIR-DEVCLASS`"
```

```
        maxlength="30" size="30" >
</p>
<p>
<INPUT TYPE="submit" name="~OkCode=LIST"
value=`BUTTON_FIND.label`>
<INPUT TYPE="submit" name="~OkCode=/NEX"
value=`BUTTON_QUIT.label`>
</p>
</FORM>
`~MESSAGELINE`
</BODY>
</html>
```

The second template lists some of the data records of the internal table. The access form is similar to that used to read the values for the list of possible entries.

Because all the fields of a column possess identical names, the ITS indexes the data records. You can depict the field contents with the REPEAT metastatement. The statement transforms the contents of a run variable. The value becomes the number of lines in the step loop. The system determines the number of lines with the suffix .dim at the name of a table column. The use of an HTML table aligns all the fields.

```
<html>
<HEAD>
</HEAD>
<BODY>
<FORM ACTION="`wgateURL()`" METHOD="post">
<p>
<TABLE>
  `repeat with j from 1 to ITADIR-PGMID.dim`
    <tr>
      <td>
        <INPUT TYPE="text" name="ITADIR-PGMID[`j`]"
            VALUE="`ITADIR-PGMID[j]`"
            maxlength=" 4" size=" 4" > </td>
  <td>
    <INPUT TYPE="text" name="ITADIR-OBJECT[`j`]"
        VALUE="`ITADIR-OBJECT[j]`"
        maxlength=" 4" size=" 4" > </td>
  <td>
    <INPUT TYPE="text" name="ITADIR-OBJ_NAME[`j`]"
        VALUE="`ITADIR-OBJ_NAME[j]`"
        maxlength="40" size="40" > </td>
  </tr>
  `end`
</TABLE>
```

```
</p>
<p>
<INPUT TYPE="submit" name="~OkCode=FORW"
value=`BUTTON_FORW.label`>
</p>
<p>
<INPUT TYPE="submit" name="~OkCode=BACK"
value=`BUTTON_BACK.label`>
</p>
<p>
<INPUT TYPE="submit" name="~OkCode=/NEX"
value=`BUTTON_QUIT.label`>
</p>
</FORM>
`~MESSAGELINE`
</BODY>
</html>
```

For the most part, the third template corresponds to the second, but a simple text replaces the input fields. It contains no new language elements or programming techniques.

```
<html>
<HEAD>
</HEAD>
<BODY>
<FORM ACTION="`wgateURL()`" METHOD="post">
<p>
<TABLE>
   `repeat with j from 1 to ITADIR-PGMID.dim`
   <tr>
     <td>
       `ITADIR-PGMID[j]` </td>
     <td>
       `ITADIR-OBJECT[j]` </td>
     <td>
       `ITADIR-OBJ_NAME[j]` </td>
   </tr>
   `end`
</TABLE>
</p>
<p>
<INPUT TYPE="submit" name="~OkCode=BACK"
value=`BUTTON_BACK.label`>
</p>
<p>
```

```
<INPUT TYPE="submit" name="~OkCode=/NEX"
value=`BUTTON_QUIT.label`>
</p>
</FORM>
`~MESSAGELINE`
</BODY>
</html>
```

Testing the application

After performing the actual test of the application, you can make minor changes and test an important characteristic of step loop functions. Regardless of the actual number of data records to be displayed, the size of the HTML page on the monitor, or the type of step loop, the HTML document displays (at the most) only the number of step loop lines defined in the screen. As long as it is acceptable for the application, you should always define step loops with a maximum length. You can use the maximum length of screen (currently 200 lines). A scroll bar automatically appears in an HTML document when the document is larger than the current screen window. If the system fills very long step loops, loading the document will take a long time. In this case, you should rebuild the application accordingly and retest it.

Summary

- The contents of a step loop are stored in fields with multiple values (vectors). You access the contents of step loops with an index.

- The number of lines defined in the screen determines the number of tables displayed on the Web.

- If no convincing reasons argue against it, generate the step loop in the screen with the maximum allowable length.

7.2.8   Example 8: The scroll interface

The previous example demonstrated only the principal use of a steep loop. Lengthening the step loop implements scrolling in long lists (an important characteristic) inadequately. Although this method is sufficient in many practical cases, it also contains a hidden danger. It may attempt to display more data records than the step loop can accommodate. The extra data records simply become lost.

In addition to the option of programming scrolling in step loops on your own and triggering scrolling with special pushbuttons in the screen, the ITS also offers a *Scroll Interface*. In special cases the ITS automatically generates function codes and sends them to the R/3 System. The function codes scroll through the Step loop and reads them all. Use of the scroll interface requires a special programming technique, demonstrated in this example.

This example is based on the previous one, so you can copy and enhance it. The scroll interface in version 1.0 of the ITS permits only the transfer of data from the R/3 System to the Web site; version 2.0 no longer suffers from this limitation. With version 2.0, you can now send data created in the browser to the R/3 System.

The R/3 application

This example focuses on the scroll interface. The essential structure of the application remains intact. You need to make only minor adjustments to various modules. Accordingly, you can copy program SAPMI404. Name the new program SAPMI405. The program calls transaction code IAC5. Use steploop2 as the project and scroll as the service.

As an exception to the rule, the scroll interface requires an R/3 application with an interface. In the interface (SCROLL), you can assign both virtual function keys, PF21 (FIRST PAGE) and PF23 (NEXT PAGE) any function code desired. You must evaluate both function codes in the user command module of your application. The ITS uses the function codes assigned to the two keys to scroll through the entire step loop before it generates the final HTML document. You must make the following changes to perform this task.

First, create the appropriate status. The example application uses function code FT21 for function key PF21 (Shift-F9) and function code FT23 for function key PF23 (Shift-F11). Link a module call to the flow logic of screen 100 to set the interface.

```
PROCESS BEFORE OUTPUT.
   MODULE status_0100.
 *
 PROCESS AFTER INPUT.
   MODULE user_command_0100.
```

The user command module remains unchanged. You must program only the new, additional module.

```
MODULE status_0100 OUTPUT.
 SET PF-STATUS 'SCROLL'.
ENDMODULE.                 " STATUS_0100 OUTPUT
```

Module aktual_itadir, called in screen 200, requires an enhancement. The system variable SY-LOOPC prepares the number of lines in the step loop. However, the contents of the field are valid only within a LOOP-ENDLOOP loop over the step loop. You must therefore take the value into an internal program variable for later evaluation.

```
MODULE aktual_itadir INPUT.
  MODIFY itadir FROM itadir INDEX itadir_cursor.
  loopsize = sy-loopc.
ENDMODULE.                 " AKTUAL_ITADIR INPUT
```

The user command module uses this value to get the cursor for the internal table to the next record to be displayed.

```
MODULE user_command_0200 INPUT.
  CASE okcode.
    WHEN '/NEX'.
      LEAVE TO SCREEN 0.
    WHEN 'BACK'.
      LEAVE TO SCREEN 100.
    WHEN 'FORW'.
      LEAVE TO SCREEN 300.
    WHEN 'FT21'.
      itadir_cursor = 1.
    WHEN 'FT23'.
      itadir_cursor = itadir_cursor + loopsize.
  ENDCASE.
ENDMODULE.                " USER_COMMAND_0200 INPUT
```

Screen 300 requires similar changes. Link a module to the PAI portion of the flow logic. The module determines the size of the step loop.

```
PROCESS BEFORE OUTPUT.
  LOOP AT itadir CURSOR itadir_cursor.
  ENDLOOP.
*
PROCESS AFTER INPUT.
  LOOP AT itadir.
    MODULE size_0300.
  ENDLOOP.
  MODULE user_command_0300.
```

The new module is very simple.

```
MODULE size_0300 INPUT.
  loopsize = sy-loopc.
ENDMODULE.                " SIZE_0300 INPUT
```

The user command module still must evaluate the two additional function codes.

```
MODULE user_command_0300 INPUT.
  CASE okcode.
    WHEN '/NEX'.
      LEAVE TO SCREEN 0.
    WHEN 'BACK'.
      LEAVE TO SCREEN 200.
    WHEN 'FT21'.
      itadir_cursor = 1.
    WHEN 'FT23'.
      itadir_cursor = itadir_cursor + loopsize.
  ENDCASE.
ENDMODULE.                " USER_COMMAND_0300 INPUT
```

Generating the templates

The templates to be generated do not differ from those of the previous example. You can regenerate the templates or take them from the existing project `steploop1`.

Function of the application

At the call of screen 200, the ITS recognizes the presence of an interface. If the function keys have a function code in the status, the ITS reads the codes as an indication that the screen contains more data than it can display at one time. In this case the ITS transmits the function code for function key PF23 (NEXT PAGE) to the application until one of the following occurs:

- No more step loop fields are displayed because the application has executed the EXIT FROM STEP-LOOP command.

- The contents of two sequential screens do not differ.

- The scroll function keys are no longer ready for input.

In this manner, the entire contents of the internal table supplied by the step loop are read. The ITS generates a line in the internal data area for all data records and thus also generates a line in the final HTML document.

Because the ITS must communicate with the R/3 System several times to read the entire step loop, creation of the template takes considerable longer than it did in the previous variant. Communication takes place at each screen flow. Accordingly, you should not use the scroll interface in every case.

Summary

- The ITS offer a scroll interface to read the complete contents of a step loop from an ABAP/4 application and to display the results in an HTML document.

- The interface requires creation of a status. You must supply the predefined function keys for 'first page' and 'next page' with function codes. The R/3 System must evaluate the function codes accordingly.

7.2.9   Example 9: Step loops and the mass data channel

The previous example used the screen interface to transfer data to and from the R/3 System. In addition to this screen interface, the mass data channel, available as of version 2.0 of the ITS, also exists to transfer data bidirectionally. The mass data channel offers the advantages of greater flexibility and faster transfer speed. It particularly simplifies scrolling in the data. Since data exchange no longer takes place over fields in the screen, the application behaves differently on the Web than it does in the R/3 System. Even when you add the mass data channel to the screen fields in the application and the screen fields remain operable in the R/3 System, partially different programs branches execute a call over the Web and within the R/3 System. This situation can make searching for errors far more difficult. You should therefore consider using this option only with care.

The R/3 application

For this example you can copy and then modify program SAPMI404. Name the new program SAPMI406. Call it with transaction code IAC6. Name the project steploop3 and the service rfc_step.

The program code and the screens require only minimal changes. To make sure that the macros can use the mass data channel, insert include AVWRTCXM immediately after the TOP include. You can then remove the step loops from screen 200 and 300. The pushbuttons remain. You must replace the LOOP statement in screen 200 with call two new modules in screen 200 at the LOOP statement to ensure that the data of the internal table can still be sent to and retrieved from the ITS. The following listing shows the flow logic of screen 200.

```
PROCESS BEFORE OUTPUT.
  MODULE send_itab.
*
PROCESS AFTER INPUT.
  MODULE get_itab.
  MODULE user_command_0200.
```

The send_itab module transmits the contents of internal table itadir to the ITS over the mass data channel.

```
MODULE send_itab OUTPUT.
  LOOP AT itadir.
    i = sy-tabix.
    field-set 'PGMID' i itadir-pgmid.
    field-set 'OBJECT' i itadir-object.
    field-set 'OBJ_NAME' i itadir-obj_name.
  ENDLOOP.
  field-transport.
ENDMODULE.                 " SEND_ITAB OUTPUT
```

The basic structure is similar to module input_help_0100 of program SAPMI403. However, watch out for a small trap. You must transfer an index when calling the field-set macro. You can use the number of the current data record of the internal table, stored in the system field SY-TABIX. When you call the macro, it then calls subprograms that also work with internal tables and therefore change the contents of SY-TABIX. You must therefore copy the value of SY-TABIX to a local variable before calling the macro for the first time.

You need some background knowledge to understand the get_itab module completely. The ITS keeps all data related to a user session in a data context. When you use the mass data channel to transfer data to the ITS, you add data to the data context or change it. To do so, you use macros from the include AVWRTCXM. One of these includes, field-set, builds a temporary data context within the R/3 application. The temporary data context then transmits the field-transport macro to the ITS. An internal table, tavwctx, stores the temporary context. Many macros of include AVWRTCXM work together with this internal table. If required, you can copy the entire data context of the ITS into this internal table and evaluate it there. This process naturally takes some time, so you should exercise caution when using it to transfer large quantities of data. To read the data context of the ITS, you use the function module ITS_IMPORT_CONTEXT. To read individual data fields from the internal table, evaluate them directly or with the field-query macro.

When you analyze the program, remember that the ITS can process only one-dimensional arrays. You therefore do not transfer an internal table that consists of several fields, but an array with several fields for each field of the internal table itadir.

```
MODULE get_itab INPUT.
  IF okcode <> 'BACK'.
    CALL FUNCTION 'ITS_IMPORT_CONTEXT'
      TABLES
        context          = tavwctx
      EXCEPTIONS
        its_not_available= 1
        OTHERS           = 2.
    IF sy-subrc = 0.
      LOOP AT itadir.
        i = sy-tabix.
        field-query 'PGMID'       i itadir-pgmid.
        field-query 'OBJECT'  i itadir-object.
        field-query 'OBJ_NAME'    i itadir-obj_name.
        MODIFY itadir.
      ENDLOOP.
    ENDIF.
  ENDIF.
ENDMODULE.                      " GET_ITAB INPUT
```

Screen 300 of the application must also transmit data to the ITS so that it can depict the contents of the table. You can use the existing send_itab module to transmit data to the ITS.

```
PROCESS BEFORE OUTPUT.
  MODULE send_itab.
*
PROCESS AFTER INPUT.
  MODULE user_command_0300.
```

Except for the minor changes to the HTML[Business] statements for reading the data fields transmitted over the mass data channel, both templates are similar to the previous example. Instead of accessing screen fields whose names correspond to the internal table itadir, you not access one-dimensional arrays. The following lists the template for screen 200. You can create template 300 most easily by converting the input fields into simple output fields.

```
<html>
<HEAD>
</HEAD>
<BODY>
<FORM ACTION=""`wgateURL()`"" METHOD="post">
<p>
<TABLE>
   `repeat with j from 1 to PGMID.dim`
     <tr>
       <td>
         <INPUT TYPE="text" name="PGMID[`j`]"
VALUE=""`PGMID[j]`"
               maxlength="4" size="4" > </td>
       <td>
         <INPUT TYPE="text" name="OBJECT[`j`]"
VALUE=""`OBJECT[j]`"
               maxlength="4" size="4" > </td>
       <td>
         <INPUT TYPE="text" name="OBJ_NAME[`j`]"
VALUE='`OBJ_NAME[j]`"
               maxlength="4" size="4" > </td>
     </tr>
   `end`
</TABLE>
</p>
<p>
<INPUT TYPE="submit" name="~OkCode=FORW"
value=`BUTTON_FORW.label`>
</p>
<p>
<INPUT TYPE="submit" name="~OkCode=BACK"
value=`BUTTON_BACK.label`>
</p>
<p>
<INPUT TYPE="submit" name="~OkCode=/NEX"
value=`BUTTON_QUIT.label`>
</p>
</FORM>
`~MESSAGELINE`
</BODY>
</html>
```

7.2.10 Example 10: Introduction to frame applications

Frames can increase the flexibility of and ability to view HTML applications. When using Frames, the choice of a link or selection of a pushbutton no longer exchanges the contents of the entire document, but simply restructures a small section of a window. You can update the contents of one frame independently of the other frames or windows. You can use a *subscreen* to perform a similar task in ABAP/4 applications. Programming subscreen applications and displaying them as a frame document requires increased effort. You must also consider additional conditions. The following example introduces the problem involved in steps.

Once again, we note that this R/3 application is intended only for use on the Web. Do not execute it with normal SAPGUIs except for testing. The application uses subscreens only to simplify the frame model. A comparable application that uses normal SAPGUIs would use a completely different design.

The use of frames generally produces relatively large HTML documents. Small monitors cannot always display these documents with sufficient clarity and quality. Space limitations would require each frame to have a scroll bar, and the advantages of frames disappear quickly when the browser must display several frames with scroll bars. You should therefore use frames only when they offer the user real advantages.

The R/3 application

The first frame application demonstrates only the principles of using frames. Pushbuttons in some subscreens can change the contents of other subscreens.

The application consists of a frame screen that contains three subscreens. A total of seven additional screens are available. The additional screens are programmed as subscreens and are dynamically loaded into the subscreen area of the frame screen. Figure 7.31 shows the ABAP/4 application in the test phase.

The *frame screen* of the R/3 application corresponds to a *frameset document* on the Web. Because such a frameset document divides the screen surface for the actual frame documents and does not contain any visual objects itself, the frame screen should not contain any elements that will later be displayed in the Web application.

The frame screen highlights the subscreen areas. The left subscreen (number 1000), that has constant contents, contains four pushbuttons. The pushbuttons end the application or change the contents of the lower subscreens by dynamically placing other screens there. These screen are numbered 3000, 3050 and 3100. They differ in their contents and have various pushbuttons to change the contents of the third subscreen. Three additional screens exist for the third subscreen area. The additional screens (2000, 2050, 2100) contain only a short static text.

Programming the application begins with the frame screen (screen number 100). It must contain three subscreen areas, each completely enclosed with a frame. The names of the frames (but not the subscreen areas) should be as descriptive as possible. The subscreens and the corresponding frames will later be called by these names in the HTML document. The names should indicate the function of the subscreen. Table 7.2 shows the field list of the screen.

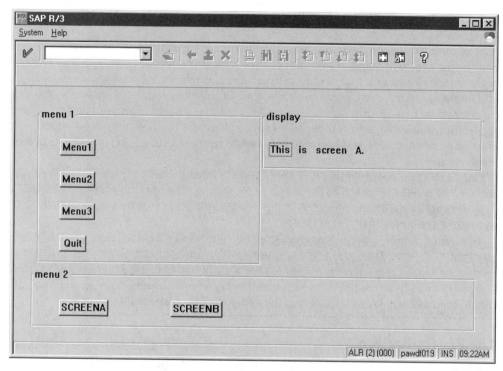

Figure 7.31   Subscreen application

Table 7.2   Field list of the frame screen

Field	Type
SUB_MENU_1	Subsc
SUB_DISPLAY	Subsc
SUB_MENU_2	Subsc
MENU_1	Box
DISPLAY	Box
MENU_2	Box
AW-DYNNR_DISPLAY	I/O
AW-DYNNR_MENU_1	I/O
AW-DYNNR_MENU_2	I/O
OKCODE	OK

Screen 1000 contains only four pushbuttons. They should trigger function codes BT01, BT02, BT03 and /NEX.

Screens 3000, 3050 and 3100 each have two pushbuttons, from which the user can generate a selection from function codes SCRA, SCRB and SCRC. The distribution on the three screens is without consequence.

Screens 2000, 2050 and 2100 contain only a static text that identifies the screen and enables you to test the application.

Screen 100, the frame screen, contains the entire source code. Only the frame screen may contain a field for the OK code in the R/3 System. The user command module evaluates the screen. In addition to handling the function codes, the flow logic of the frame screen receives additional important elements. The next section shows the flow logic.

```
PROCESS BEFORE OUTPUT.
   MODULE status_0100.
   CALL SUBSCREEN sub_menu_1 INCLUDING 'SAPMI407' aw-dynnr_menu_1.
   CALL SUBSCREEN sub_display INCLUDING 'SAPMI407' aw-dynnr_display.
   CALL SUBSCREEN sub_menu_2 INCLUDING 'SAPMI407' aw-dynnr_menu_2.
*
PROCESS AFTER INPUT.
   CALL SUBSCREEN sub_menu_1.
   CALL SUBSCREEN sub_display.
   CALL SUBSCREEN sub_menu_2.
   MODULE user_command_0100.
```

The flow logic must call the flow logic of the corresponding subscreen at the time of PBO and PAI. Implement the call with the CALL SUBSCREEN statement. The names of the corresponding subscreens are transferred to this statement at the time of PBO. The calls take place dynamically. Each run through the flow logic can also place different subscreens. The status module performs the first initialization of the corresponding fields.

```
MODULE status_0100 OUTPUT.
   IF aw-dynnr_menu_1 IS INITIAL.
      aw-dynnr_menu_1  = '1000'.
      aw-dynnr_menu_2  = '3000'.
      aw-dynnr_display = '2000'.
   ENDIF.
ENDMODULE.                " STATUS_0100 OUTPUT
```

Initialization may take place only at the first call of the application since the user command module executes all other modifications.

```
MODULE user_command_0100 INPUT.
   CASE okcode.
      WHEN '/NEX'.
         LEAVE TO SCREEN 0.
      WHEN 'SCRA'.
```

```
          aw-dynnr_display = '2000'.
      WHEN 'SCRB'.
          aw-dynnr_display = '2050'.
      WHEN 'SCRC'.
          aw-dynnr_display = '2100'.
      WHEN 'BT01'.
          aw-dynnr_menu_2 = '3000'.
      WHEN 'BT02'.
          aw-dynnr_menu_2 = '3050'.
      WHEN 'BT03'.
          aw-dynnr_menu_2 = '3100'.
    ENDCASE.
ENDMODULE.                     " USER_COMMAND_0100 INPUT
```

You can now test the application in the R/3 System. Activating the pushbuttons changes the contents in one of the subscreen areas. True application logic does not contain this example.

Working in the Web-Studio

As in the case of the other applications, you must first create a service description and a language resource. Then generate the template for the frame screen. The generator inserts size specifications for the individual frames into the FRAMSET statements. The current size of the subscreen in the frame screen serves as the basis for these specifications. The size of the subscreen areas in the screen also influences keeping or changing the specifications during the test phase. The arrangement of the frames may not necessarily agree with the desires of the programmer. These reasons make it necessary to edit the frame document.

```
<html>
<HEAD>
</HEAD>
<FRAMESET ROWS="80%, *">
  <FRAMESET COLS="50%, *">
    <FRAME NAME="MENU_1"
          SRC="`wgateURL(~FrameName="MENU_1")`"
          SCROLLING="auto">
    <FRAME NAME="DISPLAY"
          SRC="`wgateURL(~FrameName="DISPLAY")`"
          SCROLLING="auto">
  </FRAMESET>
  <FRAME NAME="MENU_2"
          SRC="`wgateURL(~FrameName="MENU_2")`"
          SCROLLING="auto">
</FRAMESET>
</html>
```

You must enter the URLs of the documents to be displayed in the frames in the `Frame` tags. This can become problematic because the R/3 application dynamically sets the various subscreens and therefore the names of the HTML documents to be inserted. Therefore, you cannot work in the HTML template with hard-coded URLs for the documents to be inserted. Instead, you should use the HTML[Business] function `wgateURL()`. This function, however, should not deliver the URL to the Web server, but a special document. You must therefore transfer a parameter to the function. The parameter sets the type of URL to be delivered more precisely. The `~FrameName` parameter name requests the return of a URL for an HTML template. The ITS determines the name of the URL from the value of the parameter.

Screen 1000 (left subscreen) offers three pushbuttons that can change the contents of the lower subscreen. An additional pushbutton ends the application.

```
<html>
<HEAD>
</HEAD>
<BODY>
<FORM ACTION="`wgateURL(~target="MENU_2",
~forceTarget="YES")`"
      METHOD="post">
<p>
<INPUT TYPE="submit" name="~OkCode=BT01"
value=`BUTTON_M1.label`>
</p><p>
<INPUT TYPE="submit" name="~OkCode=BT02"
value=`BUTTON_M2.label`>
</p><p>
<INPUT TYPE="submit" name="~OkCode=BT03"
value=`BUTTON_M3.label`>
</p>
</FORM>
<FORM ACTION="`wgateURL(~target="_top",
~forceTarget="YES")`"
      METHOD="post" target="_top">
<INPUT TYPE="submit" name="~OkCode=/NEX"
value=`BUTTON_QUIT.label` >
</FORM>

`~MESSAGELINE`
</BODY>
</html>
```

This template differs from previous examples. The URL in the FORM tag no longer consists of the address of the Web server (`ACTION="`wgateURL()`"`), but of a somewhat wider call. Actually, the URL used up until now would suffice to update the HTML document in the manner desired. Using it, however, would restructure all the frames.

If you want to change the contents of a single frame, you can avoid updating the entire frameset. In that case, the URL must specify which frame is being updated. You cannot hard code the name of the document for the frame because it depends on the current state of the application. Once again, you must use the wgateURL() function. This time, however, use it with a parameter that indicates the correct frame or subscreen. You must use a different parameter because such a URL had a different structure than the one for the frameset document.

Even when a frame and therefore the contents of a subscreen are redisplayed, the R/3 System processes the entire screen and all its subscreen. In this case the ITS sends only the contents of the updated subscreen to the browser. Only the browser or the ITS evaluate specification of a ~target parameter. The parameter has no influence on the R/3 application. The next example contains additional comments on the ~target parameter and the problems associated with it.

When ending the application, you must restructure the entire display in the browser. Doing so requires another target specification in the wgateURL function. You will find the required pushbutton in a special FORM tag. Without the tag, the system would not remove the frameset document and new documents would appear in the area of the left frame.

The other templates have a similar structure. Here, however, the presentation of a representative for each group in final form suffices.

```
<html>
<HEAD>
</HEAD>
<BODY>
<FORM ACTION="`wgateURL()`" METHOD="post">
<p>
This is subscreen A.
</p>
</FORM>
`~MESSAGELINE`
</BODY>
</html>
```

The source code of the template for screen 3000 represents screens 3000–3100.

```
<html>
<HEAD>
</HEAD>
<BODY>
<FORM ACTION="`wgateURL(~target="DISPLAY",
~forceTarget="YES")`"
        METHOD="post">
<p>
<INPUT TYPE="submit" name="~OkCode=SCRA"
value=`BUTTON_MA.label`>
<INPUT TYPE="submit" name="~OkCode=SCRB"
value=`BUTTON_MB.label`>
</p>
```

```
</FORM>
`~MESSAGELINE`
</BODY>
</html>
```

Summary

- To create a frame application, you must generate an ABAP/4 application with subscreens.

- A frame must enclose every subscreen.

- The HTML[Business] function `wgateURL()` can use different parameters. The parameters influence the structure of the URL generated by the ITS.

- The frame screen must contain fields in the following form: `AW-DYNNR_<name of frame >`.

Note

During production of this manuscript, developers at SAP were attempting to simplify the use of subscreens. In the future, subscreens will be identified with their own names, rather than with the name of a frame. The frames will thus become superfluous. It will no longer be necessary to store AW-DYNNR fields in the frame screen.

This development work may be complete by the time this book appears. Please consult the release notes when installing the ITS and SAP@Web-Studio.

7.2.11   Example 11: Frame applications and hyperlinks

Additional problems appear when programming a frame application with complex application logic. Frames are often used to display detailed information on a selection in another frame. This method requires the selection of an entry in a list and the transfer of this information to the R/3 application. Two options exist to trigger an immediate reaction from the application, without any additional user intervention:

- an additional pushbutton for each element;

- an HTML link.

Special programming techniques are required to evaluate hyperlinks. This example describes the use of HTML links.

The R/3 Application

The R/3 application is more extensive. It builds upon Examples 9 and 10. It is completely implemented as a frame application. The frame document contains three frames. Its structure is similar to that of the frame document from Example 10. The program is named `SAPMI408`. Use transaction `code IAC8` to call the program. Use `frame2` as the project name and name the service `hyperlink`.

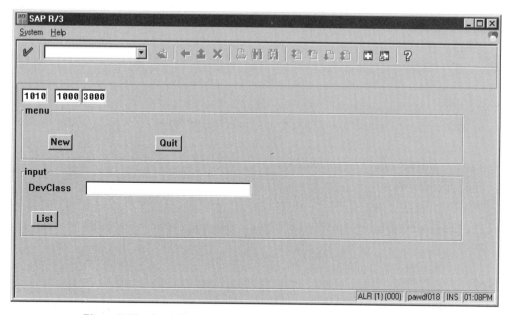

Figure 7.32   Initial screen of the frame application in the R/3 system

First, enter the name of a development class in a subscreen (Figure 7.32). The screen that contains the input field must also contain the pushbuttons. This example arranges the three subscreen areas beneath each other to simplify viewing.

After confirmation of the specification (Figure 7.33), the INPUT subscreen displays all the objects of the development class. After selection of one these entries, the OUTPUT subscreen displays the details for the object. The frame at the lower border of the window displays pushbuttons for navigation in the application.

You can create most of the application by copying elements of Examples 9 and 10. The user command module of frame screen 100 completely evaluates the function codes.

The application uses a range of fields. The data declaration for the application follows:

```
PROGRAM sapmi408 MESSAGE-ID i!.
TABLES: tadir.
DATA:
  itadir LIKE tadir OCCURS 100 WITH HEADER LINE,
  ftadir LIKE LINE OF itadir,
  aw-dynnr_input LIKE sy-dynnr,
  aw-dynnr_output LIKE sy-dynnr,
  aw-dynnr_menu LIKE sy-dynnr,
  itadir_size TYPE i,
  itadir_cursor TYPE i,
  loopsize TYPE i,
  okcode LIKE sy-ucomm.
```

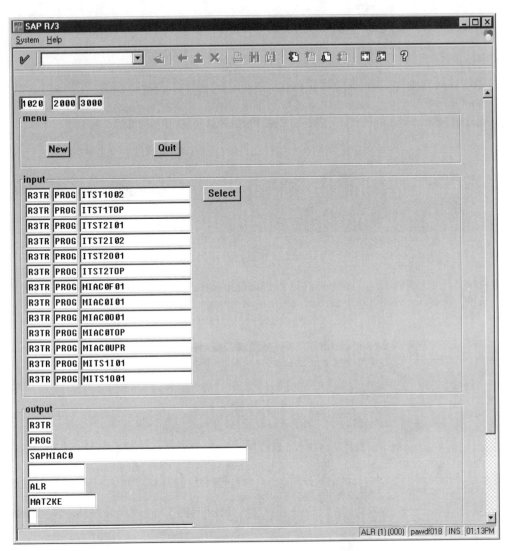

Figure 7.33   List of the TADIR entries located

The application has a frame screen that links to the required subscreens dynamically. The flow logic of the frame screen calls the subscreens and evaluates all the function codes.

```
PROCESS BEFORE OUTPUT.
  MODULE status_0100.
  CALL SUBSCREEN sub_input INCLUDING 'SAPMI408' aw-dynnr_input.
  CALL SUBSCREEN sub_output INCLUDING 'SAPMI408' aw-dynnr_output.
  CALL SUBSCREEN sub_menu INCLUDING 'SAPMI408' aw-dynnr_menu.
*
```

```
PROCESS AFTER INPUT.
   CALL SUBSCREEN sub_input.
   CALL SUBSCREEN sub_output.
   CALL SUBSCREEN sub_menu.
   MODULE user_command_0100.
```

The STATUS_0100 module sets a defined starting condition and loads an interface required by the scroll interface. Create the interface as in Example 8.

```
MODULE status_0100 OUTPUT.
   SET PF-STATUS 'SCROLL'.
   IF aw-dynnr_input IS INITIAL.
      aw-dynnr_input  = '1010'.
      aw-dynnr_output = '1000'.
      aw-dynnr_menu   = '3000'.
   ENDIF.
ENDMODULE.                    " STATUS_0100 OUTPUT
```

The USER_COMMAND_0100 module that evaluates the function codes is described later. The screen for entering the search argument (screen 1010) consists only of the TADIR-

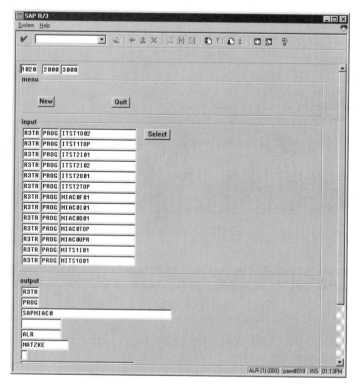

Figure 7.33   List of the TADIR entries located

DEVCLASS field and a pushbutton that triggers function code LIST. We will not treat the display of the list here. It must be created as a subscreen rather than as a normal screen.

The other subscreen differs from the screens used in Example 10. Subscreen 1000 is empty: it exists only to delete unnecessary frames.

Screen 1020 lists all the entries found in a step loop. These data records later appear as links in the HTML document. Screen 1020 should also contain a pushbutton for the function code SELE. The task of this pushbutton will be treated in more detail later. Table 7.3 shows the field list of the screen.

Table 7.3 Field list of the left subscreen

Field	Type
ITADIR-PGMID	I/O
ITADIR-OBJECT	I/O
ITADIR-OBJ_NAME	I/O
BUTTON_SELE	Push

The flow logic of the screen is relatively simple. It contains only the LOOP statement for the step loop.

```
PROCESS BEFORE OUTPUT.
  LOOP AT itadir CURSOR itadir_cursor.
    MODULE loopsize.
  ENDLOOP.
*
PROCESS AFTER INPUT.
  LOOP AT itadir.
  ENDLOOP.
```

The availability of the current size of the loop greatly affects the correct operation of the scroll interface. The contents of the corresponding system field are copied into a global data field within the LOOP statement.

```
MODULE loopsize OUTPUT.
  loopsize = sy-loopc.
ENDMODULE.                " LOOPSIZE OUTPUT
```

Screen 2000 should display details on the selected data record. The screen records only a few fields from FTADIR. The field list in Table 7.4 describes the screen with sufficient exactitude.

Table 7.4 Field list of the right subscreen

Field	Type
FTADIR-PGMID	I/O
FTADIR-OBJECT	I/O
FTADIR-OBJ_NAME	I/O
FTADIR-KORRNUM	I/O
FTADIR-SRCSYSTEM	I/O
FTADIR-AUTHOR	I/O
FTADIR-DEVCLASS	I/O
FTADIR-GENFLAG	I/O
FTADIR-EDTFLAG	I/O
FTADIR-CPROJECT	I/O
FTADIR-MASTERLANG	I/O
FTADIR-VERSID	I/O

Screen 300 controls the application. It contains two pushbuttons for the function codes NEW and /NEX. One pushbutton jumps back to the start screen; the other pushbutton ends the application. The evaluation of the function code in the frame screen clarifies the connections between the individual subscreens.

```
MODULE USER_COMMAND_0100 INPUT.
  CASE OKCODE.
    WHEN '/NEX'.
      LEAVE TO SCREEN 0.

    WHEN 'NEW'.
      AW-DYNNR_INPUT  = '1010'.
      AW-DYNNR_OUTPUT = '1000'.
      AW-DYNNR_MENU   = '3000'.
      CLEAR FTADIR.

    WHEN 'FT21'.
      ITADIR_CURSOR = 0.

    WHEN 'FT23'.
      ITADIR_CURSOR = ITADIR_CURSOR + LOOPSIZE.

    WHEN 'SELE'.
      READ TABLE ITADIR INTO FTADIR
```

```
            WITH KEY PGMID       = FTADIR-PGMID
                 OBJECT = FTADIR-OBJECT
                     OBJ_NAME    = FTADIR-OBJ_NAME.

   WHEN 'LIST'.
     SELECT * FROM TADIR INTO TABLE ITADIR
       WHERE DEVCLASS = TADIR-DEVCLASS.
     ITADIR_SIZE = SY-DBCNT.
     IF ITADIR_SIZE > 0.
       SORT ITADIR BY PGMID OBJECT OBJ_NAME.
       AW-DYNNR_INPUT   = '1020'.
       AW-DYNNR_OUTPUT = '2000'.
       AW-DYNNR_MENU    = '3000'.
     ENDIF.

   ENDCASE.
ENDMODULE.                    " USER_COMMAND_0100 INPUT
```

The manner of selecting a data record in screen 1010 within the context of function code SELE requires some explanation. The application considers the demands of the Web. The Web cannot reproduce the usual programming method of the R/3 System. That method uses an index to determine the cursor position and to read the search argument from the step loop or internal table. The browser has no ability to determine the number of the selected table line and to generate a query to the Web server based on the number. The hyperlink must therefore store all the specifications required for selection of a data record.

As already demonstrated, data exchange between the Web and the R/3 System can occur only over screen fields or, with some limitations, over the mass data channel. The fields of screen 2000 serve to transfer data and to display detailed information. The Web fills some of the fields of screen 2000 with the search arguments. It also transfers a function that introduces the search for the proper data record.

The R/3 application should reproduce this search form as exactly as possible so that during a test the R/3 System executes the exact same program code that a call on the Web does.

Generating the templates

The templates contain links to some graphics for the background and for pushbuttons. Accordingly, these templates differ from those already introduced. We will omit repeating a discussion of generating the new templates. The following source code already contains the edited final version.

The template for screen 100 serves as a frameset document.

```
<html>
<HEAD>
</HEAD>
<FRAMESET ROWS="80%, *%">
```

```
<FRAMESET COLS="50%, *%">
   <FRAME NAME="INPUT" SRC="`wgateURL(~FrameName="INPUT")`"
           SCROLLING="auto">
   <FRAME NAME="OUTPUT"
SRC="`wgateURL(~FrameName="OUTPUT")`"
           SCROLLING="auto">
  </FRAMESET>
  <FRAME NAME="MENU" SRC="`wgateURL(~FrameName="MENU")`"
           SCROLLING="auto">
</FRAMESET>
</html>
```

The template for screen 1010 requests the development class. It also loads a background and implements a graphic for the pushbuttons.

```
<html>
<HEAD>
<TITLE>Frame 2</TITLE>
</HEAD>
<BODY>
<FORM ACTION="`wgateURL()`" METHOD="post">
<p>
`TADIR-DEVCLASS.label`
<INPUT TYPE="text" name="TADIR-DEVCLASS" VALUE="`TADIR-DEVCLASS`"
       maxlength="30" size="30" >
<INPUT TYPE="submit" name="~OkCode=LIST"
value=`BUTTON_LIST.label`>
</p>
</FORM>
`~MESSAGELINE`
</BODY>
</html>
```

New language elements appear in the template for screen 1020. Hyperlinks are generated from the lines of the step loop in this template.

```
<html>
<HEAD>
<TITLE>Frame 2</TITLE>
</HEAD>
<BODY>
<FORM ACTION="`wgateURL()`" METHOD="post">
<p>
<TABLE>
   `repeat with j from 1 to ITADIR-PGMID.dim`
     <TR>
```

```
        <TD ALIGN=LEFT nowrap>
            <A HREF="`wgateURL(
                    FTADIR-PGMID=ITADIR-PGMID[j],
                    FTADIR-OBJECT=ITADIR-OBJECT[j],
                    FTADIR-OBJ_NAME=ITADIR-OBJ_NAME[j],
                    ~OkCode="SELE",
                    ~forceTarget="YES",
                    ~target="OUTPUT")`">
                `ITADIR-PGMID[j]`
                `ITADIR-OBJECT[j]`
                `ITADIR-OBJ_NAME[j]`
            </A>
        </td>
        </TR>
    `end`
</TABLE>
</p>
</FORM>
</BODY>
</html>
```

Hyperlinks trigger the proper function code. The template therefore omits the ABAP/4 function key in screen 1010 for function code SELE.

The data records contained in internal table ITADIR run with a REPEAT statement. The program does not create any input fields for individual fields. It uses the contents to build the URL of a hyperlink instead. The URL is then produced with the HTML[Business] function wgateURL(). This URL has a relatively complex structure. It contains the target address and some supplemental data. The data includes the function code (~OkCode="SELE") to be triggered in the R/3 System and the target of the hyperlink (~target="OUTPUT"). Specification of ~forceTarget="YES" must explicitly inform the ITS that the target frame changes. The apparently redundant information in the parameters ~target and ~forceTarget is necessary: different browsers require different commands to refresh a frame.

The content of individual frames changes frequently during execution of a frame application. Current state-of-the-art browsers permit you to update the contents of a frame within a frameset document. This method operates more quickly and interrupts the user less than restructuring the entire frameset document. In this method, the browser must contain information on which frame of the current frameset should display the transferred document. You can employ either of two different procedures with varying degrees of comfort to use this method. In the first procedure, the Web server can notify the browser which frame should display the document with a Target statement in the header of the HTML page. Unfortunately, only Netscape Navigator currently processes this statement, which does not belong to the official HTML standard. In the second procedure, you inform the browser which frame is to display the document when you request a new document. In this case, the URL that addresses the new document must contain an additional `Target` parameter that contains the target frame of the requested page. Since URLs are created with the metafunction `wgateURL()`, the metafunction has a `~target` parameter whose value appears in the URL with a parameter of the same name. Although the names are identical, the `Target` statement in the header and the parameter in the URL are not identical.

Although the ITS can often independently recognize the frame it is to update and generates a target specification in the header of the HTML document, you must still specify a target frame in the URL for reasons of compatibility.

You must use the `wgateURL` parameter `~forceTarget` only if the ITS cannot clearly identify the frame to update. This situation exists whenever only the content of input fields change in the target frame. This problem appears independently of the browser in use. Only the use of both statements in the form described solves the problem.

If you wish to transmit additional information, such as field contents, to the R/3 application, you can do so by filling screen fields. Specify the fields to be filled (`FTADIR-...`) and the corresponding value in the parameter list of the `wgateURL()` function. The ITS dissolves the dependencies when generating the HTML document and creates complete URLs that meet the HTML standard. The following excerpt from a template provides an example of such a URL:

```
<A HREF="/scripts/wgate.dll/hyperlink/?~State=26924.013.02.05
&FTADIR-PGMID=R3OB&FTADIR-OBJECT=DSYO&FTADIR-OBJ_NAME=DSIMG_OIAC2
&~OkCode=SELE&~forceTarget=YES&~target=OUTPUT">
```

The Internet server deletes all the specifications between `/scripts/wgate.dll/` and the closing `target="OUTPUT"` from the URL and transfers them to the ITS as parameters. The ITS evaluates the parameters so that it can fill the screen fields with values, provide the `Okcode` field with a value and then send the screen to the R/3 System. The system then evaluates the three fields, `FTADIR-PGMID`, `FTADIR-OBJECT` and `FTADIR-OBJ_NAME` in the user command module of screen 100.

For the sake of completeness, the source code of the other template follows. The template for subscreen 2000 displays details.

```
<html>
<HEAD>
<TITLE>Frame 2</TITLE>
</HEAD>
<BODY>
<p>
`FTADIR-PGMID`</p><p>
`FTADIR-OBJECT`</p><p>
`FTADIR-OBJ_NAME`</p><p>
`FTADIR-KORRNUM`</p><p>
`FTADIR-SRCSYSTEM`</p><p>
`FTADIR-AUTHOR`</p><p>
```

```
`FTADIR-DEVCLASS`</p><p>
`FTADIR-MASTERLANG`</p>
</body>
</html>
```

The template for screen 3000 contains two pushbuttons only.

```
<html>
<HEAD>
<TITLE>Frame 2</TITLE>
</HEAD>
<BODY>
<FORM ACTION="`wgateURL()`" METHOD="post">
<INPUT TYPE="submit" name="~OkCode=NEW"
value=`BUTTON_NEW.label`>
</FORM>

<FORM ACTION             ="`wgateURL(~target="_top",
~forceTarget             ="YES")`"
     METHOD              ="post" target="_top">
<INPUT TYPE="submit" name="~OkCode=/NEX"
value=`BUTTON_QUIT.label`>
</FORM>
`~MESSAGELINE`
</BODY>
</html>
```

The template for screen 1000 is completely empty.

```
<html>
<HEAD>
</HEAD>
<BODY>
</BODY>
</html>
```

Summary

- Only selected HTML elements (hyperlinks and buttons) can transmit information to the R/3 System directly. These HTML elements must therefore reproduce some ABAP/4 programming techniques (such as selecting a line of a step loop with a click of the mouse). To do so, you must adjust the R/3 application to the HTML programming model.

- You can use the metafunction `wgateURL()` to generate URLs and merge field values into them. The ITS then transfers the information into the correct screen fields.

7.2.12 Example 12: Synchronization

Up to now, we have assumed that only the pushbuttons or hyperlinks within the template operate the entire Web application. This process ensures that the data arrives at the R/3 System and that the current reply reaches the browser. The HTML document viewed by the end user therefore must reflect the current state of the R/3 application.

All browsers possess a cache that stores previous loaded pages for a particular period. The browser also has a list (the history list) that indicates all the pages it has read. Special functions in the browser permit users to scroll through the list. In some cases, the browser loads these pages from the cache, rather than requesting them from the Web server. Because the Web was initially designed for information without a status, this method accelerates access and limits the load on the network.

The function poses something of problem in the context of Internet applications. When the user selects the BACK function of the browser to jump back to an old page, the document displayed by the browser no longer reflects the current state of the R/3 application. When the user then transmits data to the R/3 System from this page, the data no longer corresponds to the current state of the application in the R/3 System. The ITS cannot redirect this data to the R/3 System and reacts with an error message.

Not all synchronization problems lead to runtime errors. In the first application (calculator), both screens have identical fields. First, perform a calculation and always use the NEW HTML button to return to the first template. Then use the browser's BACK button to move from the second screen (results display) to the first screen (value input). You can enter new values in the now current HTML document. The ITS can also transmit values to the R/3 System correctly, even though the second screen is still active in the R/3 System. No calculation is performed since the second screen does not evaluate the transferred function code. The second screen displays the (new) correct input values, but the old results.

The problem of synchronization is new to ABAP developers. It arises from the depiction of applications that require a state in a stateless medium. The problem can appear in almost all applications and therefore requires solution by adequate programming.

Solution

The ITS generates all the HTML documents of a Web application as well as their URLs. A unique state ID in the URLs enables the ITS to allocate every generated URL and therefore every HTML document (and its values) to a screen individually.

Every state corresponds to a state in an R/3 application determined by a specific screen combination. The ITS stores all the state Ids and the screen combinations that belong to them. When the browser transmits a URL to the ITS, the state information in the URL, the internal description of the state and the current state of the R/3 application allow the ITS to determine if synchronization is necessary.

Depending on the type of application and the type of synchronization problem, the ITS can solve the problem itself or inform the R/3 System that synchronization is necessary. The feature of the ITS opens the door to some options to work around the problem or to solve it. Not all variants can be applied to all applications. Choose a method that fits the application and the desired level of comfort for the user.

Error message

In some cases, synchronization of the application can or should not be guaranteed. In these cases the ITS creates an error message indicating that use of the BACK button is not permitted. To have the ITS use this method, you must set ~SyncBehaviour in the service description to NoResync.

Applications with a single screen

When an application consists of a single screen, no problems can appear. Such applications have but one URL. The application must always restart the single URL. Because the application does not (and cannot) support navigation, no synchronization problems can arise. The screen can consist of several subscreens, but the subscreens may not be exchanged dynamically. To do so, you should use a frame application. Because many Web applications have a simple structure, you can use this option frequently.

Manual synchronization

You cannot achieve completely automatic synchronization if the current frame screen of a frame application or the screen of a normal application does not agree with the state required by the Web. In such cases, the ITS transmits the function code AWSS or AWSY to the R/3 application. The ITS uses the function code AWSS when one or more screens require changes. The ITS uses function code AWSY to inform the R/3 application that the main screen must be changed.

When this function code appears, the application can call function module ITS_GET_SYNC_INFO to retrieve required information on the state of the application. It then creates synchronization by setting the subsequent screen or subscreen. This function of the ITS and the function module are available as of version 2.0 of the ITS and version 4.0 of the R/3 System. Older versions of the ITS add the name of the module pool and the screen number assumed by the transmitting HTML document to the function code. The ability of the screen protocol to use more than the normal four characters permits this feature. The application must provide a field of sufficient length to ensure that the longer function code arrives correctly at the R/3 System. This is normally the case when the OK-code field is derived with LIKE from SY-UCOMM. In this case you should evaluate on the first four characters of the function code in the user command module.

The current R/3 application must evaluate the function codes AWSS and AWSY to start the screen expected by the browser. The R/3 application therefore adjusts to the state on the Web. You can program this adjustment by jumping directly to the new screen with the LEAVE TO SCREEN command. Synchronization problems cannot always be solved schematically. For example: a user fills a virtual shopping cart by executing several dialog steps and then jumps back to the beginning of the program with the BACK button. This action can mean that the user wishes to begin entering another article. It can also mean that the user wishes to cancel previous selections and begin the process all over again. The application must react intelligently in such situations. Depending on the user's desires, it must ask a question or offer a completely different program flow. Developers must plan and reprogram the reactions of the application for every program. The function code AWSY can also trigger the appropriate actions. The actions are required in addition to purely technical synchronization: they call the correct screen.

The function module ITS_GET_SYNC_INFO is called without import parameters It returns a list of required screens in an internal table.

```
DATA: BEGIN OF SYNCINFO LIKE SITSSYNC OCCURS 10 WITH HEADER LINE.
  CALL FUNCTION 'ITS_GET_SYNC_INFO'
    TABLES
      SYNC_INFO = SYNCINFO
  EXCEPTIONS
          ITS_NOT_AVAILABLE = 1.
```

Structure SITSSYNC depicts the internal table. The following table illustrates the structure.

Table 7.5 Structure SISTSYNC

Field name	Type	Length	Meaning
SUBSC	CHAR	132	Name of a subscreen area, MAIN for the main screen
REPID	CHAR	40	Name of a module pool
DYNNR	CHAR	4	Screen number

Programming Example: Calculator

Synchronization requires only changes in the ABAP/4 source code, not in the templates. This section treats the modifications to the source code but not the application as a whole. The programming example is named SAPMI409 and is called with service IAC9 transaction IAC9 . The project is named synchronization, the service is named calc_synchro. Because the issue of synchronization has significant implications for all Web applications, this section demonstrates the older variant that works with version 1.1 of the ITS and SAP R/3 Release 3.1x. As noted, a synchronization problem appears in the calculator example. Since it is an application without subscreens, the ITS triggers the function code AWSY to synchronize the application. You can use the following universal subroutine to evaluate the function code. However, you must remember that the names of module pools can consist of more than eight characters as of release 4.0 of the R/3 Software. In any case, as of version 4.0, be sure to use function module ITS_GET_SYNC_INFO to generate the synchronization information.

```
FORM synchronize.
DATA l TYPE i.
FIELD-SYMBOLS <f> LIKE sy-dynnr.
IF okcode(4) = 'AWSY'.
  l = STRLEN( okcode ).
  l = l - 4.
  ASSIGN okcode+l(4) TO <f>.
  LEAVE TO SCREEN <f>.
ENDIF.
ENDFORM.                    " SYNCHRONIZE
```

Call the subroutine in a `SYNCHRONIZE` module that you execute as the first module at the point of PAI.

```
MODULE synchronize INPUT.
 PERFORM synchronize.
ENDMODULE.                  " SYNCHRONIZE INPUT
```

The ITS enters the name of the module pool that belongs to the screen after the fifth position of the function code. If the application uses screens from several module pools, this information also requires evaluation. Call the module in both screens. Screen 100:

```
PROCESS BEFORE OUTPUT.
  MODULE init_0100.
*
PROCESS AFTER INPUT.
  MODULE synchronize.
  CHAIN.
    FIELD: value1, value2.
    MODULE check_0100.
  ENDCHAIN.
  MODULE user_command_0100.
```

Screen 200:

```
PROCESS BEFORE OUTPUT.
*
PROCESS AFTER INPUT.
  MODULE synchronize.
  MODULE user_command_0200.
```

7.2.13   Example 13: Text areas

The HTML standard offers an input element, the *text area* that has no counterpart in the R/3 System. You can create a long, multiline text with this element. This example demonstrates how you can transfer the contents of a text area from the Web into an R/3 application with some special commands.

The R/3 application

Processing of text areas involves a special characteristic. The quantity of data delivered from the Web to the R/3 application cannot be determined in advance. Accordingly, you should use the mass data channel rather than link text areas to input elements on the screen. The connection with the lines of a step loop can lead to problems if the step loop is not large enough to record all the data delivered by the ITS.

The browser transmits the data in a text area as a character string within a field with multiple values (array). The characters in a paragraph thereby constitute a value.

The application itself is relatively simple. It requires two screens from an existing R/3 application. The first screen has only two pushbuttons: one jumps to the next screen and the other ends the application. In the second screen, a step loop over the internal table itext outputs the data read. The second screen contains two pushbuttons also. One pushbutton returns to the first screen and the other exits the application. The application is named SAPMI410 and is called with transaction code IACA. The project is named steploop4, the service is text_area.

The declaration portion of the application follows:

```
PROGRAM sapmi410.
INCLUDE avwrtcxm.
DATA:
  okcode LIKE sy-ucomm,
  itab_cursor LIKE sy-stepl,
  line_length LIKE sy-stepl,
  BEGIN OF itext OCCURS 100,
    line(60),
  END OF itext,
  ihelp LIKE itext OCCURS 10 WITH HEADER LINE,
  i TYPE i.
```

The first screen accepts the contents of the text area and writes them to the internal table itext. This process uses module get_textarea.

```
PROCESS BEFORE OUTPUT.
*
PROCESS AFTER INPUT.
  MODULE get_textarea.
  MODULE user_command_0100.
```

The field-get macro transfers data from the Web into the internal table. The ITS returns the data of a text area in a field with multiple values. All the characters up to a paragraph marker constitute a single, self-contained value. You must read field values in module get_textarea until the macro no longer returns values. You can use the DO loop to perform this task. The contents of SY-SUBRC serve as the criterion for cancelling the operation. The value of this field is set within the macro.

Unlike field-set, which expects a single field as a parameter, field-get collaborates with an internal table. The data delivered by the ITS fill the table sequentially. A help table and a second loop are required to transfer the values of a paragraph.

```
MODULE get_textarea INPUT.
  CLEAR itext. REFRESH itext.
  i = 1.
  DO.
    field-get 'TEXTAREA' i ihelp line_length.
    IF sy-subrc = 0.
      LOOP AT ihelp.
        APPEND ihelp TO itext.
      ENDLOOP.
      ADD 1 TO i.
    ELSE.
      EXIT.
    ENDIF.
  ENDDO.
ENDMODULE.                    " GET_TEXTAREA
```

The field lengths of the internal table and the width of the text area on the Web should agree (if at all possible). Doing so ensures the correct transfer of line breaks and formatting.

The user command module is very simple because it has to evaluate only two function codes.

```
MODULE user_command_0100 INPUT.
  CASE okcode.
    WHEN 'DISP'.
      LEAVE TO SCREEN 200.
    WHEN '/NEX'.
      LEAVE TO SCREEN 0.
  ENDCASE.
ENDMODULE.                    " USER_COMMAND_0100 INPUT
```

Screen 200 should output the internal table processed in screen 100 to inspect it. The flow logic of the screen basically consists of two LOOP statements to depict the step loop.

```
PROCESS BEFORE OUTPUT.
  LOOP AT itext CURSOR itab_cursor.
  ENDLOOP.

PROCESS AFTER INPUT.
  LOOP AT itext.
  ENDLOOP.
  MODULE user_command_0200.
```

The user command module enables a return to the previous screen and ending the application.

```
MODULE user_command_0200 INPUT.
  CASE okcode.
```

```
      WHEN 'BACK'.
         LEAVE TO SCREEN 100.
      WHEN '/NEX'.
         LEAVE TO SCREEN 0.
   ENDCASE.
ENDMODULE.                     " USER_COMMAND_0200 INPUT
```

The templates

The following templates represent the final revision. They emphasize a clarification of the principles involved rather than visual design.

```
<html>
<HEAD>
</HEAD>
<BODY>
<FORM ACTION="`wgateURL()`" METHOD="post">
<TEXTAREA NAME="TEXTAREA[]" ROWS="10" COLS="40">
</TEXTAREA>
<p>
<INPUT TYPE="submit" name="~OkCode=DISP" value=`BUTTON_DISP.label`>
</p>
<p>
<INPUT TYPE="submit" name="~OkCode=/NEX" value=`BUTTON_QUIT.label`>
</p>
</FORM>
`~MESSAGELINE`
</BODY>
</html>
```

Only the text area in the template offers any special interest. The `<textarea>` tag introduces the area, and the `</textarea>` tag closes it. The NAME parameter sets the name. You can choose any name desired because the area does not correspond to any R/3 field. You must, however, place the name within square brackets, [ ], as a suffix after the name. The brackets inform the ITS that the field has multiple values. The brackets provide the precondition for the ability of the `field-get` macro to read more than one value. If no brackets are present, the ITS reads only the first value of such a field. For a text area, this would mean availability of only the first paragraph from the R/3 System.

The template for screen 200 has no special characteristic. Only the contents of the current step loop are output.

```
<html>
<HEAD>
</HEAD>
<BODY>
```

```
<FORM ACTION="`wgateURL()`" METHOD="post">
<p>
<TABLE>
`repeat with j from 1 to ITEXT-LINE.dim`
<tr>
<td>
<INPUT TYPE="text" name="ITEXT-LINE[`j`]" VALUE="`ITEXT-LINE[j]`"
       maxlength="60" size="60" >
</td>
</tr>
`end`
</TABLE>
</p>
<p>
<INPUT TYPE="submit" name="~OkCode=BACK"
value=`BUTTON_BACK.label`>
</p>
<p>
<INPUT TYPE="submit" name="~OkCode=/NEX"
value=`BUTTON_QUIT.label`>
</p>
</FORM>
`~MESSAGELINE`
</BODY>
</html>
```

Summary

- The contents of text areas must be transferred into individual lines of an internal table.

- Use the `field-get` macro to read the data.

- Identify the text area in the template as an array by appending square brackets [ ] to the name.

7.2.14   Checkboxes

This section provides some information on the use of checkboxes. It does not, however, introduce specific examples. Given the knowledge gained in the previous examples, you should have no problem creating such an application on your own.

Depict the checkboxes in the R/3 application as simple character fields of length 1. Assign the fields the value 'X' in the HTML template. The definition of a checkbox would therefore appear as follows:

```
<INPUT TYPE=checkbox name = "check1" value="X" >
```

Beware of a small trap here. If fields are empty, the browser does not transfer them to the Web server and therefore to the R/3 application. Thus, the ITS cannot reset the contents of marked checkboxes. This inability becomes annoyingly evident when you run a screen several times and thus reset the marked checkboxes. An additional statement provides a workaround that must come immediately after the definition of the checkbox. Simply define a *hidden field*. These fields do not appear in the form, but their values are transferred to the server. You must declare a checkbox in IAC templates as follows:

```
<INPUT TYPE=hidden name = "check1" value=" " >
<INPUT TYPE=checkbox name = "check1" value="X" >
```

Both field names must agree with each other. If the contents of the checkbox are not transferred, the *hidden field* deletes the R/3 field. A marked checkbox overwrites the value of the *hidden field* because it is sent to the server after the checkbox.

7.3   Web RFC

The SAPGUI can communicate with the R/3 System in two ways: the DIAG channel (Dynamic Information and Actions Gateway) and the RFC channel. The RFC channel calls RFC-capable function modules of the R/3 System and is integrated into the ITS. A special service, hard-coded in the ITS, permits you to use a specific URL to call a function module in the R/3 System. The modules must refer to a default interface. The modules take parameters from an internal table and return a completely generated HTML page. The ITS then redirects the page to the browser.

7.3.1   Preconditions

A special service, XGWFC, provides direct RFC access to the R/3 System. Do not confuse this direct access with that provided by the mass data channel. A service description, XGWFC.SRVC, must exist for the ITS to execute the XGWFC service. This service description differs from the other service descriptions. Note that login and routing differences can exist, depending on the system landscape. The following except from such a file provides an example. If the global service file contains these parameters, you do not need to repeat them for service XGWFC.

```
~SystemType     R3
~RFCTraceOn     0
~xgateway       sapxgwfc.dll
~destination    ALR
~SystemType     R3
~logingroup
```

Of course, login data for the R/3 System must also be available. If the data is set separately for each service rather than in the global service file, you must supplement file XGWFC.SRVC with the appropriate parameters. The global service file must contain the following entry:

```
~XGateways      SAPXGWFC
```

With this entry, the ITS recognizes that it must load a special DLL to implement Web RFC when it starts. Standard installation automatically creates such an entry.

7.3.2   Example 14: Function module for Web RFC

With the RFC channel, you can call special function modules of the R/3 System. Within the R/3 System, these modules must be identified as RFC function modules. In a Web-RFC connection, the ITS redirects the data delivered by the function module to the Web server without changing it in any way. Accordingly, these function modules must return a complete HTML page or a binary object. External templates, such as those for dialog applications, are not presently available. The function module must work like traditional CGI applications.

Although this method is very flexible, it is also more complex than dialog programming. A Web-RFC module features a predefined interface because transfer tables must store both input and output data.

The ITS stores input data in an array and transfers it to the function module as an internal table. The table parameter is called `QUERY_STRING`, and its structure corresponds to the dictionary structure `W3QUERY`. This table stores all the fields of the current data context, both system fields and application data, in *name-value pairs*.

Table `HTML` (structure `W3HTML`) for HTML pages and `MIME` (structure `W3MIME`) for binary data handle the return of values. Fill the `CONTENT_TYPE` field with the type identification that conforms to HTML. If the module delivers binary data, you must also fill the `CONTENT_LENGTH` field with the exact length of the binary object.

Calling such a function module requires a URL in the following form:

```
http://bernd/scripts/wgate.dll?~Service=xgwfc&_function=iac_calcu-
lator&f1=33&f2=44&op=%2b
```

The URL begins with the obligatory specification of the protocol (`http://`). It includes the name of the Web server (`bernd`) and the call of the ITS (`/scripts/wgate.dll`). The server installed at your site will undoubtedly have a different name. However, a standard installation includes the access to the ITS given above and will likely correspond to the particulars of your system.

When you call the Web-RFC service, you must transfer some parameters. Append the parameters to the URL. A question mark separates the address portion of the URL from the parameters. Specify parameters in the following form:

```
Parameter_name=Value
```

The ampersand (`&`) separates individual parameters from each other. The first parameter (`~Service=XGWFC`) is intended for the ITS. It informs the ITS which service it should execute. This special service is designed to call a function module in the R/3 System. The next parameter (`_function=its_calculator`) transfers the name of the function module. The underscore (_) belongs to the parameter name. All additional parameters (f1=33, f2=44 and op=%2b) are redirected to the function module and evaluated there. Please note that a plus sign (+) has a special meaning within a URL, and you may not use it in a URL for the value to the op parameter. In place of the plus sign, use the internal HTML appearance %2b. No problems occur with the other three operands ("-", "*", "/").

Despite its simple functions, the function module is rather complicated. It requires great effort to evaluate the parameters.

```
FUNCTION IAC_CALCULATOR.
*"----------------------------------------------------------------
----
*"*"Local interface:
*"          EXPORTING
*"                VALUE(CONTENT_TYPE) LIKE W3PARAM-CONT_TYPE
*"                VALUE(CONTENT_LENGTH) LIKE W3PARAM-CONT_LEN
*"          TABLES
*"                QUERY_STRING STRUCTURE W3QUERY
*"                HTML STRUCTURE W3HTML
*"                MIME STRUCTURE W3MIME
*"----------------------------------------------------------------
----
data: feld1(50) type c,
      feld2(50) type c,
      feld3(50) type c,
      fop.
  refresh html.
  refresh mime.
  content_type = 'text/html'.
  html = '<html>'.
  append html.
  html = '<body>'.
  append html.
  html = '<h1>calculator via rfc</h1>'.
  append html.
  html = '<hr>'.
  append html.
  loop at query_string.
    case query_string-name.
      when 'F1'.
        feld1 = query_string-value.
      when 'F2'.
        feld2 = query_string-value.
      when 'OP'.
        fop   = query_string-value.
    endcase.
  endloop.
```

```
case fop.
  when '+'.
    feld3 = feld1 + feld2.
  when '-'.
    feld3 = feld1 - feld2.
  when '*'.
    feld3 = feld1 * feld2.
  when '/'.
    IF FELD2 <> 0.
      FELD3 = FELD1 / FELD2.
    ELSE.
      FELD3 = 'ERROR'.
    ENDIF.
endcase.

concatenate feld1 ' ' fop ' ' feld2 ' = ' feld3 into html.
append html.
html = '</body>'.
append html.
html = '</html>'.
append html.
ENDFUNCTION.
```

The internal table QUERY_STRING handles the input parameters for all Web-capable function modules called with RFC. The table consists of the NAME and VALUE fields. Input parameters are transferred in this table. These, however, are not only, however, the parameters in the URL, but also some ITS fields. A tilde (~) in front of the name identifies these fields. The above example does not evaluate these fields.

The example creates a simple HTML page and fills it with the results of the calculation. In actual practice, a function module called in this manner can perform very complex tasks. The last section contains information on additional possibilities offered by WEB-RFC.

7.3.3   Example 15: Standard reports on the Web

A preconfigured function module, called with Web-RFC, allows execution of all non-interactive reports and the output of the lists generated by those reports. You do not need to design the reports for use on the Web. However, output created on the Web is very poor.

Theoretically, this module could call all reports. Doing so, however, would lead to an extreme security risk. According, you should process reports on the Web only when they meet the following conditions:

- An authorization group must exist in the attributes for the report.

- The report must be entered in a release table with transaction SMW0. In the starting screen of the transaction, select ADMINISTRATION | INTERNET RELEASE | REPORTS.

The function to be called is named WWW_GET_REPORT. The _REPORT parameter is transferred to the function module; the parameter contains the name of the report to be called. If the report has a selection screen that is not to be used to input values interactively, you must transfer the corresponding selection parameters with additional parameters in the URL. (Note that the report in the next example uses a selection screen that is used to input values interactively.) You can use a preconfigured R/3 variant to transfer the parameters or specify them individually.

You must use a special procedure to name the parameter or the selection in the URL. These names do not completely correspond to the names used in the R/3 System.

For selections, the identifier in the URL uses the following pattern:

SELt_name-range

Here t stands for a letter that describes the data type of the value (see Table 7.6). The name of the selection in the R/3 System is given in with name, and range is replaced with LOW or HIGH to address one of the two fields of the selection. You use the a similar convention to name the report parameters.

PARt_name

Here, too, t stands for the data type and name for the name in the R/3 System.

Table 7.6 ID letters for data types in parameters and selections

Data type	Description
C	CHAR
D	DATE
T	TIME
I	INTEGER
F	FLOAT
P	PACKED

The source code of a report example follows:

```
REPORT iaccalcu.
DATA field3(10).
PARAMETERS: field1(10), field2(10), op.
  CASE op.
    WHEN '+'.
      field3 = field1 + field2.
    WHEN '-'.
      field3 = field1 - field2.
    WHEN '*'.
      field3 = field1 * field2.
```

```
WHEN '/'.
  IF field2 <> 0.
    field3 = field1 / field2.
  ELSE.
    field3 = 'ERROR'.
  ENDIF.
ENDCASE.
WRITE: / field1, op, field2, '=', field3.
```

The report is called with the following URL:7

```
http://bernd/scripts/wgate.dll?~Service=xgwfc&_function=www_get_re
port&_report=IACCALCU&parc_field1=12345679& parc_field2=72&
parc_op=*
```

If preconfigured variants for the report exist, you can set the variant to be executed in the URL. To do so, use the _VARIANT parameter.

7.3.4   Calling a selection screen for reports

If you do not wish to bypass the selection screen for a report or wish to fill it with fixed values, you can create an input template for the selection screen. To do so, call the report with function module WWW_GET_SELSCREEN. The URL for calling reports ITSREPO1 would then appear as follows:

```
http://bernd/scripts/wgate.dll?~Service=xgwfc&_function=www_get_se
lscreen&_report=IACCALCU
```

The HTML page generated for the selection screen (see Figure 7.34) contains two pushbuttons. One pushbutton deletes an input value, the other executes the report.

7.3.5   Additional characteristics

The Web-RFC solution cannot currently use the external templates of the ITS or its diverse HTML[Business] functions. As a substitute, you can store templates in the R/3 System and merge R/3 data into these templates. Much like external templates of the ITS, these templates have placeholders. The function module WWW_HTML_MERGER handles the merge.

The function module WWW_URL_PREFIX provides you with information comparable to that of the HTML[Business] function wgateURL(). You need this information to create portable applications.

You cannot use true interactive reports of the R/3 System on the Web without any changes. You can use some function modules (WWW_SET_URL, WWW_GET_URL) and a complex programming model for reports to create an application that behaves similarly to interactive reports. See the online documentation of SAP@Web-Studio for further details. We can omit additional remarks at this point because you can also use dialog-oriented applications to reproduce the functions of interactive reports and thereby have access to all the options offered by the ITS (Templates, HTML[Business]).

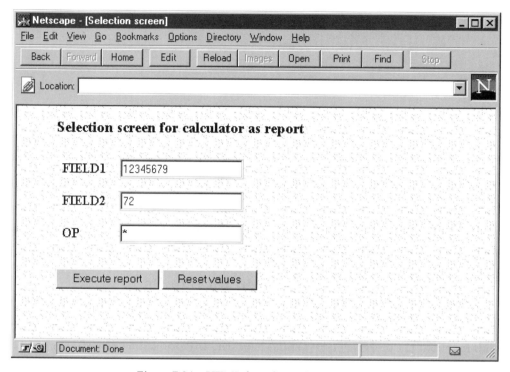

Figure 7.34   HTML form for a selection screen

7.4   Multilingual applications

The R/3 System supports the implementation of multilingual applications. You can also use these functions to design Web applications. However, note that the R/3 System covers only a portion of the required tasks. Because the application runs completely within the R/3 System, the system finds and makes available the entries in the language-dependent tables of the application in the language specified at login. The R/3 System also delivers the correct field identifiers to screen and the translated contents of numbered text elements. However, the R/3 System cannot offer language-dependent preparation of static objects that exist outside the R/3 System. Such static objects include graphics for pushbuttons or texts hard coded in the template. Some statements and parameters exist that you can use to implement language-dependence outside the R/3 System.

7.4.1   Login language

Users must specify a login language when logging into the R/3 System. You can set a login language in the service file with the LANGUAGE parameter. The user cannot deviate from this language. If the service description contains no language setting, or if LANGUAGE= overwrites the login language in the global service file, the ITS asks the user to specify a login language when it starts the service.

Whether or not the service file specifies a default language, the ITS operates with only one valid language after login.

7.4.2   Language-independent templates

If possible, templates should be language-independent. They should not contain any hard coded text or URL of language-dependent objects. Store all the objects dependent on a particular language in the proper language resource. The templates should contain only placeholders for the various objects. Since the ITS replaces the placeholders, you can use almost all HTML objects (simple text, URLs, field descriptions). When an application executes, the ITS first searches for a language resource for the login language. If it finds a resource, it uses language-independent templates for later operations. These templates do not contain a language ID in their names. The ITS expects language-dependent templates only when it cannot find an appropriate language resource.

7.4.3   Language-dependent templates

Language-dependent templates can contain any language-dependent objects. To allocate templates to a language, the names of the templates include a language ID. The ITS uses language-dependent templates whenever it cannot find a language resource.

7.4.4   Language resources and placeholders

The language resource files store objects as name-value pairs. You can maintain language resources with the Web-Studio and with a normal ASCII editor. You can also store language resources outside of the R/3 System in a form that will allow you to use the translation tools of the R/3 System.

You can insert language-dependent objects into templates much like screen fields. To distinguish between the two, prefix a hash (#) to the name. Valid placeholders in templates include:

```
`#CustomerName`
`#Street`
`#1`
`#Name`
```

7.5   Static pages

The previous described application always reflects a one-to-one correspondence between the R/3 screen and the HTML document. However, you can also link static HTML pages to such an application. These pages are called from within an HTML page without triggering any reaction in the R/3 application. Possible uses include pages with help texts, copyrights, a table of contents or similar material. Once at a static HTML page, the user must return to the HTML page that called the static page.

A standard URL calls static pages. Accordingly, a directory of the Web server must contain the pages. This directory is not identical to the directory for templates. If you use static pages frequently, you should create a structured subdirectory for them.

A special URL is required to jump from static pages back to a Web application. The URL calls the coupling program (WGATE.DLL) and transfers the name of the service as a parameter. For reasons internal to the ITS, you must end the URL with the slash character (/). No other specifications are necessary. In this special form of a call, the ITS recognizes that it must re-execute the last current R/3 screen. Because the URL that governs the return jump is static (it does not depend on the current state of the application), you can link the call to various HTML templates in an application. The ITS ensures that it always generates the correct HTML page when it jumps back. Various protective mechanisms in the ITS exclude third parties from this procedure.

7.5.1   Programming example

This example of a static page links operating instructions to the first example. Because static pages have no corresponding element in the R/3 System, the R/3 application requires no modification. The work required is limited to the HTML templates.

The simplest form of a call uses normal hyperlinks. These are used first here to demonstrate the principles.

In addition to the templates that already exist, a static HTML page is necessary. It contains a dummy text and a hyperlink for the jump back to the originating page.

```
<HTML>
<HEAD>
<TITLE>Static Text</TITLE>
</HEAD>
<BODY>
<p>
Sample for static screens
</p>
<A HREF="/scripts/wgate.dll/calc_simple/"> Back to Calculator </a>
</BODY>
</HTML>
```

To call the static page, the following call is added to both templates of the calculator example:

```
<A HREF="/help.html">Help </a>
```

No other activities are required. Note that the URL for the static page assumes the root directory of the Web server because this page is called without the ITS. Accordingly, a static page may not contain any HTML[Business] statements or placeholders for language-dependent objects.

Instead of a hyperlink, you can use a pushbutton to call the static page or to return from it. To use a pushbutton, create a `FORM tag` with a URL that points to the desired page. In this case, you must use the `GET` method for processing. The following statement calls the static page:

```
<FORM ACTION="/help.html" METHOD="get">
  <INPUT TYPE="submit" name="HELP" value="HELP">
</FORM>
```

The following statements returns to the original page:

```
<FORM ACTION="/scripts/wgate.dll/calc_simple/" METHOD="get">
  <INPUT TYPE="submit" name="BACK" value="BACK">
</FORM>
```

7.5.2   Language-dependent static pages

Because the ITS does not process the static page, no substitution of HTML enhancements (such as placeholders for language-dependent texts) takes place. If you still wish to implement language-dependence, you can only do so with an appropriate number of HTML pages called according to the user's login language. You can use various options. If you work with language-dependent templates, simply note the correct (language-dependent) URL in the template. If you work with language-independent templates (those that operate with a language resource), you can use a placeholder that stands for the correct page in the language resources. For example, an entry in a language resource for English would appear as follows:

```
HelpSite /help/CALC1/help_e.html
```

A call of this page in the language-independent template would appear as follows:

```
<FORM ACTION="`#HelpSite`" METHOD="get">
  <INPUT TYPE="submit" name="HELP" value="HELP">
</FORM>
```

The login language has no influence on the jump back to the original page. No changes are required in the original page.

Use of the HTML[Business] function `mimeURL` offers another way to address language-dependent pages and to administer the pages simply. The function expects some parameters that it combines into a URL. The function was designed to support graphic objects. Accordingly, the generated URL always refers to a subdirectory of `/SAP/ITS/MIMES`, that is located in the directory of the Web server. If you create additional directories for static pages beneath this directory, you can address them relatively simply. Language-dependence automatically implements this function. For more information, see the description of this function in the section on HTML[Business] enhancements.

7.6   Directory structure

The ITS assumes the presence of a special directory structure to store all the required data. This directory must store all objects that the ITS must access. Two root directories serve as a starting point. Installation of the ITS creates the directory and then enters in the NT registry.

One directory stores ITS objects: templates, resources and service descriptions. The default value of this directory in ITS version 1.x is `\Program Files\SAP\ITS\AGate\`. The default value for ITS version 2.0 is `\Program Files\SAP\ITS\2.0\<virtual ITS>\`. This directory has two subdirectories: `Services` and `Templates`. The service subdirectory contains the global and application-oriented service descriptions. The template directory stores the templates and language resources, and it has additional subdirectories. A subdirectory which is named after the service exists for each service. Installation of the ITS copies predefined templates for error messages and so on to another subdirectory, `SYSTEM`. The system subdirectory contains two additional subdirectories, `dm` and `pm` for the *system templates*. The ITS uses these templates to create error messages, optional login masks and similar items.

If *themes* exist for a service, a subdirectory is created in the template directory of the service. The subdirectory has a name in the form of `xx`, where `xx` is the number of the theme. In this case, either the template directory itself or the subdirectories for the theme store the templates and language resources.

The ITS does not merge some other files, such as graphics, into an HTML document. The Web server performs this task. Accordingly, a directory of the Web server, rather than the ITS directory tree, stores such files. For this reason, templates do not contain a hard coded URL for these objects. Instead, determine the URL with the `mimeURL()` function. The home directory of the Web server has a subdirectory named `\SAP\ITS\MIMES`. This directory has additional subdirectories that enable allocation of objects to services, themes and languages. This directory functions much like the template directory of the ITS. The directory structure does not explicitly support yet another subdivision, arranged according to file type (graphics, sound and so on). You can create such a directory, but must then enter the complete relative path to each file in the templates. If you were to store all the GIF files for pushbuttons in a subdirectory named `BUTTONS`, you would have to address such a file in the template as follows:

```
src="`mimeURL("BUTTONS\PLUS.GIF", ~language = "")`"
```

The ID, consisting of a path and file name, depicts the actual name of the object for all the checkin/checkout modules and transaction SIAC described in the following.

7.7   SAP@Web-Studio

Several previous examples used the Web-Studio. The Studio plays a key role for all work performed outside of the R/3 System. The use of the Web-Studio ensures the storage of all files in the directory structure required by the ITS, the storage of all objects in the R/3 System, and collaboration with the Correction and Transport System. The Web-Studio can edit all files related to ITS-based Internet applications. The Web-Studio also generates service descriptions based on entries you make in dialog boxes. You do not need to process the service descriptions manually. This section describes all the functions of the Web-Studio. Note that the discussion here focuses on version 2.0 of SAP@Web-Studio. Some of its functions, particularly checkin/checkout, currently work only in connection with R/3 Systems of release 4.0A and higher.

The Web-Studio performs the following tasks:

- administration of all external files in the form of projects;

- generation and processing of language resources;

- generation of service descriptions;

- generation of HTML templates by remote calls of R/3 functions;

- communication with the Correction and Transport System of the R/3 System and checkin/checkout functions for Web objects.

7.7.1   Checkin/checkout

The Correction and Transport System (CTS) manages all objects processed within the R/3 System. The CTS locks objects for exclusive processing by one user and enables you to transport those objects into other R/3 Systems. The various tools of the R/3 System establish connections to the CTS.

When the Web-Studio loads Web objects from the R/3 Studio for external processing, you must protect the objects from the work of other developers. Because you cannot call the CTS directly from external applications, a special procedure handles the connection between the Web-Studio and the CTS.

The Web-Studio must load all objects that it processes from the R/3 System with a checkout procedure. The Web-Studio must also return the objects to the R/3 System with a checkin procedure. Each checkout sets a flag in the R/3 System; each checkin resets the flag. Because you can check out only objects with reset flags, the procedure ensures that only one developer can work on an object at any given time. Only the developer and the computer that check out an object may check it back in.

In addition to protection from editing by multiple developers, you must also implement a connection to the CTS. All the available objects that you wish to download from the R/3 System to a local computer must be open for correction or repair. Before you can check out a Web object, you must write an open correction to the Web object with a special transaction (SIAC) in the R/3 System. If no open correction exists, the transaction creates it.

During development of an application some objects (service descriptions, templates, language resources) are stored outside of the R/3 System. These objects have no corresponding originals in the R/3 System. After testing the application, you must transport the object into the R/3 System. Transport begins from the Web-Studio. Because the objects do not yet exist in the R/3 System, you can load them without any preconditions. Once within the R/3 System, you once again use transaction SIAC to maintain the Web objects. A special menu function displays all the new objects. You must then write the objects as open for a correction. During this process, the CTS creates a TADIR entry for each new service. After it creates the TADIR entry, the CTS resets the flag that identified the object as new. You can check out new objects once they have been checked in. After the initial checkin, the objects do not have to indicate an open correction.

7.7.2 Operating the Web-Studio

The tasks of the Web-Studio are extensive and somewhat complex. The following sections describes some of the most important activities.

Interface

The Studio consists of three windows (Figure 7.35). For the left window you can set a special view of projects. The setting IAC VIEW shows the services and all the static elements for the current project. Select FILE VIEW to have an overview of all the files that belong to the project. This function displays the directory structure of the subdirectory that stores all

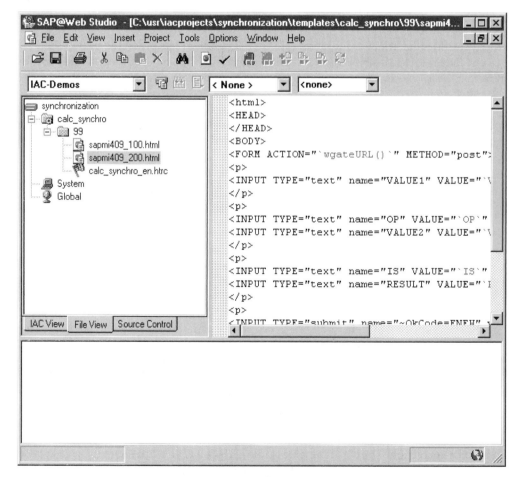

Figure 7.35   View of SAP@Web-Studio

the files for the project. SOURCE CONTROL displays all the services that exist in an R/3 System. It also permits exporting (checkout) files from the R/3 System and importing (checkin) then after editing.

In the left window, you can mark objects (nodes or individual files) with a click of the mouse. A right click calls a context menu that offers functions related to the selected object.

The right window of the Studio presents the contents of the file. Several smaller windows may appear in this area. Each window permits access to a file. However, you can edit only service descriptions, language resources and templates. The Studio depicts graphics files, but does not edit them.

The lower window, covering the entire width of the main window, displays status messages.

Basic techniques

The Studio administers all files that belong to an Internet application as projects. It stores the files in a project directory that is not identical to the ITS working directory. To test the edited files, you must transfer them into the ITS directory. The Studio names this process *Publish*. A site definition contains technical information for publishing, particularly the names of the directories involved. Accordingly, a project always requires a site definition. In practical use, the Studio requires a site for every Web server with which you work. The Studio offers tools to define both sites and projects.

Files that belong to an Internet application can be created in various ways. During development of an IAC, you can use file generators that create service descriptions, templates and language resources. Another option allows you to export the required files from the R/3 System. This option is most often the case when you modify existing applications. As a third option, you can create the files without the help of the Studio and later use the Studio to insert the files into the project.

Defining a site

Use the menu function PROJECT | SITE to process a site definition. The function displays a popup with several options. The options include functions to create and delete sites as well as input fields for all parameters. Table 7.7 displays the various parameters.

Table 7.7 Parameters for a site definition

Parameter	Meaning
WebServer	Name of the Web server that executes the application
Web Root Dir	Root directory of the Web server
UrlWGate	Portion of the URL that accesses the WGate, usually /scripts/wgate.dll. The name of the server and the portions that call a service are ignored.
ITS Host	Name of the ITS that executes the application
ITS Data Directory	Name of the ITS data directory (root directory for services and templates)

Projects

The Studio organizes the processing of IAC files in the form of projects. A project can record one or more services and the files associated with them. A special subdirectory, itself containing additional subdirectories, stores the files that belong to a given project. Set the root for the project subdirectory with the menu function OPTIONS | STUDIO PROPERTIES. This function displays a popup, in which you select DIRECTORIES. The project directory need not lie within the ITS working directory. You can therefore create the project directory in your local file system, even when the ITS is installed on a central computer on the network.

The Studio builds a complex file structure beneath the root. It first creates a subdirectory for each project that carries the name of the project. This directory contains the project file, <projektname>.itsp, that stores all project specifications. Binary objects, divided by theme and language, are located beneath this directory (named after the service).

The project directory contains two additional subdirectories, SERVICES and TEMPLATES. The SERVICES subdirectory records the service descriptions of all the services involved. In the TEMPLATES subdirectory, the Studio creates an additional directory tree for each service; a branch records the templates. As for binary objects, the subdirectory is divided according to theme and language. Figure 7.36 shows an excerpt from NT Explorer that displays the directory structure for a project with one service.

To create a new project, select the function FILE | NEW. Activate PROJECTS in the following popup and enter the name of the project. The Studio generates the required subdirectories and the project file. The project file contains all the information that the Studio requires for a project. All changes to a project, such as insertions, deletions or modifications of path names must take place with the Studio to ensure that the project file is updated. It inserts files into a project; simply copy them into the project directory.

Open an existing project with the menu function FILE | OPEN PROJECT. This function calls up a standard file selection box in which you must select a project file (ends with .ITSP). The Studio opens the project file, reads the corresponding information and then builds the project tree in the left window. When you close the project with FILE | SAVE, the Studio automatically stores all the changes to the project itself and to the corresponding files.

You can mark any desired nodes (themes, languages or the project itself) in the project tree with a click of the mouse. A right click returns a context menu that you can use to generate new files or copy existing files.

Publish

The term *publish* defines the transfer of files from the project directory into the ITS directory. Such transfer can become necessary once during the development phase of an application. After creation, all files must be tested in cooperation with a Web server. Testing requires that the ITS can access the files.

The publish function is also needed to transport IAC files into the R/3 System for storage or to export files from the R/3 System into the ITS. You can perform such transfers only with the publish function. See the section on checkin/checkout for detailed information.

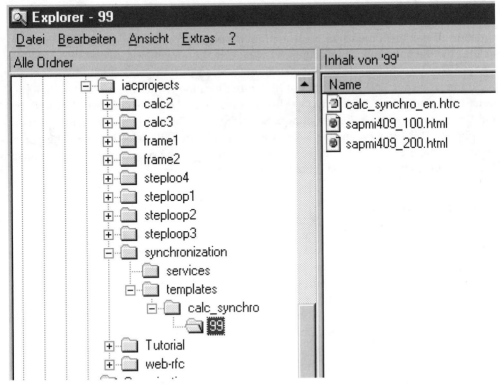

Figure 7.36   Structure of the project directory

Publish always works with the target directories specified in the site definition. To execute a *publish*, mark a node in the project tree and then use the right mouse button to call the context menu for the node. The node contains the PUBLISH function. Use the function to transfer all files within the node to the correct target directories of the ITS. Publish also works, in similar manner, for individual files.

Editing objects

Templates are pure ASCII files. The Studio processes templates with a simple text editor. The other objects (service description and language resources) consist of parameter names and values. A different editor processes those objects. The other editor displays the contents of the file in a table. A click on the parameter name (column key) displays the value of the parameter in a popup. You can then edit the value in the popup. The popup closes only when you use the enter key. You also use this popup to generate new entries. In that case, the popup also offers an input field for the name of the parameter.

A click on the pin symbol in the upper left anchors the popup to a permanent location on the screen. After you use the enter key, the popup remains visible. After you select a new entry, the popup is immediately available for editing the entry.

You must edit the entries in the service files in the same manner.

During editing, you can save files independently of each other with the FILE | SAVE function. The context menu for a file contain a function for deleting a file. This function deletes the file only from the administrative information for the project, not from the file system. The file continues to exist physically.

You may wish to add files that exist in another location within the file system to a project. Such an addition usually involves binary files. To add files to a project, click with the right mouse button to produce a popup. Select INSERT | FILE in the menu that appears in the popup. This function enables you to select the file in a file selection box. The Studio copies the file into the project directory and records it in the project file. The previously marked node in the project tree is the target location.

Checkin of new objects

New objects cannot be stored in the R/3 System as completely independent components. You must always assign them to a service. Accordingly, you must check in the service description as the first object. You can also check in all the objects of a service simultaneously. In this case, the Studio ensures that the service is imported first.

To check in a new service, use the right mouse button to select the service with FILE VIEW in Studio. Then select the ADD FILE function in the subsequent popup. The Studio determines all the objects and subobjects of the marked node and presents these objects in a selection list (see Figure 7.37).

All the objects are marked in the list. If you wish, you can exclude individual objects from the import by resetting the mark.

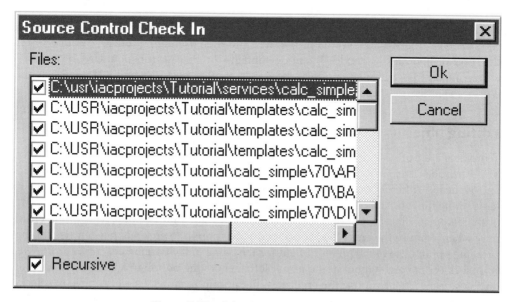

Figure 7.37   Selecting objects for checkin

After you confirm the list, you must use an additional popup to select the R/3 System that will store the objects. Figure 7.38 displays the popup.

After the import, the status window of the Studio (see Figure 7.39) displays information on the import of individual elements. The Studio notes the import status of every object in the project file. Successfully imported objects no longer appear in the object list when you attempt another import.

You can also import objects individually. The process is similar. You again mark the object with the right mouse button, but a different context menu appears. Select the ADD function in the menu.

The Studio stores information on the status of individual files in the project file. The ADD function is provided for files that you have not yet transferred into an R/3 System.

Checkin and checkout of existing objects

A connection to an R/3 System must exist to check objects in and out. To establish such a connection use TOOLS | SOURCE CONTROL | CONNECT TO R/3. The Studio displays a popup that lists all the R/3 Systems available. You must select a system from the list. The Studio

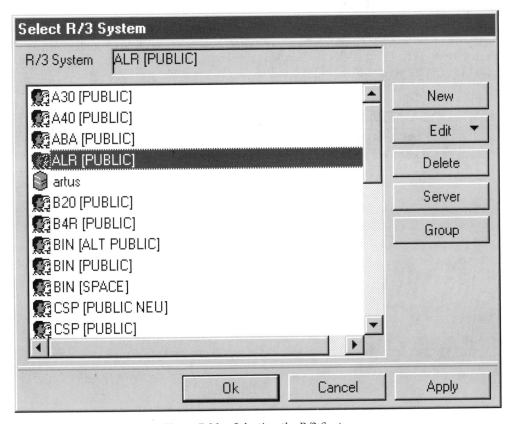

Figure 7.38   Selecting the R/3 System

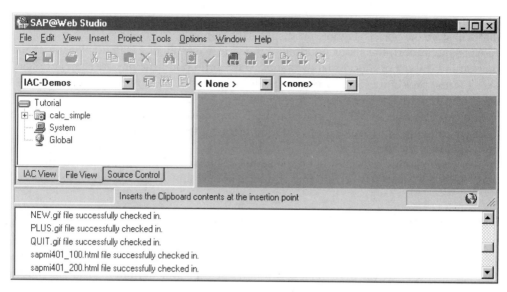

Figure 7.39   General view of SAP@Web-Studio with status notifications

then lists under SOURCE CONTROL all the services stored in that R/3 System along with their themes. When you click on a service or a theme, the Studio reads the appropriate object list and displays it in the right window (see Figure 7.40).

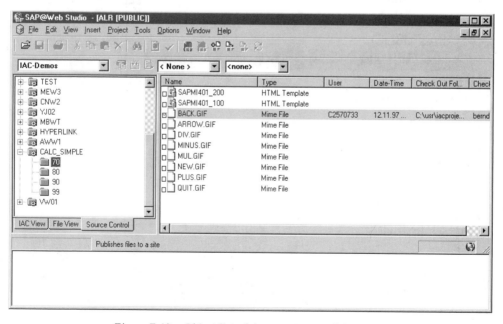

Figure 7.40   Object list of the source control function

You can mark one or more objects in the window. The context menu (right mouse button) now displays the GET and CHECK OUT functions. Use the GET function to copy an object from the R/3 System to your local project directory. This function does not change the status of the object in the R/3 System. *You cannot later rewrite this object into the R/3 System!* This function primarily exists to *publish* the files of completed applications that have been imported into an R/3 System with the Correction and Transport System and will later be transferred to the TIS and the Web server.

If you edit an object externally and then later wish to load it into the R/3 System, you must use the CHECK OUT function. This function reserves the desired objects for you in the R/3 System. No other users may check out the object. Checkout can occur only when you have previously set the object for correction or transport. The studio indicates the checked out status of an at an object has been checked object by placing a red check mark before its name.

After editing it, you must check the file back in. A red mark in File View indicates an object that has been checked out. Mark objects intended for checkin and then call the context menu with the right mouse button. The context menu provides you with a CHECK IN function. You then reconfirm the files for checkin with the popup. The status window of the Studio displays a message after checkin.

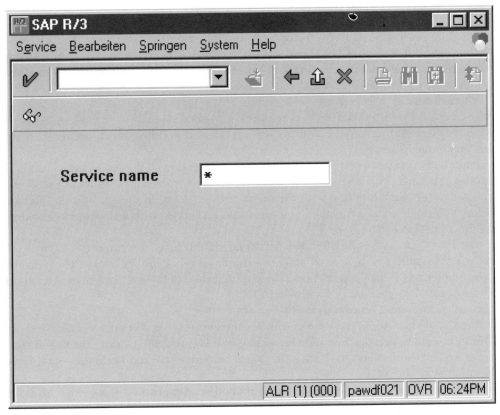

Figure 7.41   Initial screen of transaction SIAC

Note a special consideration when working with language resources. In the R/3 System, each object possesses an original language. Development of an application and generation of all language-dependent elements (text elements, headers, short texts, documentation and so on) take place in this language only. Translators at SAP later translate language-dependent elements from the original language into the target languages. The translators and the developers are not identical. Translation takes place just before delivery of the new application in a special translation system that prohibits any development work. This relatively simple procedure guarantees the consistency of language-dependent elements.

If development of an application takes place in a system owned by SAP itself, it is neither necessary nor helpful to edit more than one language resource. Accordingly, you can check in only one language resource and do so only in the original language of the service. In customer systems, however, it is often simpler to translate the language resources without the complex tools of the R/3 System. Customer systems therefore support checkin and checkout of any language resources, as long as you have set the release flag (MULTILANG) with transaction SIAC in the service.

7.8   Transaction SIAC

The R/3 transaction SIAC forms the opposite number to SAP@Web-Studio. You administer the external files that belong to an IAC with this transaction. You can use the transaction to set special files for a task or generate the task. You can also use it to modify administrative information and to delete objects.

Internally, the R/3 System administers data according to services. Accordingly the initial screen of the SIAC transaction requests a service name. The name can contain wildcards (see Figure 7.41). To edit the service selected in this manner, use the DISPLAY function or the F8 key.

In the subsequent screen (Figure 7.42), the transaction lists all the services that meet the selection specifications. The screen provides you with several functions to edit services. You can access each function with the menu and a symbol in the application toolbar. Before you can execute a function, you must select a service with a click in the marking column of the table view.

The EDIT | TRANSPORT function has particular significance. You can use it to write an entry for the entire service in an existing task or in a task that you will create. The function uses an interface to the Correction and Transport System of the R/3 System, so you must fill out some of the familiar popups of the CTS.

Another important function is EDIT | CHANGE ATTRIBUTES.

You make valid administrative entries for the entire service in an additional screen. This information includes the *multilingual* flag (see Figure 7.43). Setting this flag in customer systems allows you to check in language resources that use languages other than the original for the service.

The hierarchy overview leads you to the individual components of a service. You can enter supplemental selection criteria in a popup (see Figure 7.44) before the transaction offers you a table view with various objects. The supplemental selection criteria include

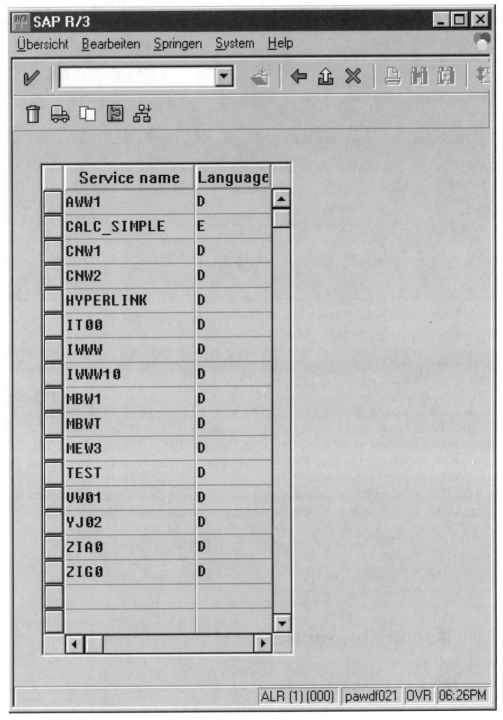

Figure 7.42   Service overview

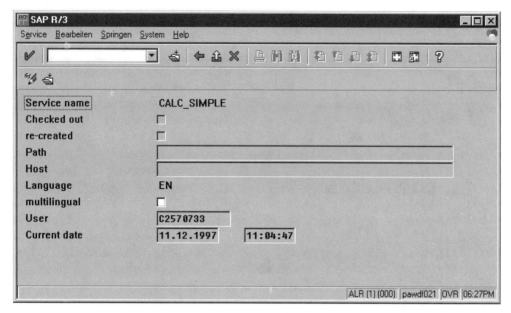

Figure 7.43   Administrative information of a service

the flag setting for objects you have checked out and for new objects. You can use wild-cards for the theme.

The transaction also lists the sub-objects in a table view. Here, too, you can call a detail screen for each object and change some of the administrative information. This ability is particularly important for the checkout flag. If necessary, you can reset the flag manually. The detail screen offers another important function: the transport connection. If you edit only sub-objects, you do not need to include the entire service in a correction. You can set individual sub-objects to correction status.

If required, a conversion of object names into a short form also takes place within transaction SIAC. To implement a transport connection, the names used internally in the R/3 System cannot exceed a predefined length. Some of the names used externally (binary files and temples) can, of course, be longer. The transaction therefore creates a unique identification from the beginning of the external name, the system name and a sequential number. The identification then appears within transaction SIAC and in the object list of the Correction and Transport System.

7.9   Naming conventions

The objects stored in the local file system receive names that must follow specific criteria. When the Web-Studio generates the objects, it names them correctly. If you make changes manually, you must observe the naming convention.

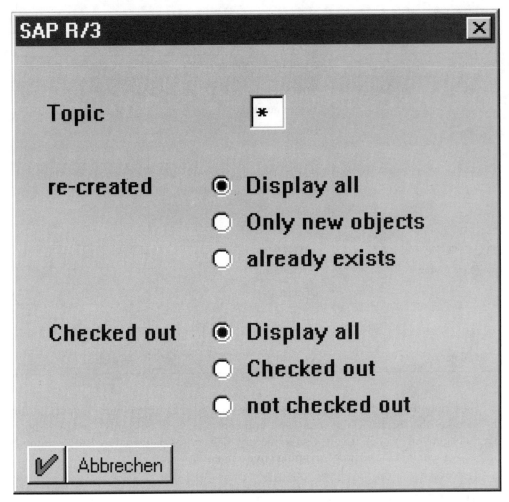

Figure 7.44   Popup with selection criteria

Internal and external names differ in their constituent parts. External names contain some information in the path name, but internal names must contain all the required information. Table 7.8 shows the structure of external names for various object types.

Internal names have importance only for the Correction and Transport System. The R/3 System itself always creates them. You cannot create internal names manually. For the sake of completeness, Table 7.9 shows the structure of internal names.

The names of the module pool and external binary files can be longer than the 20 characters indicated here. In this case, the system creates a shorter unique identifier from the longer name. The short version includes the system name and a sequential number. This short name has significance only within the R/3 System. This process has no influence on external names.

Table 7.8 External names of ITS objects

Type	Contents	Length
Templates	Name of the module pool	max. 255
	Underscore "_"	1
	Screen number	3 or 4
	Underscore	1
	"_"	
	(optional, required only when a language ID follows)	
	Language (optional)	2
Service description	Service name	1–14
Language resource	Service name	1–14
	Underscore	1
	"_"	
	Language	2
Binary data	As desired	As desired

Please note that the SAP conventions for the customer naming environment hold for the name of the service. This means that you can create and edit only services whose names begin with Y or Z. If you wish to modify the services delivered by SAP, you must first copy them into the customer naming environment.

7.10   HTML^Business

Templates include control statements for the ITS in the form of metastatements. The ITS creates these statements before it transfers HTML pages to the Web server in true HTML source code. SAP uses the term *HTML*^Business for these metastatements.

The following section describes the various groups of meta-HTML statements that exist.

7.10.1   General

So that the ITS can distinguish meta-HTML statements from true HTML source code, the metastatements must have unique identifiers. You can provide this identification by enclosing it in the `server tag` (`<server>` and `</server>`) or backticks (`` ` ``). You can include multiples statements in one of two ways. First, you can include them separately in individual tags or backticks. Second, you can include them within a tag by separating

Table 7.9 Internal names of ITS objects

Type	Contents	Length
Templates	Service name	14
	Theme	2
	Screen number	4
	Module pool	20
Supplemental for language-dependent templates	Language	1
Service description	Service name	14
Language resource	Service name	14
	Language	1
	Theme	2
Binary data	Service name	14
	Theme	2
	External name	20
Supplemental for language-dependent binary files	Language	1

the statements with a semicolon. At least an underscore must come between two statements, when backticks enclose each statement. Examples of valid HTML^{Business} statements include:

```
`repeat with j from 1 to TEXT-LINE.dim`
<server> repeat with j from 1 to ITADIR-PGMID.dim </server>
`ITADIR-PGMID[j]` `ITADIR-OBJECT[j]` `ITADIR-OBJ_NAME[j]`
```

7.10.2   Field substitutions and field attributes

Field substitutions provide the simplest form of HTML metastatements. These statements regulate both the transfer of data from screen values into HTML pages and the merging of values delivered by the browser into the input fields of the screen. In normal cases, a one-to-one correspondence exists between the screen fields and the HTML fields. The correspondence has validity for both reading from and writing to the screen. Text areas are an exception.

Each metastatement (other than reserved key words) is evaluated as the name of a screen field and replaced by its contents. If no such field exists, the ITS generates a run-time error. You can also use field contents in simple statements.

The ITS converts the contents of step loops or data transmitted over the screen RFC channel into arrays. You can access the individual elements of an array by specifying an index after the field name. Square brackets enclose the index. This allocation holds for the fields of a step loop in both directions. Data delivered by RFC is read only: you cannot transfer the fields back to the R/3 System.

If only square brackets without a specified value appear after a field name during a transfer from the HTML document to the R/3 System, the system appends the data to existing fields. The array may not become larger than the corresponding step loop on the screen, or a runtime error occurs.

If you need to limit the number of characters per field transferred from the Web to the screen, you can specify the number of characters after the field name. A colon (:) separates the specification from the filed name. A specification of length must come between the field name and the index. If you have specified a length, excessive characters are discarded. Only one exception to this rule exists. If the field is an array and no explicit index is specified (only [ ]), the extra characters are placed into a new line of the step loop. This process is required for text areas.

Example:

```
<textarea name="TEXT-LINE:20[]" cols="80">
```

You can use different attributes of the field names to determine various characteristics of the field in the R/3 System, in addition to the field contents. You insert these values into the Web page or the meta-HTML statement just as you do the actual field contents. Table 7.10 shows the available attributes.

Table 7.10 Supplemental attributes for field names

Attribute	Description
Dim	Number of values of a field
MaxSize	Maximum number of characters in a field
VisSize	Visible length of the screen field
Disabled	Field not ready for input
Label	Text for the screen field (key text)

7.10.3　Statements and conditions

The description described in the following sections use logical conditions. You can use the operators listed in Table 7.11 in these conditions and in other statements. Statements have a structure similar to those found in the C programming language.

7.10.4　Conditional substitutions

In some cases, you may have to make substitution depend on specific conditions. Depending on the contents of a field, you can use alternative lines, suppress empty fields

7.10 HTML^{Business}

Operator	Meaning
!	Negation
++	Increasing increment
--	Decreasing increment
=	Assignment
*	Multiplication
/	Division
%	Module
&&	Logical AND
+	Addition
−	Subtraction
&	Concatenation
||	Logical OR
==	Equals
!=	Does not equal
>	Larger than
<	Smaller than
>=	Greater than or equal
<=	Smaller than or equal

or change the order of arrangement of fields on the screen. You use the meta statement IF to perform these tasks. The END statement closes an IF statement. An ELSE statement within an IF statement can execute an alternative branch. You can also nest IF statements. You can combine sequential ELSE-IF statements into one ELSIF or ELSEIF command.

7.10.5 Loops

To process the contents of fields with multiple values, step loops or internal tables, you must use substitutions repeatedly. To do so, you can use two commands, REPEAT and FOR, both of which have a similar functional range. Both commands process a defined sequence of statements repeatedly.

The REPEAT statement has three basic forms. The simplest form executes a defined number of loops without using a run variable. The statement uses the following syntax:

repeat expr **times** statement **end**

This form of a statement does not permit meaningful field substitution. It serves best to insert graphic elements, blank lines and so on.

Use the second form of the REPEAT statement when you wish to output the contents of fields with multiple values in sequence. This form places the individual values after each other in an additional field. The statement uses the following syntax:

repeat with register **in** field statement **end**

The individual values of fields with multiple values or of the table field are placed in register one after the other. This statement permits editing only of a field named in the statement. If a loop processes several fields of one line in an internal table, you must use an index. Use the third form of the REPEAT statement to provide the statement with an index.

repeat with indexfield **from** expr1 **to** expr2 [**by** expr3] statement **end**

The indexfield field runs through the set of values between expr1 and expr2 in increments of 1. You can change the increment with expr3 if required. If expr1 is greater than expr2, the value of expr3 must be negative. In this manner, you can run through an internal table from the end to the beginning if required.

You can also use a FOR statement, similar to the C programming language. This statement has a functional range comparable to the REPEAT statement. The statement uses the following syntax:

for(expr1 ; expr2 ; expr3) statement **end**

Statement expr1 executes before the first run of the loop. Normally, expr1 is the assignment of a starting value for a run variable. The loop then executes. Statement expr3 executes after each execution of the loop until the logical expression expr2 is no longer met. Only one statement may exist between the semicolons. Unlike C, this syntax does not permit you to link several commands.

Table 7.12 compares the commands available for the REPEAT and the FOR statement. Because the examples come from HTML templates, they contain backticks to indicate the meta-HTML statements.

Table 7.12 Comparison of loop statements

Repeat	*for*
`repeat 10 times`	`for(i=1;i<=10;i++)`
<p></p>	<p></p>
`end`	`end`
`repeat with i in FIELD_OP`	Implementation only with the third form
<option value="`i`">	
`end`	
`repeat with i from 1 to FIELD_OP.dim`	`for(i=1; i<=FIELD_OP.dim; i++)`
<option value="`FIELD_OP[i]`"> `FIELD_BZ[I]` `FIELD_BZ[i]`	<option value="`FIELD_OP[i]`">
`end`	`end`

7.10.6   Functions

Templates can include some meta-HTML functions. The functions also have parameters that further specify the value they return. Only the use of these functions enables you to write templates that work independently of the concrete configuration of the ITS server. You can transfer only templates without hard-coded URLs or path names to graphic files and so on to other systems without any problems.

WgateURL

The `wgateURL` function determines URLs that refer to the current Web server. Three cases demand the use of this function. First, the `FORM` tag requires specification of a URL of a program that processes the contents of the form. Because the path depends on the type of ITS installation, the system should determine it dynamically. Second, use the `wgateURL` function to specify the target frame in the form or an application with multiple frames. In this case, you must generate the URL to the ITS and merge additional parameters into the URL. Third, use the function to specify a URL for a frame within a frameset document. Table 7.13 shows the parameters of the `wgateURL` function.

Table 7.13   Parameters of the wgateURL function

Parameter	Task
~OkCode	Filled with the function code triggered in the R/3 application.
~target	Filled with the name of the target frame in the FORM tag.
~FrameName	Determines the URL of a frame in a frameset document
Name of the screen field	Fills screen fields in the target frame

Syntax:

```
wgateURL(identifier = expr {, identifier = expr})
```

MimeURL

The `mimeURL` function creates links to files in the directory of the Web server and merges these files into the HTML document. This function assumes a predefined directory structure. The directory tree beneath the root directory of the Web server normally begins with the following path:

```
/sap/its/mimes
```

The path is stored in the ~URLmime parameter of the global service description.

Additional subdirectories are arranged in the following order: service, theme and language. In addition to the subdirectories that actually exist, the directory structure includes the directories SYSTEM and GLOBAL. You can store binary objects for system templates and objects for cross-service use in these directories.

The ~name parameter can contain a complete path specification, so that you can add even more subdirectories beneath the last subdirectory defined by the standard. For example, you can create subdirectories named background, button, sound and so on arrange supplementary binary files. The ITS does not check the values of the parameters, it simply combines them into a complete URL. This feature enables you to create additional subdirectories and address the objects within them with the mimeURL function.

ImageURL

The imageURL function is now obsolete. The mimeURL function has replaced it. A description of imageURL follows to enable migration of older templates.

The imageURL function specifies links to graphics files stored in the Web server directory rather than the ITS directory. You cannot use a simple, relative URL here. The URL includes parameters (see Table 7.14) that determine the type of graphics file and allocation to a service and to a theme. Except for the names, all other parameters refer to the subdirectory within the directory structure described previously. The path name follows the following pattern:

/Web_Server_Root_Directory/SAP/ITS/GRAPHICS/Type/Language/Theme/Name

If the parameter does not specify a language and a theme, the entries in the service description or the current login language apply. The ITS uses the values given in the parameters to build a URL, but does not check the values. You can therefore include additional subdirectories in the graphics directory and address them with the imageURL function.

Table 7.14 Parameters of the imageURL function

Parameter	Task
~name	Name of the file
~type	Type of graphic
~language	Language
~theme	Theme

Syntax:

imageURL(~type=expr, ~name=expr {,~theme=expr,} {,~language=expr})

ArchiveURL

The R/3 System supports optical archiving systems. These systems can store scanned documents that a special viewer then displays in the R/3 System. The archiveURL function enables you to use the functions of the iXOS archive from a Web application. Select the desired function with the `Command`, `ArchiveID` and `DocID` parameters. Consult the documentation on the Archive-DLL for further information.

Syntax:

```
archiveURL(command, archiveID=expr, docID=expr)
```

Assert

The name of a screen field is transferred as a parameter to the `Assert` function. When the R/3 application triggers an error, the system determines the position of the cursor in the field that triggered the error. It then insets a standard error text in the HTML document at the position of the corresponding `Assert` function. The system parameter `~ErrorMarker` can overwrite the error text. The service description sets the parameter. The text can contain any desired HTML statement, such as the link to a graphic. Only a simple substitution takes place, because the parameter does not evaluate HTML[Business] statements.

If the R/3 application links several fields to an error message, the assert function always recognizes only the first field name delivered by the R/3 System.

Syntax:

```
assert(Field Name)
```

Write and WriteENC

You can use the `Write` function to write field contents and other information into the HTML document. The function does not insert any separating spaces between the individual values. This limitation represents the only difference between the function and simple substitution. The `WriteENC` function works similarly, but encodes the output to a URL according to requirements. It substitutes hexadecimal code for special characters or space characters. The function is needed to create correct URLs from fields that contain these characters.

7.11   Macros and function modules for the mass data channel

The include `AVWRTCXM` contains the declarations of some macros. Communication between the R/3 application and the ITS require these macros in special cases. Previous examples have already used some of the macros. You use these macros most often in connection with the mass data channel. Please note that you cannot monitor data exchange over this channel within the Debugger.

7.11.1   The Mass Data Channel

The include `AVWRTCXM` also contains the declaration of internal table `tavwctx`. The table functions as a temporary data pool. Its structure corresponds to the data context of the ITS. You can transmit the table to the ITS. In this case, the ITS merges the contents of the table into the data context. You can also copy the data context of the ITS into the table, and thus access the entire data context within the R/3 application. All the macros described in the following use table `tavwctx`.

The transfer of the table to and from the ITS requires two function modules. You use `ITS_SET_CONTEXT` to send a table to the ITS. You must never call this function module directly. Instead, use the `field-transport` macro that provides the function module with the correct values.

You use the function module `ITS_IMPORT_CONTEXT` to read the context. This module imports the data context and stores it in an internal table. Since no macro currently exists to call this module, you must link it directly into your application.

7.11.2   FIELD-SET

You use this macro to collect any desired data into a pool. You then transmit the pool to the ITS with the `FIELD-TRANSPORT` macro.

Syntax:

field-set name index value.

You can use any desired name as `name`. The name later provides access from the template to values. The name does not have to refer to any existing field in the R/3 application. The name should include a unique sequential number so that the ITS can process several fields with the same name (arrays). The number will later serve as an index. If you transfer only one field, the specification of an index is obligatory.

The value transmitted to the ITS must be a character string. You must transform numerical values into that form.

7.11.3   FIELD-TRANSPORT

This macro transmits the data pool built with `FIELD-SET` to the ITS. To ensure that the data in the template become available immediately, you should place the two macros, `FIELD-SET` and `FIELD-TRANSPORT` at the time of PBO. You may call the `FIELD-TRANSPORT` macro repeatedly for each run during the processing cycle of the screen only from version 2.0 of the ITS.

7.11.4   FIELD-GET

You can use this macro to read field contents directly from the ITS.

FIELD-GET name index table length.

The parameter `name` represents the name of the element to be read. This macro also requires specification of an obligatory index. The third parameter transfers an internal table that will store the read value. The parameter `length`, also a field in your application, provides information on the length of the read value. Because you cannot always determine the length of data ahead of time (see text area), you cannot use a field with fixed length. If the length of the read data exceeds the length of a table line, the system automatically appends additional lines. The table is filled continuously without consideration of its structure. Accordingly, you may have to transform the data.

At each call of `field-get`, the system established a new connection to the ITS. It reads only one field each time. You cannot use wildcards or areas for the index. Efficient performance dictates that you should not use this macro to read a large number of fields.

7.11.5 FIELD-QUERY

You can use this macro to read a field from the internal data pool. You can fill the pool ahead of time by calling the function module `ITS_IMPORT_CONTEXT`. Since the function module requires only one access to the ITS, use it when you must read several fields.

FIELD-QUERY `name index field.`

Transfer the name of the context field and its index as a parameter. The parameter `field` returns the desired value.

7.11.6 FIELD-DELETE

This macro deletes a field or the value of a field with several values from the temporary data context.

Syntax:

FIELD-DELETE `field index.`

7.11.7 MIME-INFO

Some HTML commands enable you to send any data from the browser to the Web server. The server then redirects the data to the ITS, which can then send it to the R/3 application. The application uses the macro `MIME-INFO` to determine some technical data.

Syntax:

MIME-INFO `info.`

A field with the structure `SAVWMPMIME` is represented by `info`. Table 7.15 shows the makeup of the structure.

Table 7.15 Structure SAVWMPMIME

Field name	Type	Length
CONTTYPE	CHAR	255
CONTLENGTH	NUMC	10
CONTNAME	CHAR	255
CONTFNAME	CHAR	255

7.11.8 MIME-UPLOAD

This macro loads the binary data sent by the Web browser into the R/3 System.
   Syntax:

MIME_UPLOAD index data length.

The ITS transfer the data in table form. The system must read the data by line.

7.11.9 MIME-UPLOADPART

This macro works similarly to MIME-UPLOAD, but it allows you to read only one, exactly defined portion of the data. The syntax is therefore similar to the previous macros:

MIME-UPLOADPART index offset length data.

7.11.10 MIME-DOWNLOAD

You can use this macro to send any desired binary data to the Web browser over the ITS. In this case, the system does not generate a template.
   Syntax:

MIME-DOWNLOAD data length type.

7.12 Debugger

A debugger provides an important utility for the identification of errors. The ITS does not have its own tool to debug Web applications. However, you can use the Debugger in the SAP System to debug the R/3 portion of Web applications.

The ITS can redirect the data stream delivered by the R/3 System to a normal SAPGUI. The ITS appears like an application server of the R/3 System to the SAPGUI. You can thus operate the application in parallel over the Web browser and the SAPGUI. Proceed as follows to debug a Web application.

First login to the ITS of the pseudo R/3 System. To do so, create a new entry in the SAPLOGON program with the NEW pushbutton. You can describe the entry in any way you wish. The value for the APPLICATION SERVER field is the name of your Web server; the system number is 00.

You can debug only Web applications currently running. If you wish to use the Debugger while testing a Web application, log on to the pseudo R/3 System created above. A SAPGUI appears that shows the current status of the application. It also mirrors the steps executed over the Web.

Enter the command /h in the command field of the SAPGUI. This entry has two effects. First, an ITS system message appears in the Web application because the Web cannot display the debugging screen. Until you complete the debugging session, you can operate the application only with the SAPGUI. Second, the SAPGUI displays the Debugger's interface. You have access to all its functions.

Use the `continue` function to exit the debugger. You can continue the application by selecting the `continue` pushbutton within the system message of the ITS in the browser.

7.13   Important Service Parameters

Parameters in global and service-specific parameter files describe the behavior of a service. Some of these parameters are set during system initialization and should not be changed. Other parameters can or must be edited during development or at placement into the productive system. Table 7.16 lists the most important parameters and their meaning.

Table 7.16 Important parameters in service files

Parameter	Example	Meaning
~login	Murner	Login name
~client	800	Client
~language	E	Login language
~password	des26(82c2f25498c7bf2d)	Password for login to the R/3 System (DES encrypted)
~transaction	zb37	Transaction to be executed
~SyncBehaviour	NoResync	The ITS turns synchronization off
~exiturl	http:\\capitola	URL of a static HTML document, called after the orderly ending of an application.
~runtimeMode	dm or pm	Subdirectory, under \templates\system, from which system templates are taken.
~Timeout	20	Timeout in minutes
~systemName	M11	R/3 System
~loginGroup	PUBLIC	Login group for load balancing
~messageServer	Kansas	Name of the message server
~connectString	/H/kansas/S/sapdp11	Connect string to the R/3 System

8 Design techniques for HTML templates

The 4.0 versions of the browsers from Microsoft (Internet Explorer) and Netscape (Communicator) offer completely new techniques for the design of a Web page. Both browsers take fuller advantage of the multimedia potentials of the Internet. In addition to the design opportunities provided by images, video and sound, the newest versions of the browsers add expanded interaction to a Web page.

Purely static Web pages have long since failed to meet current demands. To display the most current information, today's systems generate Web pages dynamically. For example, the Web site offered by a bank must contain the most up-to-date currency rates. Developers now use various techniques, including Common Gateway Interface (CGI), Active Server Pages (ASP) or Java Data Base Connectivity (JDBC) to extract information from data dynamically and link it to the corresponding page.

In addition to its ability to create a Web page dynamically, ITS technology also permits you to access the business system directly and thus always produce up-to-date Web pages. You do not need to maintain any systems in addition to the business system. Previously, information that had reached the browser immediately became static. Older systems did not support interaction with users without a new request for an updated Web page. For example, these systems did not support expansion of a tree structure, as users expect in Windows 95.

The new techniques allow the display of information already in the browser to depend upon user entries. To show or hide this data, the techniques do not demand a new connection to the Web server. This chapter therefore treats supplementing Web pages with dynamic elements rather than generating Web pages dynamically for IACs. The following examples offer an introductory view of how you can use the techniques most advantageously:

- *Employment opportunities*
  In the *Employment Opportunities* IAC (Section 5.6.2), interested applicants can submit applications online. They must enter personal information on the form in the left window. The form contains various sections. Each section becomes visible only when users make a selection and the R/3 System sends the correct elements to the browser. Each click initiates communication with the Web server, the ITS and the R/3 System. Good performance dictates that the browser should load all the sections at one time, but display only the selected section. Communication would then take place when the user has completed the entire form and all its sections and then transmits it.

- *Web research in the DMS of the R/3 System*
  Section 6.1.2 introduced an Internet application that permits searching for documents classified according to various criteria in the *Document Management System* (DMS) of

the R/3 System. To search, the user must specify the values for the characteristics applicable to a class. After specification of a class, the application lists all the characteristics in the left window. The user enters values by specifying a characteristic. The lower part of the left window then displays a field for the input of values or a list of possible values, from which the user must make a selection. Display occurs without communication with the R/3 System in the same window. Note that the system displays the input field after the user has selected a characteristic. Navigation between the characteristics and the input of values takes places completely within the browser.

The following sections give an overview of these techniques and their use in IACs. They do not present a detailed explanation of the Web technologies. Sufficient literature exists to cover that point. However, we wish to indicate new paths that the reader may follow and to present examples of how to use these techniques in an Internet application. On this basis provided here, readers can give free reign to their creativity in designing Web pages. A basic knowledge of HTML offers an advantage. The following comments treat only the techniques that users can link directly into an HTML page. They do not cover the use of Java-Applets. Nor do they discuss the graphic design of Web pages by professional designers. We also recommend most strongly that good ergonomics depend upon successful collaboration between professional Web designers and HTML developers. The Web designer is responsible for the design and arrangement of graphic elements. The HTML developer is responsible for the technical conversion of design tools from the HTML repertoire.

8.1   Introduction

Numerous tools exist to present multimedia elements such as VRML or videos. These comments apply to techniques that the browser can interpret directly, without the use of plug-ins. JavaScript naturally represents the first and foremost technique. (In principle, we could also speak here of script language, such as Visual Basic Script. However, the following example use JavaScript as the script language. We therefore treat only JavaScript concretely.) New aspects include the use of style sheets for new ways of displaying text. The W3C organization (W3C: WWW Consortium, responsible for the standarization of Web topics as HTML (http://www.w3.org)) has standardized these style sheets. Dynamic HTML (DHTML) also enables the placement and movement of blocks of information.

   The following remarks treat only the browsers from Microsoft and Netscape, because of their large market share. These two manufacturers currently wage a 'browser war' that becomes particularly evident in the different tags used by DHTML. These remarks discuss only the techniques that both browsers can use. We indicate any differences that may exist between the browsers.

8.1.1   JavaScript

HTML was originally conceived as a way to present static information independently of the platform in use. The growing popularity of the Web, however, soon demanded interaction with users. The ability to make entries with forms that are components of HTML represents a first step in this direction. However, HTML does not support a check of the entry directly in the browser. This function demands programming. JavaScript can perform this task and process additional information. JavaScript is a simple and effective interpreter language. It works closely with HTML and was specifically developed for this purpose. The browser interprets JavaScript directly, if the user has set the browser to permit it. JavaScript therefore allows manipulation of information in HTML pages. The language is object-based and contains traditional control statements. Its syntax is similar to C/C++.

Object hierarchy

An HTML page contains several objects, data elements with characteristics and, often, data elements with functions (methods) bound to objects. Examples include frames, forms, images or checkboxes. Objects can be part of a superior object. Accordingly, objects are arranged into a hierarchy, displayed in Figure 8.1. The uppermost object is the browser window itself. A window has attributes, such as title or size. The HTML document in this window represents the next lowest object, a *document*. The tags contained in an HTML page define objects at the next level, such as *forms* or *images*.

Certain objects placed in an HTML page may themselves consist of various elements. A form, for example, consists of input fields or selection lists. In addition to the hierarchy of HTML objects, other objects, such as Date, exist. Such objects are not treated here.

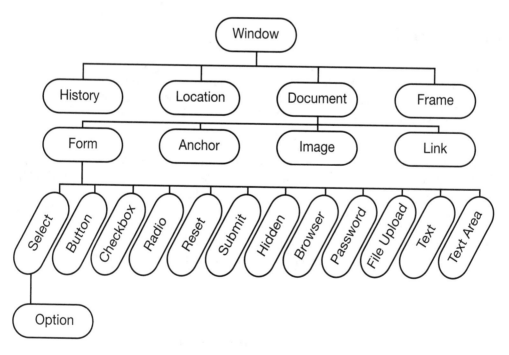

Figure 8.1   Hierarchy of HTML objects

Access to objects in HTML

The *Document Object Model* (DOM) (see the specifications of the W3C at: http://www.w3.org/DOM) defines the objects that JavaScript can manipulate. DOM is language-independent; every script language, including Visual Basic Script, can use it. Access to the characteristics or methods of an object takes place by specifying the hierarchy in the notation common to object-based languages. You can reference the object itself in various ways:

- You can assign a name with the name attribute. An image, for example:

  ```
  <IMG src="logo.gif" name="logo">
  ```

  For example, access to the attribute src takes place with this name:

  ```
  window.document.logo.src
  ```

- You can make all the objects with the same type accessible with an array. If an object has no name assigned to it, you can reference the object with the array. For example, if an HTML page contains three images, you can access the src attribute of the second image with the following:

  ```
  window.document.images[1].src (counting begins at 0).
  ```

  The numbers of the images correspond to their order of appearance in the HTML page.

The first version has an advantage: access is independent of the arrangement of the objects on the HTML page . You usually do not have to place a window object ahead, as long as you remain in the same window.

Functions, called by events, usually handle modifications to objects. An event handler (see next section) or a click on a hyperlink can trigger an event. For example, if you wish to change the image object from the last example, you must assign a new image file to the src attribute as follows:

```
function changeImage(){
    window.document.logo.src = "logo_new .gif";
}
```

Listing 8.1   JavaScript function changeImage()

You can execute the function by calling a hyperlink. Here, you do not assign the href attribute of the <A> tag a new HTML file, but the function name by specifying the script language:

```
<A href="JavaScript: changeImage();">Change Image </A>
```

Capturing events

Various events can occur during a user's interaction with an HTML page: clicking on a hyperlink or crossing over a hyperlink or an image with the mouse pointer. *Event handlers* can register these events and trigger appropriate actions. Consider the following case as an example. As the mouse pointer crosses over a hyperlink, the status line of the browser window should display an explanatory text:

```
<A href="new_dok.html" onMouseOver="window.status = "Loading docu-
ment new_doc '">Document</A>
```

The event handler onMouseOver informs the browser that an action should accompany the event *crossing the hyperlink*: placing the appropriate text in the browser's status line. (An event handler does not require specification of a script language.) You can also call the function that changes the image when crossing an image:

```
<IMG src="logo.gif" name="logo" onMouseOver = "changeImage();">
```

Additional event handlers include: onMouseOut, onClick, onLoad.

Placing JavaScript

The statements and functions of JavaScript do not belong to the language range of HTML. You must therefore specify both within the <SCRIPT> tag. So that the browser knows which script language you use, you must specify the name of the language in the language attribute of the <SCRIPT> tag. When you specify JavaScript, the browser interprets everything between these tags as JavaScript statements. No direct defaults require you to place the statement at a particular point in the HTML page. Usually, however, it is placed between the <HEAD> tags .

Example of an HTML page with JavaScript:

```
<HTML>
<HEAD>
  <TITLE>HTML with JavaScript</TITLE>
    <SCRIPT language="JavaScript">
      function changeImage(){
          document.logo.src = "logo_new .gif"
        }
    </SCRIPT>
</HEAD>
<BODY>
  Page with JavaScript<br>
  <IMG src="pictures /change.gif" name="logo"
onMouseOver="changeImage();">
</BODY>
</HTML>
```

Listing 8.2   Placing JavaScript in an HTML page

If you use the same JavaScript functions in several Web pages, you can store the functions in a separate file, rather than reprogramming them. You must then link the file to the page: use the src attribute of the <SCRIPT> tag with the URL of the file:

```
<SCRIPT language="JavaScript" src="functions.js"> </SCRIPT>
```

8.1.2 Cascading Style Sheet

The popularity of the Web has not only increased demands for interaction with the user, but also increased the desire to additional graphic design options in HTML. Microsoft and Netscape attempted to meet these demands by creating a number of proprietary enhancements to HTML. The enhancements, however, remained isolated islands. They did not lead to a standard and ran only in proprietary browsers. Web designers, of course, reacted with anger. To use the new options, designers had to double the work involved in creating a Web page or support only a single browser.

The W3C organization followed a different path in its attempt to offer additional design options. Rather than introducing new HTML tags, the W3C decided to separate contents from presentation. It developed an additional language that set the graphic representation of standard HTML tags with *style sheets*. These style sheets offer a significant advantage. Both Microsoft and Netscape support style sheets that provide a common denominator for supplemental Web design. Although the two browsers do not produce identical results, they can both interpret and display all the commands.

Syntax for assigning style sheets

Up to now, the layout of headers, `<H1>`, depended on the browser. You can now use style sheets to change the display of headers. For example, style sheets can define the size, weight and family of font. Permissible characteristics broadly cover the categories *font, text, color and background, box* and *classification*. The number of attributes for each characteristic differs. The syntax is quite simple:

```
H1 {font-size: 50px; font-weight: bolder; font-family: arial;}
```

The style sheet begins with the name of the HTML element type. Curly brackets enclose all the characteristics being set. A semicolon (;) separates the characteristics. A colon (:) introduces assignments. The assignments overwrite the default values that the browser already has for these tags. Each `<H1>` header on the HTML page will now display the new value.

Note: Style sheets interpret an HTML text block (for example with the `<DIV>` or `<SPAN>` tags) as a box. The box is later called a layer, but do not confuse this layer with the `<Layer>` tag of the Netscape browser.

Assignments with classes and identifiers

The last example assigns all the `<H1>` headers on a Web page to the same style sheet. However, should you wish to change only selected headers, you can explicitly assign a style sheet to a class. You reference the style sheet in the HTML tag with an identifier of your choice by using the `class` attribute. Nothing in the definition of the style sheet changes except the point before the identifier:

```
.classname {font-size: 30px; font-weight: bold; font-family: arial;}
```

Referencing the style sheet of a class in an HTML tag:

```
<H1 class="classname">New header </H1>
```

You can also assign style sheets with IDs. If, for example, you wish to specify the point size in a specific text block, you would:

- provide the text block with an ID;

- define a style sheet for the ID.

You can define IDs for style sheets with whatever names you desire, as long as the name is preceded by a hash sign (#).

```
#box {font-size: 20px; font-weight: bold; font-family: Courier;}
...
<DIV id="box">
    This text is inside a text block
</DIV>
```

Listing 8.3   Allocation of a style sheet with an ID

Placing style sheets

As in the case of JavaScript, no predefined rules determine where to place style sheets in HTML pages. However, we recommend placing them in the header. Because the definitions of style sheets do not display any HTML tags, you must frame them with a specific tag: <STYLE>. The following gives text/css as the type:

```
<HTML>
<HEAD>
  <STYLE TYPE="text/css">
    H1    {font-size: 50px; font-weight: bolder; font-family: Arial;}
    .header {font-size: 30px; font-weight: bold; font-family: Arial;}
    #box {font-size: 20px; font-weight: bold; font-family: Courier;}
  </STYLE>
</HEAD>
<BODY>
<H1> HTML with style sheets" </H1>
<H2 class="header">New headline </H2>
<DIV ID="box">
  Text inside a text block
</DIV>
</BODY>
</HTML>
```

Listing 8.4   Placing style sheets in an HTML page

If you wish to make defined style sheets available to several Web pages at once, you should store the definition in an external file. You can then link the file to the header of the Web page with the <LINK> tag.

```
<LINK REL=StyleSheet HREF="style.css" TYPE="text/css">
```

In addition to placing the definition of a style sheet within a <STYLE> tags, you can also specify them directly in the HTML tag:

```
<H1 style=" font-size: 50px; font-weight: bolder; font-family: arial;">
```

We recommend against this form, however, since it violates the principle of separating contents from design.

Note: Although the W3C has standardized the specification of style sheets, the Microsoft and Netscape browsers to not implement it completely. Accordingly, the following comments present only style sheets available equally to both browsers.

8.1.3 Dynamic HTML

The use of style sheets can significantly improve the design of a Web page. Style sheets, however, mean that the pages are still very static. The possibilities offered by *Dynamic HTML* (DHTML) in new browsers provide a powerful new means of designing Web pages and changing their contents dynamically. Dynamic modification takes places in the client – without reloading the page from the server. Dynamic HTML does not require support of Applets, controls or other plug-ins.

The *Document Object Model* (DOM) underwent extensive enhancement for DHTML so that a script language could address more objects as well as more characteristics and methods of objects as previously. A difference between the two browsers exists here. Microsoft Internet Explorer can access all HTML elements by characteristics and methods, but Netscape can access only a limited number of objects. However, Netscape has nonetheless expanded the capabilities of the old DOM.

Expanding the characteristics of style sheets

HTML-Objects in DHTML are based on the characteristics and attributes of the DOM as well as expansions by the style sheets. To enable a Web page to function dynamically, DHTML expands the characteristic even further. The most important elements include:

- POSITION: You can place objects in HTML pages in an absolute or relative position to the text flow.

- TOP and LEFT: You must specify the coordinates when using absolute placement. TOP indicates the distance (in pixels) from the upper edge of the Web page. LEFT specifies the distance to the left edge.

- HEIGHT and WIDTH: height and width of an object .

- Z-ORDER: If different objects lie on top of each other, this characteristic specifies their arrangement.

- VISIBILITY: You use this characteristic to specify if an object remains visible or hidden.

The standardization set by the W3C also applies to these characteristics. The term CSS Positioning (see the specifications of the W3C at: `http://www.w3.org/TR/WD-positioning`) (CSS P) sets specifications for characteristics. Both browsers have already implemented a large portion of this specification .

The principal advantage of dynamic HTML is its ability to position specific text blocks freely in an HTML page and to change the characteristics of the text blocks dynamically. Because the text blocks can be displayed at different levels, the following also refers to them as layers. The somewhat complicated formatting required by tables is no longer necessary. This section clarifies the use of such *layers* in Internet application. The treatment of modifications to HTML objects in the following is limited to a discussion of layers.

Certain tags, such as `<DIV>` or `<SPAN>` define text blocks in HTML. For JavaScript to modify these tags, they require a unique ID (see Listing 8.3).

Both browsers originally implemented a layer technique in isolation. They introduced new, non-standardized HTML tags that ran only in one browser. Standardization of style sheets and similar, if not identical, implementation in both browsers permits consideration of layer technology independently of the browsers. JavaScript can change the characteristics of the style sheets dynamically.

Access to objects and characteristics

The syntax for style sheets in both browsers is almost identical. However, each browser implements the DOM and access to objects and their characteristics with JavaScript differently:

- *Microsoft*
  Microsoft introduced a new object, `all`. You can address every HTML object with `all`. To access the style sheets of a layer in Microsoft, you must specify the `all` object and the key word `style`. You can change the `TOP` characteristic of the `box` layer in one of two ways:

  ```
  document.all["box"].style.top = 100;
  ```

  or

  ```
  document.all.box.style.top = 100;
  ```

- *Netscape*
  Netscape supports direct access to the layer and its characteristics:

  ```
  document.box.top = 100;
  ```

  Netscape has also introduced a new object: layer. You would usually use the object in the context of the new `<LAYER>` tag. You can also use this object to address text blocks that have an assigned ID:

  ```
  document.layers["box"].top = 100;
  ```

  Note: as noted above, the use of the term 'layer' in the following refers to a text block in general. Do not confuse it with the 'layer object' from Netscape.

You can still achieve independence from browsers for statements in JavaScript functions. Simply hide the differences in different variables or functions (see the section on browser-independence).

Moving layers

If JavaScript assigns a new value to the characteristics LEFT or TOP, the condition in the corresponding layer in the browser changes. If the assignment repeats in small steps until the layer has reached another condition, the layer appears to move. A recursion handles the repeated assignment and the final condition terminates repetition. The following example moves the box layer from left to right. The style sheet specifies the left starting point as 0. Each recursion moves the layer 10 pixels to the right. The recursion ends when the layer is 100 pixels from the left edge. (To simplify the presentation, the example below uses the notation from Netscape. The section on browser-independence provides examples independent of specific browsers.)

```
function moveLayer(){
   if(document.box.left < 100){
      document.box.left += 10;
      moveLayer();
   }
}
```

Listing 8.5   Moving a Layer

If you execute the recursion in this manner, the following problem appears: the browser cannot accept any new entries during the recursion. Accordingly, you should call each recursion after some time has elapsed. To do so, you can use the setTimeout() function. Call the function with the following parameters: first enter the calling function (with parameters), then specify the time interval in milliseconds before the next call. In the above example, the fourth line would change to the following:

```
setTimeout("moveLayer()", 100);
```

Expansion of the event model

Dynamic HTML also expanded the event model. The browser can register the events *MouseDown*, *MouseUp* and *MouseMove* and trigger the corresponding actions as JavaScript functions. You can use this feature for the following actions:

- *Drag&Drop*
  Selects HTML objects with the *MouseDown* event and moves them on the HTML page with *MouseMove*.

- *Individual scroll mechanism*
  If the contents of a given layer do not fit into the predefined limits, an individual scroll mechanism can move the non-visible contents. The *MouseDown* event moves the visible part of a layer.

Microsoft and Netscape implement the event model differently. Please see the literature if interested in these differences. Treating them here would take us too far from our actual interests.

Browser-independence

Each browser handles access to HTML objects differently. Accordingly, when a page loads, it should know what browser is involved. In JavaScript, you can determine the name of the browser from the `navigator` object with the `appName` characteristic. Depending on the browser, two global variants, `layerRef` and `styleSwitch`, receive different values required for later access to the objects.

```
var layerRef = "null"
var styleSwitch = "null"
function init(){
   if (navigator.appName == "Netscape") {
      layerRef="document.layers";
      styleSwitch="";
   else{
      layerRef="document.all";
      styleSwitch=".style";
   }
}
```

Listing 8.6   Browser-Independence

You can access the characteristics of an object with the set variables by using the EVAL() function. This function composes a statement from the transferred parameters and then executes it. For example, the function assigns the value 100 to the LEFT characteristic of the BOX object–independently of the browser:

```
eval(layerRef+'["box"]'+styleSwitch+'.left = 100;');
```

The Microsoft browser executes the following statement:

```
document.all["box"].style.left = 100;
```

The Netscape browser executes the following statement:

```
document.layers["box"].left = 100;
```

Another variant transfers the name of a layer to a function. The variant then composes the object name for access to methods and characteristic and allocates it to a global variable. All subsequent access to the object takes place over the global variable:

```
var layerRef = "null"; //global variable
function getLayerStyle(layerName){
  if (navigator.appName == "Netscape")
    eval("layerRef = document."+layerName);
  else
    eval("layerRef = document.all."+layerName+".style");
}
```

Listing 8.7   Additional options for browser-independence

Accordingly, `layerRef.left` provides access to the LEFT characteristic. We leave the version used to the reader. The second version increases readability, but the first does not call a function repeatedly.

8.1.4   Example

An example will clarify the comments made in the previous section. The following program displays, hides, shifts moves layers. Explanations of the individual statements are given after the program code:

```
1    <HTML>
2    <HEAD>
3    <STYLE type="text/css">
4    H1             {FONT-SIZE: 30px; }
5    .menuitem {POSITION: absolute; LEFT: 20;}
6    .submenu     {POSITION: absolute; LEFT: 100; VISIBILITY: hidden;}
7    #info         {POSITION: absolute; LEFT: 200; TOP: 10; VISIBILITY:
                    hidden;}
8    </STYLE>
9
10   <SCRIPT LANGUAGE="JavaScript">
11   var topPosition, curPosition = 10, lowerPoint=200, upperPoint=10;
12   var items=3, space=25, menuHeight=10, layerHeight=40;
13   var visibleSwitch, layer = "null";
14
15   function getLayerStyle(layerName){
16     if( navigator.appName == 'Netscape'){
17       eval("layer = document."+layerName+";");
18       visibleSwitch = "show";}
19     else{
20       eval("layer = document.all."+layerName+".style");
21       visibleSwitch = "visible"}
22   }
23
24   function setMenu(){
25     topPosition = 50;
26     for (i=1; i<=items; i++){
```

```
27        getLayerStyle("menu "+i);
28        layer.top = topPosition;
29        topPosition += menuHeight + space;
30        getLayerStyle("sub "+i);
31        if( layer.visibility == visibleSwitch ){
32          layer.top = topPosition;
33          topPosition += layerHeight + space;
34        }
35      }
36    }
37
38  function showSubItems(itemNo){
39    getLayerStyle("sub "+itemNo);
40    if( layer.visibility == visibleSwitch)
41        layer.visibility = 'hidden';
42    else
43        layer.visibility = visibleSwitch;
44    setMenu();
45  }
46
47   function show(layerName){
48     getLayerStyle(layerName);
49     layer.visibility = visibleSwitch;
50   }
51
52 function hide(layerName){
53     getLayerStyle(layerName);
54     layer.visibility = "hidden";
55   }
56
57   function setPosition(layerName, position){
58     getLayerStyle(layerName);
59     layer.top = position;
60   }
61
62   function moveDown(layerName){
63     getLayerStyle(layerName);
64     if (curPosition < lowerPoint){
65       curPosition += 10;
66       layer.top = curPosition;
67       setTimeout('moveDown("'+layerName+'")', 10);
68     }
69   }
70
71   function moveUp(layerName){
72     getLayerStyle(layerName);
```

```
73      if (curPosition > upperPoint){
74        curPosition -= 10;
75        layer.top = curPosition;
76        setTimeout('moveUp("'+layerName+'")', 10);
77      }
78    }
79  </SCRIPT>
80  </HEAD>
81  <BODY onLoad="setMenu()">
82  <H1>Plese select !</H1>
83  <DIV ID="menu 1" CLASS="menuitem ">
84    <a href="JavaScript: showSubItems(1);">Show </a>
85  </DIV>
86
87  <DIV ID="sub 1" CLASS="sub menu ">
88    <a href="JavaScript: show('info');">Show picture </a><br>
89    <a href="JavaScript: hide('info');">Hide picture </a><br>
90  </DIV>
91
92  <DIV ID="menu 2" CLASS="menuitem ">
93    <a href="JavaScript: showSubItems(2);">Place </a>
94  </DIV>
95
96  <DIV ID="sub 2" CLASS="sub menu ">
97    <a href="JavaScript: setPosition('info', 200);">Place at
bottom </a><br>
98    <a href="JavaScript: setPosition('info', 10);">Place at top
</a><br>
99  </DIV>
100
101 <DIV ID="menu 3" CLASS="menuitem ">
102   <a href="JavaScript: showSubItems(3);">Move </a>
103 </DIV>
104
105 <DIV ID="sub 3" CLASS="sub menu ">
106   <a href="JavaScript: moveDown('info');">Move down </a><br>
107   <a href="JavaScript: moveUp('info');">Move up </a><br>
108 </DIV>
109
110 <DIV ID="info">
111   <center> <img src="grin.gif"><br>
112           Move <br>the picture ! </center>
113 </DIV>
114 </BODY>
115 </HTML>
```

Listing 8.8   Sample application

This example places no values on efficient programming. It merely presents the reader with an overview of the possibilities offered by DHTML. If these HTML pages contain too much programming code for you, you can store the style sheets and the JavaScript functions in external files and link them to the header.

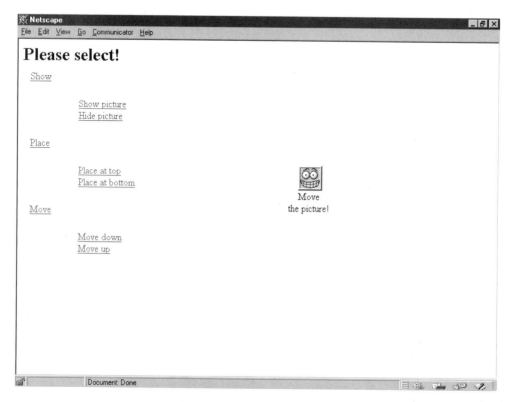

Figure 8.2   Example of DHTML

After the above example has loaded, the browser displays three menu items. Selection of a menu item displays a submenu and shifts the subordinate layers below. You can show/hide an additional layer with the subitems of the first menu, shift it with the second submenu and move it with the third.

The structure of this HTML page has three sections. The header contains the definitions of the style sheets and the JavaScript functions. The main section defines the layers.

- *Style sheets*
  You do not need to define style sheets for each individual layer of the menu. Definition of a class is far more elegant. You can assign style sheets to the layers with the class. You can define a class for items in the main menu and submenu. Specify an individual style sheet for displaying the additional layer that will move. The font size of header H1 remains unchanged.

- *JavaScript functions*
  The script area contains definitions for the individual actions of required functions, such as display, hide, shift and move (see below for descriptions). It also specifies the `getLayerStyle()` function that enables browser-independence. This function sets the global variable `layer` that handles access to the characteristics of an HTML object. (The following comments do not repeat an explanation of this global variable.)

- *Layer*
  Layers are defined in the main part of the code with the HTML tag `<DIV>`. Each menu and submenu is implemented as a unique layer. You allocate style sheets to menus with the `CLASS` attribute and to the additional layer with an ID. Each layer receives an ID for later modification.

The event handler *onLoad* initiates positioning of menu items immediately after the page has been loaded. The hyperlinks in the menu execute various actions. Event handlers are not used here. For example, you could also start an action with the *onClick* event in a hyperlink:

```
<a href="" onClick="show();">Show </a>
```

The following explains the individual functions:

Showing and hiding layers

You can show and hide layers with the functions `show()` (line 47) and `hide()` (line 52). The layer name is transferred to both functions. The transfers sets the `visibility` characteristic of the `layer` variable to `visible` or `hidden`.

Shifting layers

You can shift the position of a layer in the browser with the function `setPosition()` (line 57). In addition to the layer you wish to shift, you transfer the vertical position as a parameter. The position if assigned to the `TOP` characteristic after setting the global variable layer.

Moving layers

You can use the `moveDown()` (line 62) and `moveUp()` (line 71) functions to move the visible layer. The two functions differ only in the termination criterion and in how the position is determined. The following comments therefore treat only the `moveDown()` function. Essentially, the function changes only the vertical position of the layer. Its special features, however, concern the recursive call with the `setTimeout()` (line 67) function. A new position must be determined for each call for a move. The global variable `curPosition` stores the current position of the layer and increases it by 10 pixels for each call. The value of the variable is then assigned to the `TOP` characteristic of the layer in line 66. Recursion continues until the layer reaches a specified value (position) and the condition in line 64 is no longer true . This value is assigned to the `lowerPoint` as defined in line 11 (`upperPoint` for `moveUp()`).

The dynamic menu

You can use the hyperlinks of the main menu entries to expand or contract the menu tree. A click on a menu item calls the `showSubItem()` function (line 38) that checks if the corresponding submenu is displayed or hidden. If it is still hidden, the function displays it (and vice versa). The `setMenu()` function (line 24) implements the following positioning of the individual menu items. The idea for the expansion/contraction lies in the new position of each layer, if it is visible. The new position comes from the for `loop` in line 26, which assigns a new `TOP` position to each menu layer. The first menu entry (Show) always has the same position (here 10). The position of the second menu entry, *Move*, depends on the visibility of the first submenu. If it is visible, the menu item *Move* moves down at the value of the `layerHeight` variable plus a `space`. The `topPosition` variable always contains the current `TOP` position assigned to the layers.

  Note: The `VISIBILITY` characteristic determines if a layer is visible or not. Netscape uses `visible`, Microsoft uses `show`. Lines 18 and 21 therefore show a variable with the appropriate value.

8.1.5   Literature

The topic of generating dynamic Web pages is still relatively new. You can generally find the most extensive information in online documentation on the Web. We particularly recommend the Microsoft and Netscape sites for the latest developments and changes. These two sites, however, do not emphasize Web design that considers browser-independence. Since most Web designers do not wish to limit themselves to a particular browser, the Web contains several links to sites that treat the creation of browser-independent pages. The following links contain numerous examples and extensive information on these techniques:

- *JavaScript*
  Microsoft: Introduction, Examples, and so on

  `http://msdn.microsoft.com/scripting/`

  Netscape: JavaScript Guide, Examples and so on

  `http://developer.netscape.com/library/documentation/communicator/`
  `jsguide4/index.htm`

  JavaScript Source: Several examples

  `http://JavaScriptsource.com/`

  JavaScript Tip of the Day:

  `http://www.webreference.com/JavaScript/`

- *Style sheets*
  W3C Recommendation: Cascading style sheets, Level 1

  ```
  http://www.w3.org/pub/WWW/TR/REC-CSS1
  ```

  W3C Working Draft: Positioning HTML elements with cascading style sheets

  ```
  http://www.w3.org/pub/WWW/TR/WD-positioning
  ```

  WebReview style sheet reference:

  ```
  http://style.webreview.com/
  ```

  Web design group tutorial:

  ```
  http://www.htmlhelp.com/reference/css/
  ```

  WebReference tutorial:

  ```
  http://www.webreference.com/dev/style/
  ```

- *Dynamic HTML*
  Microsoft: Collection of overviews, technical articles and examples

  ```
  http://www.microsoft.com/workshop/author/dhtml/
  ```

  Netscape: Tutorial for DHTML in the communicator

  ```
  http://developer.netscape.com/library/documentation/communicator/
  dynhtml/index.htm
  ```

  Inside DHTML: Tutorials, examples and so on

  ```
  http://www.insideDHTML.com
  ```

  Macromedia: Page for development of browser-independent Web pages

  ```
  http://www.dhtmlzone.com
  ```

  Project Cool: Tutorials, examples and so on

  ```
  http://www.projectcool.com/developer
  ```

  WebReference: Tutorials for browser-independent Web pages

  ```
  http://www.webreference.com/dhtml/
  ```

Most of these Web sites contain references to additional sites on this topic. Currency is the primary advantage of online documentation. Both Netscape and Microsoft record new techniques or changes in these sites immediately. Given the novelty of style sheets and Dynamic HTML, very few books cover these topics in exhaustive detail. The growing acceptance of these techniques indicates that the future will bring more literature. Note, however, the following books that have already appeared:

- Nick Heinle: *Designing with JavaScript*

- Scott Isaacs: *Inside Dynamic HTML*

- Danny Goodman: *Dynamic HTML – The Definitive Reference*

Various newspapers frequently publish articles on these topics. A series of books on JavaScript already exists. We do not provide a list here.

8.2   Use in Internet applications

Business applications can also benefit from the user-driven presentation of information that a browser displays in an HTML page. In addition to the purely visual design possibilities that permit better control by users, this technique offers an additional advantage. Performance is significantly improved, since the Web browser temporarily holds all the information as soon as it loads the HTML page. No additional communication with the server is required.

8.2.1   Usage possibilities

In addition to numerous other considerations, we present the following recommendations for the use of layer technology in Internet applications of the R/3 System.

Selected display of sections

The description of the *Employment Opportunities* IAC (see Section 5.6.2) discussed the completion of application forms. Each movement between the various sections of the form required communication with the R/3 System. Depending on the network load, this repetitive communication can become both annoying and tiring. It would be far more sensible to implement each section with a layer. Only the currently active section, however, is visible to the user. Communication is required only when the user sends the entire application to the R/3 System.

The *Event Calendar* (see Section 5.6.4) IAC can also benefit from the use of layers. After a user selects an event, the IAC displays information on the price, contents or facilitator in different sections. Here, too, the information can be loaded only once and become visible only as the user requires it.

Displaying detailed information

Consider another example: the display of detailed information from elements in a list. For example, the *Employee Directory* IAC (see Section 5.6.1) can display information such as telephone number, fax number, office or building along with a list of persons. The detailed data would become visible only when the user selects a particular person. Here, however, developers must consider the size of the data involved. A list of 1,000 elements, each of which has 100 elements of additional information, would produce a huge HTML page and require a long time to load. Reasonable limits to the quantity of detail by the R/3 System can limit the length of the list. Users could then retrieve the remaining information (or a subsequent subset) with a new request of the R/3 System. Alternatively, the application could ask the user to reduce the number of results by entering a particular value as a matchcode.

Expanding and contracting

The *Web Reporting Browser, Event Calendar or Integrated Inbox* IACs can all expand and contract structures. Each click in these applications requests the corresponding substructures from the R/3 System. Yet, it would make more sense to transmit all the information to the browser at one time. The browser would then display selected portions of the data as required by the user. A click on a menu item would then display the substructure immediately, without additional communication.

Showing options or search masks

Search masks, such as those in the *Employee Directory* IAC, are required only for input. For the remaining run of the application, the masks simply occupy valuable space. You can implements these kinds of input fields with layers that appear when the user wishes to input new values. You can also make certain settings relevant for the next selection in the R/3 System with 'option layers.'

Placing help texts

Until now, users could access help texts only as complete elements in a new window of the browser. However, you can now use different layers with the desired information to present individual sections of a larger help document in an HTML page whenever the user requires help on a particular portion of the application. You place the appropriate hyperlinks on the page or use the *onClick* event handler (for images, for example). The hyperlinks refer to the corresponding help text.

Loading images

Loading images in IACs can take a considerable time, depending on the network load. The user often becomes impatient and triggers pushbuttons before the page loads completely. These actions can often lead to problems, because the user might transmit an incomplete request. You can avoid the problem, however, if the application displays the layers with input options only after the complete page loads. Placing the event handler `onLoad` in the `<BODY>` tag triggers the event that executes the corresponding functions only when the page has loaded completely. The user can now perform actions only when the browser has the complete page. In cases involving a large image, you can inform the user of the loading process by placing a text such as 'Loading image. Please wait.' in the same position as the image. When the image is complete in the browser, the application suppresses the text (with *onLoad*).

Effective design

Largely, the Internet lives on its graphical interface and multimedia possibilities. Internet applications generally offer effective design, so that users find them interesting. Display of options user-controlling settings can become more effective with layers that move or continually enlarge. If the user wishes to enter new options (filling in two fields that are currently hidden, for example), the layers can move from right to left into the middle of the display. Warnings or errors can appear as a recursively-blinking layer.

General comments

Developers of Web pages have received a powerful tool. Until now, however, the different operation of the various Web browsers can presented a problem. A number of DHTML examples exist that developers can make their own or provide the inspiration for improvements to existing applications. Even games have made use of this technology. For example, consider *Asteroid* in DHTML or *HTMLtris*, a DHTML version of Tetris.

The browser is changing from a purely display-oriented client to an application that can process some tasks in the client. Until now, complicated server-based interfaces had to implement such processing. In this period of overloaded networks, R/3 Internet applications can contribute to the browser's conversion into a client. Nonetheless, browser-based processing should not influence the application logic of the R/3 transaction itself. This technology should not overtake the inside-out design of the ITS, however, or you would lose all the advantages of transaction-oriented flow in the application.

The following introduces an example that shows the interplay of HTML[Business] and DHTML.

8.2.2   Sample application

To avoid an unnecessarily complex and complicated example, the following introduces a very simple application. It represents an index card for a customer. Table KNA1 holds all the required information in the R/3 System.

Scenario

The application queries the user for a customer number and then displays all the desired information on the customer in the browser. For a good overview, the application should display only those portions selected by a hyperlink. The same HTML page handles both query and display. The application does not require a return to a previous page to switch to another index card. The use of frames is superfluous.

This example does not provide a comfortable entry of the customer name. It would be possible here to enter a complete or partial name. If several customers match the entered criteria, the hit list could appear in a layer or in a new window of the browser. The user would then select from the hit list.

Chapter 7 treated the development of R/3 Internet applications in detail. Accordingly, we will treat only the most important sections here. The reader's creativity can name the transaction, the project in the Web-Studio, the service description and so on.

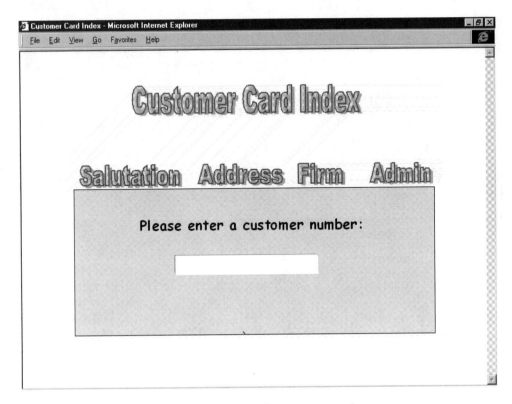

Figure 8.3   Entry of a customer number

Developing the R/3 transaction

This application requires a screen containing a field for input of the customer name and output fields for the requested customer information. The application uses the customer number to transfer a portion of the customer information from table KNA1 to the `customer` structure. The structure contains certain fields from KNA1, divided into the following sections:

Table 8.1   Sections of the Customer Index Card

Section	Fields
Salutation	`kunnr, anred, name1`
Address	`stras, ort01, telef1, telfx`
Company	`gform, umsat, uwaer, jmzah`
Administrative data	`aufsd, erdat, ernam`

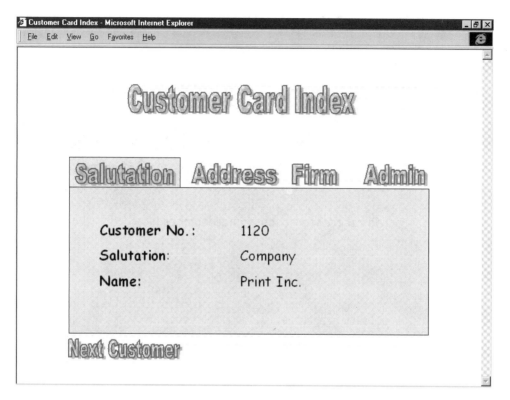

Figure 8.4   Displaying the customer index cards

The above structure will be filled after entering a correct customer number with an appropriate `select` statement. The R/3 System determines values for the customer number and displays them in the same screen as the query. The reader can expand the structure depending on the information desired. If the number does not exist and the application therefore does not find a customer, the system places an additional field on the screen: `custdata`. This field, type `char` and length 1, can record the following values: 0 – initial, no selection yet; 1 – customer found; 2 – no customer found. The field is set according to the corresponding `select` statement. HTML[Business] can use this field to place a text, such as a warning on the HTML page.

Developing the HTML page

To avoid typographical error in the structure fields, generate the appropriate template with the Web-Studio (remove the superfluous `input` tags). You must enter the following additions:

Style sheets

The sections of the customer index cards given above all have the same layout. You should therefore assign the same style sheet to every layer with the `customerinfo` class. The application also requires a layer for input of the customer number (`custinput`) and positioning the hyperlinks (`actions`):

```
.customerinfo {POSITION: absolute; TOP: 50; LEFT: 100; VISIBILITY: hidden;}
#custinput {POSITION: absolute; TOP: 50; LEFT: 100; VISIBILITY: hidden;}
#actions {POSITION: absolute; TOP: 50; LEFT: 100;}
```

Listing 8.9   Style sheets

JavaScript

The application requires the `show()` and `hide()` functions from the example in Section 8.1.4 to display and suppress sections. To show a new section, the application must hide a previously visible section. To do so, define a global variable, `curLayer` that contains the layer currently visible. The `showLayer()` function shows the selected layer and hides the current layer :

```
function showLayer(layerName){
    hide(curLayer);
    show(layerName);
    curLayer = layerName;
}
```

Listing 8.10   The showLayer() function

You must decide which layer to display while loading the HTML page. If the application started from scratch, you must also display the layer that permits input of the customer number. If customer data is already present, the application displays the layer for the first section of the customer index card (salutation). The decision is made in the init function, called with the *onLoad* event handler in the BODY tag (`<BODY onLoad="init()">`). The layer that now appears depends upon the CUSTDATA screen field:

```
function init(){
  'if( CUSTDATA == "2")'
    getLayerStyle("custinput"); <!"customer not found ">
  'else'
    getLayerStyle("anrede"); <!"customer found ">
  'end'
  layer.visibility = "visible"; <! "assignment of visibility ">
}
```

Listing 8.11   The init() function

If the user wishes to view the index card of another customer, the application must display the custinput layer and hide the current layer to provide a clear display:

```
function changeCustomer(){
  hide(curLayer); show("custinput");
}
```

Listing 8.12   The changeCustomer() function

Layer

The application requires a layer for every section of the index card. The following defines the input layer (custinput) and specifies the layer to executing actions (actions):

```
<DIV ID="salutation " CLASS=customerinfo>
    Customer No.: 'CUSTOMER-KUNNR'<br>
    Name: 'CUSTOMER-ANRED' 'CUSTOMER-NAME1'
</DIV>
<DIV ID="adress " CLASS=customerinfo >
    Street : 'CUSTOMER-STRAS'<br>
    City : 'CUSTOMER-ORT01'<br>
    Telephone : 'CUSTOMER-TELEF1', Fax: 'CUSTOMER-TELEFX'
</DIV>
<DIV ID="firm " CLASS=customerinfo >
    Type of company : 'CUSTOMER-GFORM'<br>
    Sales : 'CUSTOMER-UWAER' 'CUSTOMER-UMSAT'<br>
    Number of employees : 'CUSTOMER-JMZAH'
</DIV>
<DIV ID="actions">
  <a href=" JavaScript: newCustomer(); ">Next customer </a> |
  <a href="JavaScript: showLayer(,salutation ');">Salutation </a> |
  <a href="JavaScript: showLayer(,adress ');">Address </a> |
  <a href="JavaScript: showLayer(,firm ');">Firm </a> |
  <a href="JavaScript: showLayer(,administration ');"> adminis-
tration</a>
</DIV>
<DIV ID="custinput">
  Please enter a customer number :
  <FORM ACTION="'wgateURL()'" METHOD="post">
    Customer No.: <INPUT TYPE="text" NAME="CUSTOMER-KUNNR"
VALUE=" 'CUSTOMER-KUNNR'">
    <INPUT TYPE="submit" NAME="Okcode(INFO)" VALUE="OK ">
  </FORM>
</DIV>
```

Listing 8.13   Definition of the Layers

Utilizing dynamic creation of the HTML page

During creation of fixed HTML pages (those loaded only by the Web server), access to an HTML object must be implemented independently of the browser. However, the ITS merges information from the R/3 System into the corresponding template dynamically. You can use this procedure to implement the program code for access to an HTML object and make it dependent upon the browser in use. The global variable `userAgent`, set by the ITS, identifies the browser that transmitted the current request. The advantage here is that the ITS and the browser transmit less data between themselves. It also offers greater readability of the source text in the browser, which, in turn, simplifies searching for errors. The disadvantage is a less clear overview of the program code in the template. An example of such access:

```
'if ( userAgent == "Netscape" )'
  document.box.top = 100;
'else'
  document.all.box.style.top = 100
'end'
```

Listing 8.14   Utilizing Dynamic Creation with HTML[Business]

The reader's imagination can find further use of this possibility.

Enhancements

Although the above example depicts a very simple application, you can add the following enhancements.

Graphic design

You can substitute images for the normal text hyperlinks to various actions. You would then use a hyperlink over the image or the *onClick* event handler in the <IMG> tag. Depending upon the section currently visible, you can supply the `src` attribute of the <IMG> tag with a new image, thus triggering a dynamic exchange of images.

You can effectively display the input layer for another customer by moving the layer into the middle from top to bottom.

Displaying all tasks for a customer

You can place a display of the list of all orders for a customer in one layer as follows:

```
<DIV ID="order">
  'repeat with i from 1 to ORDER-NUMBER.dim'
    'ORDER-NUMBER[i]': 'ORDER-TYPE[i]'<br>
  'end'
</DIV>
```

Listing 8.15   Linking internal tables

Bottom line

In many cases, it is quite practicable to link HTML pages that are generated dynamically at runtime, that contain dynamic elements, and that contain current information from the productive business system of an enterprise. Users enjoy simpler operation that can lead to more informative design possibilities. Developers have at their disposal a powerful tool to develop business transactions or display information on the Internet. We can only hope that new standardization by independent groups will significantly simplify creation of dynamic Web pages. It remains true that numerous HTML pages already use DHTML techniques that will continue to grow in the future.

Glossary and list of abbreviations

ADSL

Asymmetric Digital Subscriber Line Systems. A procedure to transfer data over today's copper cable. Uses a bandwidth of 6144 MBPS, with a return channel of 640 KBPS. The bandwidth of the send and receive channels are asymmetrical. The bandwidth can split into several channels: approximately three channels at 2048 MBPS or four channels at 1536 MBPS.

Anonymous FTP Server

See FTP.

AOL

America Online.

API

Application programming interface. A documented interface, available over libraries, for functions or services.

Archie

A research tool that you can use to search for files on public (anonymous) FTP servers. You usually search with a know segment of the file name. Archie supplies a list of possible matches. A double click on a list entry in a graphical Archie client automatically downloads the file (with FTP) onto your computer.

ArchiveLink

Standard interface between the R/3 System and archive system. Suppliers of archives must be certified for this interface.

ASCII

American Standard Code for Information Interchange. The usual process of coding (pure) texts under UNIX.

ATM

Asynchronous transfer mode. A communications procedure that assigns network bandwidth dynamically.

AUP

Abbreviation for acceptable use policy. Describes the guidelines or policies of a company for its network. It determines who can use the network for what purpose.

Backbone

A high-speed component that connects a network or a subnetwork to the Internet (or to another network).

BAPI

Business Application Programming Interface. A special function module in the R/3 System that enables the user to access selected business-oriented functions of the R/3 System.

Baud

Specifies transfer speed in steps per second. The rate usually specifies the speed in Kbaud (Kilo-baud).

BBS

Abbreviation for Bulletin Board System, an electronic bulletin board that users call up with a modem to request information. These systems/services often offer simple mail functions as well. The systems also normally permit users to post messages on the bulletin board.

BPS

Bits per second. A unit used to indicate the maximum transfer speed of transmission routes or transmission methods.

Browser

Understood on the Internet as the WWW client.

Business Document

All types of documents relevant to the business activities of an enterprise. In addition to invoices, business documents also include blueprints, for example.

Business Workflow

The cross-department and cross-workstation distribution and control of work steps.

CCI

Common Client Interface. An interface (API) introduced with Mosaic 2.0 to call and control a Web browser from external applications. The controlling application uses the CCI interface to determine (and log) the actions performed by the user in the Web browser.

CERT

Computer Emergency Response Team. An organization originally established by the United State Department of Defense (DOD) at Carnegie Mellon University. CERT studies security problems on the Internet, warns users of known gaps and dangers and provides information on solutions.

CGI

Common Gateway Interface. An API interface between a WWW server and applications that communicate with each other to serve interactive WWW pages. Examples of such pages include those with forms or with contents that change dynamically.

Chat

An electronic discussion forum on the Internet. Chat allows several persons to 'converse' on the Internet. Communication takes place with texts that users enter on their keyboards and that then appear on the screens of all participants.

CIM

CompuServe Information Manager. The user interface of the CompuServe online service.

CIX

Commercial Internet Exchange. An association of Internet providers for the support and expansion of the Internet. CIX processes agreements between Internet providers on the commercial use of the Internet and on the conditions that govern how providers exchange information and messages.

Client

The program that runs locally on your computer. It gathers information from a server program and displays it on your computer.

CPS

Customer and Partner System. IAC demo system of SAP. You can test the IACs delivered by SAP on this system.

CRS

Computer Reservation System.

CSS

Cascading Style Sheets. Style Sheets provided by the W3C for HTML documents to design new type of HTML pages. Goal: separation of contents and design.

Cyberspace

A term to describe the Internet culture.

DARPA

Defense Advanced Research Project Agency. A division of the United States Department of Defense that created a early version of the Internet, the ARPANET.

DES

Data Encryption Standard. A standardized encryption procedure developed in the USA.

DHTML

Dynamic HTML. Technique to design dynamic HTML pages in the browser.

Dial-in

An Internet connection over a modem. If necessary, the connection uses a telephone line to establish contact with the Internet. The procedure is also called dial-up.

Dial-up

Corresponds to dial-in.

Digest

A paper summary of several contributions to a news group or a mailing list. Message digest (MD) refers to the digital checksum of an electronic document or of a file. You can later use the MD to determine if the file has changed because of technical difficulties or by intent.

Digital cash

Or d-cash. Describes money that users can transfer electronically on the Internet. Also known as electronic cash or e-cash.

Digital ID

See Digital signature.

Digital signature

A digital suffix to digital information that identifies the sender or author of the information. This portion of a message is usually stored in a special, encrypted format so that it cannot be falsified. You can use the originator's public key to check the authenticity and accuracy of the message.

DMS

A proprietary Document Management System in the R/3 System. It uses classes and attributes to classify and store documents in the R/3 System.

DNS

Domain Name Service. The service converts a computer name (in text) into an IP address and vice versa, converting an IP address into a computer name.

DOM

Document Object Model. Standard set by the W3C for access with a script language to objects of an HTML page.

Domain

Portion of the naming hierarchy of the Internet.

Domain name server

This server converts domain names into IP addresses.

Download

Load data or files from a server onto a local system. The opposite process is an upload.

DSA

Abbreviation for Digital Signature Algorithm (see DSS).

DSS

Digital Signature Standard. A standard defined by the US government for digital signatures or digital identification. A digital signature is stored in encrypted form and can be checked with the public key of the sender/author. DSS Digital Signature Algorithm (DSA) is used for encryption. For various reasons, DSS has found little acceptance in industry.

DTS

Digital Time Stamp Service. A network service that supplies a digital confirmation of a specific time for a document. Certification of digital documents requires such a service.

EBONE

European Backbone Consortium. A group of several European research networks joined to build a backbone infrastructure for the exchange of data. The EBONE network has three hierarchy levels. The highest level is a very fast backbone network that connects individual EBONE Code Sites (ECS) to each other and to the backbone network in the USA. Larger countries usually have an ECS: the ECRC in Munich for Germany and additional ECS in Geneva, Vienna, Paris and Stockholm. An ECS has fast connections to the second level, Internet service providers. The providers then create the network for their customers as POPs at the third level.

EC

Electronic Commerce. Conducting business electronically.

E-cash

A process to transfer money electronically on the Internet. Also known a digital cash or d-cash.

EDI

Electronic Data Interchange. Coordinates the exchange of business data between two enterprises. EDI uses specific standards: EDIFACT, ODETTE and so on.

EFF

Electronic Frontier Foundation. An American association concerned with the social and legal aspects of the increasing use of computer communications. The foundation seeks to counter the increased control of the state on network operation. It also works against the attempts of many governments to 'tap' encrypted data or to forbid encryption entirely, as is the case in France.

E-mail

Electronic Mail. An electronic message sent over a network.

EMM

Electronic Marketplace Manager.

EPSF

Abbreviation for Encapsulated PostScript File, a PostScript file subject to certain limitations. The file contains a mostly stand-alone PostScript program, one that does not build upon specific environments and does not change its own environment. EPSF files usually contain graphics that can be inserted into other PostScript files, created with word processing programs. The new PostScript file displays both the surrounding text and the inserted graphics when output to a PostScript printer or an appropriate projector.

FAQ

Abbreviation for Frequently Asked Questions. Frequent inquiries from users and answers from experts on common questions on the Internet. Located on anonymous FTP servers and in newsgroups.

Finger

A program that displays the user names of individual users or several users on another system. In addition to names, the information usually includes the full name, telephone number and (on internal systems) office location.

Firewall

A software wall to protect against unauthorized access to a system. A special computer system implements access to the Internet and contains special protective mechanisms. The mechanisms determine who has access to the system and who monitors access on a regular basis. The software is also called firewall software. It also logs illegal attempts to gain access.

Flame

An insult on the Internet, usually appearing as an answer to a message or an electronically expressed opinion.

FQDN

Fully Qualified Domain Name, the complete, text Internet address of a host computer. Usually differs (greater length) from the host name on the local network.

Freeware

Software made available at no cost. Users may copy and give away the software without charge, as long as the entire packet (including any documentation) and the author's copyright remain intact.

FSTC

Financial Service Technology Consortium, an association of more than 65 banks, technology firms and governmental agencies to develop special technologies in common for the financial industry. The consortium is currently working on a procedure for secure money transfer on the Internet and other online services. The procedure uses a chipcard (and reader) for legitimization. The card identifies the user and contains the user's digital signature.

FTP

Abbreviation for File Transfer Protocol. The protocol permits the transfer of files to remote computers over an Internet connection.

FYI

For Your Information. Technical documents or descriptions on the Internet that comment on a subject informally, rather than from a highly technical viewpoint.

Gateway

A system that serves as a bridge between two different networks.

GIF

Graphic Interchange Format. A file format developed by CompuServe to store images on a grid (black and white or color). This format has become the standard for grid images in HTML.

Gopher

A distributed, hierarchically arranged information system, available on the Internet. It provides access to various data.

GSM

Global System for Mobile telecommunications. A uniform mobile system that meets specific criteria: good speech quality, low equipment and service costs, support for hand-held units and ISDN compatibility. Serves as the standard for all of Europe and supports SMS.

Home page

The initial page seen by users when the select a WWW server or the page used by enterprises, organizations or individuals to represent themselves on a server.

Hotlist

A list of interesting or often visited Web pages that users create in their browsers to make accessing the pages simpler.

HTML

HyperText Markup Language. Describes the syntax of WWW documents in the Internet environment.

HTML+

An enhanced form of HTML. HTML 3.2 has replaced the term. See also: *http://www.w3.org*.

HTML-Business

A collection of metastatements stored in templates and required by the ITS to merge current field values.

HTTP

HyperText Transfer Protocol defines the protocol between a Web server and a Web client. A variant for secure transmissions is SHTTP.

Hyper-G

A hypertext language. A competitive development to HTML, it is also compatible with HTML in many respects. In some ways, however, it goes beyond HTML. It permits bi-directional links and hyperlinks. Hyper-G offers significantly more powerful formatting options than HTML does.

HyperLinks

Cross-references in a hypertext document. If a user clicks on such a reference, the display automatically jumps to the place or the document referenced. HTML documents use this technology.

Hypertext

A special form of documents that contain hyperlinks. If a user clicks on such a link, an action, dependent upon the type of link, is triggered. HTML documents are these type of hypertext document.

IAB

Internet Architecture Board. A portion of the ISOC, it is responsible for the continued development of Internet protocols.

IAC

Internet Application Component. An IAC consists of an R/3 transaction and the external files (templates, language resources, and so on) needed for an Internet connection.

IANA

Internet Assign Numbers Authority. This assigns the standard port numbers for Internet services.

IDES

International Demonstrating and Education System. A sample company in the R/3 System, preconfigured by SAP. You can use the company to test various modules and to perform training.

IETF

Internet Engineering Task Force. This group is responsible for the short-term technical development of the Internet and has numerous subgroups.

Image map

A process you can use in HTML documents to store hyperlinks with a graphic. The image map sets the part of the graphic that reacts to a hyperlink and the link assigned to a graphic area.

Interlaced GIF

A special GIF format that builds raster images in shifts. A browser first displays such an image in coarse definition and then displays it in its final form. This format permits early recognition of the image by the user, who can then terminate the transfer if the information is uninteresting.

IP

Internet Protocol or Internet Provider (see ISP).

IPP

Internet Presence Provider. Another term for the operator of a POP.

IP spoofing

An attempt to break into another computer on the Internet. The sender changes the IP header to include an IP address that belongs to someone else. The sender hopes, illegally, to obtain special access rights.

IPv6

Internet Protocol Version 6. The new version of the Internet protocol approved in April, 1994 by the IETF. IP New Generation (Ipng) is a synonym. The previous version is known as Ipv4. An important characteristic is the ability to use 128-bit IP addresses (Ipv4 uses 32 bits). The new protocol was designed to provide better authentication and the ability to encrypt data transmitted over the Internet. Ipv6 can coexist with Ipv4. General use of Ipv6 (on the Internet, for example) may well occur beyond 2000.

IRC

Internet Relay Chat. Several persons can carry on a dialog (much like a conference) on the Internet.

IRTF

Internet Research Task Force. This portion of the ISOC is responsible for the long-term technical development of the Internet.

ISO

International Standard Organization. The international corollary to the German DIN.

ISO 8859/1

Describes the coding of text characters with an 8-bit code. Also called Latin Alphabet No. 1 or simply Latin-1. The lower 128 positions of the code correspond to ASCII code; the higher 128 positions (not completely filled) contain special characters and most Western European special characters (diacritical marks) such as German umlauts, the German double-S character (ß), French accents, Greek characters and mathematical symbols.

ISOC

Internet Society. The ISOC coordinates the technical development of the Internet. A forum for the development of new Internet applications, it also includes organizations such as the IAB, IETF and IRTF. For more information see: *www.isco.org*.

ISP

Internet Service Provider. A term to describe firms that offer access to the Internet commercially.

ITS

Internet Transaction Server. The gateway between the R/3 System and the World Wide Web.

JPEG

Abbreviation for coding or compressing images according to the recommendations of the Joint Photographic Experts Group. The procedure was developed to store halftone and color images and permits reductions of data volume at a factor of two to (approximately) 50. Except for a special version (JPEG+), the process does not protect completely against loss. For example, an image compressed with JPEG cannot be decompressed into its original quality. During compression, users can select between maintaining the best possible image quality or allowing the greatest possible compression factor. Users who opt for lowered quality can use a rather high compression factor, 50–100. An even more complex process for image sequences (motion pictures), MPEG (see MPEG) works similarly.

Knowboat

The Knowboat Information Service supports searching for data (such as Internet addresses) on persons.

Listserv

A mailing list server. A server that distributes e-mail from a mailing list to its members.

Login

'Signing in' or 'on' to a computer by specifying a login (user) name. Login also refers to the ID or a known way of accessing a computer (system).

Mailing list

A discussion forum that distributes members comments by e-mail.

MAN

Metropolitan Area Network, a citywide (usually fast) network.

Mbone

A protocol used on the Internet to implement multicast messages (messages with several recipients). This protocol is required for conferences (video, audio and whiteboard) with several participants. The network routers must have enhanced functions.

MBPS

Megabaud per second. A unit to specify transmission speed.

MD

Message Digest. A sum of the digits or a hash function on a message or on a text. If you have the MD of digital information, you can check the authenticity of the message. Various procedures have established themselves to provide an MD for secure messages and texts. These procedures include MD2 (RFC 1319), MD3 (RFC 1320) and MD5 (RFC 1321). All use 128-bit sum of the digits.

Micropayment

Payment procedure for very small amounts, generally between 0.01 cents and 5 dollars. Unlike larger payments, these electronic transactions require very low handling fees per payment.

MIME

Multipurpose Internet Mail Extensions. These extensions enable transmission of formatted, multimedia mail messages and attaching files to the e-mail. A MIME message can consist of various individual components, each of which may have a different format. For texts, MIME specifies the coding used. S/MIME (Secure MIME), a variant of MIME, was developed by a group of mail suppliers (including Microsoft, RSA and Lotus) to transmit encrypted messages. S/MIME offers a high level of confidentiality for e-mail messages.

MPEG

Means of coding or compressing image sequences (motion pictures) according to the recommendations of the Motion Photographic Experts Group. The process enables a reduction of the data volume by a factor of 20–100.

MSN

Microsoft Network.

Multicasting

The ability to send a message simultaneously to several addresses (recipients).

Netfind

A system (client and server on the network) to search for e-mail addresses of persons on the network.

Netiquette

A combination of net(work) and etiquette. Defines acceptable behavior on the Internet.

Netnews

News areas or discussion area/forums on the Internet (or Usenet) open for public access.

Newbie

A new member of a newsgroup.

Newsgroup

A group dedicated to a topic on Usenet.

NIC

Network Information Center. The organization assigns IP addresses worldwide, but delegates assignment for each country to a central instance. In Germany, the instance is DE-NIC (Deutsche [German] Network Information Center) at the University of Karlsruhe. The university also runs the primary nameserver that contains all the systems connected to the German Internet. For further information, see *www.nic.de*.

NIST

National Institute of Standards, the American version of the international ISO or the German DIN.

NNTP

Network News Transfer Protocol, used on the Internet to distribute information from newsgroups.

NOC

Network Operation Center, the headquarters of a network that usually provides support to users.

NSA

National Security Agency, an American agency concerned with the security of messages between American agencies. Concerns include encryption and decryption. The NSA develops new algorithms for use by governmental agencies and the military. It creates standards in the security area and tests procedures to break (decrypt) the messages of other governmental security agencies and of commercial enterprises.

NSFNET

National Science Foundation Network, a very large American research institute. It represents an essential portion of the American Internet.

Offline

Activities that take place without an active connection to a computer or to the network.

OLR

Off line reader. A program that reads/displays news information without an active connection to the network. An OLR saves online costs. Of course, the reader must first transfer the news to a local system.

PD

See Public domain.

PEM

Privacy Enhanced Mail. An enhancement to Internet mail that encrypts information when it is transmitted and decrypts it when it is received.

PGP

Pretty Good Privacy. A public key encryption and authentication procedure that offers rather good, but not perfect, confidentiality. PGP involves free software available in the public domain. PGP has been ported to numerous different systems.

PICS

Platform for Internet Content Selection. The ability to add information to a HTML document that classifies its contents. You can then search specifically for particular contents or protect certain contents from access.

PIN

Personal information number. Often describes a second form of user identification at login or a password.

Ping

A program to test very primitive connections on the Internet. The program transmits an IP packet to another computer and measures the number of packets returned by the other computer and how long the process took.

POP

Point of Presence: a dial-in point to the network.

Port Number

Computers on a network offer services on their servers over different addresses. The input to each address is known as a port. Services are therefore addressed over the port number.

PPP

Point to Point Protocol. A connection protocol or serial connections and frequently used for a TCP/IP connection over modem stretches.

Proxy host

A dedicated computer that runs the Internet client software. It functions for the Internet as the representative of an entire network behind it, which is no longer visible to the Internet. Proxy hosts seek to guarantee high security for the local network against an attempted break-in from the Internet.

Public domain

Software available free of charge to everyone. Often abbreviated as PD.

RFC

Request for comment. New protocols and services are introduced by RFC documents on the network. The documents ask users to evaluate the suggestions. For example, RFC 822 describes the Internet Mail Message Header and RFC 821 covers the SMTP protocol. For an Internet glossary, see RFC 1392 or *ftp://internic.net/pub/rfc/rfc1392.txt*.

RGB

Red, green and blue. You can create (almost) all other colors (with differing intensities) from these three primary colors. All colors on a monitor are created in this manner. Printing, however, uses the CMYK process.

RIFF

Raster Image File Format. A format frequently used on the PC and Macintosh to store raster images.

RIPE

Research Internet Protocol Europeans. A group of European Internet providers that reaches the agreements needed to operate the Internet in Europe.

Roaming

On the Internet, roaming means the ability to dial in to the Internet from any possible location. Up until now, this ability required users to agree on a special Internet tariff with their providers. The providers, in turn, had to negotiate a corresponding agreement among themselves. Users employ either different call-in points or numbers (and must therefore have the list) or special call-in numbers, such as 800 (toll-free) numbers, that permit users to call in for the cost of a local call. This concept is directed at persons who travel frequently.

Robot

A program, usually in the e-mail environment, that receives messages, evaluates them and automatically generates an answer or initiates some other action.

RSA

An encryption process developed by the mathematicians R. Rivest, A. Shamir and L. Adleman (Public Key Process). Since its development, RSA has become a standard for encryption RSA Data Security, Inc., possesses licensing rights for the RSA algorithm.

RTF

Rich Text File Format. A format developed by Microsoft to exchange formatted text between different applications and systems. Numerous word processing programs can both import and export this format. Unfortunately, it supports only a very limited transfer of graphics.

SAP automation

Technology for remote control of an R/3 application over its application interfaces. Also enables applications over the Internet.

SAPGUI

Client (user interface) for operating the R/3 System.

Secure courier

A data format for financial transactions with fixed fields. Netscape developed the format with MasterCard. It uses a very strong encryption process to secure the contents: a current key length of 768 bits, to expand to 1024 bits in the future. In spite of the secure encryption, the software can be exported from the United States because it is applicable only to financial data.

Secure MIME

See MIME

SGML

Standard Generalized Markup Language. A markup language for documents that describes the contents without fixing their appearance. The WWW language HTML works best with the basic principles of version 3 of SGML. Currently, great interest in SGML exists.

Shareware

Software that users can copy and try out free of charge. Users can usually also copy and distribute it without cost. If users wish to employ the software after the test phase, they should register as users and pay a shareware fee (usually between $10 and $50) to the author.

SHTTP

Secure Hypertext Transport Protocol. An HTTP protocol developed by Terisa Systems, Inc., to transmit data securely (without the possibility of espionage) on the WWW. It defines new elements for HTML to transmit data in a form securely. S-HTTP offers a framework for three cryptographic methods: a digital signature that guarantees the data integrity of the message, data encryption that secures the confidentiality of the data, and authentication that can check the identity of the sender.

Signature

One or more lines with personal information on the sender. Users normally add them to the end of an e-mail message. They can provide the full name, address and telephone number of the sender.

SLIP

Serial Line IP. A connection protocol similar to PPP for serial connections. It is often used as the basis for a TCP/IP connection over modem stretches.

Smiley

'Faces' created from ASCII characters. They express the author's mood. Examples include :-) to indicate happiness and :-((to indicate sadness.

SMS

Short Message Service. Bidirectional service to send short alphanumeric message (up to 160 bytes) with the *store-and-forward* process.

SMTP

Simple Mail Transport Protocol. The normal protocol on the Internet to exchange mail between mail servers. RFC 821 deals with SMTP. The POP3 protocol normally handles communications between the mail server and the mail client.

SSL

Secure Sockets Layer. A process developed by Netscape that prohibits scouting for data on a network. It aims at guaranteeing secure transmission of data over a network and thus provides secure financial transactions for electronic commerce.

Store-And-Forward

Process for transmitting messages with intermediate buffers. If the system cannot establish a connection to the recipient, it places the message in temporary storage. When a connection exists, the system automatically sends it to the intended recipient.

STT

Secure Transaction Technology. An encryption method developed by Microsoft and Visa for secure transmission of payments (including a digital signature). Microsoft also offers APIs and wants to use SST in the future in its own operating systems and applications.

SysOp

System Operator.

T1

Network connection with a speed of 1544 MBPS.

T3

Network connection with a speed of 45 MBPS.

TCP

Transmission Control Protocol. An essential, basic protocol of the Internet that provides the foundation for higher server protocols.

Telnet

An Internet protocol that enables a dialog session on a remote computer. Telnet usually refers to the client.

Thread

For the ITS, a thread is the internal distribution of the load on the AGate. Thread is also the topic of a discussion group, usually a newsgroup.

TIFF

Tag Image File Format, a data format for raster images. The format is many-sided and expandable. It can record various raster sizes, raster depths, color rasters and additional information. The format supports storage of pure black and white images, graphics with gray values (such as photographs), and color graphics in faster format. Recent definitions also permit fax-compressed image.

Topic

The subject of a discussion on the Internet.

Tunneling

On the Internet, tunneling refers to a procedure that encapsulates data on one side in a different format and then expands it on the other side. The procedure permits transparent transmission of data over a transport leg when the data normally cannot run through the transport protocol without problems. Consider this case, for example. You encapsulate encrypted data in a mail format, thereby changing the encrypted data into ASCII format, and then change it back to the original format upon receipt. You can thus use the ASCII-oriented Internet mail protocol to transmit encrypted data, an activity not supported by the protocol. The same is true if you wish to transfer data from an telnet session.

Unicode

Coding for texts or text characters. Similar to ASCII, but uses a 16-bit code for each character. Unicode includes all the characters of European languages as well as the large Chinese and Japanese 'alphabets.'

URL

Uniform Resource Locator. A standardized form to name a resource on the Internet. Hyperlinks in HTML documents are built from URLs.

UUCP

Stands for UNIX to UNIX COPY. An early method of exchanging information, mail and files between UNIX systems.

VA

Value-added.

VAN

Value added network. Usually a closed network for special tasks. The network operator adds value by redirecting the information or special transformation of the basic network services.

VAS

Value-added service.

Veronica

An Internet program for searching in Gopher space.

VRML

Virtual Reality Modeling Language. A language to model 3-D worlds that can be used within Web browsers.

W3

See WWW.

W3C

World Wide Web Consortium. An organization at the Massachusetts Institute of Technology (MIT) in Cambridge, Massachusetts to coordinate the future development of the WWW.

WAIS

Wide Area Information Service. WAIS permits a full text search in distributed text databases.

Web

See WWW.

Web-Studio

Tool to generate HTML templates, service descriptions and language resources in the context of an SAP Internet connection.

Whiteboard

An application that allows several users to access a common, virtual screen and make entries on it. During an electronic conference, participants can communicate over the screen to draw and discuss contexts in common.

Whois

The Whois Internet program permits searching for the e-mail address of an Internet user whose (Internet) name is known.

WWW

World Wide Web. Alternative terms are Web or W3.

WYSIWYG

What you see is what you get. A screen display of a document that shows the appearance of the printed document.

X.25

An OSI standard for data exchange.

X.400

An OSI standard for e-mail or electronic messaging exchange. X.400 competes with the SMTP normally used on the Internet to exchange e-mail between two mail servers. X.400 is significantly more complex (and therefore slower) but also partially more powerful than SMTP. Only the MIME enhancement of SMTP makes the two procedures remotely comparable. X.400 is used far more often in Europe than in the United States.

X.435

An OSI standard to exchange EDI messages over X.400. EDI-VANs increasingly use X.435.

X.500

An OSI standard for directory services. It defines the protocol between individual X.500 servers and clients. The directory service stores information on objects that may be information on persons, companies, applications, terminals or distributed lists. Although part of the OSI concept, X.500 can be used outside of X.400.

X.509

CCITT Standard for digital ID. A digital identification proving that information (such as an e-mail) truly comes from the sender or author specified.

Zine

Online magazine.

ZIP

An archiving and compression format used on PCs by the popular PKZIP program (along with pkunzip and winzip).

Bibliography

Aboba, B. (1993) *The Online User's Encyclopedia: Bulletin Boards and Beyond*. Reading: Addison-Wesley.

Buck-Emden, Rüdiger and Galimow, Jürgen (1996) *SAP R/3 System: A Client/Server Technology*. Trans. Audrey Weinland. Harlow: Addison-Wesley.

Bundesministerium für Wirtschaft (1995) *Die Informationsgesellschaft*. Bonn: Zeitbild-Verlag.

Cameron, Bobby (1996) The prudent approach to R/3. In *Forrester Packaged Applications Report*, Vol. 1, April.

Cameron, Debra (1995) *The Internet: A Global Business Opportunity*. Charleston, South Carolina: Computer Technology Research Corp.

Cameron, Debra (1995) *Implementing the Internet for Business*. Charleston, South Carolina: Computer Technology Research Corp.

Cook, David and Sellers, Deborah (1995) *Launching a Business on the Web*. Indianapolis: Que Corporation.

Emery, Vince (1995) *How to Grow Your Business on the Internet*. Scottsdale, Arizona: Coriolis Group.

Gartner Group (1995) In side at a glance: The World Wide Web – understanding its retailing value. In *Gartner Group This Week*, Vol 11, July 26.

Gartner Group (1997) Fünf Irrtümer über Web-Technologien. In *Gartner Group ITips-Informationen für den IT-Professional*, Vol. 10, October.

Isaacs, Scott (1997) *Inside Dynamic HTML*. Microsoft Press.

Hall, Devra (1995) *net.Genesis: Build a Web Site*. Rocklin: Prima Online.

Heinle, Nick (1991) *Designing with JavaScript*. Sebastopol: O'Reilly.

Goodman, Danny (1998) *Dynamic HTML – the Definitive Reference*. Sebastopol: O'Reilly.

Kuhlen, Rainer (1991) *Hypertext, ein nicht-lineares Medium zwischen Buch und Wissensbank*. Berlin: Springer Verlag.

Kuhlen, Rainer (1996) *Informationsmarkt: Chancen und Risiken der Kommerzialisierung von Wissen*. Constance: UVK, Universitätsverlag.

Lipps, Peter (1996) SAP@Web: SAP R/3 im Internet und Intranet. In *Kongreßband Exponet 96*. Starnberg: dc congresse + fachmessen GmbH.

Matzke, Bernd (1996) *ABAP/4: Anwendungsentwicklung im SAP-System R/3*. Bonn: Addison-Wesley.

Pincince, Thomas J. et al. (1996) The Full Service Intranet. In *Forrester Research Network Report*, Vol. 10, March.

R/3 System Release 3.1 (1996) *Business on the Internet*. SAP AG.

R/3-Internet-Anwendungskomponenten (1997) Release 3.1H; Online Help. SAP AG.

Resnick, Rosalind and Taylor, Dave (1994) *The Internet Business Guide*. Indianapolis: Sams Publishing.

Riehm, U., Wingert, B., Böhle, K., and Gabel-Becker, I. (1992) *Elektronisches Publizieren:. Eine kritische Bestandsaufnahme*. Berlin: Springer Verlag.

SAP@Web Installation (1996) *Installationsanleitung zum Release 3.1 FCS*. Product number 51000502. SAP AG.

Scheller, Martin; Boden, Klaus-Peter; Geenen, Andreas and Kampermann, Joachim (1994) *Internet: Dienste und Werkzeuge*. Berlin: Springer Verlag.

Weisman, David E., Trevino, Victor B. and Sweet, Susan R. (1996) Payments on the Web. In *Forrester Money & Technology Strategies*, Vol 1.

Index